Invitation to Mathematics

Authors and Advisors

L. Carey Bolster
Supervisor of Mathematics
Baltimore County Public Schools
Towson, Maryland

Warren Crown
Associate Professor of Mathematics
Education
Rutgers University
New Brunswick, New Jersey

Robert Hamada
Instructional Specialist, Mathematics
Los Angeles Unified School District
Los Angeles, California

Viggo Hansen
Professor, Mathematics Education
California State University
Northridge, California

Mary Montgomery Lindquist
Professor of Mathematics Education
Columbus College
Columbus, Georgia

Charles McNerney
Professor of Mathematics
University of Northern Colorado
Greeley, Colorado

William Nibbelink
Professor and Chairman
Division of Early Childhood and
Elementary Education
University of Iowa
Iowa City, Iowa

Glenn Prigge
Professor of Mathematics
University of North Dakota
Grand Forks, North Dakota

Cathy Rahlfs
Math Coordinator K–12
Humble Independent School District
Humble, Texas

David Robitaille
Head, Department of Mathematics
and Science Education
University of British Columbia
Vancouver, British Columbia, Canada

James Schultz
Associate Professor of Mathematics
The Ohio State University
Columbus, Ohio

Sidney Sharron
Formerly, Supervisor Instructional Materials
Los Angeles Unified School District
Los Angeles, California

Jane Swafford
Professor of Mathematics
Northern Michigan University
Marquette, Michigan

Irvin Vance
Professor of Mathematical Sciences
New Mexico State University
Las Cruces, New Mexico

David E. Williams
Director of Mathematics Education
Division of Mathematics
School District of Philadelphia
Philadelphia, Pennsylvania

James Wilson
Professor of Mathematics Education
University of Georgia
Athens, Georgia

Robert Wisner
Professor of Mathematical Sciences
New Mexico State University
Las Cruces, New Mexico

Scott, Foresman and Company

Editorial Offices: Glenview, Illinois

Regional Offices: Sunnyvale, California •
Tucker, Georgia • Glenview, Illinois •
Oakland, New Jersey • Dallas, Texas

Teacher Consultants for Grade 4

Guadalupe Flores
Stonewall Elementary School
804 Stonewall Street
San Antonio, Texas

Annie Mayes
Indianapolis Public Schools
120 East Walnut Street
Education Center, Room 402
Indianapolis, Indiana

Acknowledgments

For permission to reproduce indicated information on the following pages, acknowledgment is made to:

Riddles on page 341 from THE AMERICAN RIDDLE BOOK, edited by Carl Withers and Dr. Sula Benet. Reprinted by permission of Harper & Row, Publishers, Inc.

For permission to reproduce photographs on the following pages, acknowledgment is made to:

14–15 Courtesy Sea World **30–31** Bill Benoit/ATOZ IMAGES **40–41** Craig Aurness-Pony Express/WEST LIGHT **42–43** Tom Carroll/ALPHA/FPG **64** Larry West **68–69** Marty Stouffer Productions/ANIMALS ANIMALS **78–79** Courtesty IBM **158–159** Bill Ross/ WEST LIGHT **168–169** Ray Hillstrom Photography **174** Courtesy NASA **192** Martha Bates/STOCK BOSTON, INC. **264–265, 266** Courtesy NASA **308** Joe Craighead/ ATOZ IMAGES

Editorial development, design, art and photography by: Scott, Foresman staff, Norman Perman, Inc.; Brown & Rosner Design/Gene Rosner/Debra Scambia Coley; Meyer Seltzer Design/Illustration

Bautzmann, Roland; Blake, Gerrie; Bleck, Catherine; Brooks, Nan; Carr, Ted; Cochran, Bobbye; Collins, Britt Taylor; Faitage, Nick; Hamilton, Laurie; Herbert Gotsch Studios, Inc.; Hirtenstein, Virginia; K & S Photo Graphics; Knize, Karl; Kock, Carl; Maniates, Cynthia; Martin, Richard; Masheris, Robert; Meyer Seltzer Design/Illustration; Moody, Roy; Petersen, William; Ralph Cowan, Inc.; Renaud, Phil; Schaefer, Ray; Seymour, Ron; Signorino, Slug; Smith, Ray; Snyder, John; Sumichrast, Jozef; Suyeoka, George; tek/nēk, inc.; A. J. Thomas Midwest Cash Register Co.

ISBN: 0-673-23904-7

vii

Addition and Subtraction Facts

$$14 - 5 = 9$$

Using Numbers

On her way to the Numberville Dog Show, Peggy noticed that numbers are used in many ways.

Here are some of the ways Peggy saw numbers in use.

COUNT

MEASURE

ORDER

LABEL

Try For each picture, tell if the number is used to count, to measure, to order, or to label.

a.

b.

c. 2, 4, 6, 8, 10

Practice For each picture, tell if the number is used to count, to measure, to order, or to label.

Apply On the sign, which numbers are used

10. to count?

11. to measure?

12. to order?

13. to label?

More Practice Set 1, page 352 3

Comparing and Ordering Numbers

A. Compare the weights of the beagle and the sheepdog.

Compare 30 and 55. Use this number line.

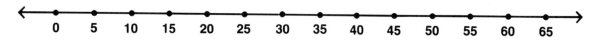

| 0 | 5 | 10 | 15 | 20 | 25 | 30 | 35 | 40 | 45 | 50 | 55 | 60 | 65 |

30 is to the left of 55, so
30 is less than 55.

30 < 55

The beagle weighs less than
the sheepdog.

55 is to the right of 30, so
55 is greater than 30.

55 > 30

The sheepdog weighs more than
the beagle.

B. Give the weights of the three dogs in order from least to greatest.

Find 30, 15, and 55 on the number line above.

In order from least to greatest, the weights are 15, 30, 55.

Try

a. Write two number sentences to compare 5 and 16. Use < and >.

b. Write the numbers in order from least to greatest.

65   7   42   98

Practice   Write two number sentences to compare each pair of numbers. Use < and >.

1. 5 and 25

2. 60 and 45

3. 35 and 17

4. 54 and 65

5. 63 and 82

6. 29 and 33

7. 71 and 7

8. 98 and 2

9. 68 and 55

10. 47 and 94

11. 13 and 17

12. 36 and 31

Write the numbers in order from least to greatest.

13. 15   8   14

14. 12   9   6

15. 98   81   73

16. 28   13   30

17. 50   41   33

18. 20   16   49

19. 83   52   63   55

20. 60   35   47   68

21. 15   47   17   43

22. 74   60   59   77

23. 51   58   41   54

24. 89   96   84   86

Apply   _Use data from a table._ Solve each problem.

Which dog weighs more?

25. Springer spaniel or boxer

26. Doberman pinscher or collie

27. Labrador retriever or collie

28. Poodle or Doberman pinscher

29. Boxer or collie

Dog	Weight (pounds)
Springer spaniel	43
Boxer	85
Doberman pinscher	93
Collie	57
Labrador retriever	97
Poodle	21

∗30. Give the weights of the six dogs in order from least to greatest.

31. _Find the facts._ Which dog is taller, a springer spaniel or a boxer?

Addition Basic Facts

A. On May 23, 1977, the Milwaukee Brewers hit 6 home runs in one game. The Boston Red Sox hit 5 home runs in the same game. How many home runs were hit in that game?

Find 6 + 5.

$$\begin{array}{c} 6 \\ +5 \\ \hline 11 \end{array} \quad \longleftarrow \text{Addend} \longrightarrow \quad \begin{array}{c} 5 \\ +6 \\ \hline 11 \end{array}$$

$$\longleftarrow \text{Addend} \longrightarrow$$

$$\longleftarrow \text{Sum} \longrightarrow$$

11 home runs were hit in that game.

 Mental Math

B. These strategies can help you remember addition facts.

Count on from the greater number.

$$6 \cdot 7, 8, 9$$
$$6 + 3 = 9$$

Use doubles.

$$7 + 7 = 14$$
$$\text{So, } 8 + 7 = 15$$
$$8 + 7 = 15$$

$$5 + 1 + 6$$
$$6 + 6$$
$$5 + 7 = 12$$

Use 10 to Add 8 or 9.

$$10 + 4$$
$$9 + 5 = 14$$

$$10 + 2$$
$$8 + 4 = 12$$

Discuss Does the order in which you add two numbers change the sum?

What is the sum when you add 0 and another number?

Try Add.

a. 5
   +7

b. 6
   +8

c. 0
   +5

d. 8
   +1

e. 9 + 8

f. 7 + 6

g. 4 + 8

Practice Add.

1. 3
   +4

2. 8
   +0

3. 2
   +7

4. 1
   +9

5. 4
   +2

6. 5
   +3

7. 6
   +4

8. 5
   +5

9. 1
   +6

10. 0
   +7

11. 2
   +8

12. 4
   +4

13. 9
   +5

14. 3
   +7

15. 6
   +0

16. 7
   +8

17. 2
   +5

18. 6
   +3

19. 7
   +7

20. 0
   +1

21. 9
   +9

22. 7 + 1

23. 3 + 3

24. 9 + 4

25. 3 + 8

26. 6 + 6

27. 9 + 6

28. 8 + 8

29. 3 + 2

30. 6 + 2

31. 4 + 9

32. 5 + 8

33. 9 + 3

34. 8 + 9

35. 7 + 4

36. 8 + 7

37. 7 + 9

38. 6 + 7

39. 5 + 9

Apply Solve each problem.

40. In one All-Star Game, the American League scored 9 runs. The National League scored 7 runs. How many runs were scored in all?

41. The New York Giants won 5 World Series. They lost 4 more World Series than they won. How many World Series did they lose?

42. David Lopes had 77 stolen bases in 1975. He had 63 stolen bases in 1976. In which of these years did he have fewer stolen bases?

43. **CALCULATOR** Estimate the total number of runs scored by all 26 major league teams last Saturday. Use a newspaper and a calculator to check your estimate.

Subtraction Basic Facts

A. Randy had 17 baseball cards. He gave 9 cards to Jane. How many cards did he have left?

Find 17 − 9.

$$\begin{array}{r} 17 \\ -\ \ 9 \\ \hline 8 \end{array}$$ **Difference**

Randy had 8 cards left.

Discuss What is the difference when you subtract a number from itself? when you subtract zero from another number?

B. These strategies can help you remember facts.

Count back from the greater number.   ⑧•⑦,⑥   **8 − 2 = 6**

Count up from the lesser number.   ⑤•⑥,⑦ Mental Math   **7 − 5 = 2**

Use 10 to subtract 9.   17 − 10   **16 − 9 = 7**

Try   Subtract.

a. $\begin{array}{r} 5 \\ -2 \end{array}$ **b.** $\begin{array}{r} 11 \\ -\ 4 \end{array}$ **c.** $\begin{array}{r} 7 \\ -3 \end{array}$

d. 15 − 8   **e.** 18 − 9

f. 6 − 0   **g.** 7 − 7

Practice Subtract.

1. 5
− 4

2. 7
− 1

3. 13
− 8

4. 11
− 9

5. 6
− 2

6. 8
− 3

7. 15
− 6

8. 14
− 5

9. 7
− 6

10. 9
− 7

11. 10
− 3

12. 12
− 4

13. 4
− 4

14. 8
− 8

15. 16
− 8

16. 11
− 2

17. 3
− 0

18. 9
− 0

19. 10
− 6

20. 12
− 7

21. 11
− 5

22. 13 − 4

23. 14 − 9

24. 10 − 8

25. 9 − 4

26. 12 − 9

27. 14 − 7

28. 12 − 6

29. 13 − 6

30. 11 − 3

31. 17 − 8

32. 10 − 2

33. 13 − 9

34. 15 − 9

35. 13 − 7

36. 11 − 6

37. 15 − 7

38. 14 − 8

39. 16 − 9

40. Look at Exercises 1–39 on page 7. Look at Exercises 1–39 that you just completed. Explain why you would or would not use a calculator to find the sums or differences.

Apply Solve each problem.

41. Kenji had 16 baseball cards. He gave 7 of them away. How many baseball cards did he have left?

42. Don has 49 baseball cards. Nina has 97 cards. Who has the greater number of cards?

43. Bert has 15 cards to trade. Marta has 9 cards to trade. How many more cards does Bert have to trade than Marta?

44. Jim put 6 baseball cards on page 8 of his scrapbook and 5 cards on page 9. How many baseball cards did he put on pages 8 and 9 of his scrapbook?

45. **CALCULATOR** Press: 7 [+] [=] [=] [=] [=]. What happened on your calculator?

46. **CALCULATOR** Press: 2 [M+] 3 [M+] [MR] What is the display?

47. Work with another student to find how many triangles are in this figure.

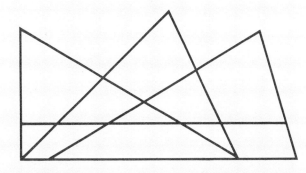

ERIC'S GUESSING GAME

A guessing game was played at Eric's birthday party. Eric had put a total of 10 chips in two cans. Each can had at least one chip. A prize was won for guessing the correct number of chips in each can. *Show all the different guesses you could make.*

Use chips or other objects to show one way that the chips might be in the two cans.

1. If you put 3 chips in the first can and 7 chips in the second can, would 7 chips in the first can and 3 chips in the second can be another way?

2. List all of the different ways that the chips could be put in the cans.

3. Use a table like the one below to list all the ways 10 chips could be put into two cans.

Number of chips in the first can	Number of chips in the second can
9	1
8	—
7	—
6	—
.	.
.	.
.	.

4. How many ways are there to put the chips into 2 cans?

5. If there were 12 chips to put into 2 cans, how many different ways would there be?

6. If there were 15 chips to put into 2 cans, how many different ways would there be?

7. If there were 100 chips to put into 2 cans, how many different ways would there be?

8. Write a rule about the number of ways any number of chips can be put into 2 cans.

.

Ordering Events

For each activity, write the steps in order.

1. Rinse dishes.

Scrape dishes.

Dry dishes.

Wash dishes.

2. Talk to person.

Dial number.

Look up number.

Ask for person.

3. Put bread in oven and bake.

Find recipe and ingredients.

Mix ingredients and preheat oven.

Measure ingredients.

4. Write the steps in order that you would use to set a table.

Families of Facts

A. These four number sentences make up a *family of facts*.
The numbers used are 4, 6, and 10.

Mental
Math

Use families of facts as a strategy to help you
remember basic facts.

If you remember 4 + 6 = 10, you can use the
family of facts to remember 6 + 4 = 10, 10 − 6 = 4, and 10 − 4 = 6.

B. Some families of facts have only two number sentences and use only two numbers.

$$8 + 8 = 16$$
$$16 - 8 = 8$$

Try

a. Tell which fact does not belong to the family.

$$3 + 5 = 8$$
$$5 + 3 = 8$$
$$8 + 0 = 8$$
$$8 - 5 = 3$$
$$8 - 3 = 5$$

b. Write a family of facts using the given numbers.

7, 6, 13

Practice Tell which fact does not belong to each family.

1.
$5 + 6 = 11$
$11 - 5 = 6$
$11 - 6 = 5$
$6 + 5 = 11$
$6 - 5 = 1$

2.
$4 + 3 = 7$
$7 - 4 = 3$
$3 + 4 = 7$
$3 + 3 = 6$
$7 - 3 = 4$

3.
$8 - 2 = 6$
$2 + 8 = 10$
$8 + 2 = 10$
$10 - 2 = 8$
$10 - 8 = 2$

4.
$7 - 1 = 6$
$6 - 1 = 5$
$7 - 6 = 1$
$6 + 1 = 7$
$1 + 6 = 7$

Write a family of facts using the given numbers.

5. 15, 7, 8   **6.** 7, 3, 10   **7.** 9, 3, 6   **8.** 5, 2, 3   **9.** 4, 9, 5

10. 6, 14, 8   **11.** 7, 12, 5   **12.** 1, 6, 5   **13.** 5, 10   **14.** 9, 18

15. 17, 8, 9   **16.** 5, 8, 13   **17.** 8, 16   **★18.** 0, 4   **★19.** 8, 0

MAINTENANCE

Add or subtract.

1.
$$\begin{array}{r} 13 \\ -4 \\ \hline \end{array}$$

2.
$$\begin{array}{r} 11 \\ -9 \\ \hline \end{array}$$

3.
$$\begin{array}{r} 7 \\ +9 \\ \hline \end{array}$$

4.
$$\begin{array}{r} 3 \\ +3 \\ \hline \end{array}$$

5.
$$\begin{array}{r} 12 \\ -9 \\ \hline \end{array}$$

6.
$$\begin{array}{r} 10 \\ -7 \\ \hline \end{array}$$

7.
$$\begin{array}{r} 5 \\ +5 \\ \hline \end{array}$$

8. $2 + 6$ **9.** $9 - 6$ **10.** $15 - 8$ **11.** $4 + 8$ **12.** $7 + 3$ **13.** $14 - 8$

14. $17 - 9$ **15.** $4 + 9$ **16.** $3 + 5$ **17.** $4 - 0$ **18.** $7 - 7$ **19.** $6 + 9$

20. $1 + 8$ **21.** $8 + 8$ **22.** $5 + 6$ **23.** $11 - 5$ **24.** $14 - 7$ **25.** $18 - 9$

Three or More Addends

A. *Career* Shirley is the keeper at the penguin house. She takes care of 4 emperor penguins, 9 adelie penguins, and 6 gentoo penguins. How many penguins does she care for?

Find $4 + 9 + 6$.

$$\begin{array}{r} 4 \\ 9 \\ + 6 \\ \hline 19 \end{array}$$

Look for a sum of 10.
$4 + 6 = 10$
Then it is easy to add $10 + 9$.

Mental Math

Shirley cares for 19 penguins.

B. Find $3 + 2 + 8 + 4$.

$$\begin{array}{r} 3 \\ 2 \\ 8 \\ + 4 \\ \hline 17 \end{array}$$

Find a sum of 10. $8 + 2 = 10$

Find $3 + 4$. $3 + 4 = 7$

Add $10 + 7$. $10 + 7 = 17$

Try Add.

a.
$$\begin{array}{r} 2 \\ 5 \\ +7 \\ \hline \end{array}$$

b.
$$\begin{array}{r} 2 \\ 4 \\ +3 \\ \hline \end{array}$$

c.
$$\begin{array}{r} 3 \\ 2 \\ +7 \\ \hline \end{array}$$

d.
$$\begin{array}{r} 6 \\ 9 \\ 1 \\ +2 \\ \hline \end{array}$$

e. $9 + 2 + 5 + 1 + 2$

Mental Math

Practice Add.

1.
$$\begin{array}{r} 7 \\ 2 \\ +3 \\ \hline \end{array}$$

2.
$$\begin{array}{r} 4 \\ 5 \\ +5 \\ \hline \end{array}$$

3.
$$\begin{array}{r} 6 \\ 7 \\ +3 \\ \hline \end{array}$$

4.
$$\begin{array}{r} 4 \\ 6 \\ +9 \\ \hline \end{array}$$

5.
$$\begin{array}{r} 2 \\ 8 \\ +1 \\ \hline \end{array}$$

6.
$$\begin{array}{r} 9 \\ 2 \\ +1 \\ \hline \end{array}$$

7.
$$\begin{array}{r} 3 \\ 6 \\ 3 \\ +4 \\ \hline \end{array}$$

8.
$$\begin{array}{r} 6 \\ 2 \\ 5 \\ +4 \\ \hline \end{array}$$

9.
$$\begin{array}{r} 3 \\ 4 \\ 5 \\ +5 \\ \hline \end{array}$$

10.
$$\begin{array}{r} 8 \\ 2 \\ 1 \\ +3 \\ \hline \end{array}$$

11.
$$\begin{array}{r} 1 \\ 6 \\ 3 \\ 1 \\ +2 \\ \hline \end{array}$$

12.
$$\begin{array}{r} 4 \\ 5 \\ 3 \\ 2 \\ +1 \\ \hline \end{array}$$

13. $7 + 5 + 1$

14. $5 + 6 + 4$

15. $7 + 1 + 6 + 3$

16. $2 + 2 + 3 + 9$

17. $8 + 3 + 5 + 1 + 2$

18. $5 + 3 + 5 + 3 + 2$

Apply Solve each problem.

19. In the morning, Nora cleaned 4 lion cages and 3 elephant cages. In the afternoon, she cleaned 6 cages. How many cages did she clean that day?

20. Sam fed 3 teaspoons of mush to a baby macaw in the morning, 4 teaspoons at noon, 5 teaspoons in the evening, and 6 teaspoons at night. How many teaspoons of mush did Sam feed to the macaw that day?

*21. At one zoo there are 2 polar bears. There are 3 more brown bears than polar bears, and 2 more black bears than brown bears. How many bears are at this zoo?

22. *Thinking skills* Write $1 + 2 + 3 + 4 + 5 + 6 + 7 + 8 + 9$. Look for sums of 10. What is the sum of the 9 digits?

Problem Solving | Choose the Operation

When Mrs. Hadley's class visited the zoo, each student was assigned to a group. There were 6 students in Mrs. Hadley's group, 5 students in Mrs. Zeman's group, and 5 students in Mr. Cater's group. How many students in all went to the zoo?

Read | Read the problem. What facts are given? What are you asked to find?

Facts: Groups of 6, 5, and 5 students

Find: Number of students in all.

Plan | What can you do to solve the problem?

Think of combining the groups into one group. Add to find how many in all. Find $6 + 5 + 5$.

Solve | Carry out the plan.

$$\begin{array}{r} 6 \\ 5 \\ + 5 \\ \hline 16 \end{array}$$

Answer | Answer the question.

There were 16 students who went to the zoo.

Look Back | Read the question. Does the answer make sense?

The answer must be greater than the number in any of the groups. 16 is greater than 6 or 5. 16 is reasonable.

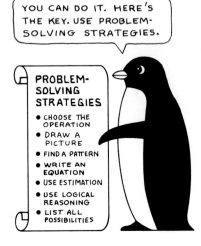

YOU CAN DO IT. HERE'S THE KEY. USE PROBLEM-SOLVING STRATEGIES.

PROBLEM-SOLVING STRATEGIES
- CHOOSE THE OPERATION
- DRAW A PICTURE
- FIND A PATTERN
- WRITE AN EQUATION
- USE ESTIMATION
- USE LOGICAL REASONING
- LIST ALL POSSIBILITIES

Try Tell whether you *add* or *subtract*. Then find the answer.

a. There are 9 boys and 7 girls in Mrs. Hadley's class. How many more boys than girls are there?

b. Pedro saw 6 sea lions. He saw 4 more seals than sea lions. How many seals did he see?

Apply Tell whether you would *add* or *subtract* to find the answer.

1. Pamela saw  brown bears and ● black bears. How many bears did she see in all?

2. Sharon saw ▦ lions. Mark saw ● lions. How many more lions did Mark see than Sharon?

Tell whether you *add* or *subtract*. Then find the answer.

3. Gina saw 8 geese in the pond at the children's zoo. Ana saw 6 more geese than Gina. How many geese did Ana see?

4. Mr. Cater's group visited 3 areas of the zoo before lunch, and 4 areas after lunch. How many areas did they visit in all?

5. Ann saw 13 snakes and 5 lizards in the reptile house. How many fewer lizards than snakes did she see?

6. The keeper said there were 15 camels. 7 of them were outside. How many camels were inside?

7. At the bird house, Paul saw 5 cockatoos. He saw 3 more parrots than cockatoos. How many parrots did he see?

8. Mrs. Zeman's group bought 12 bags of peanuts. They fed 8 bags to the monkeys. How many bags did they have left?

9. There were 2 baby chimps, 1 baby squirrel, 3 bear cubs, and 1 tiger cub in the zoo nursery. How many animals were in the zoo nursery?

★10. The keeper gave each lion 2 chunks of meat that weighed 5 pounds each. How many pounds of meat did she give each lion?

11. **CALCULATOR** The 4 elephants at the zoo weigh 9,189 pounds, 7,976 pounds, 7,452 pounds and 8,048 pounds. What is the total weight of the elephants?

Missing Addends

When the tour started, there were 6 passengers on
Nick's tram. At the first stop, no one got off the tram.
After the first stop, there were 15 passengers on board.
How many passengers boarded the tram at the first stop?

Write a number sentence.
Use n for the number that
boarded at the first stop.

Number on board at the start	Number that boarded at the first stop	Number on board after the first stop
6 $+$	n $=$	15

Subtract to find the
missing addend.

$$15 - 6 = 9$$

$$n = 9$$

9 passengers boarded the tram at the first stop.

Try Give each missing addend.

a. $3 + n = 7$ **b.** $n + 5 = 9$ **c.** $9 + n = 11$ **d.** $n + 8 = 15$

Practice Give each missing addend.

1. $6 + n = 13$ **2.** $7 + n = 11$ **3.** $n + 2 = 5$ **4.** $n + 6 = 8$

5. $n + 5 = 10$ **6.** $n + 9 = 17$ **7.** $5 + n = 7$ **8.** $1 + n = 5$

9. $9 + n = 9$ **10.** $0 + n = 0$ **11.** $n + 4 = 10$ **12.** $n + 4 = 12$

13. $n + 7 = 8$ **14.** $n + 3 = 4$ **15.** $8 + n = 16$ **16.** $7 + n = 14$

17. $n + 9 = 18$ **18.** $n + 8 = 13$ **★19.** $5 = 5 + n$ **★20.** $2 = 2 + n$

Apply Solve each problem.

21. Last year, the zoo tram stopped at 9 different areas on each tour. Now it stops at 13. How many new stops were added?
($9 + n = 13$)

22. The reptile house received 5 new crocodiles. Now there are 12. How many crocodiles were there before?
($n + 5 = 12$)

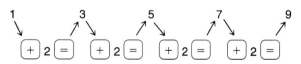

Here is a list of numbers. Tell what rule was used each time to get the next number.

1 3 5 7 9   ⊕ 2 ⊜ is the rule.

For each list, use your calculator to find the rule and the missing numbers.

1. 0 4 8 12 ▨ ▨

2. 17 15 13 ▨ ▨

3. 18 15 12 ▨ ▨

4. 1 4 ▨ ▨ 13

5. ▨ ▨ 15 11 ▨

6. 0 ▨ ▨ 15 ▨

7. ▨ 9 18 ▨ ▨

8. ▨ ▨ 48 40 ▨

9. ▨ 14 ▨ 26 ▨

Chapter 1 Test

Tell if the number in each picture is used to count, to measure, to order, or to label.

1.  **2.**

3. Write a number sentence to compare 5 and 26. Use >.

4. Write a number sentence to compare 61 and 26. Use <.

Write the numbers in order from least to greatest.

5. 72   65   85

6. 21   10   19   8

7. 87   95   83   92

Add.

8. 6
   + 4

9. 7
   + 6

10. 4
    + 5

11. 8
    + 6

12. 5
    + 7

13. 9
    + 8

14. 7 + 4   **15.** 5 + 3   **16.** 9 + 0

Subtract.

17. 7
   − 2

18. 14
    − 6

19. 8
   − 0

20. 15
    − 8

21. 12
    − 7

22. 18
    − 9

23. 16 − 7   **24.** 13 − 5   **25.** 11 − 3

Write a family of facts using the given numbers.

26. 4, 2, 6   **27.** 5, 6, 11

Add.

28. 9
    5
   + 1

29. 3
    7
   + 4

30. 8
    4
    2
   + 5

Tell whether you *add* or *subtract*. Then solve each problem.

31. There were 7 boys and 8 girls at the party. How many children were at the party?

32. In the first game, 9 runs were scored. 4 runs were scored in the second game. How many more runs were scored in the first game than in the second game?

33. A bird laid 5 eggs. Only 3 eggs hatched. How many eggs did not hatch?

Give each missing addend.

34. $n + 8 = 13$ **35.** $3 + n = 9$

CHALLENGE

Number Patterns

An interesting sequence of numbers was discovered by the famous mathematician, Fibonacci.

The Fibonacci sequence begins with these numbers.

1   1   2   3   5   8   13 . . .

More numbers in this sequence can be found by using an addition pattern.

Answer each question to help you find the pattern.

1. What is the sum of the first and second numbers of the sequence?

2. What is the third number of the sequence?

3. What is the sum of the second and third numbers of the sequence?

4. What is the fourth number of the sequence?

5. What is the sum of the third and fourth numbers of the sequence?

6. What is the fifth number of the sequence?

7. What pattern do you see?

8. Write the next four numbers in the Fibonacci sequence.

   1   1   2   3   5   8   13   ▨   ▨   ▨   ▨

9. Find the addition pattern in this sequence.

   1   1   1   3   5   9   17 . . .

10. Find the next four numbers in the sequence in Exercise 9.

RACE RESULTS

Five friends ran in a race. Runner B finished the race right behind Runner E. Runner D finished last. C finished ahead of A. Two runners finished between A and C. *Who won the race? In what order?*

1. Below is a picture showing the order of Runners B and E. Draw the picture on your paper. Show where Runner D should be.

2. Complete the picture. Show where Runners A and C should be.

3. Who won the race?

4. In another race among 5 runners, O finished ahead of both P and M. N finished right behind O. Two runners finished between Q and P. In what order did they finish? Who won the race?

Numbers and Place Value

125

Letters are used to write words. *Digits* are used to write numbers.

0, 1, 2, 3, 4, 5, 6, 7, 8, and 9 are all the digits that are used.

A. During a five-minute run, Amy made a tally of the number of laps run by each team member. Then she used digits to write each number.

NAME	TALLY	LAPS
DOROTHY	IIII	4
AMBROSE	⊹⊦⊦ I	6
JILL	III	3
GUADALUPE	⊹⊦⊦ II	7
GREG	⊹⊦⊦	5

B. John wrote this two-digit number to show that the entire team ran a total of *twenty-five* laps.

25

tens digit ⌐↑ ↑⌐ ones digit

c. Work with three other students. Turn to pages 438–441 for help on group work. Each student in your group should put two handfuls of beans into one pile. Count the beans. When you are finished counting, discuss these questions.

1. How did you count the beans?

2. How can you show the total number of beans without using digits?

Now write the total number of beans using digits.

3. When is it useful to use tally marks?

4. When is it useful to use digits?

d. Work with your group. Use the digits 1, 2, 3, 4, 5, 6, 7, 8, or 9 to write a two-digit number. Write another two-digit number using the same digits. Discuss these questions.

5. How are these numbers different?

6. How are they the same?

e. Play a digit game with your group.
- Make a spinner that shows the digits 0–9.
- Each player draws two boxes that are next to each other.
- Players take turns spinning the spinner 2, 3, or 4 times. Players will write two of the digits from their spins in the boxes to make a two-digit number.
- For each spin, players must decide if they want to write the number in a box. They must also decide which box is the best box to write the number in.
- The player who makes the greatest two-digit number wins the game.

Try to play the game so that the player with the least number wins the game.

Try to play the game using three digits out of four spins.

7. How is it different to play the game this way?

Hundreds, Tens, and Ones

A. Ted and Claudia each drew a picture to show the number of fourth graders in Bay School. Each picture shows 1 hundred, 2 tens, and 8 ones.

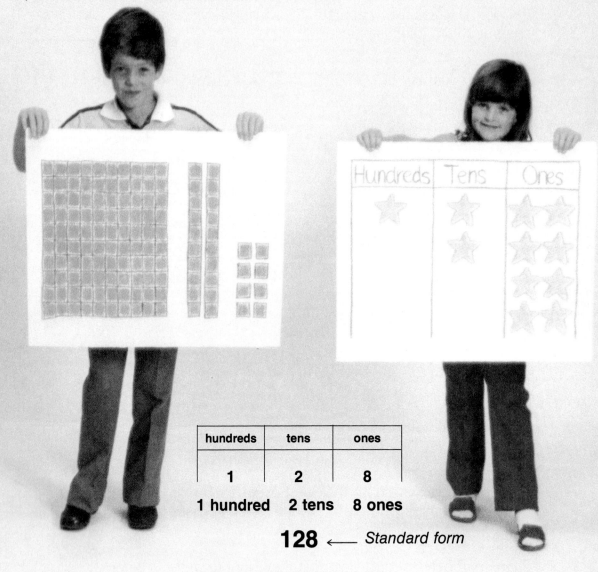

hundreds	tens	ones
1	2	8
1 hundred	2 tens	8 ones

128 ⟵ *Standard form*

one hundred twenty-eight

B. What does each digit mean in 564?

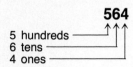

564

5 hundreds
6 tens
4 ones

Try Write each number in standard form.

a. 3 hundreds 5 tens

b. 6 hundreds 8 ones

c. two hundred ninety

d. Tell what the 6 means in 642.

e. Write 374 in words.

Practice Write each number in standard form.

1. 4 hundreds 5 tens 3 ones

2. 7 hundreds 4 tens 9 ones

3. 5 hundreds 8 tens

4. 3 hundreds 5 ones

5. fifty-eight

6. seventy-nine

7. six hundred twelve

8. two hundred fifteen

9. nine hundred fifty

10. three hundred sixty

11. nine hundred two

Tell what the 3 means in each number.

12. 63　　**13.** 30　　**14.** 532　　**15.** 362　　**16.** 236　　**17.** 813　　**18.** 390

Write each number in words.

19. 41　　**20.** 53　　**21.** 308　　**22.** 503　　**23.** 410　　**24.** 670　　**25.** 915

Apply Without repeating a digit in a number, use the digits 4, 6, and 1 to write as many three-digit numbers as you can with

26. 4 as the ones digit.

27. 1 as the hundreds digit.

28. 6 as the tens digit.

29. 4 as the hundreds digit.

30. Use the digits 2, 9, and 5 to write as many three-digit numbers as you can. Do not repeat a digit in a number.

31. Use the digits 5, 7, and 8 to write as many three-digit numbers as you can. Do not repeat a digit in a number.

★32. Write the greatest number you can, using the digits 3, 0, and 9. Do not repeat a digit.

★33. Write the least number you can, using the digits 1, 9, and 8. Do not repeat a digit.

Thousands

The population of Bayview is two thousand, seven hundred fifty-four.

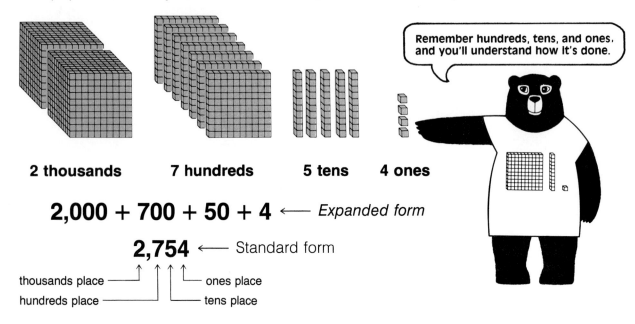

2 thousands   **7 hundreds**   **5 tens**   **4 ones**

Remember hundreds, tens, and ones, and you'll understand how it's done.

2,000 + 700 + 50 + 4 ← *Expanded form*

2,754 ← Standard form

thousands place ——┐
hundreds place ———┘   └— tens place
                └— ones place

Try   Write each number in standard form.

a. 9,000 + 200 + 60   **b.** 3,000 + 40 + 8   **c.** one thousand, four hundred

d. Write 7,123 in words.   **e.** Write 2,507 in expanded form.

Practice   Write each number in standard form.

1. 9,000 + 700 + 20 + 5   **2.** 6,000 + 400 + 30 + 9   **3.** 5,000 + 20 + 8

4. 3,000 + 800 + 90   **5.** 2,000 + 600 + 5   **6.** 8,000 + 300

7. three thousand, seven hundred eighty-five

8. four thousand, three hundred sixty-two

9. one thousand, six hundred ten

10. six thousand, two hundred twelve

11. seven thousand, one hundred six

12. five thousand, forty-nine

13. one thousand, ninety-eight

14. eight thousand, five

For each number, tell what digit is in the given place.

15. 6,812 (hundreds)   **16.** 4,319 (ones)   **17.** 6,401 (thousands)

18. 3,528 (tens)   **19.** 7,395 (thousands)   **20.** 1,076 (hundreds)

Write each number in words.

21. 530   **22.** 304   **23.** 267   **24.** 1,000   **25.** 9,250   **26.** 8,751

Write each number in expanded form.

27. 685   **28.** 412   **29.** 7,813   **30.** 1,986   **31.** 5,042   **32.** 6,107

Apply   Solve each problem.

33. The population of Redfield is three thousand, two hundred forty-seven. Write this number in standard form.

34. Redfield is 15 miles from Bayview. Clifton is 8 miles closer to Bayview. How far is Clifton from Bayview?

35. The population of Clifton is two thousand, eighty-one. Write this number in standard form.

★36. The population of Myerville is the greatest four-digit number possible using all the digits 3, 4, 9, and 1. What is the population of Myerville?

37. **CALCULATOR** Enter the number 6,385 on your calculator. Change the number to 6,785 by adding one number. What is the number?

Comparing Numbers

A. The table shows the lengths of two floating bridges in the state of Washington. Which is longer, Evergreen Point Bridge or Hood Canal Bridge?

Floating bridge	Length of main span in feet
Evergreen Point	7,518
Hood Canal	6,471

Compare 7,518 and 6,471.

7,518 ● **6,471** Compare the thousands digits.
7 is greater than 6.

7,518 > 6,471 7,518 is greater than 6,471.

Evergreen Point Bridge is longer than Hood Canal Bridge.

B. Compare 2,390 and 2,587.

2,390 ● **2,587** The thousands digits are the same.

2,390 ● **2,587** Compare the hundreds digits.
3 is less than 5.

2,390 < 2,587 2,390 is less than 2,587.

Try Compare the numbers. Use < or >.

a. 273 ● 292   **b.** 5,964 ● 5,962   **c.** 7,846 ● 7,839

Practice Compare the numbers. Use < or >.

1. 782 ● 389   **2.** 517 ● 611   **3.** 587 ● 593

4. 235 ● 229   **5.** 8,207 ● 7,065   **6.** 1,972 ● 2,875

7. 1,638 ● 1,730   **8.** 9,136 ● 9,218   **9.** 372 ● 370

10. 415 ● 417   **11.** 1,675 ● 1,658   **12.** 3,964 ● 3,961

Apply For each problem, tell which bridge is longer. Use the information in the table.

13. Benjamin Franklin or Ambassador

14. Williamsburg or Bear Mountain

15. Benjamin Franklin or Bear Mountain

16. Williamsburg or Brooklyn

Suspension bridge	Length of main span in feet
Benjamin Franklin	1,750
Williamsburg	1,600
Bear Mountain	1,632
Ambassador	1,850
Brooklyn	1,595

Ordering Numbers

The four longest suspension bridges in North America are listed in this table.

Bridge	Location	Length of main span in feet
George Washington	New York	3,500
Golden Gate	California	4,200
Mackinac	Michigan	3,800
Verrazano-Narrows	New York	4,260

A. List the lengths in order from least to greatest.

First, write the thousands digits in order. Complete each number as soon as you know its order.

3	The thousands digits are the same. Write the hundreds digits in order.	35	Complete each number.	3,500
3		38		3,800
4	The thousands digits are the same. The hundreds digits are the same.	42	Write the tens digits in order. Complete each number.	4,200
4		42		4,260

The lengths in order from least to greatest are 3,500 feet, 3,800 feet, 4,200 feet, and 4,260 feet.

B. Study the patterns. Think of counting by thousands, by hundreds, and by tens.

467	742	976
1,467	842	986
2,467	942	996
3,467	1,042	1,006
4,467	1,142	1,016
5,467	1,242	1,026

Each number is 1,000 greater than the number before it.

Each number is 100 greater than the number before it.

Each number is 10 greater than the number before it.

Try

a. Write 1,568, 1,572, and 1,621 in order from greatest to least.

b. Give the number that is 10 greater than 597.

Practice Write the numbers in order from least to greatest.

1. 162   357   283   **2.** 423   315   248   **3.** 546   637   532

4. 768   854   835   **5.** 1,384   2,925   1,274   **6.** 1,354   1,267   1,282

7. 256   249   273   268   **8.** 716   724   705   734

9. 1,405   1,487   1,326   1,314   **10.** 3,657   3,472   3,470   3,381

Write the numbers in order from greatest to least.

11. 781   693   892   **12.** 189   341   256   **13.** 458   315   409

14. 627   683   725   **15.** 7,689   7,456   8,122   **16.** 3,984   4,923   3,856

17. 576   595   583   568   **18.** 266   284   220   244

19. 1,476   1,412   1,502   1,320   **20.** 8,655   8,740   8,622   8,625

Write the number that is 1,000 greater.

21. 4,582   **22.** 2,702   **23.** 1,936   **24.** 8,029   **25.** 980

Write the number that is 100 greater.

26. 640   **27.** 113   **28.** 1,898   **29.** 2,480   **30.** 964

Write the number that is 10 greater.

31. 750   **32.** 210   **33.** 4,209   **34.** 6,206   **35.** 1,893

Apply Solve each problem.

36. The Quebec Bridge is 1,800 feet long. The Tacoma-Narrows Bridge is 1,000 feet longer. How long is the Tacoma-Narrows Bridge?

37. *Write a problem.* Write a problem comparing the lengths of two bridges. Solve the problem.

Rounding: Nearest Ten and Nearest Hundred

The Jensen family went on a bus tour. There were 47 people on the bus. They traveled 329 miles the first day. The Jensens spent $450 on the tour. When Mr. Jensen wrote these facts in his diary, he used *rounded numbers*.

A. Round 47 to the nearest ten.
Use this number line.

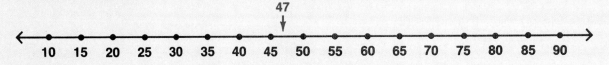

47 is between 40 and 50, but it is closer to 50.

Round 47 up to 50.

B. Round 329 to the nearest hundred.
Use the number line below.

329 is between 300 and 400, but it is closer to 300.

Round 329 down to 300.

C. Round 450 to the nearest hundred.
Use the number line below.

450 is exactly halfway between 400 and 500.

Round 450 up to 500.

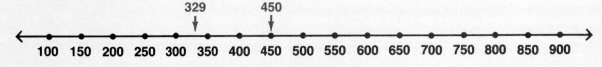

Try Round each number to the nearest ten.

a. 33　　　**b.** 695　　　**c.** 942　　　**d.** 508

Round each number to the nearest hundred.

e. 640　　　**f.** 250　　　**g.** 391　　　**h.** 817

Practice Round each number to the nearest ten.

1. 74　　　**2.** 92　　　**3.** 85　　　**4.** 36

5. 18　　　**6.** 12　　　**7.** 43　　　**8.** 25

9. 432　　**10.** 807　　**11.** 397　　**★12.** 98

Round each number to the nearest hundred.

13. 378　　**14.** 542　　**15.** 439　　**16.** 267

17. 150　　**18.** 846　　**19.** 235　　**20.** 750

21. 654　　**22.** 109　　**23.** 504　　**★24.** 987

Add or subtract.

1. $15 - 7$　　**2.** $8 + 3$

3. $9 + 5$　　**4.** $13 - 6$

5. $8 + 4$　　**6.** $5 + 5$

7. $17 - 9$　　**8.** $6 + 3$

9. $14 - 6$　　**10.** $15 - 9$

11. $9 + 7$　　**12.** $11 - 4$

13. $12 - 5$　　**14.** $9 + 9$

15. $13 - 9$　　**16.** $12 - 3$

17. $7 + 7$　　**18.** $5 + 8$

19. $8 + 9$　　**20.** $11 - 7$

Rounding: Nearest Hundred and Nearest Thousand

A. Round the number on each sign to the nearest thousand.

In each number, the thousands digit is 2, so each number is between 2,000 and 3,000.

To round to the nearest thousand, look at the hundreds digit.

2,237   **2,736**   **2,504**

The hundreds digit is less than 5. The thousands digit stays the same.

The hundreds digit is greater than 5. Add 1 to the thousands digit.

2 + 1 = 3

The hundreds digit is 5. Add 1 to the thousands digit.

2 + 1 = 3

2,000   **3,000**   **3,000**

B. Round 1,637 and 1,650 to the nearest hundred.

Each number is between 1,600 and 1,700.

To round to the nearest hundred, look at the tens digit.

1,637   The tens digit is less than 5. Round down.
↓
1,600

1,650   The tens digit is 5. Round up.
↓
1,700

Try

a. Round 3,492 to the nearest thousand.

b. Round 5,973 to the nearest hundred.

Practice Round each number to the nearest thousand.

1. 3,468 **2.** 6,723 **3.** 8,144 **4.** 2,890 **5.** 3,507

6. 6,402 **7.** 1,076 **8.** 2,500 **9.** 7,682 **★10.** 974

Round each number to the nearest hundred.

11. 276 **12.** 341 **13.** 3,728 **14.** 4,689 **15.** 2,509

16. 8,057 **17.** 7,163 **18.** 5,021 **19.** 6,984 **★20.** 89

Apply _Use data from a table._ Solve each problem. Round the population of each town to the nearest thousand.

21. Barrington **22.** Cary **23.** East Alton

Round the population of each town to the nearest hundred.

24. Rochelle **25.** Salem **26.** Shelbyville

Illinois town	Population
Barrington	9,029
Cary	6,640
East Alton	7,123
Rochelle	8,982
Salem	7,813
Shelbyville	5,259

★27. Round the population of Salem to the nearest ten.

CALCULATOR

To answer each question, follow the directions, and turn your calculator upside down.

1. What kind of clothes did the giant wear? Enter the number that is 100 less than 1,018.

2. What did the giant use boats for? Enter 38,495. Add 14,550.

THE SUM GAME

John and Sara are playing a game with a set of 6 cards with the numbers 1, 2, 3, 4, 5, and 6 written on them. Sara gave John three of the cards and kept the other three cards for herself. The person with the higher sum wins a point. *What are the possible sums that John and Sara could have?*

What sums do you think John and Sara might get most often?

Find a partner and play the game that John and Sara were playing. Use 6 cards with each of the numbers from 1 to 6 written on them. Take turns dealing 3 cards to each other. Add the numbers on the 3 cards and write the sum on a piece of paper. The person with the higher sum wins a point. Do this 10 times. The person with the most points wins.

1. What numbers did you get for the sum? If you played the game again, which sum do you think would occur most often? Give reasons for your guess.

2. Compare the sums that you and your partner found with those of others in the class. Based on this information, which sums do you think would occur most often?

3. Work with your partner to find all possible sums. List all ways each sum can be made with the six cards.

4. Which three cards have the smallest sum? What is this sum?

5. Which cards would have a sum of 7? Is there more than one way of getting this sum?

6. Which cards would have a sum of 8? Is there more than one way of getting this sum?

7. Which cards would have a sum of 9? How many ways can you get this sum?

8. What is the largest possible sum?

9. Which sums occur most often? How many times do they occur?

10. Look back at your prediction of which sums would occur most often. Did your guess include the sums listed in Problem 9?

BASIC: Quotation Marks in PRINT Statements

A *computer program* is a set of instructions that tells a computer what to do. A computer does a program in the order of the line numbers.

```
10 PRINT "COMPUTER PROGRAM"
```
 — line number

The computer will print only what is in quotation marks.

END tells the computer to stop. It is not printed.

```
20 PRINT "IS WRITTEN IN"
10 PRINT "THIS PROGRAM"
40 END
30 PRINT "BASIC LANGUAGE."
```

When this program is run on a computer, this is printed.

```
THIS PROGRAM
IS WRITTEN IN
BASIC LANGUAGE.
```

Tell what would be printed for each program.

```
1. 20 PRINT "VERY FAST."
   10 PRINT "COMPUTERS ARE"
   30 END
```

```
2. 20 PRINT "COMPUTER KNOW?"
   30 END
   10 PRINT "WHAT DOES A"
```

```
3. 40 END
   20 PRINT "ONLY WHAT YOU"
   10 PRINT "A COMPUTER KNOWS"
   30 PRINT "TELL IT."
```

Information is often organized by putting it in a table. This table shows how the population and the land area of eight counties in Nevada might be organized in a reference book.

Name of county	Population	Land area in square miles
Esmeralda	777	3,570
Eureka	1,198	4,182
Humboldt	9,434	9,702
Lander	4,082	5,621
Mineral	6,217	3,765
Pershing	3,408	6,001
Storey	1,459	262
White Pine	8,167	8,904

Read Mrs. Lauer's class was studying Nevada. Which has more land area, Esmeralda County or Mineral County?

Plan The information needed is in the table given above. Locate the numbers that give the land area of the two counties. Compare the numbers to find which county has more land area.

Solve Find the name *Esmeralda* in the first column of the table. Move across to the column for land area. The number is 3,570. The number for Mineral is 3,765. 3,570 < 3,765

Answer Mineral County has more land area.

Look Back Check to see that you have read the table correctly.

40

Try Solve each problem. Use the table on page 40.

a. Find the populations of Mineral, Humboldt, and White Pine counties. List them in order from greatest to least.

b. Find the population of Esmeralda County to the nearest hundred.

Apply Solve each problem. Use the table on page 40.

1. Find the land area of Esmeralda County to the nearest thousand square miles.

2. Find the population of Storey County to the nearest hundred.

3. Find the land area of Storey County to the nearest ten square miles.

4. Which is less, the population of Storey County or the population of Eureka County?

5. Which is less, the land area of Mineral County or the land area of Esmeralda County?

6. To the nearest thousand square miles, what is the land area of Pershing County?

7. To the nearest thousand, what is the population of Mineral County?

8. Find the land areas of Eureka, Storey, and Lander counties. List them in order from least to greatest.

9. Which counties have more people than square miles of land?

★10. If the population of each county was rounded to the nearest thousand, which counties would appear to have the same population?

11. **CALCULATOR** What is the total population of the eight counties listed in the table?

Ten-Thousands and Hundred-Thousands

A. In 1980, Alabama produced about two hundred seventy-five thousand bales of cotton. Write this number in standard form.

hundred-thousands	ten-thousands	thousands	hundreds	tens	ones
2	7	5	0	0	0

200,000 + 70,000 + 5,000 ⟵ Expanded form

275,000 ⟵ Standard form

B. Tell what the 3 means in each number.

364,152
↑——— 3 hundred-thousands

932,470
↑——— 3 ten-thousands

Try Write each number in standard form.

a. forty-four thousand, six hundred seventeen

b. 100,000 + 20,000 + 7,000 + 40 + 3

c. Tell what the 8 means in 84,375.

d. Tell what the 5 means in 563,274.

Practice Write each number in standard form.

1. 40,000 + 6,000 + 300 + 20 + 9

2. 300,000 + 50,000 + 7,000

3. 600,000 + 70,000 + 5,000 + 90

4. 80,000 + 5,000

5. seventy-two thousand, five hundred sixty-four

6. fifty-one thousand, eight hundred twenty-three

7. three hundred forty-five thousand, nine hundred

8. six hundred twelve thousand, five hundred forty

9. five hundred twenty-one thousand

10. nine hundred thirty-two thousand

Tell what the 4 means in each number.

11. 31,490

12. 45,271

13. 421,863

14. 304,295

15. 142,705

16. 470,958

17. 745,680

18. 19,456

19. 82,543

20. 803,754

Apply For problems 21–22, write the given number in standard form.

21. In 1980, Georgia produced about eighty-six thousand bales of cotton.

22. In 1980, Oklahoma produced about two hundred five thousand bales of cotton.

23. *Estimation* South Carolina produces about 100,000 bales of cotton each year. Tell whether this number is exact or estimated.

24. **CALCULATOR** Enter 3,124 on your calculator. Without using the clear [c] key, change the 2 to 8, and the 1 to 6 so the display shows 3,684. How can you do this?

Millions

A. In 1980, Arizona produced about six hundred eighty-four million, four hundred eighty thousand pounds of cotton. Write this number in standard form.

hundred-millions	ten-millions	millions	hundred-thousands	ten-thousands	thousands	hundreds	tens	ones
6	8	4	4	8	0	0	0	0

684,480,000 ← Standard form

B. Tell what the 5 means in each number.

563,208,174
↑——— 5 hundred-millions

357,702,148
↑——— 5 ten-millions

65,342,000
↑——— 5 millions

Try Write each number in standard form.

a. seven million, two hundred eleven thousand, nine hundred forty-one

b. six hundred fourteen million, five hundred ten thousand, eight

Tell what the 3 means in each number.

c. 3,456,000   **d.** 4,539,275   **e.** 32,908,150   **f.** 903,861,547

Practice Write each number in standard form.

1. six hundred twelve million, nine hundred seventy-six thousand, four hundred sixteen

2. one hundred eighty-two million, six hundred seventeen thousand, eight hundred seven

3. nine million, one hundred three thousand, two hundred twelve

4. four million, three hundred ten thousand, nine hundred eighteen

5. twenty-seven million, fifty-two thousand, nineteen

6. ninety-eight million, twenty-one thousand, seventy-eight

Tell what the 5 means in each number.

7. 5,027,431   **8.** 52,324,009   **9.** 540,916,278   **10.** 65,092,781

11. 17,205,148   **12.** 3,510,264   **13.** 2,057,267   **14.** 573,681,042

15. 43,518,240   **16.** 2,350,491   **17.** 625,403,981   **18.** 508,672,304

Apply   Solve each problem.

19. In 1980, New Mexico produced about 54,720,000 pounds of cotton. Write this number in words.

20. In 1980, Mississippi produced about 548,640,000 pounds of cotton. Write this number in words.

21. Of the 10 leading cotton-growing countries in the world, 4 are in the Western hemisphere. How many are in the Eastern hemisphere?

22. *Estimation* The cotton gin was invented by Eli Whitney in 1793. Is this an estimated number? Write *yes* or *no*.

23. In 1980, the world produced about sixty-four million three hundred thousand bales of cotton. Write this number in standard form.

24. *Thinking skills* How many hundred-thousands are in one million? How many ten-thousands are in one million? How many thousands are in one million?

25. **CALCULATOR** Display the greatest number you can show on your calculator by using just one key. Write this number in words.

Using six darts, Joshua made a score of 14 points. Could he have made the same score with

26. five darts?

27. four darts?

28. three darts?

29. two darts?

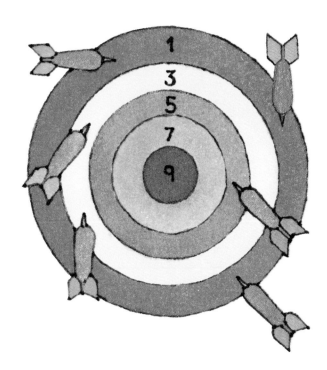

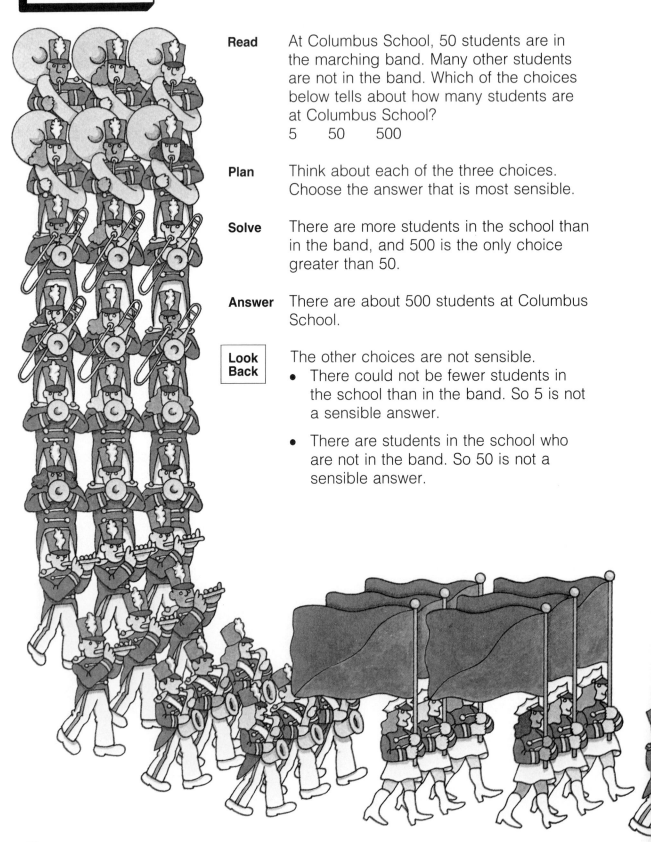

Problem Solving | Give Sensible Answers

Read At Columbus School, 50 students are in the marching band. Many other students are not in the band. Which of the choices below tells about how many students are at Columbus School?

5   50   500

Plan Think about each of the three choices. Choose the answer that is most sensible.

Solve There are more students in the school than in the band, and 500 is the only choice greater than 50.

Answer There are about 500 students at Columbus School.

Look Back The other choices are not sensible.

- There could not be fewer students in the school than in the band. So 5 is not a sensible answer.

- There are students in the school who are not in the band. So 50 is not a sensible answer.

Try *Estimation* Choose the most sensible answer.
Explain why the other choices are not sensible.

a. How many times does the school band practice each week?
5   50   500

b. The 50 band members sit in rows. About how many are in each row?
1   10   100

Apply *Estimation* Choose the most sensible answer.
Explain why the other choices are not sensible.

1. The Columbus School Band had a concert. How many people came?
2   200   200,000

2. What was the cost of a ticket to the Columbus School Band concert?
$1 $10 $100

3. How many of the 50 band members play the drums?
6   60   600

4. How many minutes does the school band practice each day?
4   45   450

5. Jamie practices her flute at home every day. How many hours does she practice at home each week?
7   17   70

6. During the school year, the band plays once a month at a school assembly. How many times each year do they do this?
1   5   10

7. The band members are raising money for 50 new uniforms. How much do they need to raise?
$3 $30 $3,000

8. The band members had a car wash to raise money. How much did they charge to wash a car?
$2 $20 $200

9. The band played at a school football game. The stands were filled. About how many people were there?
8   18   800

10. Fill in the blanks with numbers that are sensible answers. Then explain why each number is sensible.

Columbus School has an orchestra with ▨ members. There are ▨ members who play stringed instruments. The orchestra made about ▨ at its last concert when each ticket cost ▨ and about ▨ people attended. The orchestra played ▨ pieces of music which took about ▨ hours.

Chapter 2 Test

Use digits to write each number.

1. ///   **2.** fifteen   **3.** sixty

Write each number in standard form.

4. 3 hundreds 4 tens 9 ones

5. two hundred sixteen

6. 4,000 + 600 + 70 + 5

7. one thousand, three hundred ten

8. 40,000 + 2,000 + 900 + 80 + 3

9. five hundred twelve thousand

10. one million, six hundred twelve thousand, two hundred nineteen

Tell what the 3 means in each number.

11. 937   **12.** 3,075

13. 234,268   **14.** 3,056,274

Compare the numbers. Use < or >.

15. 362 ● 354

16. 6,137 ● 2,845

17. 2,450 ● 2,470

Write the numbers in order from least to greatest.

18. 372   286   465

19. 142   137   147   236

20. 3,859   3,961   2,847

Round to the nearest ten.

21. 46   **22.** 132

Round to the nearest hundred.

23. 610   **24.** 1,793

Round to the nearest thousand.

25. 2,175   **26.** 8,521

Use this table to solve each problem.

Name of county	Population	Land area in square miles
Esmeralda	777	3,570
Eureka	1,198	4,182

27. Find the population of Eureka County to the nearest hundred.

28. Which of the two counties shown has the greater land area?

Choose the most sensible answer.

29. The smallest class in Columbus School has 25 students. How many students are in the largest class?

15   25   35

30. The 3 fourth-grade classes went on a field trip. How many students went?

8   80   800

Billions

To breathe *one billion* times, you would have to live to be about 100 years old.

billions	hundred-millions	ten-millions	millions	hundred-thousands	ten-thousands	thousands	hundreds	tens	ones
1	0	0	0	0	0	0	0	0	0

1,000,000,000 ⟵ Standard form

These facts show about how much one billion really is.

- 1,000,000,000 days is about 2,737,909 years.
- 1,000,000,000 hours is about 114,080 years.
- 1,000,000,000 minutes is about 1,901 years.
- 1,000,000,000 seconds is about 31 years, 8 months, 8 days.

Write each number in standard form.

1. The population of the world is about four billion, six hundred million people.

2. Light travels at a speed of about sixteen billion, ninety-six million miles per day.

3. The United States produces about one hundred thirty billion gallons of oil per year.

4. The United States produces about six billion, two hundred eighty million pounds of cotton per year.

5. The United States produces about eight billion, two hundred million, nine hundred fifty thousand bushels of corn per year.

6. The world produces about nine hundred thirteen billion, eight hundred million gallons of oil per year.

CAT PUZZLE

Janice, Barbara, Lynn, and Margaret each own a cat. The cats' names are Juggles, Bingo, Lovey, and Muff.

Each of the cats has a name that begins with a letter different from the first letter of its owner's name.

Bingo's owner is one of Margaret's best friends. Janice doesn't know Muff's owner, but she took care of Lynn's cat, Juggles, while Lynn was on vacation. *Who owns which cat?*

1. Who owns Juggles?

2. Can Janice own Muff?   Can Margaret?

3. Who owns Muff?

4. Can Margaret own Bingo?

5. Who owns Bingo?

6. Who owns which cat?

YOU CAN DO IT. HERE'S THE KEY. USE PROBLEM-SOLVING STRATEGIES.

PROBLEM-SOLVING STRATEGIES
- DRAW A PICTURE
- MAKE A TABLE
- USE PHYSICAL MODELS
- USE LOGICAL REASONING
- WORK BACKWARD

$$26 + 8 = 34$$

Estimating Sums: Mental Math

A. There were 476 students at Lakeview School in 1955. There are now 113 more students at Lakeview than in 1955. About how many students are at Lakeview now?

Estimate 476 + 113.

Be smart. Estimate when you calculate.

$$476 + 113$$
$$\downarrow \qquad \downarrow$$
$$500 + 100 = 600$$

Round 476 and 113 to the nearest hundred. Then add.

Actual sum
```
  476
+ 113
─────
  589
```

There are about 600 students at Lakeview now.

B. Estimate each sum to the nearest thousand.

$5,530 + 2,641 = $ ▨▨▨ (Both numbers are rounded up.) Actual sum: 8,171

$5,430 + 2,341 = $ ▨▨▨ (Both numbers are rounded down.) Actual sum: 7,771

$5,530 + 2,341 = $ ▨▨▨ (One number is rounded up. One number is rounded down.) Actual sum: 7,871

Try *Estimation* Estimate each sum. First round both numbers to the given place.

a. 56 + 47 (nearest ten)

b. 314 + 525 (nearest hundred)

c. 7,305 + 1,671 (nearest thousand)

d. 2,376 + 542 (nearest hundred)

e. `CALCULATOR` Use your calculator to find the actual sums for Exercises a–d. Compare each actual sum with its estimated sum. What can you say about the actual sum of two numbers and their estimated sum
- if both numbers are rounded up to get the estimated sum?
- if both numbers are rounded down to get the estimated sum?
- if one number is rounded up and the other is rounded down to get the estimated sum?

Practice *Estimation* Estimate each sum.

First round both numbers to the nearest ten.

1. 12 + 17   2. 31 + 22   3. 68 + 21   4. 51 + 42   5. 45 + 37

6. 41 + 26   7. 27 + 42   8. 58 + 29   9. 528 + 21   10. 82 + 312

First round both numbers to the nearest hundred.

11. 671 + 218   12. 452 + 113   13. 529 + 410   14. 602 + 325

15. 238 + 311   16. 213 + 284   17. 503 + 2,310   18. 1,636 + 252

First round both numbers to the nearest thousand.

19. 6,242 + 2,731   20. 4,175 + 1,214   21. 7,865 + 1,132

22. 2,006 + 6,482   23. 2,345 + 5,132   24. 2,468 + 3,531

25. For Exercises 1–10, write whether you think the actual sum will be *greater than* or *less than* the estimated sum. If you cannot tell, write *cannot tell*. Explain your reasoning to another student.

Apply *Estimation* Solve each problem by finding the actual answer. Then estimate to see if your answer is reasonable.

26. Clark School's cafeteria served 165 hot lunches and 432 sandwich plates. How many meals were served in all?

27. At Lakeview, 202 milk tickets were sold. 37 more lunch tickets than milk tickets were sold. How many lunch tickets were sold?

28. Bus A travels 21 miles each morning picking up students for Clark Middle School. In the afternoon, it follows the same route. Find the total number of miles Bus A travels each day.

Renaming for Addition

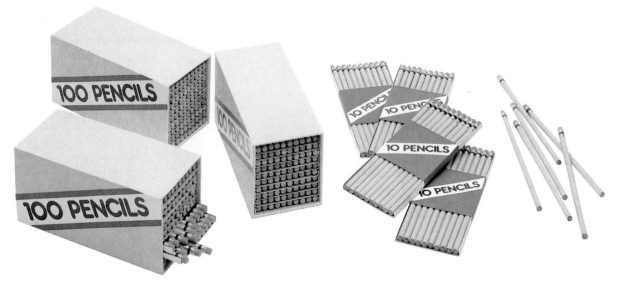

Rename 2 hundreds 14 tens 6 ones. Write the standard form.

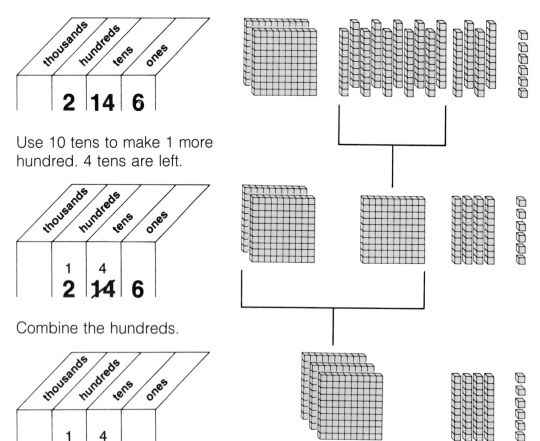

thousands	hundreds	tens	ones
2	**14**	**6**

Use 10 tens to make 1 more hundred. 4 tens are left.

thousands	hundreds	tens	ones
	1	4	
2	**14**	**6**

Combine the hundreds.

thousands	hundreds	tens	ones
	1	4	
2	**14**	**6**

346 ←Standard form

Try Rename. Write the standard form.

a.

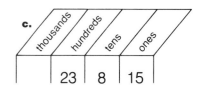
b.

c.

Practice Rename. Write the standard form.

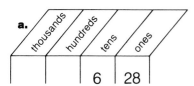
1.

2.

3.

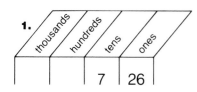
4.

5.

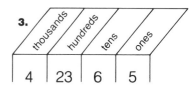
6.

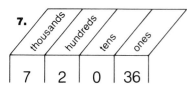
7.

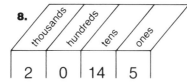
8.

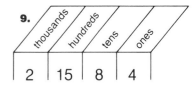
9.

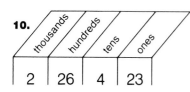
10.

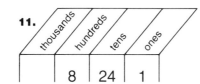
11.

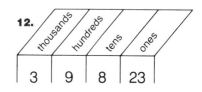
12.

Apply Solve each problem.

13. There are 3 boxes of 100 pens, 14 packs of 10 pens, and 5 single pens on the shelf. How many pens are on the shelf?

14. *Write a problem.* Tom started with 6. He used the rule "add 5" to get 6, 11, 16, 21. Start with a number, make a rule, list the numbers, and have another student discover the rule.

Addition: One Renaming

For Music Week, 238 students from the Clark School choruses joined 126 students from the Lakeview School choruses for a program of folk songs.

Remember hundreds, tens, and ones, and you'll understand how it's done.

A. Is it reasonable to say that there were about 1,000 students in the combined choruses? Explain why or why not.

In this book you will often be asked to work in groups. Turn to pages 438–441 for instructions on group work.

Work in groups of 4 and write a paragraph that explains how estimation can help you decide if an answer is reasonable.

About how many students were in the combined choruses?

B. Exactly how many students were in the combined choruses?

Find 238 + 126.

Add the ones.		Add the tens.	Add the hundreds.
$\overset{1}{2}3\mathbf{8}$ $+12\mathbf{6}$ $\overline{\mathbf{4}}$	Rename 14 ones as 1 ten 4 ones.	$\overset{1}{2}\mathbf{3}8$ $+1\mathbf{2}6$ $\overline{\mathbf{6}4}$	$\overset{1}{\mathbf{2}}38$ $+\mathbf{1}26$ $\overline{\mathbf{3}64}$

There are 364 students in the combined chorus.

Look at your estimate in Example A.
Is 364 students a reasonable answer?

Oh my Darling,
Oh my Darling,
Oh my Darling,
Clementine,
You are lost
And gone forever.
Dreadful sorry,
Clementine.

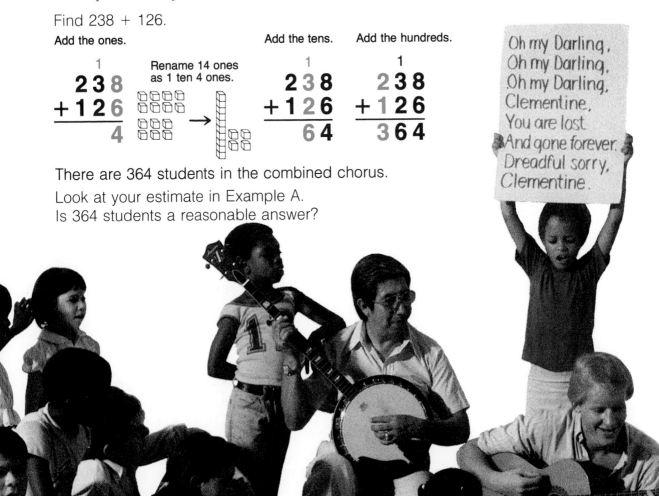

Try Work in groups. Add. Explain why your answers are reasonable.

a. 43
       +19

b. 19
       +43

c. 4,825
       +2,963

d. 3,471 + 286

e. Compare exercises a and b. What does this show you about adding two numbers?

Practice *Choosing a Computation Method* Calculator, Paper and Pencil, Mental Math
Add. Choose a method to find each answer. Tell which method you used.

1. 78
       + 15

2. 23
       + 58

3. 53
       + 19

4. 47
       + 26

5. 314
       + 295

6. 645
       + 126

7. 382
       + 255

8. 437
       + 256

9. 6,513
       + 2,585

10. 2,578
        + 6,331

11. 7,801
        + 1,557

12. 2,632
        + 1,557

13. 628
        + 91

14. 372
        + 85

15. 3,745
        + 342

16. 28 + 45

17. 259 + 113

18. 6,851 + 2,746

Mental Math

Mental math Add mentally. Write only the sum.

19. 50 + 30

20. 412 + 67

21. 6,000 + 800

22. 804 + 73

23. 76 + 21

24. 100 + 500

25. 1,350 + 4,602

26. 268 + 20

Apply *Choosing a Computation Method* Calculator, Paper and Pencil, Mental Math, Estimation
Choose a method to solve each problem. Tell which method you used.

27. The combined chorus had 18 more girls than boys. There were 173 boys. How many girls were there?

28. The chorus sang 13 folk songs. Of these, 8 were American folk songs. The rest were Mexican. How many were Mexican songs?

29. The chorus gave a concert for 452 people on Friday and for 346 people on Saturday. Is it reasonable to say that 500 people attended the two performances? Explain why or why not.

30. The combined chorus practiced together twice during Music Week. Each practice lasted 45 minutes. How many minutes did they practice together during that week?

Addition: More Than One Renaming

The Cardozo High School Band traveled by bus to California to march in the Rose Bowl Parade. They traveled 1,987 miles going and 2,108 miles coming back by a different route. How many miles did the band travel in all?

Find 1,987 + 2,108.

> Estimate using rounding:
> 2,000 + 2,000 = 4,000

Add the ones.	Add the tens.	Add the hundreds.	Add the thousands.
$\begin{array}{r} 1 \\ 1,987 \\ +\ 2,108 \\ \hline 5 \end{array}$	$\begin{array}{r} 1 \\ 1,987 \\ +\ 2,108 \\ \hline 95 \end{array}$	$\begin{array}{r} 1\ \ 1 \\ 1,987 \\ +\ 2,108 \\ \hline 095 \end{array}$	$\begin{array}{r} 1\ \ 1 \\ 1,987 \\ +\ 2,108 \\ \hline 4,095 \end{array}$
Rename 15 ones as 1 ten 5 ones.		Rename 10 hundreds as 1 thousand 0 hundreds.	

The band traveled 4,095 miles in all.

Try Add.

a. 368
    + 593

b. 2,687
    + 2,951

c. 5,783
    +   768

d. 7,980 + 485

Practice Add.

1. 297
    + 493

2. 629
    + 282

3. 366
    + 435

4. 452
    + 258

 **Be smart.
Estimate when
you calculate.**

5. 593
  + 668

6. 386
  + 857

7. 2,615
  + 5,846

8. 6,548
  + 3,624

Choosing a Computation Method Calculator, Paper and Pencil, Mental Math
Add. Choose a method to find each answer. Tell which method you used.

9. 8,735
  +2,883

10. 6,674
  +2,751

11. 4,367
  +2,435

12. 2,179
  +5,320

13. 3,487
  +3,666

14. 5,636 + 2,889

15. 694 + 36

16. 385 + 15

17. 7,463 + 4,859

18. 6,878 + 8,342

19. 1,782 + 956

20. 8,127 + 386

21. 853 + 279

22. 4,680 + 7,976

Apply   *Choosing a Computation Method*   Calculator, Paper and Pencil, Mental Math, Estimation
Choose a method to solve each problem. Tell which method you used.
Explain to another student why you chose that method.

23. The Central High School Band traveled 1,329 miles to the Orange Bowl Parade. The return trip was 1,397 miles. How many miles did the band travel in all?

24. The Willis High School Band traveled 1,017 miles to the Cotton Bowl Parade and 895 miles home. Did the band travel more or less than 2,000 miles in all?

25. Did the Central High School Band travel farther going to the Orange Bowl Parade or returning home? Use the information in Problem 23.

26. A band on tour made trips of 524 miles, 687 miles, 321 miles, 1,029 miles, and 476 miles. How many miles did the band travel?

Three or More Addends

A. *Career* Dr. Mike Madaus is a children's dentist. On Monday he saw 8 patients for fillings, 5 patients for tooth removals, and 12 patients for routine checkups. How many patients did Dr. Mike see on Monday?

Find 8 + 5 + 12.

Add the ones.

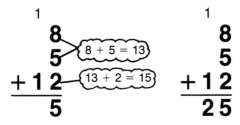

$$
\begin{array}{r}
1 \\
8 \\
5 \\
+12 \\
\hline
5
\end{array}
$$

8 + 5 = 13
13 + 2 = 15

Add the tens.

$$
\begin{array}{r}
1 \\
8 \\
5 \\
+12 \\
\hline
25
\end{array}
$$

Dr. Mike saw 25 patients on Monday.

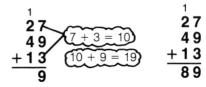

Mental Math

B. Find 27 + 49 + 13.

Look for sums of 10 to help you add mentally.

Add the ones.

$$
\begin{array}{r}
1 \\
27 \\
49 \\
+13 \\
\hline
9
\end{array}
$$

7 + 3 = 10
10 + 9 = 19

Add the tens.

$$
\begin{array}{r}
1 \\
27 \\
49 \\
+13 \\
\hline
89
\end{array}
$$

Try Add.

a.
$$
\begin{array}{r}
3 \\
7 \\
+24 \\
\hline
\end{array}
$$

b.
$$
\begin{array}{r}
639 \\
527 \\
+256 \\
\hline
\end{array}
$$

c.
$$
\begin{array}{r}
6,509 \\
2,872 \\
+1,969 \\
\hline
\end{array}
$$

d. 26 + 358 + 497 + 32

Practice Add.

1. $\begin{array}{r} 2 \\ 6 \\ +37 \end{array}$	**2.** $\begin{array}{r} 37 \\ 5 \\ +19 \end{array}$	**3.** $\begin{array}{r} 24 \\ 37 \\ +56 \end{array}$	**4.** $\begin{array}{r} 46 \\ 17 \\ +65 \end{array}$

5. $\begin{array}{r} 37 \\ 28 \\ +15 \end{array}$	**6.** $\begin{array}{r} 79 \\ 27 \\ +18 \end{array}$	**7.** $\begin{array}{r} 410 \\ 361 \\ +233 \end{array}$	**8.** $\begin{array}{r} 432 \\ 371 \\ +754 \end{array}$

Choosing a Computation Method

Calculator, Paper and Pencil, Mental Math
Choose a method to solve each problem.
Tell which method you used.

9. $\begin{array}{r} 105 \\ 562 \\ +347 \end{array}$	**10.** $\begin{array}{r} 392 \\ 747 \\ +741 \end{array}$	**11.** $\begin{array}{r} 3{,}162 \\ 6{,}392 \\ +4{,}861 \end{array}$	**12.** $\begin{array}{r} 1{,}322 \\ 1{,}074 \\ +7{,}429 \end{array}$

13. $\begin{array}{r} 63 \\ 24 \\ 43 \\ +36 \end{array}$	**14.** $\begin{array}{r} 97 \\ 52 \\ 13 \\ +28 \end{array}$	**15.** $\begin{array}{r} 306 \\ 245 \\ 124 \\ +212 \end{array}$	**16.** $\begin{array}{r} 1{,}971 \\ 1{,}834 \\ 3{,}256 \\ +1{,}123 \end{array}$

17. $76 + 52 + 62$

18. $42 + 17 + 38 + 13$

19. $217 + 485 + 812$

20. $392 + 647 + 423 + 125$

21. $482 + 67 + 145$

22. $36 + 745 + 801 + 25$

Apply Solve each problem.

23. It took Dr. Mike 10 minutes to examine Estela's teeth, 19 minutes to clean her teeth, and 18 minutes to fill a tooth. How many minutes did all of this take?

24. Dr. Mike saw 25 patients on Monday, 19 on Tuesday, 22 on Thursday, and 21 on Friday. How many patients did he see during those four days?

25. A filling costs $33 and X rays cost $24. Which costs more, a filling or X rays?

CALCULATOR

Numbers like 545, 3,883, and 21,012 are called _palindromes_. In a palindrome, the digits are in the same order whether you read from left to right, or from right to left.

A palindrome can be made by using addition. A calculator can help with the addition. Follow these steps.

- Enter a number on your calculator.

- Reverse the digits and add.

- If the sum is not a palindrome, continue to reverse the digits and add.

Press:　48 $\boxed{+}$ 84 $\boxed{=}$

Display:　_132_　（132 is not a palindrome.）

Press:　$\boxed{+}$ 231 $\boxed{=}$

Display:　_363_　（363 is a palindrome.）

Make a palindrome from each number.

1. 63　　**2.** 29

3. 79　　**4.** 86

5. 235　　**6.** 529

7. 7,543　　**8.** 5,716

Practice: Addition

Choosing a Computation Method Calculator, Paper and Pencil, Mental Math ·
Add. For Exercises 1–28, choose a method to find each answer.
Tell which method you used.

1. 87
   + 5

2. 46
   + 38

3. 746
   + 235

4. 234
   + 562

5. 573
   + 292

6. 543
   + 278

7. 729
   + 484

8. 5,201
   + 3,698

9. 3,754
   + 4,629

10. 6,784
    + 3,662

11. 5,048
    + 1,736

12. 3,625
    + 947

13. 1,708
    + 392

14. 6,872
    + 553

15. 4,636
    + 382

16. 83
    71
    + 46

17. 97
    72
    + 81

18. 157
    538
    + 226

19. 248
    578
    + 436

20. 4,625
    4,019
    + 1,268

21. 38 + 43

22. 754 + 72

23. 369 + 223

24. 3,073 + 1,552

25. 896 + 344

26. 634 + 48

27. 4,853 + 395

28. 7,639 + 1,586

Apply Solve each problem.

29. Last week Dr. Mike filled 27 teeth. He filled 17 more teeth this week than last week. How many teeth did he fill this week?

30. Dr. Mike has 367 "No Cavities" stickers and 258 "Good Checkup" stickers to give patients. How many stickers does he have in all?

31. *Estimation* During Dental Week Dr. Mike talked to 257 students and 105 parents. Estimate how many people he talked to in all. First round each number to the nearest hundred.

32. Aaron's dental appointment lasted 37 minutes. His brother's appointment lasted 15 minutes longer. How long did his brother's appointment last?

33. Each week Dr. Mike's office is open 8 hours per day for 3 days, and 10 hours per day for 2 days. How many hours is his office open each week?

34. **CALCULATOR** A float in the Rose Bowl Parade was decorated with 4,650 red flowers, 5,465 white flowers, 4,270 yellow flowers, and 3,845 orange flowers. How many flowers in all were used on the float?

35. _Mental math_ By age nine, Terri had lost 10 teeth. By age twelve, she had lost 10 more teeth. How many teeth did she lose in all?

36. Joanie and her mother drive in from Newberry to see the dentist. The trip is 78 miles each way. How many miles is the round trip?

Be smart. Estimate when you calculate.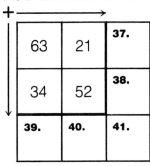

Add across. Add down.

+ ⟶

63	21	**37.**
34	52	**38.**
39.	**40.**	**41.**

+ ⟶

46	45	**42.**
27	47	**43.**
44.	**45.**	**46.**

+ ⟶

74	29	**47.**
25	57	**48.**
49.	**50.**	**51.**

+ ⟶

118	109	**52.**
296	272	**53.**
54.	**55.**	**56.**

+ ⟶

185	49	**57.**
289	98	**58.**
59.	**60.**	**61.**

+ ⟶

47	689	**62.**
68	153	**63.**
64.	**6 5.**	**66.**

67. `CALCULATOR` Make the display show 50. Use only these keys: 4, 5, ＋, ＝.

68. `CALCULATOR` Do Problem 67 again, using the same keys. Use the _least_ number of keys. Compare key sequences with your classmates.

69. Becky has 57 cents.

She has 11 coins.

She has at least one quarter, one dime, one nickel, and one penny.

Work with another student to find how many of each of the coins Becky has.

Estimating Differences: Mental Math

In the mid-1950s, there were 479 pairs of Kirtland warblers found in North America. By the early 1970s, only 216 pairs could be found. About how many fewer pairs of Kirtland warblers were found in North America in the early 1970s?

Estimate 479 − 216.

479 − 216

⬇   ⬇

500 − 200 = 300

Round 479 and 216 to the nearest hundred. Then subtract.

Actual difference

$$\begin{array}{r} 479 \\ -\ 216 \\ \hline 263 \end{array}$$

There were about 300 fewer pairs of Kirtland warblers in the early 1970s.

Try *Estimation* Estimate each difference. First round both numbers to the given place.

a. 58 − 32 (nearest ten)

b. 847 − 115 (nearest hundred)

c. 5,727 − 4,025 (nearest thousand)

d. 148 − 43 (nearest ten)

e. 8,645 − 412 (nearest hundred)

f. 1,256 − 893 (nearest hundred)

Practice *Estimation* Estimate each difference.

First round both numbers to the nearest ten.

1. 59 − 17   **2.** 79 − 32   **3.** 48 − 22   **4.** 84 − 21   **5.** 67 − 42

6. 38 − 13   **7.** 142 − 31   **8.** 179 − 74   **9.** 197 − 76   **10.** 186 − 51

First round both numbers to the nearest hundred.

11. 863 − 202   **12.** 487 − 153   **13.** 654 − 103   **14.** 328 − 214

15. 1,336 − 215   **16.** 1,564 − 463   **17.** 1,792 − 681   **18.** 1,846 − 523

First round both numbers to the nearest thousand.

19. 7,846 − 2,635   **20.** 1,985 − 1,213   **21.** 5,468 − 4,467

22. 4,673 − 1,051   **23.** 6,095 − 2,032   **24.** 8,500 − 2,500

Apply *Estimation* Solve each problem by finding the actual answer. Then estimate to see if your answer is reasonable.

25. In 1912, there were only 88 whooping cranes in Texas and Louisiana. 32 of them were in Louisiana. How many were in Texas?

26. In 1982, Hawaii had 27 kinds of endangered birds. The rest of the United States had 23 other kinds. How many kinds of endangered birds were in the entire United States in 1982?

27. *Find the facts.* In Cary, a rally to save birds was attended by 4,120 of its citizens. Use data from the table on page 37 to tell about how many citizens did not attend.

Renaming for Subtraction

A. Rename 356 to show 10 more ones.

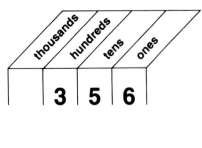

1 ten is 10 ones.
There are 16 ones in all.

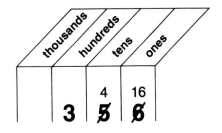

thousands	hundreds	tens	ones
3	5	4	16 6

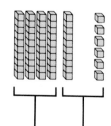

Remember hundreds, tens, and ones,
and you'll understand how it's done.

B. Rename 3,027 to show 10 more tens.

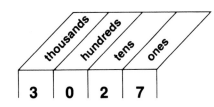

thousands	hundreds	tens	ones
3	0	2	7

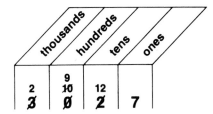

thousands	hundreds	tens	ones
2 3	9 10 0	12 2	7

Try Rename to show

a. 10 more tens.

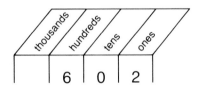

thousands	hundreds	tens	ones
	6	0	2

b. 10 more hundreds.

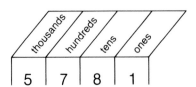

thousands	hundreds	tens	ones
5	7	8	1

c. 10 more ones.

thousands	hundreds	tens	ones
7	4	0	5

Practice Rename to show 10 more ones.

1.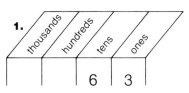

2.

3.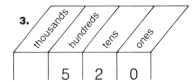

4.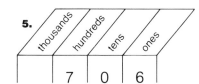

5.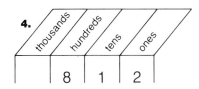

6.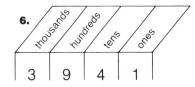

Rename to show 10 more tens.

7.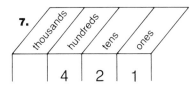

8.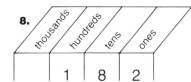

9.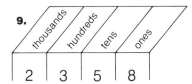

10.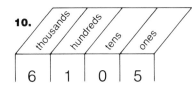

11.

12.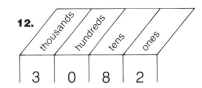

Rename to show 10 more hundreds.

13.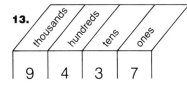

14.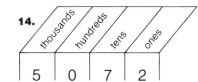

15.

Apply Solve each problem.

16. Tom had 6 bunches of 10 roses and 5 single roses. He took one bunch of 10 roses and put them with the single roses. Then how many bunches of 10 and single roses did he have?

17. Tom had 2 boxes of 100 tulip bulbs and 4 bags of 10 bulbs. He took 100 bulbs from one box and put them into bags of 10. Then how many boxes of 100 and bags of 10 did he have?

Subtraction: One Renaming

The National Zoo in Washington, D.C., has two giant pandas.
The male weighs 126 kilograms. The female weighs 109 kilograms.
How much more does the male weigh than the female?

Find 126 − 109. Estimate the difference by rounding
each number to the nearest ten. 130 − 110 =

Rename to show 10 more ones.		Subtract the ones.	Subtract the tens. Subtract the hundreds. There are no hundreds left.
1 16		1 16	1 16
12̸6̸	2 tens 6 ones = 1 ten 16 ones	12̸6̸	12̸6̸
− 1 0 9		− 1 0 9	− 1 0 9
		7	17

The male panda weighs 17 kilograms more than the female.
Check to see if the exact answer is close to the estimate. Why
is it important to estimate before you subtract?

Try For exercises a–d, estimate each difference. Then
subtract to find the exact answer and compare it to your
estimate to see if your answer is reasonable.

a. 84
  − 37

b. 624
  − 372

c. 8,435
  − 5,183

d. 245 − 26

e. Suppose you estimate an answer to a subtraction problem
   to be 7,600 and when you subtract you get an exact answer
   of 6,567. Is your answer reasonable? Why or why not?

Practice Subtract.

1. 54
  −27

2. 97
  −59

3. 90
  −64

4. 927
  −681

5. 763
  −427

6. 635
  −250

7. 7,634
  −6,182

8. 9,147
  −5,643

Choosing a Computation Method Calculator, Paper and Pencil, Mental Math
Subtract. Choose a method to find each answer.
Tell which method you used.

9. 734
   − 61

10. 6,735
    − 392

11. 4,375
    − 854

12. 8,763
    − 239

13. 5,327
    −1,152

14. 250 − 136

15. 4,137 − 1,029

16. 2,738 − 1,654

17. 826 − 54

Mental math Subtract mentally. Write only the difference.

18. 8,000 − 6,000

19. 572 − 300

20. 98 − 45

21. 731 − 401

  Mental Math

22. 9,865 − 7,000

23. 50 − 20

24. 800 − 700

Apply Solve each problem.

25. The two giant pandas arrived at the National Zoo in 1972. The zoo had opened 82 years earlier. In what year did the National Zoo open?

26. _Estimation_ The National Zoo covers an area of 173 acres. The St. Louis Zoo covers an area of 83 acres. Estimate how many more acres are covered by the National Zoo than by the St. Louis Zoo. First round both numbers to the nearest ten.

27. Let a be any number. Choose a number for b so that b is less than a. Put your numbers in the sentences below.
$a + b = b + a$ $a − b = b − a$
Are both of the sentences true? Explain why or why not. What can you say about the sentences when a and b are equal?

Subtraction: More Than One Renaming

Laurie and Jennifer Takata went to the zoo in their city. They saw 315 mammals and 167 birds. How many more mammals did they see than birds?

Find 315 − 167.

Estimate using rounding:
300 − 200 = 100

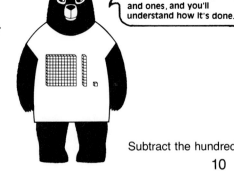

Remember hundreds, tens, and ones, and you'll understand how it's done.

Rename to show 10 more ones. Subtract the ones.

```
  0 15
3 1̸ 5̸
-1 6 7
──────
      8
```

1 ten 5 ones = 0 tens 15 ones

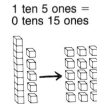

Rename to show 10 more tens. Subtract the tens.

```
    10
2 0̸ 15
3 1̸ 5̸
-1 6 7
──────
    4 8
```

3 hundreds 0 tens = 2 hundreds 10 tens

Subtract the hundreds.

```
    10
2 0̸ 15
3 1̸ 5̸
-1 6 7
──────
1 4 8
```

Laurie and Jennifer saw 148 more mammals than birds.

Try Subtract.

a. 736
      − 349

b. 8,127
      − 675

c. 7,194
      − 1,856

d. 340 − 93

70

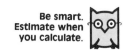
Practice   Subtract.

1. 543
     − 76

2. 350
     − 65

3. 817
     − 429

4. 450
     − 179

5. 684
     − 288

6. 8,157
     − 663

7. 5,975
     − 678

8. 2,597
     − 789

9. 6,783
     − 1,975

10. 7,194
     − 1,857

11. 732
     − 67

12. 852
     − 496

13. 340 − 68

14. 3,192 − 275

15. 4,255 − 1,718

16. 6,718 − 3,826

Apply   Solve each problem.

17. The zoo has 173 birds. Of these, 19 are parrots. How many birds other than parrots are there?

18. On Saturday, 6,145 people visited the zoo. On Sunday, 1,387 fewer people came than on Saturday. How many people came on Sunday?

19. *Estimation* The zoo aquarium has 38 fish that live in fresh water and 53 fish that live in salt water. About how many fish does the zoo aquarium have in all? Choose the best estimate.

 80   90   100

★20. The zoo has 43 ducks in its duck pond. 17 of the ducks are mallards, and 12 of them are wood ducks. How many other ducks are in the pond?

21. *Thinking skills* Fill in the missing numbers in the addition square.

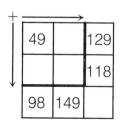

Round each number to the nearest ten.

1. 48   **2.** 172

3. 315   **4.** 87

5. 91   **6.** 624

Round each number to the nearest hundred.

7. 819   **8.** 493

9. 125   **10.** 657

11. 2,572   **12.** 1,209

Round each number to the nearest thousand.

13. 3,416   **14.** 6,540

15. 7,381   **16.** 1,253

17. 2,940   **18.** 4,286

Compare the numbers. Use < or >.

19. 65 ● 57

20. 76 ● 93

21. 352 ● 355

22. 849 ● 846

23. 1,048 ● 1,163

24. 6,281 ● 6,820

Subtraction: Renaming with Zeros

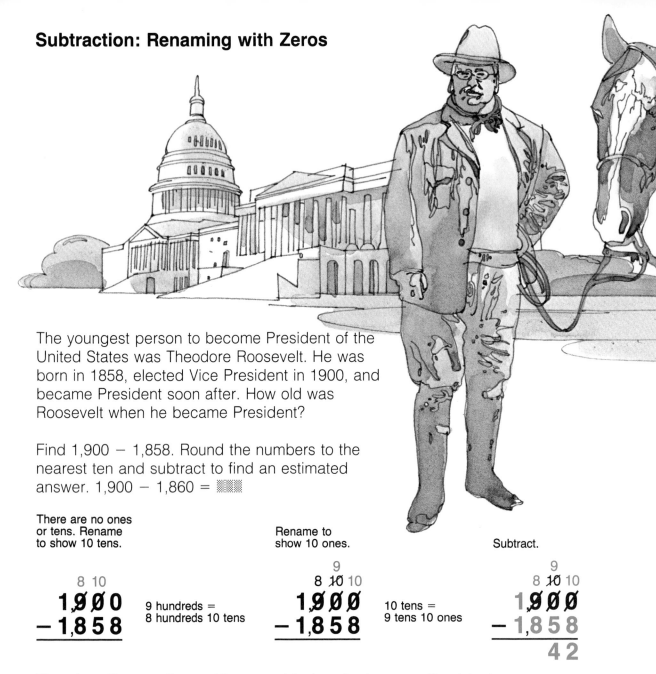

The youngest person to become President of the United States was Theodore Roosevelt. He was born in 1858, elected Vice President in 1900, and became President soon after. How old was Roosevelt when he became President?

Find 1,900 − 1,858. Round the numbers to the nearest ten and subtract to find an estimated answer. 1,900 − 1,860 = ▒▒▒

There are no ones or tens. Rename to show 10 tens.

```
    8 10
  1,9 0̸ 0
− 1,8 5 8
```
9 hundreds = 8 hundreds 10 tens

Rename to show 10 ones.

```
       9
     8 1̸0̸ 10
  1,9̸ 0̸ 0̸
− 1,8  5 8
```
10 tens = 9 tens 10 ones

Subtract.

```
       9
     8 1̸0̸ 10
  1,9̸ 0̸ 0̸
− 1,8  5 8
        4 2
```

Theodore Roosevelt was 42 years old when he became President.
Compare the estimated answer with the actual answer.
Was the actual answer close to the estimated answer?
What does this tell you?

Try Estimate the answer to each of the exercises. Then find the actual answer and compare it to its estimated answer to check for reasonableness.

a. 807
   −129

b. 300
   −167

c. 8,004
   − 563

d. 4,000 − 1,256

e. 2,401 − 53

72

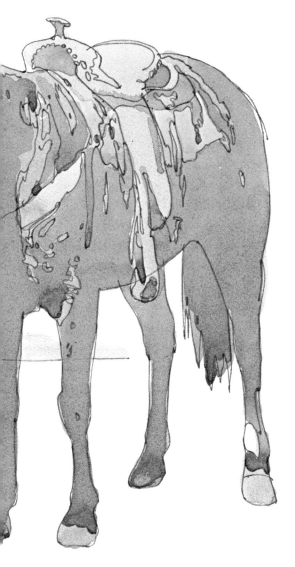

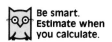
Be smart.
Estimate when
you calculate.

1. 605
    − 439

2. 403
    − 174

3. 500
    − 286

4. 700
    − 351

5. 204
    − 117

6. 800
    − 529

7. 504
    − 67

8. 706
    − 38

9. 300
    − 99

10. 800
     − 76

11. 408
     − 29

12. 503
     − 56

13. 6,902
     − 3,425

14. 5,801
     − 3,682

15. 2,600
     − 1,344

16. 6,700 − 5,379   17. 2,030 − 269

18. 7,020 − 443   19. 2,004 − 372

20. 5,002 − 661   21. 3,076 − 83

22. 1,027 − 45   23. 6,000 − 1,278

Apply   Solve each problem.

24. John F. Kennedy was another young President. He was born in 1917 and elected President in 1960. How old was he when he was elected President?

25. The oldest person to be elected President was Ronald Reagan. He was born in 1911 and elected in 1980. How old was he when he was elected President?

26. Thomas Jefferson was elected President in 1800 at the age of 57. What was the year of his birth?

27. Abraham Lincoln was born in 1809 and elected President at the age of 51. In what year was he elected President?

28. **CALCULATOR** Press: 75 − 30 CE 40 CE 25 = .
    What happened on your calculator?

THE SOCK DRAW

Claudia was getting dressed for a party when a storm caused the lights to go out. She still needed to find a matching pair of socks. She knew that she had only 3 colors of socks in the drawer—white, yellow, and blue. Her brother said, "Just take several, and then when we get in the car you can pick out a matching pair." *What is the least number of socks that she should take to be sure of having a matched pair?*

Work in groups of 4. In this book you will often be asked to work in groups. Turn to pages 438–441 for instructions on group work.

We could act out this problem by using different colored counters to represent the socks. Place 6 counters, 2 of each color, in an envelope or some other container and draw out some "socks" one at a time until two of the same color are drawn.

1. How many socks did your group draw before two of one color were drawn?

2. Compare the results of your group with those of other groups. What was the least number of draws found by a group in your class? What was the greatest number of draws?

Repeat the experiment two more times. Compare your results with those of other groups.

3. How many socks do you think Claudia should take? Give reasons for your decision.

4. Suppose that Claudia had 4 different colors of socks. How many socks should she take to make sure that she would have a matching pair?

5. If Claudia had socks of 6 different colors, how many socks should she take?

6. Claudia is taking a present to the party. She has almost finished wrapping it. She wants to decorate the package with 3 stickers of the same color. She has stickers of 4 different colors in a bag. What is the least number of stickers that she should take so that she will be sure to have 3 stickers of one color?

BASIC: Addition and Subtraction in PRINT Statements

When this program is run on a computer, the numbers are added and only the answer is printed.

This is printed.

```
10 PRINT 243+119
20 END
```
```
362
```

For this program, the numbers are subtracted and the answer is printed.

This is printed.

```
10 PRINT 845-286
20 PRINT 756-397
30 END
```
```
559
359
```

Tell what would be printed for each program.

1.
```
10 PRINT 325+295
20 END
```

2.
```
10 PRINT 756-397
20 END
```

3.
```
10 PRINT 196+242
20 PRINT 5124+1683
30 END
```

4.
```
10 PRINT 289-191
20 PRINT 2763-1825
30 PRINT 563+108
40 END
```

*5.
```
10 PRINT "THE SUM IS"
30 PRINT "THE DIFFERENCE IS"
40 PRINT 503-75
20 PRINT 67+98+35
50 END
```

75

Checking Addition and Subtraction

Isabel Diaz works in the school library. Whenever she uses addition or subtraction in her work, she checks her answers.

A. Isabel uses addition to check subtraction.

Check:

```
  654          375
− 279        + 279
─────        ─────
  375          654
```

B. Isabel uses subtraction to check addition.

Check:

```
  476          601
+ 125        − 125
─────        ─────
  601          476
```

Discuss How can you use addition to check addition?

Try Check each answer. Tell whether it is right or wrong.
If it is wrong, give the correct answer.

a.	b.	c.	d.	e.
478	837	6,300	276	4,506
+ 972	− 84	− 2,164	− 88	+ 1,293
1,440	753	4,136	192	5,799

Practice Check each answer. Tell whether it is right
or wrong. If it is wrong, give the correct answer.

1.	2.	3.	4.	5.
61	346	526	3,728	8,833
+ 59	+ 183	+ 295	+ 4,963	+ 1,079
110	529	721	8,591	9,912

6.	7.	8.	9.	10.
81	623	365	9,516	2,009
− 68	− 89	− 174	− 1,624	− 1,378
13	634	191	8,112	731

Add or subtract. Watch the signs.
Check each answer.

11.	12.	13.	14.	15.
289	756	196	503	682
− 191	− 397	+ 242	− 75	+ 357

16.	17.	18.	19.	20.
5,124	3,298	7,048	5,006	7,324
+ 638	+ 2,043	− 563	− 2,317	+ 1,676

Apply Solve each problem. Check your answers.

21. The school library has 3,050 books. 598 of them are now checked out. How many books are left in the library?

22. The library has 1,478 fiction books and 1,756 nonfiction books. How many fiction and nonfiction books does the library have?

23. In January, 805 library books were checked out. In February, 769 library books were checked out. How many more library books were checked out in January than in February?

24. `CALCULATOR` A library system has bookmobiles containing 5,645 books, 4,780 books, and 6,930 books. The main library building contains 17,250 books. How many books in all are in this library system?

Addition and Subtraction of Money

The "zebra stripes" on most supermarket products are bar codes. When read by a scanner, the codes identify the product to the store's computer. The computer contains price information that is then automatically rung on the cash register.

0 |||||||||||||||||||||
    36000 290
    PRODUCT CODE

A. The computer scanner read codes for $1.59 and $3.27. What total was rung on the cash register?

Find $1.59 + $3.27.

$$\begin{array}{r} \$1.59 \\ +\ 3.27 \\ \hline \end{array} \quad \begin{array}{r} 159 \\ +327 \\ \hline 486 \end{array} \quad \begin{array}{r} \$1.59 \\ +\ 3.27 \\ \hline \$4.86 \end{array}$$

The total was $4.86.

B. The cash register total for Kenji's order was $2.89. He paid for it with a $5.00 bill. How much money did Kenji get back?

Find $5.00 − $2.89.

$$\begin{array}{r} \$5.00 \\ -\ 2.89 \\ \hline \end{array} \quad \begin{array}{r} 500 \\ -289 \\ \hline 211 \end{array} \quad \begin{array}{r} \$5.00 \\ -\ 2.89 \\ \hline \$2.11 \end{array}$$

Kenji got back $2.11.

C. **CALCULATOR** One day Jody did some grocery shopping for both her mother and her grandfather. Her mother's groceries cost $18.38 and her grandfather's cost $7.98. How much more did her mother's groceries cost than her grandfather's? Use a calculator to find $18.38 − $7.98.

Press: 18 $\boxed{\cdot}$ 38 $\boxed{-}$ 7 $\boxed{\cdot}$ 98 $\boxed{=}$

Try Add or subtract.

a. $53.25
  + 7.85

b. $10.00
  − 6.24

c. $29.26
  − 4.94

Practice Add or subtract.

1. $8.54
  + 0.23

2. $5.42
  + 4.68

3. $43.49
  + 24.77

4. $16.32
  − 4.93

5. $89.35
  − 34.82

6. $73.91
  − 6.47

Choosing a Computation Method
Calculator, Paper and Pencil, Mental Math
Choose a method to solve each problem.
Tell which method you used.

7. $5.99
  + 0.17

8. $79.18
  + 32.82

9. $0.98
  + 0.49

10. $5.25
  − 0.98

11. $5.00
  − 2.62

12. $86.45
  − 52.82

Apply *Choosing a Computation Method*
Calculator, Paper and Pencil, Mental Math, Estimation
Choose a method to solve each problem.
Tell which method you used. Explain to
another student why you chose that method.

13. Judy has $10.00. Can she buy nuts for
$5.65 and dried fruit for $4.39?

14. The cash register total for Ramona's
order was $6.45. She paid for it with a
$10.00 bill. How much money did she
get back?

15. Wayne bought grocery items costing
$1.73, $2.45, $3.27, $0.89, $1.19, $0.66,
and $0.53. What was the total?

16. Amy bought a roast for $7.78 and fruit
for $3.85. To the nearest dollar, what
was the total?

Practice: Addition and Subtraction

Choosing a Computation Method Calculator, Paper and Pencil, Mental Math
For Exercises 1–43, choose a method to find each answer.
Tell which method you used. Add.

1. 38
    + 45

2. 262
    + 178

3. 582
    + 255

4. 4,238
    + 3,922

5. 9,881
    + 4,073

6. 874
    + 67

7. 2,362
    + 574

8. 71
    67
    + 24

9. 526
    812
    + 114

10. 4,861
    3,674
    + 2,233

11. 954 + 76

12. 581 + 295

13. 4,860 + 853

14. 2,535 + 485

Subtract.

15. 64
    − 26

16. 548
    − 59

17. 453
    − 124

18. 384
    − 177

19. 6,007
    − 4,253

20. 8,143
    − 1,287

21. 6,780
    − 4,273

22. 8,003
    − 547

23. 4,259
    − 172

24. 4,600
    − 1,439

25. 665 − 88

26. 4,516 − 925

27. 8,346 − 153

28. 8,500 − 723

Add or subtract. Watch the signs. Check each answer.

29. 643
    − 292

30. 234
    + 681

31. 304
    − 215

32. 385
    + 89

33. 284
    − 57

34. 740
    − 461

35. 500
    − 347

36. 763
    + 442

37. 5,683
    + 4,148

38. 2,493
    − 1,507

39. 7,835
    + 5,392

40. $4.64
    − 2.83

41. $3.27
    + 2.78

42. $60.97
    + 74.35

43. $84.06
    − 33.74

44. 603 − 216

45. 854 + 467

46. 4,704 + 137

47. 3,490 − 192

Mental math Add or subtract mentally. Mental Math

48. 641 + 235

49. 827 − 603

50. 9,000 + 500

51. 740 − 200

Estimation Estimate each answer.

First round both numbers to the nearest ten.

52. 127 + 48   **53.** 45 + 21   **54.** 82 − 49   **55.** 71 + 83   **56.** 184 − 92

First round both numbers to the nearest hundred.

57. 386 − 153   **58.** 263 + 415   **59.** 3,097 − 587   **60.** 1,424 + 562

First round both numbers to the nearest thousand.

61. 6,245 − 3,112   **62.** 7,705 + 2,187   **63.** 2,838 − 1,217

Apply Solve each problem.

Be smart.
Estimate when
you calculate.

64. Carmen bought 24 apples, 15 pears, and 36 plums. How many pieces of fruit did she buy altogether?

65. Carl bought groceries costing $7.43. He paid for them with a $10.00 bill. How much money did he get back?

66. There are 345 food stores in the city and 679 in the suburbs. How many stores are there in the city and the suburbs in all?

67. The Johnsons spent $58.52 for food one week. The next week they spent $62.35 for food. How much did they spend for food in those two weeks?

68. **CALCULATOR** The cash register tape at the right does not show the price of the bread. How much did the bread cost? How did you use your calculator to get the answer? Is there another sequence you could have used? Explain your method to another student.

grocery	2.49
grocery	1.67
meat	5.74
bread	
dairy	1.38
dairy	1.89
Total	14.95

69. _Estimation_ One grocery store chain has 2,842 stores and another has 1,127. About how many more stores does the larger chain have? Choose the best estimate.

2,000   3,000   4,000

Problem Solving | Write an Equation

An *equation*, like a number sentence, can be used to show how the parts of a problem are related.

In 1860, the mail was carried across the West by the Pony Express. The journey took 8 to 10 days.

The Pony Express trail covered a distance of 995 miles from St. Joseph, Missouri, to Green River in the Utah Territory. The distance covered from Green River to Sacramento, California, was 971 miles. What was the total distance covered by the Pony Express trail?

Read　Facts: 995 miles, 971 miles
Find: Total distance

PROBLEM-
SOLVING
STRATEGIES
● CHOOSE THE
  OPERATION
● DRAW A
  PICTURE
● FIND A
  PATTERN
● WRITE AN
  EQUATION
● USE
  ESTIMATION
● MAKE A
  TABLE

Plan　Write an addition equation to show that joining the two parts of the journey gives the total distance. Use *n* for the total distance.

Distance from St. Joseph to Green River		Distance from Green River to Sacramento		Total distance
995	**+**	**971**	**=**	**n**

Solve

$$\begin{array}{r} 995 \\ +\ 971 \\ \hline 1{,}966 \end{array}$$

Estimate:
1,000 + 1,000 = 2,000

n = **1,966**

Answer　The total distance covered by the trail was 1,966 miles.

Look Back　The estimate of 2,000 miles is close to 1,966 miles. The answer is reasonable.

82

Try Write an equation. Then give the answer.

a. When most horses cost about $48 each, Pony Express horses cost about $150. How much more did a Pony Express horse cost?

b. A rider weighed about 125 pounds. He carried about 20 pounds of mail and 8 pounds of supplies. What was the total weight?

Apply Write an equation. Then give the answer.

1. There were 80 Pony Express riders. One trip across the trail used 26 of these riders. How many riders were not used on that trip?

2. Four riders were used between Green River and Camp Floyd. The distances they rode were 78, 54, 76, and 77 miles. What was the total distance they traveled?

3. On the first day, the riders rode 263 miles. On the last day, they rode 195 miles. How much shorter was the ride on the last day than on the first?

4. In 1860, it cost about $160 per pound to send mail by Pony Express. The cost in 1861 was $32 per pound. How much more did it cost in 1860?

5. Bill Cates rode 92 miles. Tommy Ranahan rode 52 miles farther than Bill. How far did Tommy ride?

6. Jack Keetley rode 105 miles. Dan Wescott rode 28 miles less than Jack. How far did Dan ride?

7. Bart Riles rode 119 miles of the trail from Fort Churchill to Ruby Valley. Jay Kelley rode the remaining 118 miles. What was the distance from Fort Churchill to Ruby Valley?

8. In 1861, it cost $32.00 to send one pound of mail by Pony Express. In 1983, it cost $2.58 to send one pound of mail. How much more did it cost in 1861 than in 1983?

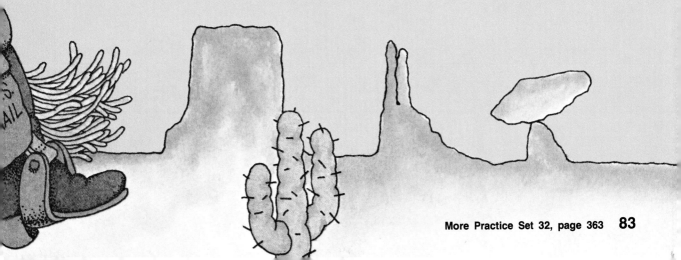

Chapter 3 Test

Estimate each answer. First round both numbers to the nearest ten.

1. 67 + 32   **2.** 88 − 43

Estimate each answer. First round both numbers to the nearest hundred.

3. 281 + 314   **4.** 743 − 212

Rename. Write the standard form.

5.

thousands	hundreds	tens	ones
5	7	24	3

Add.

6. 327
   + 58

7. 1,406
   + 2,534

8. 273
   + 149

9. 5,845
   + 3,627

10. 36
    42
   + 58

11. 363
    257
   + 195

Rename to show 10 more tens.

12.

thousands	hundreds	tens	ones
4	1	9	6

Subtract.

13. 85
   − 36

14. 637
   − 208

15. 5,203
   − 4,270

16. 634
   − 275

17. 902
   − 546

18. 4,007
   − 2,519

Check each answer. Tell whether it is right or wrong. If it is wrong, give the correct answer.

19. 6,029
   − 4,258

   1,831

20. 453
   + 507

    960

Add or subtract.

21. $8.67
   − 3.94

22. $35.26
   + 24.74

Write an equation. Then give the answer.

23. Rosa bought a camera for $68.49 and a case for $9.75. How much did she spend in all?

24. It is 2,762 miles from New York to San Diego. From New York to Seattle it is 2,815 miles. How much farther from New York is it to Seattle than to San Diego?

25. It is 965 miles from Boston to Chicago and 996 miles from Chicago to Denver. How far is it from Boston to Denver through Chicago?

Mental Math Strategies

Kay is a wizard at math. Often, she can do addition and subtraction mentally.

This is how Kay does it.

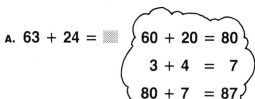

Compute mentally. Use your mind to save you time.

A. 63 + 24 = ▨
> 60 + 20 = 80
> 3 + 4 = 7
> 80 + 7 = 87

The answer is 87.

B. 98 + 56 = ▨
> 98 is 2 less than 100.
> 100 + 56 = 156
> 156 − 2 = 154

The answer is 154.

C. 58 + 37 = ▨
> 58 + 30 = 88
> 88 + 7 = 95

The answer is 95.

D. 132 − 97 = ▨
> 97 is 3 less than 100.
> Add 3 to both numbers.
> 135 − 100 = 35

The answer is 35.

E. 78 − 35 = ▨
> 78 − 30 = 48
> 48 − 5 = 43

The answer is 43.

Find each sum or difference mentally.

1. 52 + 37	**2.** 99 + 43	**3.** 86 − 45	**4.** 132 − 99	**5.** 47 − 19
6. 68 − 27	**7.** 28 + 44	**8.** 44 + 37	**9.** 124 − 98	**10.** 97 + 58
11. 17 + 46	**12.** 76 − 18	**13.** 28 + 47	**14.** 73 − 56	**15.** 157 − 97
16. 145 + 96	**17.** 253 + 38	**18.** 224 + 398	**19.** 402 + 167	**20.** 532 − 299

ZELDA'S USED CARS

Zelda buys and sells used toys. She bought a model car for 50¢ and later sold it for 60¢. A customer told her that he wanted to buy that same model to complete his collection. He was willing to pay 85¢. Zelda bought back the car for 75¢ and then sold it to him for 85¢. *Did Zelda make or lose money? How much?*

1. When Zelda bought the car for 50¢ and sold it for 60¢, did she make or lose money? How much?

2. When Zelda bought the car back for 75¢ and sold it for 85¢, did she make or lose money? How much?

3. How much money did she make or lose in all?

4. If Zelda bought a model car for 20¢, sold it for 40¢, and bought it back for 50¢, how much would she have to sell it for to make 30¢ altogether?

YOU CAN DO IT. HERE'S THE KEY. USE PROBLEM-SOLVING STRATEGIES.

PROBLEM-SOLVING STRATEGIES
- MAKE A TABLE
- FIND A PATTERN
- USE PHYSICAL MODELS
- USE LOGICAL REASONING
- WORK BACKWARD
- LIST ALL POSSIBILITIES
- TRY AND CHECK
- DRAW A DIAGRAM
- MAKE A GRAPH

Cumulative Test, Chapters 1–3

Give the letter for the correct answer.

1. Which number sentence is correct?

   A 27 > 51   **C** 17 < 51
   B 7 > 15   **D** 71 < 37

2. Add.   **A** 9
                 B 8

    3   **C** 10
   + 6   **D** 3

3. Subtract.   **A** 8
                 B 7

    9   **C** 6
   − 2   **D** 11

4. Add.   **A** 17
                 B 9

    6   **C** 13
    3   **D** 15
   + 4

5. Tell whether you *add* or *subtract*. Solve the problem.

There were 6 girls and 8 boys at the party. How many students were at the party?

   A Subtract; 14 students
   B Add; 14 students
   C Add; 2 students
   D Subtract; 2 students

6. Find the missing addend.
   $5 + n = 12$

   A 8   **B** 16   **C** 7   **D** 17

7. Give the standard form for two hundred thirty-seven.

   A 37   **C** 237
   B 327   **D** 273

8. Give the standard form for $8,000 + 200 + 11$.

   A 8,112   **C** 8,021
   B 8,211   **D** 8,210

9. Which number sentence is correct?

   A 4,383 < 3,265
   B 9,110 < 1,919
   C 7,829 > 7,842
   D 4,283 > 4,274

10. Round 436 to the nearest ten.

   A 430   **C** 400
   B 440   **D** 500

11. Round 3,482 to the nearest thousand.

   A 3,000   **C** 3,500
   B 3,400   **D** 4,000

12. What does the 2 mean in 203,734?

   A 2 ten-thousands
   B 2 tens
   C 2 hundred-thousands
   D 2 ones

13. Choose the most sensible answer.

The smallest class in Jonesville School has 20 students. How many students are in the largest class?

A 10   **B** 15   **c** 20   **D** 30

14. Rename. Give the standard form.

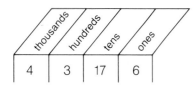

thousands	hundreds	tens	ones
4	3	17	6

A 4,377   **c** 4,476
B 4,496   **D** 4,386

15. Add.

248
+ 346

A 594
B 593
c 694
D 584

16. Add.

564
+ 289

A 843
B 853
c 753
D 743

17. Add.

48
25
+ 83

A 146
B 143
c 113
D 156

18. Subtract.

438
− 292

A 246
B 146
c 166
D 266

19. Subtract.

460
− 78

A 382
B 412
c 82
D 392

20. Subtract.

500
− 119

A 319
B 491
c 391
D 381

21. Add.

$7.25
+ 1.96

A $9.21
B $8.11
c $8.21
D $9.11

22. Choose the equation that should be used to solve the problem. Then solve the problem.

Mrs. Toruella drove 248 miles on Monday and 311 miles on Tuesday. How many more miles did she drive on Tuesday than on Monday?

A $311 + 248 = n$; 559 miles
B $311 + 64 = n$; 375 miles
c $248 − 63 = n$; 185 miles
D $311 − 248 = n$; 63 miles

Tuesday, January 3, 4:15 P.M.

Time: Clock

A. Show the times 3:00, 3:25, and 3:52 on a standard clock and on a digital clock.

The short hand is the hour hand. It moves from one number to the next in 60 minutes, or 1 hour.

The long hand is the minute hand. It moves from one number to the next in 5 minutes.

The minute hand moves from one small mark to the next in 1 minute.

3:00 A.M., 3:25 A.M., and 3:52 A.M. are between *midnight* and *noon*.

3:00 P.M., 3:25 P.M., and 3:52 P.M. are between noon and midnight.

B. At 8:30, how many minutes is it until 9:50?

C. What time will it be 45 minutes later than 6:55?

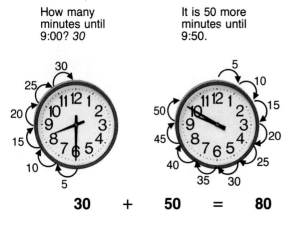

How many minutes until 9:00? *30*

It is 50 more minutes until 9:50.

30 + 50 = 80

At 8:30, it is 80 minutes until 9:50.

Count the minutes to get to 7:00.

Continue counting until you have counted 45 minutes in all.

The time will be 7:40.

Try Write the time shown. Then write the time indicated under the clock.

a.

3 hours later

b.

20 minutes later

c.

12 minutes later

Practice Write the time shown. Then write the time indicated under the clock.

1.

4 hours later

2.

30 minutes later

3.

15 minutes later

4.

40 minutes later

5.

14 minutes later

6.

9 minutes later

Apply Solve each problem.

7. Band practice begins at 3:30 and lasts until 4:45. How many minutes does band practice last?

8. The concert lasts for 2 hours and 30 minutes. It will begin at 7:30 P.M. When will it end?

9. Kristi goes to sleep at 9 P.M. She wakes up at 7 A.M. How many hours does she sleep?

10. Lunch period begins at 11:45 and ends at 12:15. How many minutes is lunch period?

11. The school day starts at 9 A.M. It ends at 3:00 P.M. How many hours long is the school day?

12. Eduardo started jogging at 3:45. He jogged for 35 minutes. What time did he stop?

Time: Calendar

January						
S	M	T	W	T	F	S
	1	2	3	4	5	6
7	8	9	10	11	12	13
14	15	16	17	18	19	20
21	22	23	24	25	26	27
28	29	30	31			

February						
S	M	T	W	T	F	S
				1	2	3
4	5	6	7	8	9	10
11	12	13	14	15	16	17
18	19	20	21	22	23	24
25	26	27	28			

March						
S	M	T	W	T	F	S
				1	2	3
4	5	6	7	8	9	10
11	12	13	14	15	16	17
18	19	20	21	22	23	24
25	26	27	28	29	30	31

April						
S	M	T	W	T	F	S
1	2	3	4	5	6	7
8	9	10	11	12	13	14
15	16	17	18	19	20	21
22	23	24	25	26	27	28
29	30					

May						
S	M	T	W	T	F	S
		1	2	3	4	5
6	7	8	9	10	11	12
13	14	15	16	17	18	19
20	21	22	23	24	25	26
27	28	29	30	31		

June						
S	M	T	W	T	F	S
					1	2
3	4	5	6	7	8	9
10	11	12	13	14	15	16
17	18	19	20	21	22	23
24	25	26	27	28	29	30

July						
S	M	T	W	T	F	S
1	2	3	4	5	6	7
8	9	10	11	12	13	14
15	16	17	18	19	20	21
22	23	24	25	26	27	28
29	30	31				

August						
S	M	T	W	T	F	S
				1	2	3	4
5	6	7	8	9	10	11
12	13	14	15	16	17	18
19	20	21	22	23	24	25
26	27	28	29	30	31	

September						
S	M	T	W	T	F	S
						1
2	3	4	5	6	7	8
9	10	11	12	13	14	15
16	17	18	19	20	21	22
23	24	25	26	27	28	29
30						

October						
S	M	T	W	T	F	S
	1	2	3	4	5	6
7	8	9	10	11	12	13
14	15	16	17	18	19	20
21	22	23	24	25	26	27
28	29	30	31			

November						
S	M	T	W	T	F	S
				1	2	3
4	5	6	7	8	9	10
11	12	13	14	15	16	17
18	19	20	21	22	23	24
25	26	27	28	29	30	

December						
S	M	T	W	T	F	S
						1
2	3	4	5	6	7	8
9	10	11	12	13	14	15
16	17	18	19	20	21	22
23	24	25	26	27	28	29
30	31					

The 12 months of the year are named on this calendar.

The days of the week are Sunday, Monday, Tuesday, Wednesday, Thursday, Friday, and Saturday.

Here is a table to help you measure time.

60 seconds = 1 minute	7 days = 1 week	366 days = 1 leap year
60 minutes = 1 hour	12 months = 1 year	10 years = 1 decade
24 hours = 1 day	365 days = 1 year	100 years = 1 century

Try Use the calendar on page 92 for Exercises a and b.

a. Which day of the week is May 26?

b. Give the date of the third Monday in November.

c. *Estimation* Choose the most sensible answer.

Jean's older sister is 16 (days, weeks, years) old.

Practice Use the calendar on page 92 for Exercises 1–14.
Name the day of the week for each date.

1. April 2

2. June 5

3. May 11

4. February 7

5. October 18

6. March 24

7. July 24

8. November 21

Name the date for each day.

9. Second Thursday in December

10. Third Wednesday in September

11. First Tuesday in February

12. Fourth Sunday in January

13. One week from March 8

14. Two weeks from August 27

Estimation For Exercises 15 to 18, choose the most sensible answer.

15. Sid slept 10 (minutes, hours, days) last night.

16. Fran walks to school in 20 (minutes, hours, months).

17. There are about 4 (days, weeks, years) in 1 month.

18. April has 30 (days, weeks, months).

19. `CALCULATOR` How many minutes are in one year? Use the table on page 92.

20. `CALCULATOR` How many seconds are in one year? Use your answer to Problem 19 and the table on page 92.

Apply Solve the problem.

21. Tammy has at least 20 pennies in her piggy bank. When she counts the pennies by 5s, there are 4 left over. When she counts them by 3s, there is 1 left over. What is the least number of pennies that she can have?

Centimeter and Decimeter

The *centimeter* and the *decimeter* are metric units of length.

A. The length of this bolt is about one centimeter (1 cm).

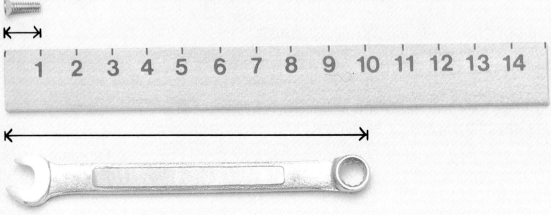

B. The length of this wrench is about one decimeter (1 dm).
1 dm = 10 cm

Try

a. *Estimation* Estimate the length to the nearest centimeter. Then measure it.

_____

b. *Estimation* Tell if the measure is sensible. Write *yes* or *no*.

A pencil is about 1 dm long.

Estimation

Practice *Estimation* Estimate each length to the nearest centimeter. Then measure it.

1. _____

2. _____

3. _____

4. _____

Estimation Tell if the measure is sensible. Write *yes* or *no*.

5. This textbook is about 2 cm thick.

6. A toothbrush is about 16 cm long.

7. Your thumb is about 5 dm long.

8. A pony stands about 15 dm high.

9. A piece of chalk is about 7 dm in length.

10. A hockey stick is about 10 cm long.

Apply Measure each length to the nearest centimeter.

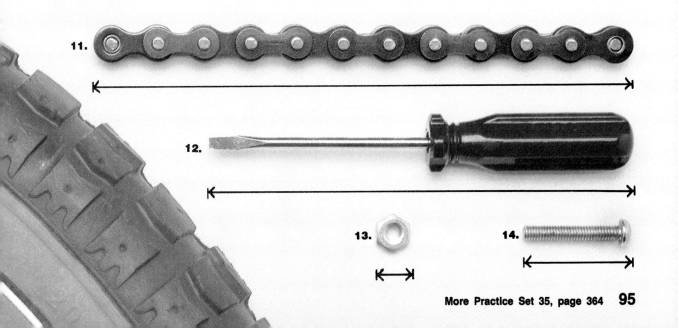

11.

12.

13.

14.

Meter and Kilometer

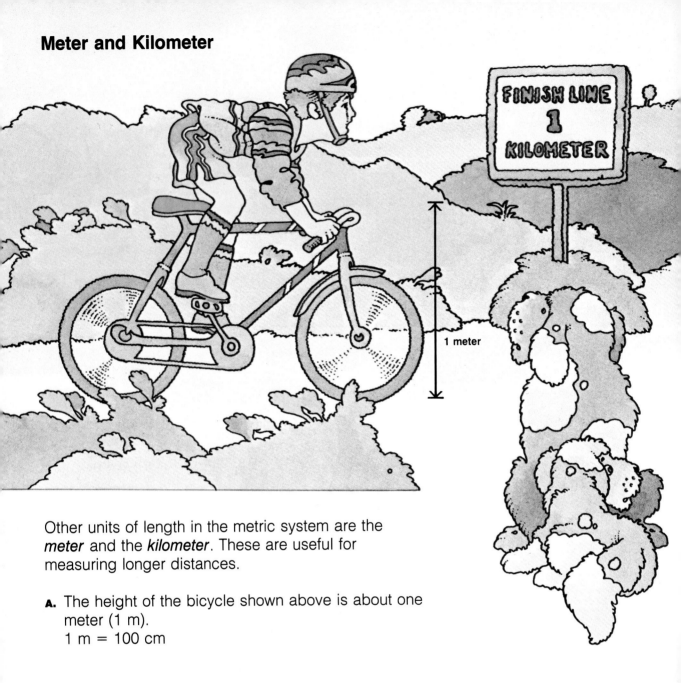

1 meter

Other units of length in the metric system are the *meter* and the *kilometer*. These are useful for measuring longer distances.

A. The height of the bicycle shown above is about one meter (1 m).
1 m = 100 cm

B. The total length of 571 bicycles is about one kilometer (1 km).
1 km = 1,000 m

Try

a. *Estimation* Would you use centimeters, meters, or kilometers to measure the height of a basketball hoop?

b. *Estimation* Choose the most sensible measure for the height of a basketball player.

2 cm   2 m   2 km

Practice *Estimation* Would you use centimeters, meters, or kilometers to measure

Estimation

1. the height of a house?

2. the distance to France?

3. the length of your shoe?

4. the length of a soccer field?

5. the width of your classroom?

6. the distance an airplane flies in an hour?

Estimation Choose the most sensible measure.

7. Length of a cat

   3 cm   3 dm   3 km

8. Height of a mountain

   2 cm   2 m   2 km

9. Width of a door

   1 dm   1 m   1 km

10. Length of a jump rope

   2 cm   2 dm   2 m

11. Distance traveled on a bus

   15 cm   15 m   15 km

12. Height of a golf trophy

   30 cm   30 m   30 km

Apply Solve each problem.

13. Of the 27 bicycles needing repair in his shop, Mr. Branson fixed 14. How many still need to be repaired?

14. Yuriko paid $4.59 for a bicycle tire. Keith's tire cost $1.40 more than Yuriko's tire. How much did Keith's tire cost?

Gram and Kilogram

Career Dr. Masumi Kato is a veterinarian. She often uses metric units of weight. Two of these units are the *gram* and the *kilogram*.

A. A nugget of this dog food weighs about one gram (1 g).

B. The puppy weighs about one kilogram (1 kg).
1 kg = 1,000 g

Try

a. _Estimation_ Would you use grams or kilograms to measure the weight of a table tennis ball?

b. _Estimation_ Choose the more sensible measure for the weight of a bowling ball.

7 g   7 kg

Estimation

Practice

Estimation Would you use grams or kilograms to measure the weight of

1. a dollar bill?

2. a desk?

3. a bicycle?

4. a paper clip?

5. a television set?

6. a banana?

Estimation Choose the more sensible measure.

7. 9-year-old boy

38 g   38 kg

8. Screwdriver

57 g   57 kg

9. Can of nuts

370 g   370 kg

10. Watermelon

3 g   3 kg

11. Dime

2 g   2 kg

12. Roller skate

1 g   1 kg

Apply   _Choosing a Computation Method_   Calculator, Paper and Pencil, Mental Math, Estimation

Choose a method to solve each problem. Tell which method you used.

13. Snoops, a basset hound, weighs 13 kg. Mac, an Irish setter, weighs 16 kg more than Snoops. How much does Mac weigh?

14. This week, Dr. Kato treated 37 cats. She treated 8 fewer dogs than cats. How many dogs did she treat this week?

15. A small puppy ate 135 g of the 200 g of food it needs each day. How many more grams of food should it eat today?

16. A beagle ate 350 g of food. A German shepherd ate 600 g of food. How much food did the two dogs eat?

Milliliter and Liter

Milliliter and *liter* are metric units used for measuring amounts of liquid.

A. To guard against disease, medicine is often put into a newborn animal's eyes with an eyedropper. An eyedropper holds about one milliliter (1 mL).

B. The medicine is stored in a bottle that holds about one liter (1 L).
1 L = 1,000 mL

Try

a. *Estimation* Would you use milliliters or liters to measure the amount of water a kitchen sink holds?

b. *Estimation* Choose the more sensible measure for a flower vase.

2 mL   2 L

Estimation

Practice   *Estimation* Would you use milliliters or liters to measure the amount of liquid each container holds?

1. Ink bottle

2. Swimming pool

3. Soup can

4. Bathtub

5. Drinking cup

6. Car fuel tank

7. Washing machine

8. Teaspoon

9. Baby bottle

Estimation Choose the more sensible measure.

10. Fish tank

17 mL   17 L

11. Ice-cube tray

450 mL   450 L

12. Spoon

5 mL   5 L

13. Bucket

8 mL   8 L

14. Milk glass

250 mL   250 L

15. Mixing bowl

3 mL   3 L

Apply   Solve each problem.

16. A bottle had 975 mL of medicine in it. Dr. Kato used 525 mL of the medicine. How much medicine is left in the bottle?

17. This month Dr. Kato has treated 28 horses. Last month she treated 37 horses. How many horses has Dr. Kato treated in the last two months?

18. An adult male horse has 40 teeth. An adult female horse has 4 fewer teeth than a male. How many teeth does an adult female horse have?

19. *Find the facts.* Find a juice container that gives the amount of juice in milliliters. How many milliliters of juice does the container hold?

20. **CALCULATOR**   Dr. Kato was finding the total amount of one type of medicine. She added 175 mL + 335 mL + 285 mL. The display showed 813. The answer is incorrect. She pressed two keys out of order. What two keys did she press out of order?

Practice: Metric Measures

Estimation Estimate each length to the nearest centimeter. Then measure it.

1. _____

2. _____

3. _____

4. _____

5.

6.

Estimation Choose the more sensible measure.

7.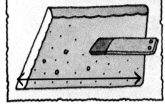

   30 m   30 km

8.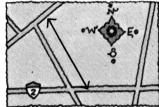

   16 dm   16 km

9.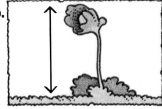

   2 cm   2 dm

10.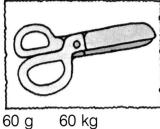

   60 g   60 kg

11.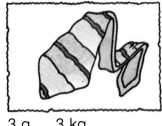

   3 g   3 kg

12.

   4 g   4 kg

13.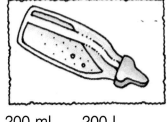

   200 mL   200 L

14.

   4 mL   4 L

15.

   2 mL   2 L

Apply Read through the problem situation given below. Then answer Problems 16–17.

Mr. Abel and his class are on a walking tour of their city. They come to an old bridge. Mr. Abel asks his students to measure the length of the bridge.

"How can we measure the bridge?" asks Sally. "We didn't bring any measuring tools."

"Yes we did," answers Billy. "We can use our feet. And I have a piece of chalk. Mr. Abel will let us borrow his watch that has a second hand."

Mr. Abel adds, "I know that the width across the palm of my hand is about 10 centimeters."

Doug says, "I can take little steps, putting the heel of one foot against the toe of the other. I can walk across the bridge that way."

Jane says, "That will take too much time. You should take the biggest steps that you can. But we need to know how long each step is. Or we can think of a way to measure using Mr. Abel's watch."

Work as a group to find out how to measure the bridge. Talk about these questions.

16. How can a piece of chalk help Mr. Abel's class measure the length of the bridge?

17. How can a watch with a second hand help the class to measure the bridge?

Explain to your class how your group would measure the bridge. Discuss and compare your methods and solutions with other groups.

Tell what the 2 means in each number.

1. 427 **2.** 285

3. 902 **4.** 2,481

5. 3,924 **6.** 3,206

Add or subtract.

7. 36 + 23 **8.** 43 + 52

9. 57 + 35 **10.** 29 + 31

11. 354 + 287 **12.** 646 + 589

13. 87 − 45 **14.** 73 − 48

15. 52 − 27 **16.** 68 − 46

17. 354 − 287 **18.** 646 − 589

19. 437 + 286 + 189

20. 276 + 548 + 168

21. 691 + 217 + 534

22. 514 + 223 + 659

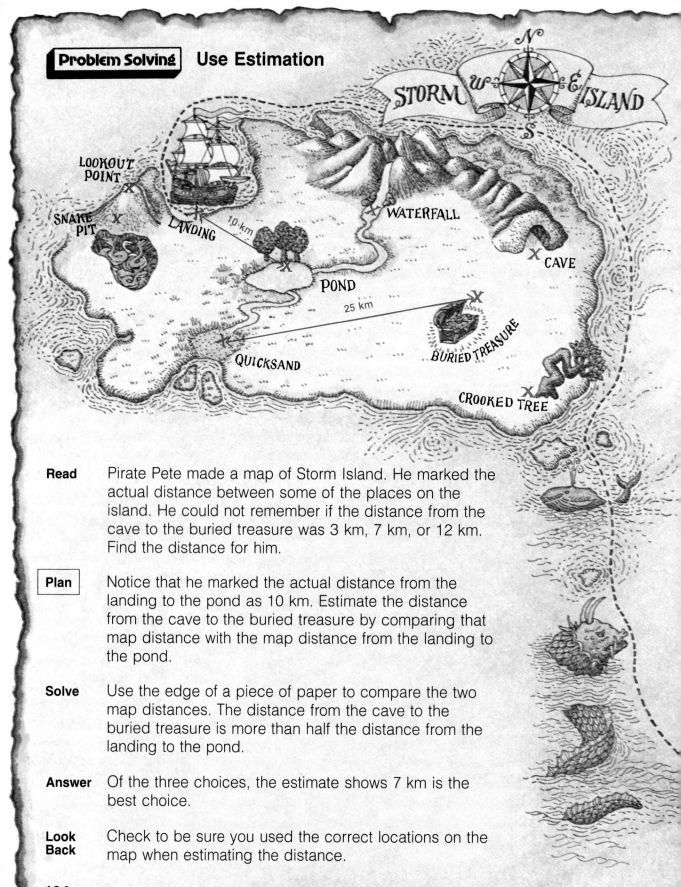

Problem Solving **Use Estimation**

Read Pirate Pete made a map of Storm Island. He marked the actual distance between some of the places on the island. He could not remember if the distance from the cave to the buried treasure was 3 km, 7 km, or 12 km. Find the distance for him.

Plan Notice that he marked the actual distance from the landing to the pond as 10 km. Estimate the distance from the cave to the buried treasure by comparing that map distance with the map distance from the landing to the pond.

Solve Use the edge of a piece of paper to compare the two map distances. The distance from the cave to the buried treasure is more than half the distance from the landing to the pond.

Answer Of the three choices, the estimate shows 7 km is the best choice.

Look Back Check to be sure you used the correct locations on the map when estimating the distance.

Try *Estimation* Solve each problem. Use the map on page 104.

a. Is the actual distance from the lookout point to the quicksand less than or greater than the actual distance from the landing to the pond?

b. Choose the most sensible estimate for the actual distance from the lookout point to the quicksand.

5 km   10 km   17 km

Apply *Estimation* Solve each problem. Use the map on page 104.

1. Is the actual distance from the lookout point to the snake pit less than or greater than the actual distance from the landing to the pond?

2. Choose the most sensible estimate for the actual distance from the lookout point to the snake pit.

3 km   10 km   15 km

3. Is the actual distance from the cave to the crooked tree less than or greater than the actual distance from the landing to the pond?

4. Choose the most sensible estimate for the actual distance from the cave to the crooked tree.

4 km   10 km   13 km

Look at the map. Notice that the actual distance from the quicksand to the buried treasure is 25 km. Choose the most sensible estimate for the actual distance from the

5. landing to the waterfall.

17 km   25 km   30 km

6. quicksand to the crooked tree.

9 km   25 km   30 km

7. pond to the waterfall.

3 km   10 km   25 km

*8. waterfall to the buried treasure.

7 km   13 km   30 km

Inch and Foot

The *inch* and *foot* are customary units for measuring length.

A. The width of each slice of the sandwich shown below is about one inch (1 in.).

B. The length of the whole sandwich is about one foot (1 ft.).

1 ft. = 12 in.

Try *Estimation* Estimate each length to the nearest inch. Then measure it.

a. _____

b. _____

Estimation Tell if each measure is sensible. Write *yes* or *no*.

c. A pencil is about 8 feet long.

d. Your thumb is about 2 inches long.

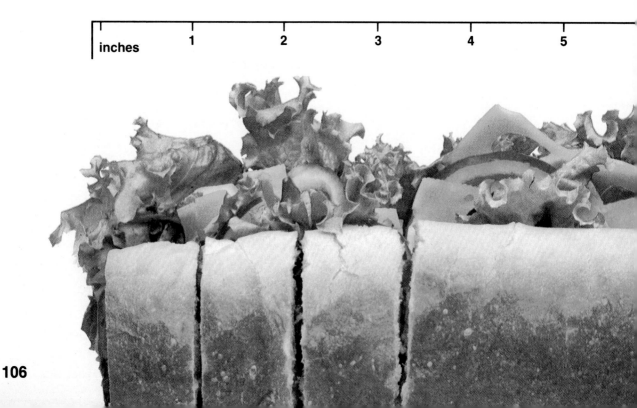

inches   1   2   3   4   5

Practice *Estimation* Estimate each length to the nearest inch. Then measure it.

1. _____   2. _____

3. _____

4. _____

Estimation Tell if each measure is sensible. Write *yes* or *no*.

5. Your shoe is about 6 inches long.

6. A student is about 9 feet tall.

7. A telephone pole is about 20 inches tall.

8. A tennis racket is about 2 feet long.

Apply Solve each problem.

9. Diego made a party sandwich 32 inches long. He and his guests ate 26 inches of it. How much of the sandwich was left?

10. Diego hung streamers for a party. He used 35 feet of red paper, 27 feet of blue paper, and 21 feet of white paper. How many feet of paper did he use?

Yard and Mile

1 yard

Other customary units of length are the *yard* and the *mile*. These are useful for measuring longer distances.

A. The length of a golf club is about one yard (1 yd.).
1 yd. = 3 ft.

B. It would take 1,760 golf clubs laid end to end to measure about one mile (1 mi.).
1 mi. = 1,760 yd.

Try

a. *Estimation* Would you use inches, feet, yards, or miles to measure the distance from the earth to the sun?

b. *Estimation* Choose the most sensible measure for the height of a room.

3 in.   3 yd.   3 mi.

Practice *Estimation* Which unit would you use to measure the

Estimation

1. height of a desk?

   (inches or miles)

2. distance between bus stops?

   (feet or miles)

3. height of a flagpole?

   (feet or miles)

4. distance run in a race?

   (inches or yards)

5. distance to the South Pole?

   (yards or miles)

6. width of a TV screen?

   (inches or yards)

Estimation Choose the most sensible measure.

7. Length of a football

   12 in.   12 ft.   12 yd.

8. Distance to first base

   90 in.   90 ft.   90 mi.

9. Height of a chalkboard

   3 in.   3 ft.   3 mi.

10. Length of the Delaware River

    390 in.   390 ft.   390 mi.

11. Length of a bike path

    8 ft.   8 yd.   8 mi.

12. Height of a man

    2 ft.   2 yd.   2 mi.

13. Width of a book

    8 in.   8 ft.   8 yd.

14. Length of a car

    5 in.   5 yd.   5 mi.

Apply   Solve each problem.

15. The first nine holes of one golf course are 2,845 yards. The last nine holes are 2,408 yards. How long is the entire course?

16. The first hole is 311 yards. The second hole is 374 yards. How much longer is the second hole than the first hole?

Ounce, Pound, and Ton

The cook at the school cafeteria uses ground beef in many school lunches.

A. The lunch menu often includes meatballs. A meatball weighs about one *ounce* (1 oz.).

B. Sometimes, the cook prepares hamburgers. Four hamburgers weigh about one *pound* (1 lb.).
1 lb. = 16 oz.

C. The *ton* is used to measure very large weights. From one ton of ground beef, the cook could make about 8,000 hamburgers or 32,000 meatballs.
1 ton = 2,000 pounds

2000 lb.

110

Try

a. *Estimation* Would you use ounces, pounds, or tons to measure the weight of a fourth-grade student?

b. *Estimation* Choose the most sensible measure for the weight of a delivery truck.

3 ounces   3 pounds   3 tons

Practice   *Estimation* Would you use ounces, pounds, or tons to measure the weight of

Estimation

1. a hand-held calculator?

2. an airplane?

3. a chimpanzee?

4. a sandwich?

5. an orange?

6. a kitchen table?

7. a tent?

8. a locomotive?

9. a rocket?

Estimation Choose the most sensible measure.

10. Guitar

8 ounces   8 pounds   8 tons

11. Egg

2 ounces   2 pounds   2 tons

12. Elephant

6 ounces   6 pounds   6 tons

13. Ship

35 ounces   35 pounds   35 tons

14. Watch

8 ounces   8 pounds   8 tons

15. Typewriter

20 ounces   20 pounds   20 tons

Apply   *Choosing a Computation Method*   Calculator, Paper and Pencil, Mental Math, Estimation
Choose a method to solve each problem. Tell which method you used.

16. A cook's helper used 17 pounds of apples from a 50-pound sack. Are there more or less than 30 pounds of apples left?

17. A cook used 45 pounds of pork and 60 pounds of beef in chop suey. How many pounds of meat did the cook use?

18. A spaghetti lunch costs 65¢. A hamburger costs 10¢ more. How much does a hamburger cost?

19. The cook prepared 15 pounds of hamburgers and 3 fewer pounds of meatballs. How many pounds of meatballs did the cook prepare?

20. The cook was born in October of 1959. How many months old is the cook today?

Using Problem-Solving Strategies, page 417
More Practice Set 42, page 366   111

Cup, Pint, Quart, and Gallon

The *cup*, the *pint*, the *quart*, and the *gallon* are customary units for measuring liquids.

A. This container holds one cup (1 c.).

1 c.

B. This container holds one pint (1 pt.).

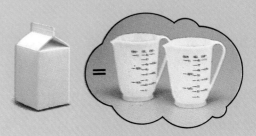

1 pt. = 2 c.

C. This container holds one quart (1 qt.).

1 qt. = 2 pt.

D. This container holds one gallon (1 gal.).

1 gal. = 4 qt.

Try

a. *Estimation* Would you use cups or gallons to measure the amount of liquid a soup bowl holds?

b. *Estimation* Choose the most sensible measure for a car's fuel tank.

18 c.   18 pt.   18 gal.

Practice *Estimation* Choose the unit you would use to measure the amount of liquid each container holds.

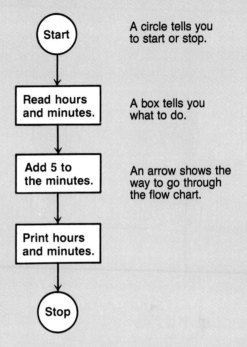

Estimation

1. Dog's water bowl

   (cup or gallon)

2. Swimming pool

   (quart or gallon)

3. Cream pitcher

   (cup or quart)

4. Ice-cube tray

   (pint or gallon)

Estimation Choose the more sensible measure.

5. Milk-shake glass

   1 pt.   1 gal.

6. Water cooler

   10 c.   10 gal.

7. Water glass

   1 c.   1 qt.

8. Sand pail

   2 c.   2 qt.

9. Baby's bottle

   1 c.   1 gal.

10. *Find the facts.* Use data from the table on page 5 to tell how much more a boxer weighs than a collie.

COMPUTER

Flow Charts

A flow chart shows the steps to use to solve a problem. This flow chart shows how to find the time 5 minutes after a given time.

Start — A circle tells you to start or stop.

Read hours and minutes. — A box tells you what to do.

Add 5 to the minutes. — An arrow shows the way to go through the flow chart.

Print hours and minutes.

Stop

1. What step comes before adding 5 to the minutes?

2. What step comes after adding 5 to the minutes?

Use the flow chart to give the time 5 minutes after

3. 3:08.   4. 6:41.

5. 11:15.   6. 2:25.

7. Make a flow chart that finds the time 10 minutes after a given time.

★8. Why won't the flow chart work if the time you read is 11:55?

More Practice Set 43, page 367

THE CATERPILLAR CRAWL

A caterpillar is at the bottom of a jar that is 10 centimeters high and 5 centimeters across. The jar has a lid with holes in it. Each day, the caterpillar crawls up 3 centimeters. Each night, he slips down 2 centimeters. *How long will it take the caterpillar to touch the lid of the jar?*

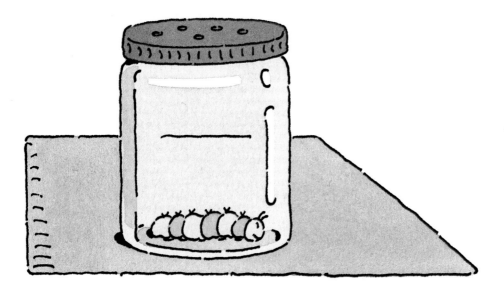

1. How high must the caterpillar crawl to touch the lid of the jar?

2. How high can the caterpillar crawl during the first day?

3. How high can the caterpillar crawl in 2 days?

4. How high can the caterpillar crawl in 5 days?

5. How many days will it take the caterpillar to touch the lid of the jar?

Find a partner and explain to him or her how you solved this problem. Compare the ways that you and your partner used to solve this problem with methods used by others.

JOHNSON'S MEAT MARKET PRICES

Baked Ham	$2.78 per lb.
Whole Chicken	$0.54 per lb.
Beef Liver	$0.59 per lb.
Boston Beef Roast	$1.89 per lb.
Smoked Sausage	$1.99 per lb.
Turkey Breast	$2.79 per lb.

Choose a method to solve the following problems.

6. A snail is trying to climb out of a 12-meter well. He crawls up 3 meters each day and slides back 2 meters each night. How long will it take him to climb out of the well?

Use your calculator to complete these orders.

1.	3 lb. of chicken	
2.	2 lb. of sausage	
3.	1 lb. of liver	
4.	2 lb of roast	
5.	1 lb. of ham	
6.	total	

7. If the same snail falls into a 15-meter well, how long will it take him to climb out of the well?

8. The poor snail fell into another well. This time it took him 16 days to climb out. How deep was the well?

9. Another caterpillar can crawl up 4 centimeters each day. Each night, he slips down 2 centimeters. How long will it take him to touch the lid of the jar that is 10 centimeters high?

7.	2 lb. of ham	
8.	3 lb. of roast	
9.	1 lb. of sausage	
10.	3 lb. of turkey	
11.	2 lb of chicken	
12.	total	

Temperature: Celsius and Fahrenheit

A sign at the Bagley Bank shows temperature in degrees *Celsius* (°C) and in degrees *Fahrenheit* (°F).

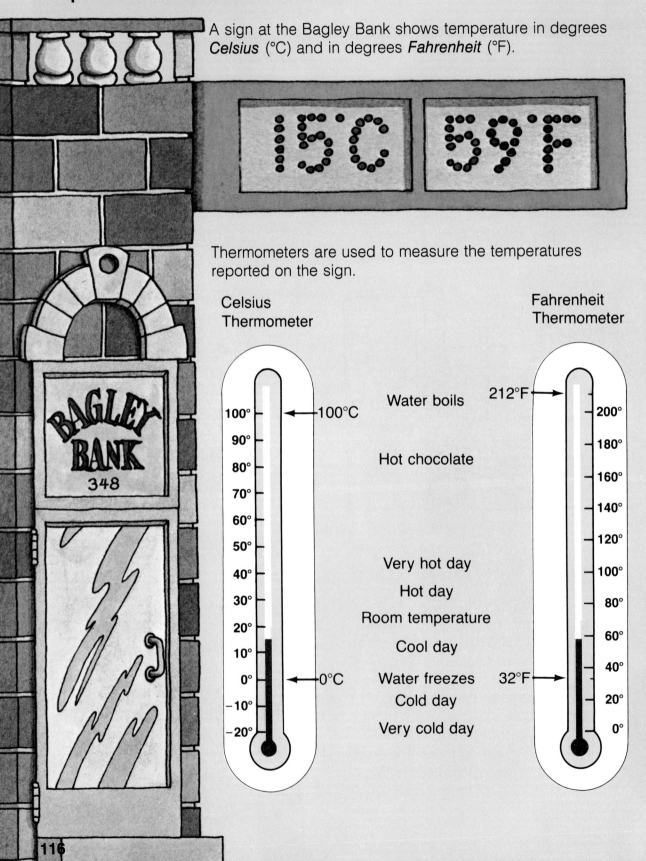

Thermometers are used to measure the temperatures reported on the sign.

Celsius Thermometer

Fahrenheit Thermometer

Water boils

Hot chocolate

Very hot day

Hot day

Room temperature

Cool day

Water freezes

Cold day

Very cold day

100°C

0°C

212°F

32°F

BAGLEY BANK 348

Try

a. *Estimation* Choose the more sensible measure for the temperature in ice-skating weather.

25°F   84°F

b. *Estimation* Give the more sensible measure. Use C (Celsius) or F (Fahrenheit).

Tom is going on a picnic. It is 25°▨.

Practice   *Estimation* Choose the more sensible measure.

1. Temperature of a school room

   32°F   68°F

2. Snowman-building weather

   28°F   84°F

3. Temperature of hot chocolate

   78°F   170°F

4. Swimming weather

   30°F   85°F

5. Hiking weather

   18°C   55°C

6. Temperature of swimming-pool water

   27°C   85°C

7. Temperature during a blizzard

   −15°C   15°C

8. Temperature of warm dinner rolls

   50°C   125°C

Estimation Give the more sensible measure.
Use C (Celsius) or F (Fahrenheit).

9. Casey is painting his house. The temperature is 22°▨.

10. Violet is taking a bath. The water's temperature is 104°▨.

11. Tom is shoveling snow off the walk. The temperature is 28°▨.

12. Glen set the thermostat in his house at 68°▨.

13. Alvin is playing football. The temperature is 45°▨.

14. Joel is drinking ice water. The water's temperature is 3°▨.

15. Carol is sunbathing. The temperature is 25°▨.

16. Emilia is boiling water to cook eggs. The water is 100°▨.

17. *Mental math* In the morning, the temperature was 39°F. By noon it was 49°F. How many degrees had the temperature risen?

18. *Mental math* In the morning, the temperature was 14°C. By afternoon, it had gone up 5°C. What was the afternoon temperature?

Chapter 4 Test

1. Write the time shown on the clock.

2. What time will it be 15 minutes later than the time shown on the clock above?

May						
S	**M**	**T**	**W**	**T**	**F**	**S**
		1	2	3	4	5
6	7	8	9	10	11	12
13	14	15	16	17	18	19
20	21	22	23	24	25	26
27	28	29	30	31		

3. What is the date of the third Monday in May?

4. What day of the week is May 24?

Measure the length to the nearest centimeter.

5. _____

Measure the length to the nearest inch.

6. _____

Choose the most sensible measure.

7. Length of your thumb

6 cm   6 dm   6 m

8. Height of a volleyball net

2 dm   2 m   2 km

9. Weight of a pencil

5 g   5 kg

10. Amount of liquid a bowl holds

2 mL   2 L

11. Height of a giraffe

17 in.   17 ft.   17 mi.

12. Length of a bicycle race

2 ft.   2 yd.   2 mi.

13. Weight of a tennis racket

2 ounces   2 pounds   2 tons

14. Amount of water a wading pool holds

15 c.   15 gal.

15. Temperature of a shower room

30°F   90°F

16. Sledding weather

2°C   34°C

17. Choose the most sensible estimate for the distance from the tent to the rock.

3 km   5 km   8 km

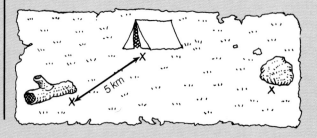

Estimation Strategies

A rough estimate can be obtained by using the *front-end* digits. The estimate can be *adjusted* by *grouping* the remaining digits.

Estimation

Estimate the total cost.

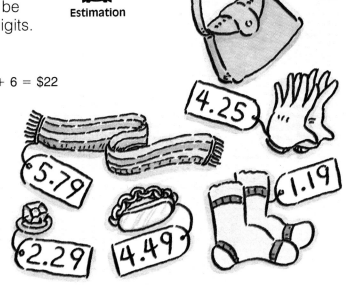

$$1 + 5 + 4 + 2 + 4 + 6 = \$22$$

Socks	$ **1** . **1 9**
Scarf	**5** . **7 9** ← About $1
Gloves	**4** . **2 5**
Ring	**2** . **2 9** ← About $1
Bracelet	**4** . **4 9**
Purse	**6** . **0 0**
Tax	**0** . **9 5** ← About $1

Total cost: About $25

Estimate each sum.

1. ┌─ 1,500
129
915
+ 508

2. ┌─ 4,000
4, 625 ← About 1,000
562
+ 918 ← About 1,000

3. ┌─ 11,000
2, 375
182 ⎞ About 1,000
+ 9, 757

4.
346
457
203
+ 512

5.
107
912
700
+ 523

6.
498
315
103
+ 97

7.
3,813
1,044
2,110
+ 1,219

8.
2,221
1,356
1,583
+ 9,940

9.
54
62
90
93
+ 11

10.
437
217
825
614
+ 143

11.
281
203
94
112
+ 215

12.
2,113
1,024
3,050
124
+ 1,272

13.
11,035
31,116
20,135
11,846
+ 20,913

14.
$3.85
2.19
0.45
1.58
+ 4.05

15.
$5.29
6.18
4.75
3.09
+ 5.19

16.
$8.05
4.33
1.52
6.25
+ 0.93

17.
$2.16
4.87
2.45
1.29
+ 5.00

18.
$5.75
2.32
7.05
1.80
+ 6.99

A FAMILY HIKE

The Kubistas are going to hike from Frontier Park to Round Lake. They are leaving the park at 9:00 in the morning and plan to hike 3 miles an hour. They plan to spend 2 hours at the lake, then return to Frontier Park on the same trail. *What time can they expect to be back at the park?*

On this map, 1 inch represents 1 mile.

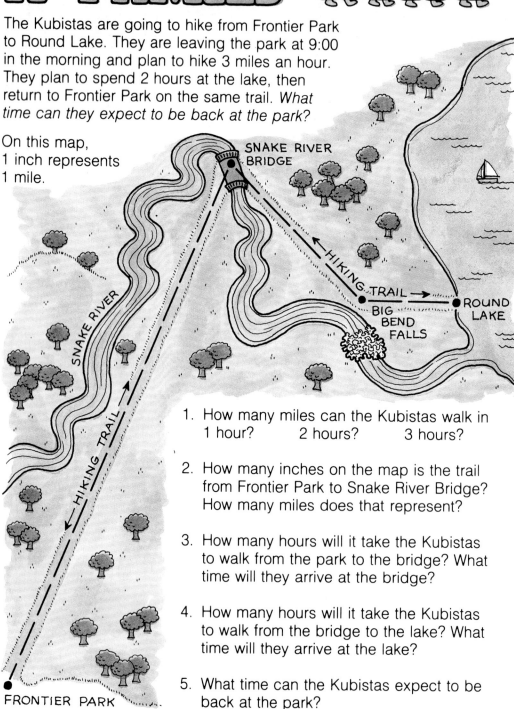

1. How many miles can the Kubistas walk in 1 hour?   2 hours?   3 hours?

2. How many inches on the map is the trail from Frontier Park to Snake River Bridge? How many miles does that represent?

3. How many hours will it take the Kubistas to walk from the park to the bridge? What time will they arrive at the bridge?

4. How many hours will it take the Kubistas to walk from the bridge to the lake? What time will they arrive at the lake?

5. What time can the Kubistas expect to be back at the park?

Multiplication Facts

4
x2

8

Meaning of Multiplication

A. If a school play is held in a gym, a seating plan needs to be made.

Work in groups of four. Each group should first make a drawing of a school gym with a stage. Their group should draw a model of a seating plan. You can use graph paper or counters to help you.

As you work on your seating plan, remember the following:

- everyone must be able to see the stage;
- ushers need an orderly arrangement to find each individual seat;
- there must be enough room for people to get to and from their seats comfortably;
- there must be the same number of seats in each row.

What were some other things your group considered when it made the seating plan? Share your findings with other groups in the class.

Your group must also order folding chairs for the play.
How many chairs are needed for your seating plan? You can
use a calculator to help you.

1. How did you find the total number of chairs needed?

2. Can you compute the answer another way? Why or why not?

Trade your plans with another group. Have them find the
total number of chairs needed. Discuss how each group
found their answer. Compare your methods.

B. The chart shows the number of tickets sold
for the school play each night during its run.
The chart covers the years 1984–1986.

Discuss the following questions with your
group. You can use the calculator to help you
find the answers.

	1984	1985	1986
Monday	210	210	158
Tuesday	210	194	143
Wednesday	210	194	165
Thursday	210	194	165
Friday	210	210	200

3. In what year were the most tickets sold?

4. From the table, what do you notice about the number of tickets sold each year?

5. How did you find the totals for each year? Is there another way to compute the totals? Why or why not?

6. How can you check your answers?

Discuss multiplication and addition with your group.
How are they alike? How are they different?

2 and 3 in Multiplication

A. There are 5 houses on each of the 2 sides of Maple Lane. How many houses are on Maple Lane?

Think of 2 groups of 5.

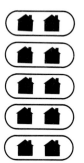

$$2 \times 5 = 10$$

Factor ↑ ↑   ↑ Product

Or, think of 5 groups of 2.

$$5 \times 2 = 10$$

There are 10 houses on Maple Lane.

B. Find 3×3.

Think of 3 groups of 3.

$$3 \times 3 = 9$$

124

Try Copy and complete the multiplication sentence for each picture.

a.

2 × 4 = ▨

b.

3 × 2 = ▨

Multiply.

c. 2 × 2   d. 4 × 3   e. 2 × 6   f. 3 × 5   g. 6 × 3   h. 7 × 2

Practice Copy and complete the multiplication sentence for each picture.

1.

6 × 2 = ▨

2.

3 × 7 = ▨

Multiply.

3. 5 × 2   4. 2 × 7   5. 7 × 3   6. 8 × 3   7. 2 × 3   8. 2 × 5

9. 9 × 3   10. 2 × 9   11. 3 × 6   12. 4 × 2   13. 5 × 3   14. 3 × 7

15. 9 × 2   16. 3 × 8   17. 3 × 9   18. 8 × 2   19. 3 × 3   20. 2 × 8

Apply Solve each problem.

21. The 2 sides of Maple Lane are lined with trees. There are 7 trees on each side. How many trees are on Maple Lane?

22. Each of the 4 corner houses on Maple Lane has 2 sidewalks. How many sidewalks do the corner houses have in all?

23. Of the 10 houses on Maple Lane, 3 houses have red roofs. How many houses on Maple Lane do not have red roofs?

★24. On each of the 2 sides of Maple Lane, 3 of the trees are birch trees, and 4 are maple trees. How many more maple trees than birch trees are on Maple Lane?

25. **CALCULATOR** Press: 3 [×] [+] 9 [=]. What happened on your calculator?

4 and 5 in Multiplication

A. Pat built a display case for his shell collection. How many sections are in the case?

Think of 4 groups of 5.

4 × 5 = 20

Or, think of 5 groups of 4.

5 × 4 = 20

There are 20 sections in the display case.

B. You can write multiplication facts another way.

```
  4 ← Factor ⟶    5
× 5 ← Factor ⟶  × 4
─────            ─────
 20 ← Product ⟶  20
```

126

c. Skip counting is a strategy that can help you remember a fact. **Mental Math**
To find 5 × 4, count 4 groups of 5.

5	,	**10**	,	**15**	,	**20**
1 group of 5		2 groups of 5		3 groups of 5		4 groups of 5

Try Multiply.

a. 8
×4

b. 6
×5

c. 9 × 4

d. 7 × 5

Practice Multiply.

1. 3
×5

2. 6
×4

3. 5
×5

4. 2
×5

5. 4
×2

6. 8
×4

7. 9
×3

8. 8
×5

9. 4
×3

10. 3
×6

11. 5
×2

12. 4
×4

13. 5
×3

14. 9
×5

15. 7
×4

16. 5
×6

17. 4
×8

18. 5
×7

19. 4
×5

20. 5
×8

21. 2
×4

22. 2 × 8

23. 4 × 9

24. 3 × 4

25. 3 × 8

26. 4 × 7

27. 6 × 3

28. 5 × 9

29. 7 × 2

30. 4 × 6

31. 9 × 2

32. 5 × 4

33. 3 × 3

Apply Solve each problem.

34. Pat has 4 shells in each of the 4 corner sections. How many shells are in the corner sections?

35. In each of 2 sections of the case, there are 5 turban shells. How many turban shells are in these sections?

36. Pat has 6 tiger cowrie shells in his case. If he places 5 more in the case, how many tiger cowrie shells will there be in Pat's case?

37. Pat has 2 moon shells in each of the 4 sections in the third row. How many moon shells are there in the third row?

38. **CALCULATOR** Press: 3 ⊗ 4 ⊜ ⊜ ⊜ ⊜ ⊜.
What does the display show? What happened on your calculator?

6 in Multiplication

Career Alan Johnson is a baker. When he bakes
biscuits, he places 6 biscuits in a row and fits
7 rows on a pan. How many biscuits does
he put on each pan?

A. Think of
7 groups of 6.

$$7 \times 6 = 42$$

 Mental
Math

B. Use doubling to
remember a fact.

3 sevens = 21
3 sevens = 21
6 sevens = 42

He puts 42 biscuits on each pan.

Try Multiply.

a.
$$\begin{array}{r} 8 \\ \times 6 \\ \hline \end{array}$$

b.
$$\begin{array}{r} 6 \\ \times 6 \\ \hline \end{array}$$

c.
$$\begin{array}{r} 6 \\ \times 9 \\ \hline \end{array}$$

d. 6×3

e. 2×6

f. 6×5

Practice Multiply.

1. 4
    ×6

2. 6
    ×2

3. 8
    ×6

4. 3
    ×6

5. 8
    ×3

6. 9
    ×6

7. 6
    ×7

8. 6
    ×3

9. 4
    ×3

10. 5
    ×6

11. 2
    ×6

12. 6
    ×6

13. 6
    ×8

14. 5
    ×8

15. 6 × 4

16. 3 × 9

17. 9 × 6

18. 6 × 2

19. 6 × 7

20. 2 × 8

21. 5 × 6

22. 7 × 2

23. 6 × 6

24. 4 × 6

25. 6 × 9

26. 5 × 7

27. 2 × 9

28. 6 × 5

29. 9 × 4

30. 6 × 8

31. 3 × 6

32. 7 × 6

Apply Solve each problem.

33. When baking muffins, Alan uses pans that have 6 rows with 4 muffins in each row. How many muffins are in each pan?

34. The bakery had 24 loaves of whole wheat bread when it opened in the morning. By noon 16 loaves were sold. How many loaves were left?

35. Alan needs to make 100 loaves of bread. If he makes 6 batches of rye bread with 5 loaves in each batch, will he have enough loaves? Why or why not?

36. Alan made a pan of dinner rolls. There were 5 dinner rolls in each of 4 rows and another row of 3 dinner rolls. How many dinner rolls did he make?

37. **[CALCULATOR]** **Press:** 6 ⓧ 2 ⌷ 3 ⌷ 5 ⌷ 8 ⌷
    Explain your displays.

38. Remove 4 toothpicks to make 4 triangles that are the same size.

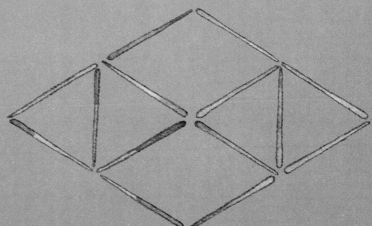

Using Problem-Solving Strategies

STACKS AND STACKS OF CANS

Jose brought his can collection to show his class. He displayed the cans by stacking them in the shape of a triangle. On the top of the stack was 1 can. On the next row down were 2 cans. The third row had 3 cans. *If Jose used 6 rows, how many cans did he show altogether?*

Work in a group with 3 other students. In your group, discuss how you plan to solve this problem. If you have more than one idea, try to solve the problem in more than one way.

1. How many cans did Jose show?

2. How did you solve the problem? Did other students in your group solve the problem in a different way?

3. Compare the methods your group used with the methods other groups used to solve the problem.

130

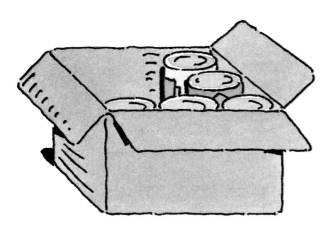

BASIC: Multiplication in PRINT Statements

In BASIC, the symbol * is used for multiplication.

A semicolon at the end of a PRINT statement makes the next PRINT statement in the program print on the same line.

When this program is typed into a computer, the numbers are multiplied and the answers are printed on one line.

4. Which method do you like the best? Why do you like this method the best?

```
10 PRINT 5*6;
20 PRINT 8*9
30 END
```

This is printed.

```
30 72
```

Use your favorite method or other methods to solve the following problems.

5. Jose brought some more cans to class. He stacked them in the shape of a triangle as before. This time, Jose used 8 rows. How many cans did he show now?

6. Other students in Jose's class brought in more cans. They added these to Jose's stack, keeping the shape of a triangle. The cans now were stacked into 12 rows. How many cans were stacked?

7. More cans were brought to class. There were now 120 cans altogether. How many rows would be needed to stack the cans in the shape of a triangle?

8. Do you still like your favorite method the best? Explain your answer.

Tell what would be printed for each program.

1. ```
10 PRINT 7*8
20 END
```

2. ```
10 PRINT 4*8;
20 PRINT 5*8
30 END
```

3. ```
10 PRINT 3*6
20 PRINT 0*7
30 END
```

4. ```
10 PRINT "PRODUCTS"
20 PRINT 5*9;
30 PRINT 2*7
40 END
```

*5. ```
30 PRINT 6*6
10 PRINT 6+6
40 END
20 PRINT 6-6;
```
```

0 and 1 in Multiplication

Play multiplication concentration!
Play the game with 3 other students. Use a calculator if you need to.

Here are the rules:

- Each group use 14 index cards. Write each of the digits 0, 1, 2, 3, 4, 5, and 6 on two cards.
- Mix the cards up. Place them in rows face down on a desk.
- Each player choose a number between 12 and 81. Announce your number to the group. This number is your *goal number* for the game. The object of the game is to reach your goal number exactly.
- Every player starts with 3 as a multiplier. Take turns selecting a card. Multiply the number on the card by 3. Write down the product. This is your score for this turn.
- Return the card to the same place. Make sure that it is face down.
- On your next turn, select a card. Multiply your present score by the number on that card. The product is your score for this turn. Return the card.
- If your point total for any turn is 0, start over.
- The first player to hit his or her goal number two times wins the game. If no player reaches his or her goal number after 10 turns, stop the game. Then have each player choose a new goal number and start the game over.

After playing the game once, discuss it with your group.

1. What strategy did you use to get back into the game if you went over your goal number?

2. Are there any goal numbers that are impossible to reach? Why or why not?

3. What is the quickest way to hit your goal number a second time?

Play the game again. Use what you have discussed to change your strategy. Will you change your goal number? Why or why not?

Round to the nearest ten.

1. 63 **2.** 87 **3.** 29

4. 284 **5.** 592 **6.** 815

Round to the nearest hundred.

7. 237 **8.** 598

9. 7,589 **10.** 4,601

Round to the nearest thousand.

11. 1,084 **12.** 4,138

13. 7,320 **14.** 5,652

Add or subtract.

15.	541 + 26	**16.** 281 + 19	**17.** 658 − 32
18.	823 + 472	**19.** 732 − 410	**20.** 406 − 319
21.	631 − 158	**22.** 590 + 287	**23.** 900 − 273
24.	83 94 + 216	**25.** 72 419 + 263	**26.** 194 639 + 402

27. 1,640 − 799 **28.** 3,105 + 286

29. 3,000 − 420 **30.** 4,203 − 874

7 in Multiplication

Heather read a book about good eating habits. She read that she should drink 8 glasses of water a day. How many glasses of water should she drink in 7 days?

Find 7×8.

Think of 7 groups of 8.

$7 \times 8 = 56$

Heather needs to drink 56 glasses of water in 7 days.

Try Multiply.

a. 6 $\times 7$	**b.** 4 $\times 7$	**c.** 7 $\times 7$	**d.** 7×9	**e.** 7×3	**f.** 8×7

Practice Multiply.

1. $\begin{array}{r} 2 \\ \times 7 \\ \hline \end{array}$
2. $\begin{array}{r} 9 \\ \times 7 \\ \hline \end{array}$
3. $\begin{array}{r} 7 \\ \times 4 \\ \hline \end{array}$
4. $\begin{array}{r} 7 \\ \times 7 \\ \hline \end{array}$
5. $\begin{array}{r} 6 \\ \times 7 \\ \hline \end{array}$
6. $\begin{array}{r} 4 \\ \times 4 \\ \hline \end{array}$
7. $\begin{array}{r} 8 \\ \times 6 \\ \hline \end{array}$

8. $\begin{array}{r} 0 \\ \times 7 \\ \hline \end{array}$
9. $\begin{array}{r} 9 \\ \times 6 \\ \hline \end{array}$
10. $\begin{array}{r} 7 \\ \times 6 \\ \hline \end{array}$
11. $\begin{array}{r} 5 \\ \times 7 \\ \hline \end{array}$
12. $\begin{array}{r} 7 \\ \times 2 \\ \hline \end{array}$
13. $\begin{array}{r} 4 \\ \times 6 \\ \hline \end{array}$
14. $\begin{array}{r} 8 \\ \times 7 \\ \hline \end{array}$

15. 5×6
16. 1×7
17. 7×8
18. 7×0
19. 9×3
20. 7×1

21. 7×3
22. 4×5
23. 7×5
24. 5×5
25. 3×7
26. 7×9

27. 4×7
28. 6×7
29. 9×4
30. 4×6
31. 8×7
32. 7×6

Apply _Choosing a Computation Method_ Calculator, Paper and Pencil, Mental Math, Estimation
Choose a method to solve each problem. Tell which method you used.

33. Heather eats 3 slices of bread each day. Is a 24-slice loaf enough bread for 7 days?

34. Heather ate 3 servings of vegetables a day for a week. How many servings of vegetables did she eat in those 7 days?

35. Heather eats 2 servings of protein each day. Does she eat enough protein if she should be eating 15 servings a week?

36. How many eggs in all are there in 7 dozen eggs?

8 in Multiplication

Jeffrey bought 9 ears of
corn at the vegetable stand.
Each ear of corn cost 8¢. How
much did Jeffrey spend for the corn?

A. Think of 9 groups of 8.

$$9 \times 8 = 72$$

B. Use a product you know to remember a fact.
To find 9×8, think of 8×8 plus one more 8.

$9 \times 8 = 72$ (64 + 8)

Jeffrey spent 72¢ for the corn.

Mental Math

Try Multiply.

a. 8
     ×9

b. 8
     ×4

c. 8×6

d. 8×8

Practice Multiply.

1. 2
     ×8

2. 5
     ×8

3. 8
     ×0

4. 7
     ×8

5. 7
     ×6

136

6. $\begin{array}{r} 8 \\ \times 8 \end{array}$	**7.** $\begin{array}{r} 8 \\ \times 5 \end{array}$	**8.** $\begin{array}{r} 5 \\ \times 9 \end{array}$	**9.** $\begin{array}{r} 3 \\ \times 8 \end{array}$	**10.** $\begin{array}{r} 8 \\ \times 1 \end{array}$	**11.** $\begin{array}{r} 6 \\ \times 5 \end{array}$

12. $\begin{array}{r} 8 \\ \times 9 \end{array}$

13. $\begin{array}{r} 8 \\ \times 3 \end{array}$ **14.** $\begin{array}{r} 9 \\ \times 8 \end{array}$ **15.** $\begin{array}{r} 5 \\ \times 8 \end{array}$ **16.** $\begin{array}{r} 3 \\ \times 6 \end{array}$ **17.** $\begin{array}{r} 4 \\ \times 8 \end{array}$ **18.** $\begin{array}{r} 8 \\ \times 6 \end{array}$ **19.** $\begin{array}{r} 7 \\ \times 9 \end{array}$

20. 0×8 **21.** 8×5 **22.** 8×2 **23.** 3×9 **24.** 4×8 **25.** 2×8

26. 8×7 **27.** 1×8 **28.** 4×7 **29.** 6×8 **30.** 8×0 **31.** 8×3

32. 8×1 **33.** 8×8 **34.** 8×4 **35.** 5×7 **36.** 7×8 **37.** 9×8

Apply   Solve each problem.

38. At the stand, carrots are sold in bunches of 8. How many carrots are in 4 bunches?

39. Jeffrey spent $3.85 at the vegetable stand. How much change did he receive from $5.00?

40. Mrs. Martinez bought 6 pounds of tomatoes and 4 pounds of onions. How many pounds of vegetables did she buy?

41. _Find the facts._ How many small squares are there in each row of a checkerboard? How many rows of squares are there? How many small squares are on a checkerboard?

Using Problem-Solving Strategies, page 418
More Practice Set 51, page 369 **137**

9 in Multiplication

Rosita and Manuel decided to make spool figures for gifts. They made 9 clowns. For each clown they used 9 spools. How many spools did they use for the clowns?

Find 9×9.

Think of 9 groups of 9.

$9 \times 9 = 81$

They used 81 spools for the clowns.

Try Multiply.

a. $\begin{array}{r} 9 \\ \times 3 \\ \hline \end{array}$
b. $\begin{array}{r} 5 \\ \times 9 \\ \hline \end{array}$
c. $\begin{array}{r} 9 \\ \times 7 \\ \hline \end{array}$

d. 8×9
e. 9×0
f. 6×9

138

Practice Multiply.

1. 7
×9

2. 3
×9

3. 9
×4

4. 1
×9

5. 7
×6

6. 9
×0

7. 5
×9

8. 9
×1

9. 9
×7

10. 2
×9

11. 8
×5

12. 9
×9

13. 9
×5

14. 8
×7

15. 9×2 **16.** 5×6 **17.** 9×8 **18.** 4×9 **19.** 0×9 **20.** 8×8

21. 9×3 **22.** 5×9 **23.** 7×8 **24.** 6×9 **25.** 8×9 **26.** 7×4

27. 7×9 **28.** 3×8 **29.** 9×4 **30.** 6×8 **31.** 9×6 **32.** 9×9

Apply _Choosing a Computation Method_ Calculator, Paper and Pencil, Mental Math, Estimation
Choose a method to solve each problem. Tell which method you used.
Discuss your thinking with another student.

33. Rosita made 9 spool pigs. For each pig, she used 7 spools. How many spools did Rosita use to make the spool pigs?

34. Manuel used 45 spools making horses. Rosita made 5 horses using 8 spools for each horse. Who used more spools making horses?

35. Manuel had 20 spools. He needed 13 spools for a giraffe and 8 spools for a horse. Did he have enough spools?

36. There are 20 spools in each box. Rosita wants to make 1 giraffe, 3 horses, and 2 pigs. She thinks she needs 6 boxes. Is this reasonable? Why or why not?

CALCULATOR

Use your calculator to find each product. Then add the digits in the product. What do you notice?

$9 \times 382 = 3,438$ $3 + 4 + 3 + 8 = 18$

1. 9×52 **2.** 9×68 **3.** 9×37 **4.** 9×84 **5.** 9×99

6. 9×16 **7.** 9×578 **8.** 9×627 **9.** 9×112 **10.** 9×813

11. 9×633 **12.** 9×987 **13.** 9×135 **14.** 9×333 **15.** 9×789

Practice: Multiplication Facts

The Brooks family played a multiplication game using two spinners.

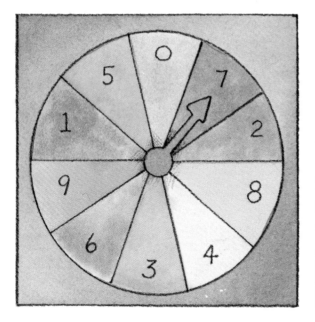 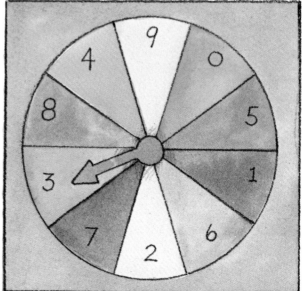

On each turn, the player spun both spinners and multiplied the numbers. The product was the player's score for that round.

Find each player's score for each round.

Player	First round	Second round	Third round	Fourth round	Fifth round
Mr. Brooks	**1.** 3 × 4	**2.** 6 × 3	**3.** 8 × 4	**4.** 1 × 2	**5.** 4 × 6
Mrs. Brooks	**6.** 6 × 4	**7.** 1 × 7	**8.** 2 × 8	**9.** 6 × 0	**10.** 3 × 7
Chad	**11.** 4 × 9	**12.** 5 × 0	**13.** 7 × 6	**14.** 5 × 8	**15.** 3 × 2
Julie	**16.** 5 × 3	**17.** 9 × 6	**18.** 8 × 1	**19.** 2 × 6	**20.** 5 × 5
Todd	**21.** 9 × 3	**22.** 2 × 5	**23.** 9 × 0	**24.** 7 × 8	**25.** 1 × 4

Find the total points for each player.

26. Mr. Brooks   **27.** Mrs. Brooks   **28.** Chad   **29.** Julie   **30.** Todd

*31. Who had the highest score?

Multiply.

32. $\begin{array}{r} 2 \\ \times 3 \end{array}$	**33.** $\begin{array}{r} 7 \\ \times 4 \end{array}$	**34.** $\begin{array}{r} 8 \\ \times 6 \end{array}$	**35.** $\begin{array}{r} 0 \\ \times 7 \end{array}$	**36.** $\begin{array}{r} 7 \\ \times 7 \end{array}$	**37.** $\begin{array}{r} 6 \\ \times 7 \end{array}$	**38.** $\begin{array}{r} 1 \\ \times 9 \end{array}$
39. $\begin{array}{r} 0 \\ \times 4 \end{array}$	**40.** $\begin{array}{r} 7 \\ \times 3 \end{array}$	**41.** $\begin{array}{r} 8 \\ \times 8 \end{array}$	**42.** $\begin{array}{r} 4 \\ \times 3 \end{array}$	**43.** $\begin{array}{r} 7 \\ \times 1 \end{array}$	**44.** $\begin{array}{r} 0 \\ \times 1 \end{array}$	**45.** $\begin{array}{r} 9 \\ \times 9 \end{array}$
46. $\begin{array}{r} 9 \\ \times 7 \end{array}$	**47.** $\begin{array}{r} 5 \\ \times 9 \end{array}$	**48.** $\begin{array}{r} 9 \\ \times 1 \end{array}$	**49.** $\begin{array}{r} 0 \\ \times 0 \end{array}$	**50.** $\begin{array}{r} 3 \\ \times 9 \end{array}$	**51.** $\begin{array}{r} 8 \\ \times 7 \end{array}$	**52.** $\begin{array}{r} 9 \\ \times 8 \end{array}$

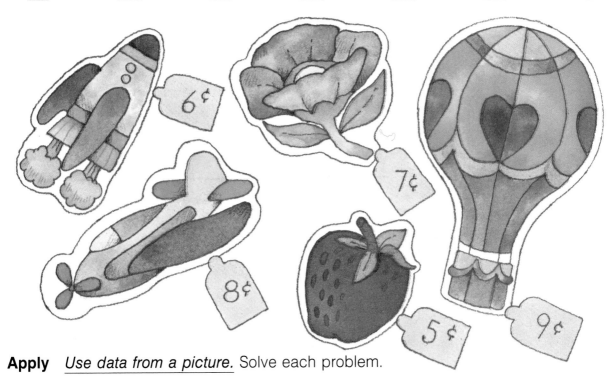

Apply *Use data from a picture.* Solve each problem.

53. How much do 6 strawberry stickers cost?

54. How much more is an airplane sticker than a rocket sticker?

55. Sherry bought 8 balloon stickers. How much did she spend?

56. Paul bought a rocket sticker, a balloon sticker, and a strawberry sticker. How much did he spend?

★57. Katie bought 2 flower stickers, 3 strawberry stickers, and 2 airplane stickers. How much change did she receive from 50¢?

58. *Thinking skills* If the product of two numbers is 36, what could the two numbers be?

Problem Solving Write a Problem

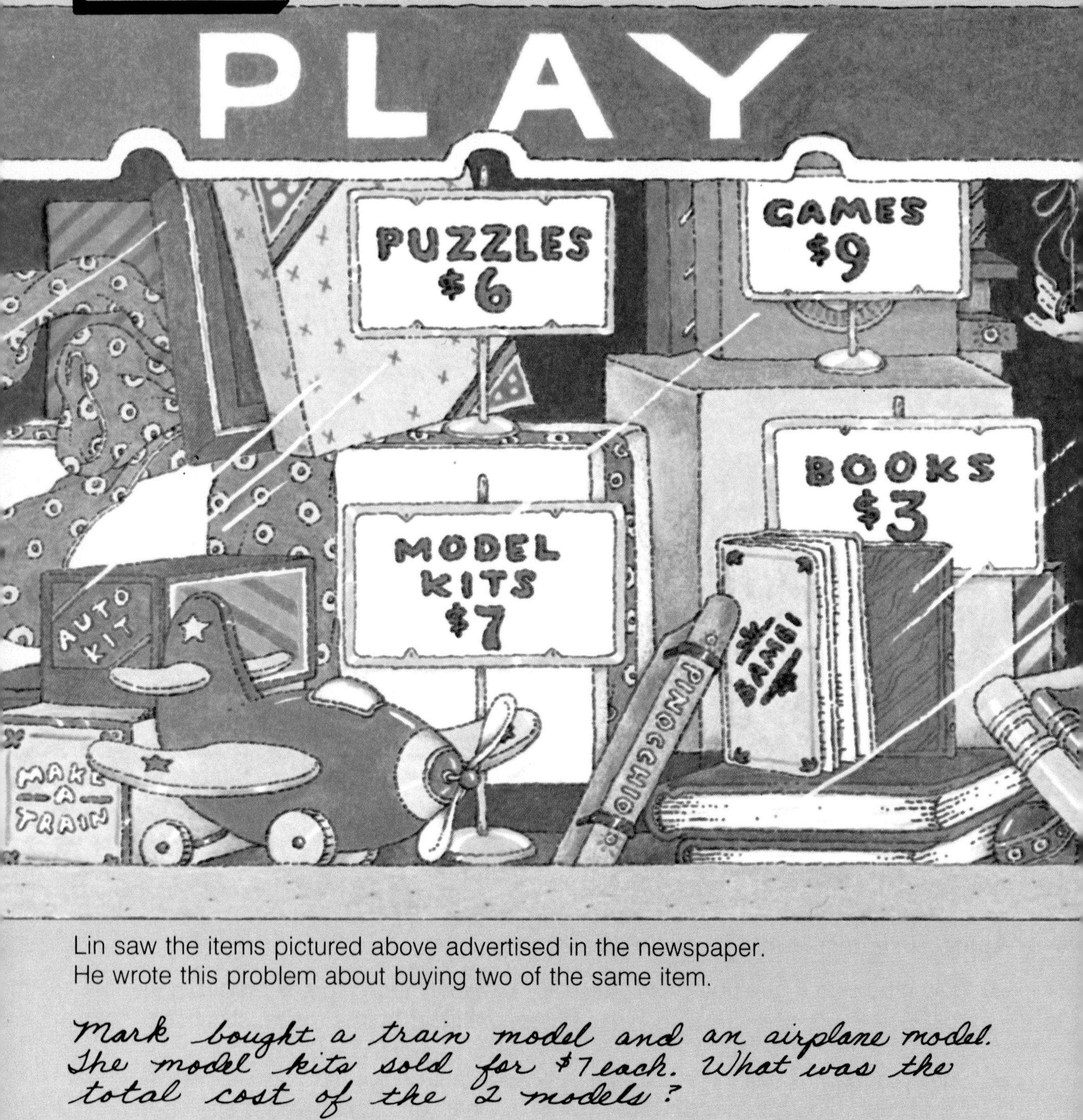
PLAY
PUZZLES
$6
GAMES
$9
MODEL
KITS
$7
BOOKS
$3
AUTO
KIT
MAKE
A
TRAIN
PINOCCHIO
BAMBI

Lin saw the items pictured above advertised in the newspaper. He wrote this problem about buying two of the same item.

Mark bought a train model and an airplane model. The model kits sold for $7 each. What was the total cost of the 2 models?

Try Write a problem about

a. buying a puzzle and a game.

b. the change received from $20 when buying two of the same item.

Apply Write a problem about

1. buying a book and a doll.

2. the change received from $10 when paying for a record.

3. which of two items costs more.

4. buying two different items.

5. how much more one item costs than another.

6. the sale price of an item when it is on sale for $1 off the regular price.

7. the change received from $20 when buying two different items.

*8. deciding if you have enough money to buy two of a certain item.

Chapter 5 Test

Copy and complete each sentence for the picture below.

(X X X X)
(X X X X)
(X X X X)

1. $4 + 4 + 4 = $ ▥

2. $3 \times 4 = $ ▥

Multiply.

3. 4 ×2

4. 3 ×3

5. 2 ×7

6. 3 ×8

7. 2 ×2

8. 7 ×3

9. 4 ×4

10. 5 ×5

11. 4 ×6

12. 5 ×4

13. 9 ×4

14. 7 ×5

15. 6 ×8

16. 3 ×6

17. 7 ×6

18. 0 ×1

19. 2 ×1

20. 1 ×6

21. 4 ×0

22. 6 ×0

23. 5 ×1

24. 4 ×7

25. 7 ×8

26. 2 ×7

27. 8 ×9

28. 4 ×8

29. 8 ×8

30. 5 ×9

31. 9 ×3

32. 7 ×9

Use the information above to write a problem about

33. buying two tote bags.

34. the change received when buying an item.

CHALLENGE

Multiples

$1 \times 5 = 5$

$2 \times 5 = 10$

$3 \times 5 = 15$

$4 \times 5 = 20$

$5 \times 5 = 25$

Laurel counted her pennies by putting them in stacks of 5.
5, 10, 15, 20, 25 are *multiples* of 5.
The next four multiples of 5 are 30, 35, 40, 45.

Complete each table.

Multiples of 6

×	1	2	3	4	5	6	7	8	9
6	**1.**	**2.**	**3.**	**4.**	**5.**	**6.**	**7.**	**8.**	**9.**

Multiples of 8

×	1	2	3	4	5	6	7	8	9
8	**10.**	**11.**	**12.**	**13.**	**14.**	**15.**	**16.**	**17.**	**18.**

Tell if each number is a multiple of 3. Write yes or no.

19. 18   **20.** 7   **21.** 27   **22.** 16   **23.** 25   **24.** 12

145

A DIZZY GAME BOARD

Tina is playing a game on the large board below. She starts in the square with the star and moves through all the squares in the directions shown by the arrows. She may not enter a square more than once. She wants to locate the sixty-eighth square without actually counting all the squares along her path. *Can she do it?*

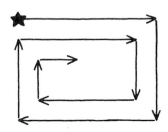

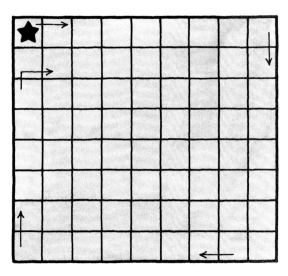

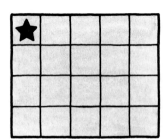

1. Copy the small game board on a piece of paper. Then trace a path all the way around to the last square. Mark that square with an "X".

2. How many squares are on the small gameboard?

3. Can you now locate the eighteenth square? Shade it in.

4. Copy the large game board and follow the same procedure to find the last square on the large board. Mark it with an "X". How many squares are on the board?
Shade in the sixty-eighth square.

PROBLEM-SOLVING STRATEGIES
- DRAW A PICTURE
- MAKE A TABLE
- USE PHYSICAL MODELS
- SOLVE A SIMPLER PROBLEM
- WORK BACKWARD

Multilpication

$6 \times 20 = 120$

Multiplying Tens, Hundreds, and Thousands: Mental Math

A. The city hall has 4 stories. On the north side, there are 10 offices on each story. How many offices are on the north side?

Think of 4 groups of 10.

You can add. $10 + 10 + 10 + 10 = 40$

Or, you can multiply. **$4 \times 10 = 40$** $(4 \times 1 \text{ ten} = 4 \text{ tens})$

There are 40 offices on the north side of the city hall.

Compute mentally. Use your mind to save you time.

B. The patterns below show an easy way to multiply with multiples of 10, 100, or 1,000.

$8 \times 2 = 16$
$8 \times 20 = 160$
$8 \times 200 = 1,600$
$8 \times 2,000 = 16,000$

$5 \times 8 = 40$
$5 \times 80 = 400$
$5 \times 800 = 4,000$
$5 \times 8,000 = 40,000$

Discuss What is an easy way to multiply a number by 10? by 100? by 1,000?

C. Look for products that are multiples of 10 to make your multiplication easier.

Find $4 \times 3 \times 5$.

$$4 \times 3 \times 5$$
$$4 \times 5 \times 3$$
$$20 \times 3$$
$$60$$

$4 \times 3 \times 5 = 60$

Try Multiply.

a. 7×20 **b.** 34×100 **c.** $5 \times 4{,}000$ **d.** $4 \times 7 \times 5$

Practice Multiply.

Mental Math

1. 8×1 **2.** 8×10 **3.** 8×100 **4.** $8 \times 1{,}000$

5. 3×10 **6.** 6×100 **7.** 9×100 **8.** $5 \times 1{,}000$

9. 46×1 **10.** 46×10 **11.** 46×100 **12.** $46 \times 1{,}000$

13. 3×4 **14.** 3×40 **15.** 3×400 **16.** $3 \times 4{,}000$

17. 6×5 **18.** 6×50 **19.** 6×500 **20.** $6 \times 5{,}000$

21. 9×10 **22.** 9×20 **23.** 9×30 **24.** $9 \times 3{,}000$

25. $7 \times 5 \times 6$ **26.** $8 \times 5 \times 9$ **27.** $8 \times 7 \times 5$ **28.** $5 \times 2 \times 7$

29. $5 \times 9 \times 6$ **30.** $5 \times 5 \times 4$ **31.** $2 \times 8 \times 5$ **32.** $4 \times 4 \times 5$

33. $9 \times 5 \times 4$ **34.** $2 \times 9 \times 5$ **35.** $5 \times 8 \times 8$ **36.** $6 \times 3 \times 5$

Apply Solve each problem.

37. There are 20 offices on the first floor of the city hall. 4 people work in each of these offices. How many people work in the offices on the first floor?

38. An office building has 8 stories. Each story has 30 windows. How many windows does this building have?

39. A department store has 20 display windows. 9 of them have been decorated for Spring. How many windows are not decorated for Spring?

★40. In an office building, 10 offices have 2 telephones each, and 20 offices have 3 telephones each. How many telephones do these offices have in all?

Multiplication: No Renaming

In this book you will often be asked to work in groups.
Turn to pages 438–441 for instructions on group work.

A. *Career* Tom Amber is a fireman. Last week he spoke about fire prevention to 3 groups of students. There were 42 students in each group. How many students did he speak to last week?

Work in groups of 4.

Find 3 × 42. Use rounding to estimate the answer.

3 × 40 = ▨

Use place-value materials to find the actual answer.

Show 3 groups of 42.
How many tens are there in all?
How many ones?

Use your place-value materials to show the product in standard form. What is 3 × 42?

Tom Amber spoke to ▨ students last week.

Is your answer reasonable? Why?

B. Continue to work in your group.

Find 4 × 72.

Estimate the product before you begin working with your place-value materials.

What is 4 × 72?

Is your answer close to the estimated product? Is your answer reasonable?

Try Multiply. Work in groups. First estimate the product. Then use place-value materials to find the actual answer. For each exercise, check if the actual answer is close to the estimate. Is your answer reasonable? Why or why not?

a. 21
$\times$ 3

b. 83 $\times$ 2

c. 432
$\times$ 2

d. 221 $\times$ 4

Practice Work in groups. Use place-value materials to find each product.

1. 31
$\times$ 2

2. 22
$\times$ 4

3. 62
$\times$ 3

4. 40
$\times$ 7

5. 93
$\times$ 2

6. 60 $\times$ 8

7. 31 $\times$ 6

8. 112 $\times$ 4

9. 333 $\times$ 2

10. 301 $\times$ 3

Apply Solve each problem.

11. On the fire truck, there were 3 hoses, each 400 feet long. If these hoses were hooked together, how far would they reach?

12. You want to explain multiplication to a younger student who has only studied addition. How would you explain that 15 $\times$ 7 equals 105, using addition?

13. Use your place-value materials to find 2 $\times$ 49. Explain how you got your answer.

Multiplication: One Renaming

A. There are 3 fire stations in the city. Each fire station has 24 firefighters. How many firefighters are there?

Find 3 × 24. Estimate the product. 3 × 24 is about ▓.

Work with two other students. Use place-value materials to show 3 groups of 24. Mix the groups together to make one group. Are there enough ones to exchange for another ten? How many tens are there in all? Show the number in standard form. What is 3 × 24?

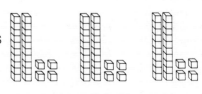

There are ▓ firefighters.

B. Continue to work in your group. Use place-value materials to find 5 × 314. First estimate the product.
Keep a step-by-step record of how you used your place-value materials to find the product.
Is your answer reasonable? Why or why not?

Compare the steps your group used to find the product to the steps used by another group. Are they the same? If not, take turns explaining each method to the other group.

Try Work in groups. Estimate the answer to each exercise. Then use place-value materials to find the actual product.

a. 25
    × 9

b. 44
    × 7

c. 42
    × 8

d. 314
     × 6

e. 8 × 421

f. 382 × 4

g. Each of you choose at least one of the Exercises a–f and explain to the others why your answer is reasonable.

Practice Work in groups. Estimate the answer to each exercise. Then use place-value materials to find the actual product.

1. 17
    × 4

2. 24
    × 3

3. 64
    × 7

4. 58
    × 5

5. Here is a way to record your work in Example A. Use the pictures to explain each step.

Step 1

$$24 \times 3$$

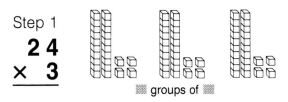

▨ groups of ▨

Step 2
Multiply the ones.

$$\overset{1}{2}4 \times 3 \over 2$$

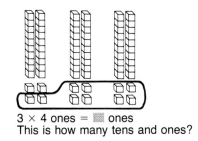

3 × 4 ones = ▨ ones
This is how many tens and ones?

Step 3
Multiply the tens.

$$\overset{1}{2}4 \times 3 \over 72$$

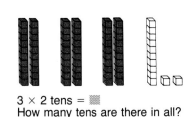

3 × 2 tens = ▨
How many tens are there in all?

Multiply. Use place-value materials and record your work.

6. 81 × 8

7. 39 × 2

8. 113 × 5

9. 627 × 3

10. 517 × 4

11. 381 × 5

12. 462 × 4

13. 832 × 3

14. 581 × 6

15. 1,217 × 4

Find each product without using place-value materials.

16. 219 × 3

17. 3,151 × 5

18. 741 × 5

19. 982 × 4

20. 5,211 × 7

21. 8 × 37

22. 45 × 9

23. 6 × 47

24. 615 × 2

Apply *Choosing a Computation Method* Calculator, Paper and Pencil, Mental Math, Estimation
Choose a method to solve each problem. Tell which method you used.

25. Last week, firefighter Diana Ortega worked 3 shifts of 24 hours each. Did she work more or less than 75 hours last week?

26. Each of the 9 fire stations has 15 bunks for its firefighters. How many bunks are there in all the fire stations?

27. Last year, Stations A, B, and C had 874 calls, 937 calls, and 629 calls. How many calls did the stations have in all?

28. If 450 feet of 3-inch wide hose is hooked up to 300 feet of 4-inch wide hose, will the hose reach 800 feet?

X	1	2	3	4	5	6	7	8	9	10	11	12
1	1	2	3	4	5	6	7	8	9	10	11	12
2	2	4	6	8	10	12	14	16	18	20	22	24
3	3	6	9	12	15	18	21	24	27	30	33	36
4	4	8	12	16	20	24	28	32	36	40	44	48
5	5	10	15	20	25	30	35	40	45	50	55	60
6	6	12	18	24	30	36	42	48	54	60	66	72
7	7	14	21	28	35	42	49	56	63	70	77	84
8	8	16	24	32	40	48	56	64	72	80	88	96
9	9	18	27	36	45	54	63	72	81	90	99	108
10	10	20	30	40	50	60	70	80	90	100	110	120
11	11	22	33	44	55	66	77	88	99	110	121	132
12	12	24	36	48	60	72	84	96	108	120	132	144

magnificent Multiplication TABLE

Read   There are many number patterns formed by the factors and products in multiplication. Some patterns can be found in a multiplication table. What pattern is made by the sums of the digits in the products for the factor 3?

YOU CAN DO IT. HERE'S THE KEY. USE PROBLEM-SOLVING STRATEGIES.

PROBLEM-SOLVING STRATEGIES
• CHOOSE THE OPERATION
• DRAW A PICTURE
• FIND A PATTERN
• WRITE AN EQUATION
• USE ESTIMATION
• MAKE A TABLE

Plan   Write the products shown in the table above for the factor 3. Where there is a 2-digit product, add the digits. Look for a pattern. Can a rule be used to find the next number? Do a group of numbers keep repeating?

Solve

Products:	3	6	9	12	15	18	21	24	27	30	33	36
Sums of digits:	3	6	9	3	6	9	3	6	9	3	6	9

Answer   The pattern is 3, 6, 9.

Look Back   Be sure you wrote the products in order and added correctly.

Try Solve each problem.

In the products for the factor 9, what pattern is made by

a. the ones digits?

b. the sums of the digits? If the digits have a 2-digit sum, add again to get a 1-digit sum.

Apply Solve each problem.

What pattern is made by the ones digits in

1. the products for the factor 5?

2. the products for the factor 4?

3. the products for the factor 8?

In the products for the factor 11, what pattern is made by

4. the ones digits?

5. the sums of the digits? If there is a 2-digit sum, add again to get a 1-digit sum.

In the products for the factor 12, what pattern is made by

6. the ones digits?

7. the sums of the digits? If there is a 2-digit sum, add again to get a 1-digit sum.

★8. In the products for the factor 5, what pattern is made by the sums of the digits?

This 2-by-2 square has been cut from a multiplication table. Notice the products of the numbers on the diagonals. They are the same.

2	3
4	6

$2 \times 6 = 12$

$3 \times 4 = 12$

Use your calculator to find out if this pattern is true for larger squares.

2	3	4
4	6	8
6	9	12

1. $2 \times 6 \times 12 = $ ▨

2. $4 \times 6 \times 6 = $ ▨

3	6	9	12
4	8	12	16
5	10	15	20
6	12	18	24

3. $3 \times 8 \times 15 \times 24 = $ ▨

4. $12 \times 12 \times 10 \times 6 = $ ▨

Are the products of the numbers on the diagonals equal for the

5. 3-by-3 square above?

6. 4-by-4 square above?

7. Choose a 5-by-5 square on the multiplication table. Is the pattern true for this square?

Multiplication: More Than One Renaming

A. If 185 visitors entered the San Diego Wild Animal Park each hour, how many visitors entered in 3 hours?

Find 3 × 185.

> Estimate using rounding:
> 3 × 200 = 600

Work in a group. Show each step in the computation with place-value materials.

Put 3 groups of 185 together. How many ones are there in all? This is how many tens and ones?

Multiply the ones.

$$\begin{array}{r} 1 \\ 18\mathbf{5} \\ \times\ \ \ \ \mathbf{3} \\ \hline \mathbf{5} \end{array}$$

3 × 5 = ▦

15 = ▦ ten ▦ ones

Now put the tens together. How many tens are there in all? This is how many hundreds and tens?

Multiply the tens.

$$\begin{array}{r} 2\ 1 \\ 1\mathbf{8}5 \\ \times\ \ \ \ \mathbf{3} \\ \hline \mathbf{5}\,5 \end{array}$$

3 × 8 tens = ▦ tens

24 tens + 1 ten = ▦ tens
25 tens = ▦ hundreds ▦ tens

How many hundreds are there in all?

Multiply the hundreds.

$$\begin{array}{r} 2\ 1 \\ \mathbf{1}85 \\ \times\ \ \ \ \mathbf{3} \\ \hline \mathbf{5}\,55 \end{array}$$

3 × 1 hundred = ▦ hundreds

3 hundreds + 2 hundreds = ▦ hundreds

555 visitors would enter in 3 hours.
Look at the estimate. Is 555 a reasonable answer?

B. **CALCULATOR** Press 185 ⊕ 185 ⊜ ⊕ 185 ⊜.
Compare this to the computation in Example A.
Write a generalization about the relationship between multiplication and addition.

Test your generalization by finding 367 × 4 both ways.

Try Multiply. Work in groups. Show the computation with your place-value materials.

a. 143
   × 4

b. 279
   × 3

c. 2 × 376

d. Look at the key sequence for the calculator in Example B. Write another key sequence which uses ⊕ and ⊜ that can be used to find 3 × 185.

Practice Multiply.

1. 236
   × 4

2. 123
   × 8

3. 216
   × 7

4. 177
   × 5

5. 238
   × 3

6. 229
   × 4

7. 134
   × 6

8. 974
   × 3

9. 127
   × 5

CALCULATOR Use a calculator to find each product.

10. 4,127
    × 6

11. 4,671
    × 2

12. 2,516
    × 9

13. 3 × 8,159

14. 1,517 × 5

Choosing a Computation Method Calculator, Paper and Pencil, Mental Math
Choose a method to find each answer. Tell which method you used.

15. 1,670
    × 4

16. 1,925
    × 3

17. 1,516
    × 5

18. 1,139
    × 6

19. 5,187
    × 4

20. 8 × 114

21. 2 × 398

22. 2,187 × 4

23. 6,274 × 3

Apply Solve each problem.

24. Each monorail train at the Wild Animal Park carries 125 people. How many people can 6 of these trains carry?

25. The plan for the Wild Animal Park was started in 1959. The park opened 13 years later. In what year did the park open?

26. *Mental math* A baby elephant gains about 2 pounds a day. How much will the baby elephant gain in 30 days?

27. By the end of 1978, 36 cheetahs were born at the park. A cheetah can run 26 meters per second. How many meters can a cheetah run in 9 seconds?

Multiplication: Renaming with Zeros

Mr. and Mrs. Rivera traveled by plane to San Diego. Their tickets cost $206 each. How much did the Riveras pay for 2 tickets?

Find 2 × 206. 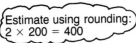 Estimate using rounding: 2 × 200 = 400

A. Work in groups of 4. Use your place-value materials. Explain to someone in your group how to find 2 × 206. What is the answer?

B. Now study the computation. Answer the questions with other students in your group.

Multiply the ones.

```
    1
  2 0 6
×     2
      2
```
2 × 6 = ▨
How many tens and ones is this?

Multiply the tens.

```
    1
  2 0 6
×     2
    1 2
```
2 × 0 tens = ▨ tens
How many tens are there in all? Why?

Multiply the hundreds.

```
    1
  2 0 6
×     2
  4 1 2
```
2 × 2 hundreds = ▨ hundreds
How many hundreds are there in all?

The Riveras paid $412 for their plane tickets. Is this answer reasonable? How do you know?

Try Work in groups. Show the computation with your place-value materials.

a.
```
  179
×   4
```

b.
```
  209
×   3
```

c. 2 × 390

d. 105 × 4

Practice Multiply.

1.
```
  301
×   6
```

2.
```
  402
×   7
```

3.
```
  520
×   9
```

4.
```
  860
×   3
```

5.
```
  400
×   6
```

6.
```
  560
×   5
```

7.
```
  601
×   8
```

8.
```
  302
×   5
```

9.
```
  750
×   8
```

| **10.** 6,027
×   5 | **11.** 3,410
×   4 | **12.** 2,002
×   5 | **13.** 7,050
×   6 | **14.** 8,007
×   8 |

Apply *Choosing a Computation Method* Calculator, Paper and Pencil, Mental Math, Estimation
Choose a method to solve each problem. Tell which method you used.

15. In a jewelry shop in San Diego, Mrs. Rivera saw gold bracelets that sold for $205 each. Could she buy 3 of the bracelets for $600?

16. The San Diego Trolley has a 32-mile round trip to the Mexican border. How far does the trolley travel in 6 round trips to the border?

17. Some of the houses that still stand today in San Diego's Old Town were built in 1829. How old were these houses in 1980?

18. At Sea World, a trained whale performs in a 3,000-seat stadium. How many people in all can be seated to see 4 shows?

19. What number multiplied by itself gives the product 34,969?

MAINTENANCE

Multiply.

1. 7 × 2	**2.** 3 × 6
3. 9 × 3	**4.** 1 × 5
5. 7 × 6	**6.** 3 × 4
7. 5 × 5	**8.** 8 × 6
9. 4 × 0	**10.** 3 × 8
11. 4 × 7	**12.** 5 × 4
13. 8 × 8	**14.** 2 × 4
15. 6 × 9	**16.** 8 × 2
17. 6 × 6	**18.** 9 × 5

Practice: Multiplication

Multiply.

Find the pattern of answers in each row.

Row A

| 1. | 41 × 3 | 2. | 26 × 9 | 3. | 115 × 3 | 4. | 76 × 6 | 5. | 63 × 9 |

Row B

| 6. | 56 × 9 | 7. | 63 × 8 | 8. | 72 × 7 | 9. | 84 × 6 | 10. | 126 × 4 |

Row C

| 11. | 23 × 9 | 12. | 34 × 9 | 13. | 45 × 9 | 14. | 56 × 9 | 15. | 67 × 9 |

Row D

| 16. | 27 × 5 | 17. | 123 × 2 | 18. | 51 × 7 | 19. | 78 × 6 | 20. | 193 × 3 |

Row E

| 21. | 131 × 2 | 22. | 121 × 3 | 23. | 116 × 4 | 24. | 113 × 5 | 25. | 111 × 6 |

Row F

| 26. | 101 × 5 | 27. | 103 × 5 | 28. | 105 × 5 | 29. | 107 × 5 | 30. | 109 × 5 |

Row G

| 31. | 617 × 2 | 32. | 2,263 × 3 | 33. | 469 × 5 | 34. | 384 × 9 | 35. | 2,839 × 2 |

Mental math Multiply mentally. Write only the product.

Mental Math

36. 6×40 37. 7×200 38. $5 \times 3,000$ 39. 12×10

40. 8×50 41. 9×900 42. $25 \times 1,000$ 43. 5×400

44. 59×100 45. 35×10 46. 7×800 47. $3 \times 9,000$

48. $6 \times 4 \times 5$ 49. $7 \times 2 \times 5$ 50. $5 \times 9 \times 8$ 51. $5 \times 5 \times 4$

160

Regular Bus Double-Decker Bus Minibus

Apply _Use data from a picture._ Solve each problem.

52. Cityville has 8 regular buses. How many passengers can ride on all 8 buses at one time?

53. How many more passengers can ride on a double-decker bus than on a regular bus?

54. There are 6 minibuses in Cityville. How many passengers can ride on the 6 minibuses at one time?

55. Cityville has 3 double-decker buses. How many passengers can ride on the 3 double-decker buses at one time?

56. There are 39 passengers on the top deck of a double-decker bus and 47 passengers on the bottom deck. How many more passengers can the bus hold?

57. **CALCULATOR** Greenville has 24 regular buses, 12 minibuses, and no double-decker buses. How many passengers can ride on all these buses at one time?

Multiplying Multiples of 10: Mental Math

A. Ron Morris owns a food stand in the park. He ordered 60 boxes of plastic spoons with 200 spoons in each box. How many plastic spoons did he order?

Find 60 × 200.

60 × 200 = 12,000 $\boxed{6 \times 2 = 12}$

Ron Morris ordered 12,000 plastic spoons.

Study these patterns.

B. 1 × 80 = 80
10 × 80 = 800
100 × 80 = 8,000
1,000 × 80 = 80,000

C. 40 × 5 = 200
40 × 50 = 2,000
40 × 500 = 20,000
40 × 5,000 = 200,000

**Compute mentally.
Use your mind
to save you time.**

*When you multiply numbers that end in zero, first
multiply the digits that are not zero. Then write as
many zeros in the product as there are in the factors.*

Try Multiply.

a. 20 × 4   **b.** 8 × 7,000   **c.** 40 × 30   **d.** 20 × 400   **e.** 200 × 50

Practice Multiply.

1. 3 × 60   **2.** 30 × 60   **3.** 300 × 60   **4.** 3,000 × 60   **5.** 30 × 6

6. 8 × 50   **7.** 80 × 50   **8.** 800 × 50   **9.** 8,000 × 50   **10.** 5 × 800

11. 7 × 80   **12.** 40 × 80   **13.** 200 × 60   **14.** 800 × 3   **15.** 60 × 70

16. 90 × 5   **17.** 10 × 60   **18.** 7 × 400   **19.** 30 × 9,000   **20.** 200 × 5

21. 60 × 4   **22.** 90 × 90   **23.** 60 × 800   **24.** 50 × 600   **25.** 80 × 700

Apply Solve each problem.

26. Mr. Morris ordered 30 packages of
paper cups with 40 cups in each
package. How many cups did he
order?

27. There are 500 straws in each box.
How many straws are in 20 boxes?

Estimating Products: Mental Math

A. City workers planted 28 trees in a park. Each tree cost $52. About how much did the trees cost in all?

Estimate 28 × 52.

28 × 52   Round both 28 and 52
  ↓   ↓   to the nearest 10.
                Then multiply.
30 × 50 = 1,500

The trees cost about $1,500 in all.

B. Estimate 34 × 62.

34 × 62   Round both 34 and 62
  ↓   ↓   to the nearest 10.
                Then multiply.
30 × 60 = 1,800

Discuss Is the actual product more or less than the estimate?

PINE
CITYVILLE PARK DISTRICT

TULIP

Try *Estimation* Estimate each product.

a. 58 × 6 ⟨60 × 6⟩   **b.** 7 × 81   **c.** 63 × 27   **d.** 36 × 48

Practice *Estimation* Estimate each product.

Be smart.
Estimate when you calculate.

1. 3 × 42   **2.** 4 × 89   **3.** 19 × 52   **4.** 31 × 67   **5.** 56 × 91
⟨3 × 40⟩   ⟨4 × 90⟩   ⟨20 × 50⟩   ⟨30 × 70⟩   ⟨60 × 90⟩

6. 83 × 2   **7.** 6 × 67   **8.** 74 × 27   **9.** 24 × 81   **10.** 43 × 55

11. 7 × 35   **12.** 4 × 18   **13.** 11 × 92   **14.** 44 × 68   **15.** 89 × 88

16. 56 × 3   **17.** 8 × 42   **18.** 32 × 38   **19.** 36 × 54   **20.** 15 × 81

21. 9 × 21   **22.** 76 × 5   **23.** 57 × 22   **24.** 88 × 17   **25.** 29 × 52

Apply Solve each problem.
Estimation Use estimation for Problems 26–29.

26. City workers planted rose bushes that cost $6 each. Estimate the total cost of 84 rose bushes.

27. Estimate the total cost of 25 pine trees at $39 each.

28. A lilac bush costs $23. A magnolia tree costs $87. Estimate how much more a magnolia tree costs than a lilac bush.

29. City workers planted 195 bushes that cost $15 each and 98 flower bulbs that cost $2 each. Estimate the total cost.

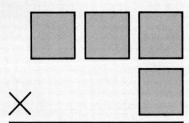

Using all of the digits 2, 5, 8, and 9 in the problem at the left,

30. how many different products can you make?

31. what is the greatest product you can make?

32. what is the least product you can make?

Multiplication: Two-Digit Numbers

A. *Career*   Mary Miller, a computer engineer, programmed the computer to show a blue rectangle with 11 rows of 12 squares on the screen. Work in groups of 4. Use grid paper to draw this rectangle. How can you find the number of squares without counting them individually? What is 11 × 12?

Try   Work in groups. Use grid paper to show each answer.

a.   14
    ×16

b. 48 × 30

c. 26 × 38

B. To learn about computers, Mary went to school for 20 weeks. She spent 32 hours a week in classes. How many hours did she spend in classes altogether?

Find 20 × 32.   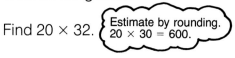 Estimate by rounding. 20 × 30 = 600.

```
  3 2     Multiply
× 2 0     by 0 ones.
    0     0 × 32 = ▨
```

```
  3 2     Multiply
× 2 0     by 2 tens.
6 4 0     2 tens × 32 = ▨
```

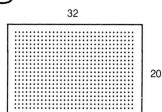

Mary spent 640 hours in classes.
Is this answer reasonable? Why?

C. Find 28 × 32.

```
  3 2     Think of 28 as
× 2 8     20 + 8
2 5 6     8 × 32 = ▨
```

```
  3 2
× 2 8
2 5 6
6 4 0     20 × 32 = ▨
```

```
  3 2
× 2 8
2 5 6
6 4 0
8 9 6     256 + 640 = ▨
```

28 × 32
(20 + 8) × 32
↑   ↑
Parentheses are used to show 28 as the sum of 20 + 8.

Practice   Multiply.

1.   37
    ×40

2.   75
    ×50

3.   19
    ×80

4.   67
    ×20

5.   56
    ×30

6.   24
    ×90

7.   58
    ×17

8.   34
    ×25

9.   32
    ×43

10.   67
    ×56

11.   98
    ×81

12.   72
    ×39

13.   42
    ×33

14.   65
    ×41

15.   84
    ×52

16.   59
    ×75

17. 68 × 61

18. 49 × 23

19. 37 × 16

20. 81 × 44

21. After you have completed Exercises 1–20, get in groups and take turns explaining why your answers are reasonable.

For Exercises 22–25, work in groups. Use grid paper.

22. Show 16 × 35 = (10 + 6) × 35.
What is 16 × 35?
What is (10 × 35) + (6 × 35)?

23. Show 35 × 16 = (30 + 5) × 16.

24. Show 35 × 16 = (30 + 5) × (10 + 6).

25. Look at the figure at the right. How many squares are there? Write a sentence to show this. Compare your sentences. Are they the same? If not, explain your sentences to one another.

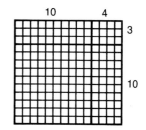

Apply   Solve each problem.

26. Mary worked with a magnetic printer that printed 87 lines per minute. How many lines can it print in 60 minutes?

27. Mary worked 48 hours last week and 39 hours this week. How many more hours did she work last week?

28. *Estimation* A printer printed 88 characters per second for 42 seconds. Estimate how many characters it printed.

29. A laser printer prints 12,000 lines per minute. How many lines can it print in 30 minutes?

30. *Thinking skills* Explain an easy way to multiply 2 × 16 × 50.

31. *Find the facts.* Work with another student. Discuss how to get an estimate for the number of letters on a page in a book. Then choose a book. Select a page in it and give an estimate of the number of letters on that page.

Multiplication: Two-Digit and Three-Digit Numbers

A. Computer-controlled robots are used in many factories. In 1982, Great Britain had about 500 programmable robots. Japan had 28 times as many. About how many programmable robots did Japan have?

Find 28 × 500.

Estimate using rounding.
30 × 500 = ▦

$$
\begin{array}{r}
500 \\
\times\ 28 \\
\hline
4000 \\
10000 \\
\hline
14,000
\end{array}
$$

8 × 500 = 4,000
20 × 500 = 10,000
4,000 + 10,000 = 14,000

In 1982, Japan had about 14,000 programmable robots.

Is this answer reasonable? How can you tell? Why is it important to determine an approximate answer before multiplying?

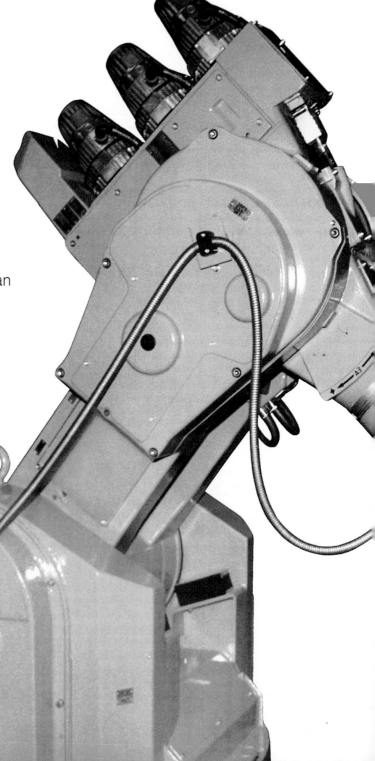

B. Find 35 × 146.

$$
\begin{array}{r}
146 \\
\times\ 35 \\
\hline
730 \\
4380 \\
\hline
5,110
\end{array}
$$

An estimate can be a range.
Round both numbers down.
30 × 100 = 3,000
Round both numbers up.
40 × 200 = 8,000
The product is between 3,000 and 8,000.

Try Multiply.

Be smart. Estimate when you calculate.

a. 400
× 62

b. 108
× 74

c. 320
× 18

d. Find 18 × 542. First estimate by finding the range. Then find the actual product. Is your actual answer within the range?

Practice Multiply.

1. 300
× 41

2. 800
× 35

3. 243
× 30

4. 317
× 40

5. 103
× 65

6. 370
× 81

7. 432
× 13

8. 826
× 44

9. 707
× 29

10. 281
× 18

11. 195
× 32

12. 275
× 64

13. 324
× 96

14. 807
× 75

15. 765
× 42

16. 581
× 39

17. 819
× 53

18. 565
× 65

19. Get together with three other students and explain to one another why your answers to Exercises 1–18 are reasonable.

Apply *Choosing a Computation Method* Calculator, Paper and Pencil, Mental Math, Estimation
Choose a method to solve each problem. Tell which method you used.
Explain to another student why you chose that method.

20. A robot can assemble a part in 110 seconds. How long will it take the robot to assemble 3,115 parts?

21. A robot can handle 400 machine parts per hour. How many parts could it handle in 20 hours?

22. If a robot worked 16 hours per day, how many hours would it work in 365 days?

23. The first mechanical adding machine was made in 1642. Robots first worked in factories 315 years later. What year was this?

24. A certain robot can move 19 feet per second. Can it move 1,000 feet in 50 seconds?

25. One type of robot can weld 50 connections per minute. How many connections can this robot weld in 60 minutes?

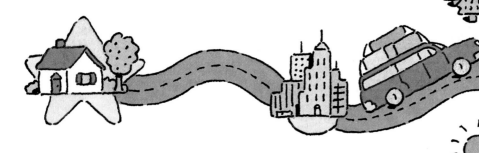

FAMILY VACATIONS

Work in a group with three other students. Choose two of the following problems to solve in your group. Discuss with your group why each problem was chosen, how you plan to solve each problem, why your method will work, and if the same method can be used for both of the problems. When the problems have been solved, present your work to the rest of the class. If another group has solved the same problem, compare the problem-solving methods used.

1. Betty Scott has $24 in savings, and her brother Tom has $12. They would like to save more money for their vacation. If Betty can save $3 a week and Tom can save $5 a week, how long will it take until Tom has the same amount of savings as Betty?

2. The Scotts and their neighbors, the Mitchells, are both going on vacations. The two families are traveling in opposite directions. The Scotts drive about 50 miles each hour, and the Mitchells drive about 45 miles each hour. How long will it take them to be 285 miles apart if they start at the same time?

3. Betty likes to collect post cards on her vacations. She can get one post card for a nickel or six post cards for a quarter. How much will it cost Betty to buy 20 post cards?

4. The first day, Tom bought 1 souvenir. The second day, he bought 2 souvenirs. The third day, he bought 3 souvenirs, and so on. How many souvenirs did Tom buy after 7 days on vacation?

5. Betty also bought some souvenirs. At one store, she spent one half of her money. Then she went to another store and spent one half of what was left. After that, she had 24 cents. How much money did she have at the start?

6. The Scotts stopped to camp for a few days. Tom and Betty went to cut some firewood. If it takes 12 minutes to cut a log into 3 pieces, how long will it take to cut a log into 4 pieces?

7. Mr. Scott, Tom, and Betty are trying to get across a river in a small boat that holds only 150 pounds at a time. Mr. Scott weighs 150 pounds; Tom weighs 85 pounds; and Betty weighs 65 pounds. How can all three get across the river?

COMPUTER

BASIC: REM Statements

REM statements allow remarks to be put into a program. These remarks are for the person reading the program. The computer ignores REM statements. A REM statement may be anywhere in a program before END and must have a line number.

```
10 REM MULTIPLY BY 5
20 PRINT 10*5;
30 PRINT 15*5;
40 PRINT 22*5
50 END
```

1. Tell what would be printed for the program above.

2. Write a program that will print your name, age, and grade on separate lines. Use a REM statement before each PRINT statement.

3. Tell what would be printed for the program you wrote for Exercise 2.

4. Write a program that will print the answers to the following exercises on one line. Use a REM statement to give a brief description of the program.

   212 × 34   331 × 23   525 × 12

5. Tell what would be printed for the program you wrote for Exercise 4.

Multiplication: Money

A. Beto and Lina each earned $2.73. How much do they have in all?

Use play money to display $2.73 on your desk. Combine your money with that of another student who has $2.73. Exchange coins for dollar bills as much as possible in order to find the total amount of money.

Explain how you combined the coins and bills and then exchanged coins for bills. Were you concerned with the decimal point?

What is 2 × $2.73?

Beto and Lina went to see a professional baseball game at the Astrodome in Houston. Each ticket cost $3.50.

B. Would $10.00 be enough to pay for two tickets?

When determining how much money is needed, estimate to the next higher dollar. Why?

$3.50 rounds to $4.00.
2 × $4.00 = $8.00

$10.00 would be enough for two tickets.

C. How much did they actually pay for the two tickets?

Find 2 × $3.50.

Think of $3.50 as 350 cents. Multiply. Write the answer in dollars and cents.

$$\begin{array}{r} \$3.50 \\ \times\ \ \ \ 2 \\ \hline \end{array} \qquad \begin{array}{r} 350 \\ \times\ \ \ 2 \\ \hline 700 \end{array} \qquad \begin{array}{r} \$3.50 \\ \times\ \ \ \ 2 \\ \hline \$7.00 \end{array}$$

Beto and Lina paid $7.00 for the two tickets.

D. Find 3 × 42¢. **Mental Math**

You can multiply mentally
by thinking of 42¢ as 40¢ + 2¢.
(3 × 40) + (3 × 2)
   120   +   6   = 126
Write the answer as dollars
and cents. $1.26

Try Multiply. Use play money for
Exercises a–c.

a. $0.06
   ×   7

b. $0.15
   ×   11

c. $1.39
   ×   6

d. 14 × $4.08

e. `CALCULATOR` 7 × 97¢
Press: 7 ⨯ · 97 =

Practice Multiply.

1. $0.02
   ×   4

2. $0.27
   ×   3

3. $0.81
   ×   9

4. $1.33
   ×   6

5. $4.05
   ×   7

6. $8.60
   ×   35

7. $0.13
   ×   28

8. $0.75
   ×   14

9. $1.50
   ×   61

10. $7.36
    ×   15

Mental math Multiply mentally. Write only the product.   **Mental Math**

11. 9 × 51¢

12. 3 × 83¢

13. 2 × 64¢

14. 4 × 52¢

Choosing a Computation Method Calculator, Paper and Pencil, Mental Math
Choose a method to find each product. Tell which method you used.

15. 16 × $0.43

16. 47 × $0.29

17. 38 × $1.07

18. 4 × $2.50

19. 20 × $0.58

20. 70 × $0.36

21. 14 × $2.49

22. 67 × $3.65

Apply _Use data from a table._ Use the prices to find the cost of

23. 4 pennants.

24. 10 programs.

25. 6 hats.

26. 20 baseball
cards

27. a hat and a
T-shirt

28. 3 hats and
6 T-shirts.

Item	Price
Program	$1.25
Pennant	$2.95
Hat	$3.75
T-shirt	$6.50
Baseball Card	$0.05

29. Jeremy wants to buy 7 pennants. Can he pay for them
with a twenty-dollar bill? Explain why or why not.

30. `CALCULATOR` Mr. Drew bought one of each item for
each of his 3 grandchildren. What was the total cost?

Problem Solving — Choose the Operation

Marie and Tony visited the Lyndon B. Johnson Space Center in Houston, Texas. They took a walking tour that included the Skylab Mission Building.

In the Skylab Mission Building, Marie learned that the first Skylab Mission lasted 28 days. The third mission lasted 3 times as long as the first. How many days did the third Skylab Mission last?

Read
Facts: First mission, 28 days
third mission, 3 times as long
Find: Number of days for third mission

Plan
Since the third mission lasted 3 times as many days as the first mission, use multiplication. Find 3×28.

Solve

$$\begin{array}{r} 28 \\ \times\ 3 \\ \hline 84 \end{array}$$

Estimate: $3 \times 30 = 90$

Answer
The third Skylab Mission lasted 84 days.

Look Back
The estimate of 90 days is close to 84 days. The answer is reasonable.

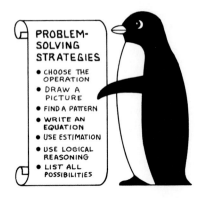

PROBLEM-SOLVING STRATEGIES
- CHOOSE THE OPERATION
- DRAW A PICTURE
- FIND A PATTERN
- WRITE AN EQUATION
- USE ESTIMATION
- USE LOGICAL REASONING
- LIST ALL POSSIBILITIES

Try Tell whether you *add*, *subtract*, or *multiply*.
Then find the answer.

Be smart.
Estimate when
you calculate.

a. The crew members of the first Skylab Mission ate a total of 9 meals a day. How many meals did they eat in 28 days?

b. The first powered aircraft flight took place in 1903. 58 years later man first flew in space. What year was the first manned space flight?

Apply Tell whether you *add*, *subtract*, or *multiply*.
Then find the answer.

1. During the first fifteen years of manned space flights, 34 Soviet cosmonauts and 41 American astronauts were launched into space. How many people traveled in space during those years?

2. The first Skylab Mission made 405 orbits around the earth. The second mission made 859 orbits. How many fewer orbits did the first mission make?

3. On the third Skylab Mission, each crew member exercised for 90 minutes each day. How many minutes did each member exercise in 84 days?

4. On the Skylab Missions, each astronaut was allowed one shower per week. Only 3 quarts of water were allowed for each shower. How many quarts of water were used for 12 showers?

5. Marie bought a model of an Apollo spacecraft for $8.75. How much change did she receive from $10.00?

6. Tony wanted to buy two books about space. One cost $4.85 and the other cost $2.95. How much would they cost altogether?

7. Directors of the Skylab Mission had planned for the astronauts to work 565 hours gathering data about the sun. The actual time spent on this was 755 hours. How many more hours than planned were spent gathering data about the sun?

8. *Estimation* A mid-sized car is about 15 feet long. The space shuttle *Enterprise* is about 8 times this length. Estimate the length of the *Enterprise*.

★9. The first Skylab Mission lasted 28 days. The second mission was planned to last twice as long. How long was the second Skylab Mission planned to last?

10. *Write a problem.* Write a problem about a space mission for which you can estimate the answer. Then solve the problem.

Chapter 6 Test

Multiply.

1. 5 × 40

2. 29 × 100

3. 63
× 3

4. 802
× 4

5. 5,314
× 2

6. 73
× 6

7. 384
× 2

8. 6,532
× 3

9. 135
× 5

10. 324
× 7

11. 2,683
× 3

12. 304
× 8

13. 4,006
× 9

14. 6,037
× 4

Solve each problem. Use these products for the factor 6.

6   12   18   24   30   36   42

15. What pattern is made by the ones digits?

16. What pattern is made by the sums of the digits?

Estimate each product.

17. 6 × 43

18. 37 × 45

Multiply.

19. 10 × 80

20. 50 × 60

21. 70 × 300

22. 4 × 700

23. 84
× 30

24. 76
× 15

25. 512
× 47

26. 907
× 62

27. $0.85
× 29

28. $1.49
× 5

Tell whether you *add*, *subtract*, or *multiply*. Then find the answer.

29. A large airplane has 264 passenger seats. How many passengers can the plane carry in 4 trips?

30. Another airplane can seat 127 passengers. 39 seats are empty. How many passengers are on the plane?

Choosing a Computation Method — Calculator, Paper and Pencil, Mental Math, Estimation

Sometimes an estimate is good enough for an answer.
Other times an exact answer is needed.

The students in Grades 4, 5, and 6 are planning a
boat trip. They can get a boat that holds up to
150 passengers or one that holds up to 300 passengers.

There are 83 people from Grade 4 going on the boat
trip, 75 are going from Grade 5, and 78 from Grade 6.

A. Estimate to determine which
size boat is needed.

$$83 + 75 + 78$$
$$\downarrow \quad \downarrow \quad \downarrow$$
$$80 + 80 + 80 = 240$$

The boat for 300 passengers
is needed.

B. Compute to find the exact number
of tickets needed.

$$\begin{array}{r} 83 \\ 75 \\ + 78 \\ \hline 236 \end{array}$$

They need 236 tickets.

For each problem, tell if you would estimate or find an exact answer.
If you find an exact answer, tell if you would use a calculator, paper
and pencil, or mental math. Then find the answer.

1. A map shows that to get from home
to Mt. Morris, the Bradys must travel
312 miles, 208 miles, and 406 miles.
About how far is it to Mt. Morris?

2. Three music classes have
61 students, 56 students, and
49 students. How many song
books are needed if each student
is to have a book?

3. Laura has $10 to spend. Can she buy
3 records that cost $3.98 each?

4. Sam bought a shirt for $21.50 and a
tie for $13.95. How much did he pay
including $1.77 tax?

5. Tom earns $1.75 an hour mowing
lawns. How much does he earn in
4 hours?

6. An airplane flies about 510 miles per
hour. About how many miles does it
fly in 3 hours?

7. One car on a train has 84 seats. If
59 people get on that car, how many
seats will be empty?

8. A restaurant sells about
95 hamburgers each day. Will the
3,000 hamburgers in the freezer be
enough for 28 days?

PAINT BY NUMBER

In a certain town, there is a street on which the houses are numbered in order starting with 1, 2, 3, 4, . . .

The town hired Bill Jones to paint each house number on the curb in front of the house.

Bill was paid $1 for each digit that he painted, and he was paid $576 in all.

How many houses are on that street?

1. How much would Bill have earned if there were

   9 houses?   10 houses?

2. How much would he have earned if there were

   14 houses?   24 houses?

3. Bill earned $576. How many houses are on that street?

Cumulative Test, Chapters 1–6

Give the letter for the correct answer.

1. Which number sentence is correct?

   A 45 > 92   **c** 28 < 36
   B 45 < 36   **D** 92 < 28

2. Subtract.

            A 4
            B 3
   10   **c** 12
 – 7   **D** 17

3. Add.

           A 20
           B 18
   2   **c** 19
   6   **D** 12
   7
+ 4

4. Tell whether you *add* or *subtract*. Solve the problem.

There were 12 books on the shelf. Only 4 books remain. How many books were taken?

   A Add; 16 books
   B Subtract; 8 books
   c Subtract; 16 books
   D Add; 8 books

5. What does the 2 mean in 6,213?

   A 2 ones   **c** 2 hundreds
   B 2 tens   **D** 2 thousands

6. Round 136 to the nearest hundred.

   A 200   **c** 100
   B 140   **D** 130

7. Add.

          A 1,867
          B 1,877
  868   **c** 1,967
  492   **D** 1,977
+ 617

8. Subtract.

          A 183
          B 173
  551   **c** 273
– 378   **D** 283

9. What time is shown on this clock?

   A 4:05   **c** 5:05
   B 1:20   **D** 1:25

10. Which day of the week is November 24?

November						
S	M	T	W	T	F	S
1	2	3	4	5	6	7
8	9	10	11	12	13	14
15	16	17	18	19	20	21
22	23	24	25	26	27	28
29	30					

   A Monday   **c** Wednesday
   B Tuesday   **D** Thursday

11. Which unit would you use to measure the length of your big toe?

   A Decimeters   **c** Centimeters
   B Meters   **D** Kilometers

12. Choose the most sensible measure for the amount of liquid in a raindrop.

   A 200 L   **c** 2 L
   B 200 mL   **D** 2 mL

13. Choose the most sensible measure for the length of a worm.

   A 8 in.   **c** 8 ft.
   B 80 in.   **D** 80 ft.

14. Multiply.

$$\begin{array}{r} 7 \\ \times\,7 \\ \hline \end{array}$$

   A 45
   B 49
   c 52
   D 56

15. Multiply.

$$\begin{array}{r} 8 \\ \times\,4 \\ \hline \end{array}$$

   A 12
   B 28
   c 34
   D 32

16. Multiply.

$$\begin{array}{r} 6 \\ \times\,9 \\ \hline \end{array}$$

   A 45
   B 15
   c 54
   D 38

17. Multiply.

$$\begin{array}{r} 32 \\ \times\,\ 3 \\ \hline \end{array}$$

   A 96
   B 35
   c 85
   D 95

18. Multiply.

$$\begin{array}{r} 56 \\ \times\,\ 2 \\ \hline \end{array}$$

   A 102
   B 187
   c 197
   D 112

19. Multiply.

$$\begin{array}{r} 406 \\ \times\,\ \ \ 4 \\ \hline \end{array}$$

   A 1,804
   B 184
   c 1,624
   D 410

20. Multiply.

50×800

   A 400
   B 40,000
   c 4,000
   D 400,000

21. Estimate the product.

42×56

   A 2,400   **c** 2,000
   B 240   **D** 200

22. Multiply.

$$\begin{array}{r} \$2.16 \\ \times\,\ \ \ \ \ 3 \\ \hline \end{array}$$

   A $4.38
   B $7.38
   c $7.48
   D $6.48

23. Tell whether you *add*, *subtract*, or *multiply*. Solve the problem.

A large airplane has 252 passenger seats. How many passengers can the plane carry in 6 trips?

   A Multiply; 1,512 passengers
   B Multiply; 1,212 passengers
   c Add; 258 passengers
   D Subtract; 246 passengers

Geometry

Points, Lines, and Segments

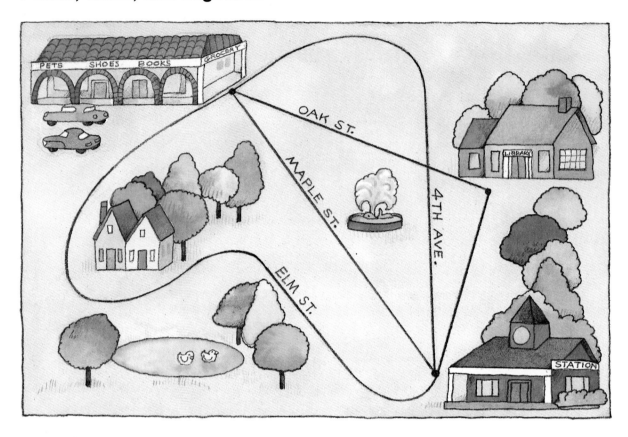

A. A city bus schedule shows these four routes from the shopping mall to the train station. What is the shortest route? Maple Street is a straight path. It is the shortest route.

The straight path from **point** A to point B is **segment** AB. This picture shows segment AB.

B. A segment is a part of a **line**. A line goes on and on, in both directions. This picture shows line CD.

Lines KL and MN are **intersecting lines**.

Lines WX and YZ are **parallel lines**.

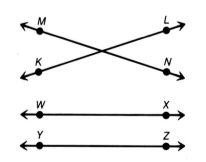

Try Name each segment or line.

a.

b.

c.

For each exercise, tell whether the lines are intersecting lines or parallel lines. Remember that lines go on and on.

d.

e.

f.

Practice Name each segment or line.

1.

2.

3.

For each exercise, tell whether the lines are intersecting lines or parallel lines.

4.

5.

6.

Apply Tell whether each picture suggests a segment, intersecting lines, or parallel lines.

7.

8.

9.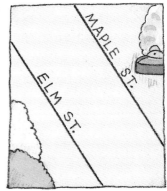

Angles

A. A *ray* is part of a line that goes on and on in one direction. When two rays have the same endpoint, they form an *angle*.

This angle is called angle *ABC* or angle *CBA*.

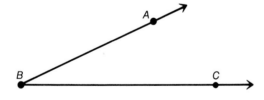

B. An angle that forms a square corner is called a *right angle*. You can test for right angles by using the square corner of a card.

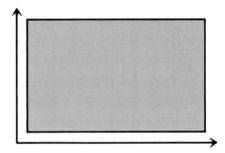

Try

a. Give two names for this angle.

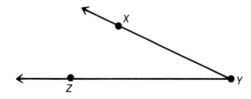

b. Is this angle a right angle? Use a card to help you decide. Write *yes* or *no*.

Practice   Give two names for each angle.

1.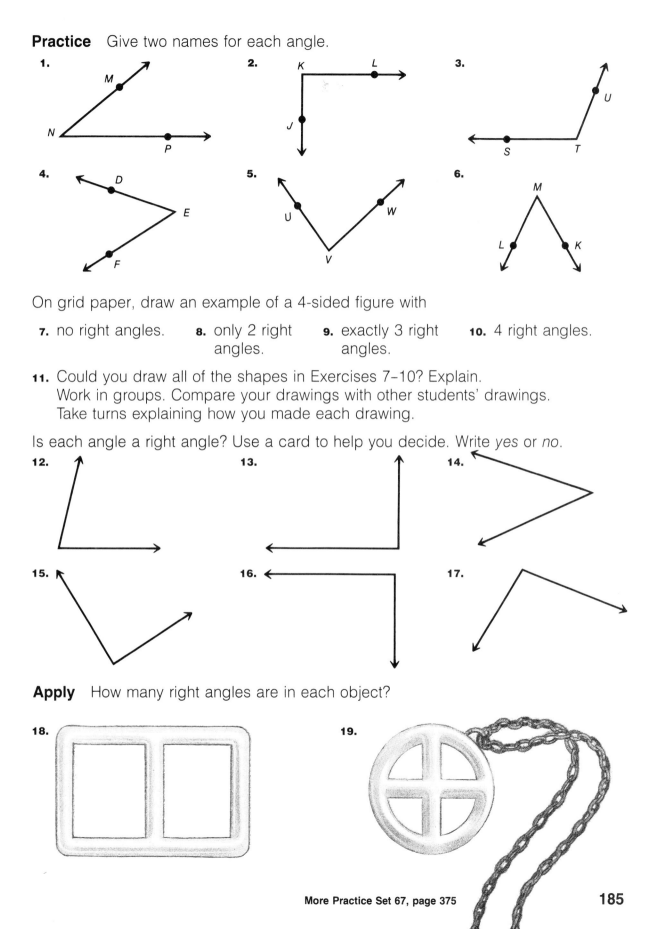

2.

3.

4.

5.

6.

On grid paper, draw an example of a 4-sided figure with

7. no right angles.   **8.** only 2 right angles.   **9.** exactly 3 right angles.   **10.** 4 right angles.

11. Could you draw all of the shapes in Exercises 7–10? Explain.
Work in groups. Compare your drawings with other students' drawings.
Take turns explaining how you made each drawing.

Is each angle a right angle? Use a card to help you decide. Write *yes* or *no*.

12.

13.

14.

15.

16.

17.

Apply   How many right angles are in each object?

18.

19.

Polygons

The shape suggested by each road sign below is a *polygon*. The sides of a polygon are segments. The sides meet to form angles.

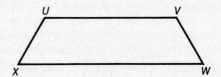

This polygon has 5 sides and 5 angles. The names of the sides are *AB*, *BC*, *CD*, *DE*, and *EA*. The names of the angles are *ABC*, *BCD*, *CDE*, *DEA*, and *EAB*.

Try

a. Tell whether this figure is a polygon. Write *yes* or *no*.

b. Name the sides and angles of this polygon.

Practice Tell whether each figure is a polygon. Write *yes* or *no*.

1.

2.

3.

For each polygon, write the number of sides and the
number of angles.

4. Triangle 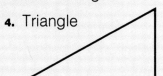 **5.** Quadrilateral 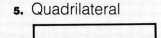 **6.** Pentagon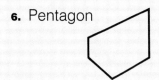

7. Hexagon 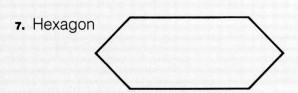 **8.** Octagon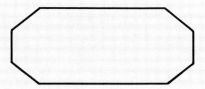

9. Name the sides and angles of this triangle.

★10. How many angles does a 9-sided polygon have?

Apply Name the road sign below that suggests each shape.

11. Triangle   **12.** Octagon   **13.** Quadrilateral   **14.** *Find the facts.* Name other road signs whose shapes are polygons.

Congruence

A. Segments that are the same length are *congruent segments*.
Are segments *AB* and *CD* congruent?

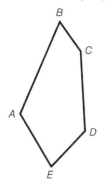

Use tracing paper to trace segment CD.
Place the tracing over segment AB.
Are the segments congruent?

B. Polygons that are the same size and shape are *congruent polygons*.
Are these polygons congruent?

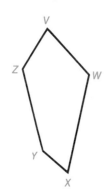

Use tracing paper to trace one of the polygons.
Place the tracing over the other polygon.
Are the polygons congruent?

C. Dot paper can be used to draw congruent figures. Draw a polygon that is congruent to the one at the right.

How do you know the polygons are congruent? How can you show that the polygons are congruent?

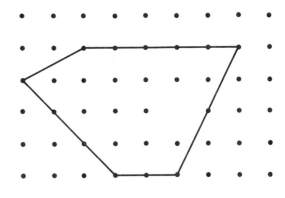

Try Use tracing paper to tell whether the segments or polygons are congruent. Write *yes* or *no*.

a.

b.

c. Use dot paper and draw two segments that are congruent. Exchange papers with another student and check each other's drawings.

Practice Use tracing paper to tell whether the segments or polygons are congruent. Write *yes* or *no*.

1.

2.

3.

4.

5.

6.

7.

8. Are all the sides of this triangle congruent?

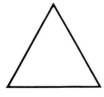

9. Use dot paper to draw two polygons that are congruent. Exchange papers with another student and check each other's drawings.

Apply Tell which shape will fit in the space.

10.

11.

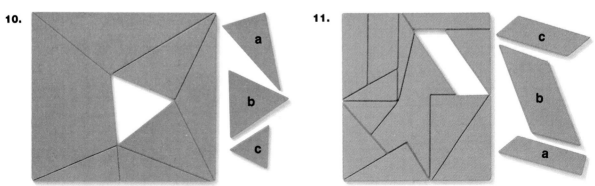

Parallelograms

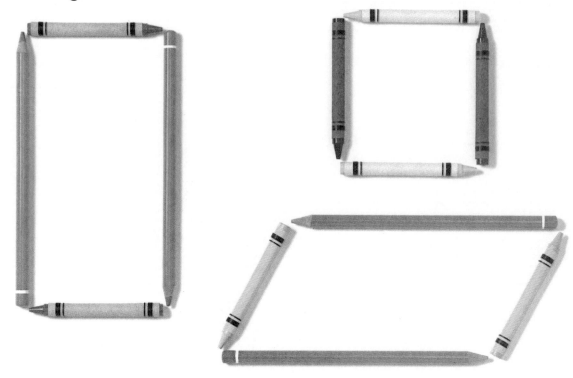

A. A *parallelogram* is a special four-sided polygon. Its opposite sides are parallel and congruent.

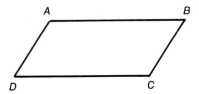

Sides *AB* and *DC* are parallel and congruent.

Sides *AD* and *BC* are parallel and congruent.

B. A *rectangle* is a special parallelogram with four right angles. These figures are rectangles.

C. A *square* is a special rectangle with four congruent sides. These figures are squares.

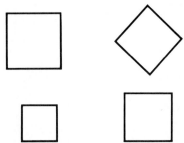

Try For each exercise, write *yes* or *no*.

a. Is this figure a parallelogram?

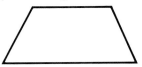

b. Is this figure a rectangle?

c. Is this figure a square?

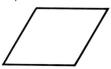

Practice Is each figure a parallelogram? Write *yes* or *no*.

1.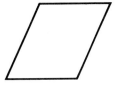

2.

3.

4.

5.

6.

7.

8.

Is each figure a rectangle? Write *yes* or *no*.

9.

10.

11.

12.

13.

14.

15.

16.

Is each figure a square? Write *yes* or *no*.

17.

18.

19.

20.

Perimeter

The distance around a polygon is called its *perimeter*. The perimeter is found by adding the lengths of all the sides.

The base of the Statue of Liberty is a square. The length of each side is 91 feet. Find the perimeter.

Since the four sides of a square are the same length, you can round 91 to the nearest ten and multiply by 4 to find an estimated answer.
$4 \times 90 = $ ▨

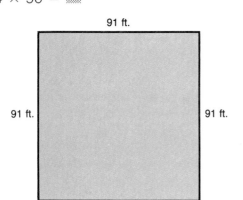

91 ft.

91 ft.

91 ft.

91 ft.

$91 + 91 + 91 + 91 = 364$

The perimeter of the base of the Statue of Liberty is 364 feet. Is the answer reasonable?
Why or why not?

Try Find the perimeter of each figure. Work in groups. Discuss ways to estimate an answer for each exercise before computing the perimeter.

a.

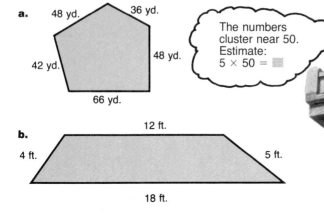

48 yd.　36 yd.
48 yd.
42 yd.
66 yd.

The numbers cluster near 50.
Estimate:
$5 \times 50 = $ ▨

b.

12 ft.
4 ft.　5 ft.
18 ft.

Practice Find the perimeter of each figure.

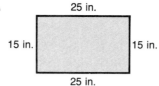

1.
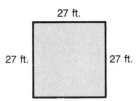
27 ft.
27 ft.
27 ft.
27 ft.

2.
25 in.
15 in. 15 in.
25 in.

3.
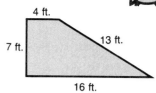
4 ft.
7 ft.
13 ft.
16 ft.

4.
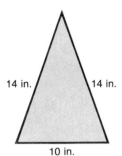
14 in. 14 in.
10 in.

5.
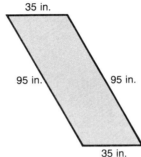
35 in.
95 in. 95 in.
35 in.

6.
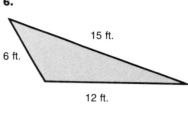
15 ft.
6 ft.
12 ft.

Apply *Choosing a Computation Method* Calculator, Paper and Pencil, Mental Math, Estimation
Choose a method to solve each problem. Tell which method you used.
For problems 7–10 find the perimeter.

7. Washington Monument
Square base of shaft

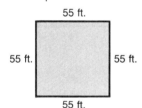
55 ft.
55 ft. 55 ft.
55 ft.

8. Lincoln Memorial
Central chamber

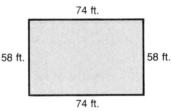
74 ft.
58 ft. 58 ft.
74 ft.

9. The lot the house is on

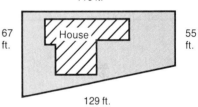
116 ft.
67 ft.
House
55 ft.
129 ft.

10. The base of a lamp that is a pentagon, 10 cm on each side.

11. *Write a problem.* Write a problem about the perimeter of something in your classroom. Then solve the problem.

12. **CALCULATOR** Make the display show 100. Use only these keys: 3, 4, 5, $+$ $=$.

MAINTENANCE

Multiply.

1.	**2.**	**3.**	**4.**	**5.**	**6.**
68	57	48	29	567	321
× 6	× 9	× 3	× 7	× 2	× 5

7. $9 \times 4{,}216$ **8.** $9{,}486 \times 2$ **9.** $6 \times \$0.36$ **10.** $\$1.32 \times 4$

Area

The *area* of a figure is the number of square units covered by the figure.

1 square centimeter

1 cm

1 cm

The *square centimeter* is a unit of area.

Jerry is making a miniature model of a farm. The barnyard covers the area shown on the grid below. What is the area of the barnyard?

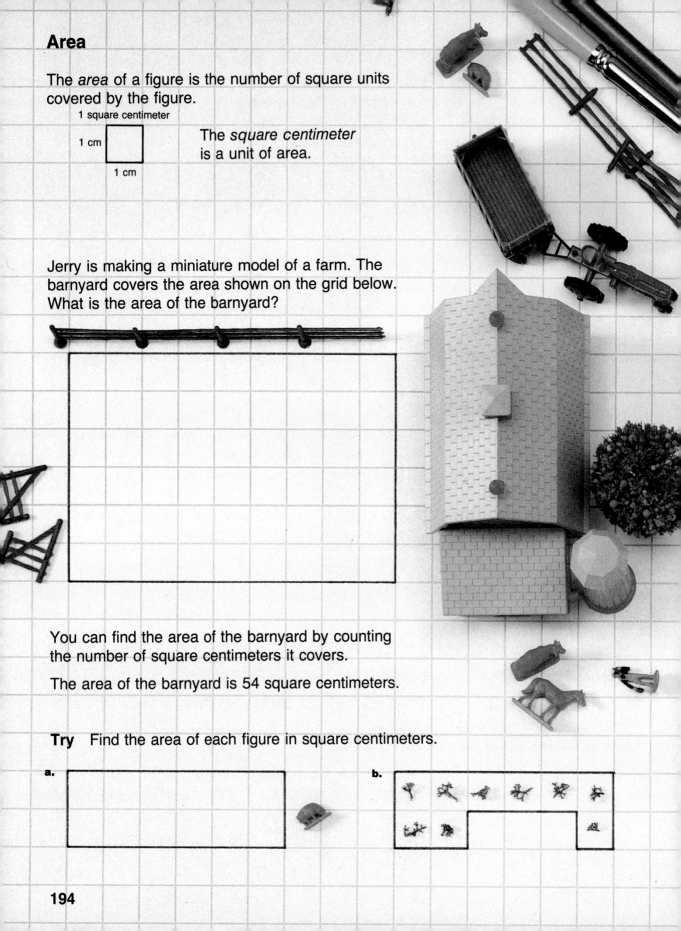

You can find the area of the barnyard by counting the number of square centimeters it covers.

The area of the barnyard is 54 square centimeters.

Try Find the area of each figure in square centimeters.

a.

b.

Practice Find the area of each figure in square centimeters.

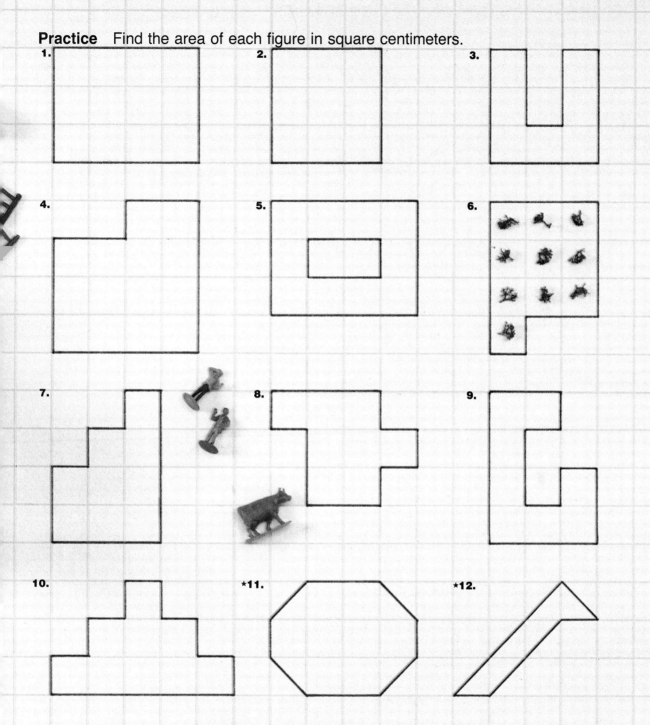

1.

2.

3.

4.

5.

6.

7.

8.

9.

10.

*11.

*12.

Apply For each problem, draw the figure on centimeter grid paper.

13. On Jerry's model farm, the floor of the barn is a rectangle that is 3 cm long and 2 cm wide. What is the area covered by the barn?

14. On Jerry's model farm, one field is a square that is 4 cm long on each side. What is the area of the field?

Cagey Cages

The lion trainer is outside the cage.
Is the lion inside the cage or outside the cage?

If you do not know, guess. Then work
Problems 1–8 to find out how you can tell.

A simple closed curve has an inside
and an outside. In the curve at the right,
points A, B, and C are in the inside.
Points D, E, and F are outside the curve.

Copy the curve, including points A–F.
Use your drawing for Problems 1–8.

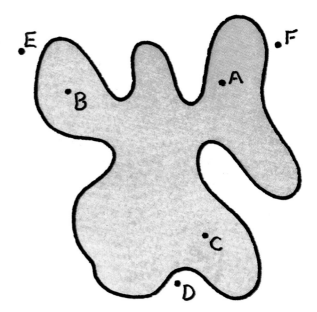

Imagine a segment between two inside points. How many times does the segment cross the curve between these points?

1. A and B
2. A and C
3. B and C

How many times does a segment cross the curve between these outside points?

4. D and F
5. D and E
6. E and F

7. How many times does a segment cross the curve going between one outside point and one inside point? Try several pairs of points to help you answer the question.

8. If you know the location of one point, how can you determine the location of another?

9. Is the lion inside the cage or outside the cage?

10. Copy the closed figure below. Point R is outside the figure. Color the inside.

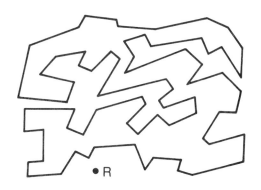

LOGO: REPEAT Commands

In LOGO, the Turtle is a small triangle on the computer screen. This turtle can follow commands that make it do special things.

The REPEAT command has two parts. The first part is a number that tells how many times to repeat a list of commands. The second part is a list of commands that are inside two brackets [ ].

REPEAT 4 [FD 30 RT 90] tells the Turtle to complete the following directions 4 times: *move forward 30 steps and turn right 90* (make a square corner).

When the turtle follows the command REPEAT 4 [FD 30 RT 90], a square is drawn. The length of each side of the square is 30 steps. Since there are 4 sides, the perimeter of the square is 120 steps.

In each exercise, the REPEAT command tells the turtle to draw a square. Find the perimeter of each square.

1. REPEAT 4 [FD 50 RT 90]

2. REPEAT 4 [FD 25 RT 90]

3. REPEAT 4 [FD 10 RT 90]

4. REPEAT 4 [FD 40 RT 90]

5. REPEAT 4 [FD 15 RT 90]

6. REPEAT 4 [FD 35 RT 90]

PROBLEM-
SOLVING
STRATEGIES
• CHOOSE THE
  OPERATION
• DRAW A
  PICTURE
• FIND A
  PATTERN
• WRITE AN
  EQUATION
• USE
  ESTIMATION
• MAKE A
  TABLE

Read   Dean is covering a bulletin board with right triangles cut from colored paper. The triangles are congruent to the red one shown. What is the area of each triangle Dean is using?

Plan   Draw the right triangle on centimeter grid paper. Count the squares to find the area.

Solve   Count the whole squares. There are 15.
Combine the half squares.

6 half squares

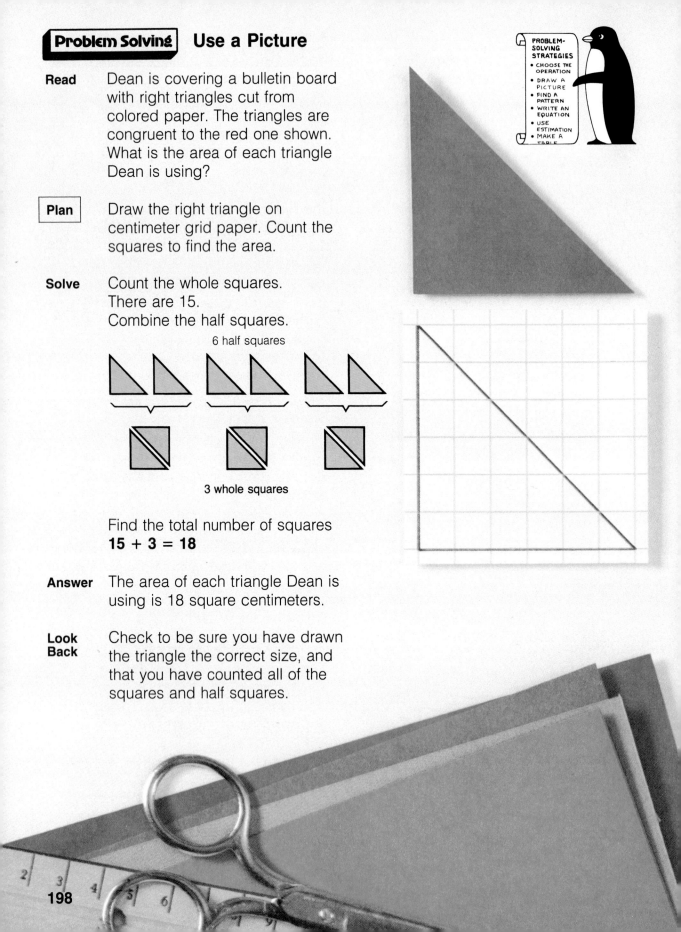

3 whole squares

Find the total number of squares
15 + 3 = 18

Answer The area of each triangle Dean is using is 18 square centimeters.

Look Back Check to be sure you have drawn the triangle the correct size, and that you have counted all of the squares and half squares.

Try

a. Find the area of this figure.

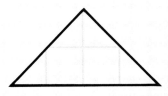

b. Trace this figure on centimeter grid paper. Then find the area.

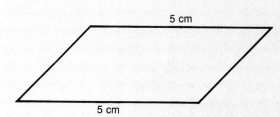

5 cm

5 cm

Apply Find the area of each figure.

1.

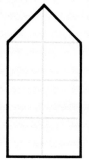

2.

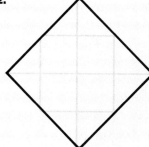

3.

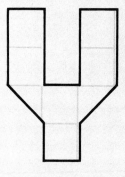

4.

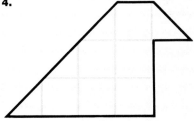

5.

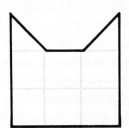

6.

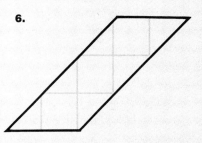

Trace each figure on centimeter grid paper. Then find the area.

7.

2 cm

4 cm

8.

3 cm

3 cm

★9.

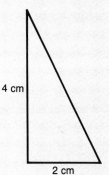

4 cm

2 cm

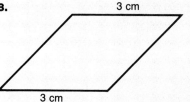

10. **[CALCULATOR]** A paper company packages colored paper in 48 sheet pads with 36 pads in a box. How many sheets of colored paper are in 75 boxes?

Circles

Wheels are shaped like *circles*.

A. Draw a circle with a compass. Your pencil mark is the circle.

Cut out the circular region. Fold it in half and draw a line on the fold. This segment is a *diameter* of the circle.

Fold again to find another diameter. The two diameters meet at the *center* of the circle. Put a dot at the center of your circle.

A segment from the center of a circle to the circle is a *radius*. Show a radius of your circle.

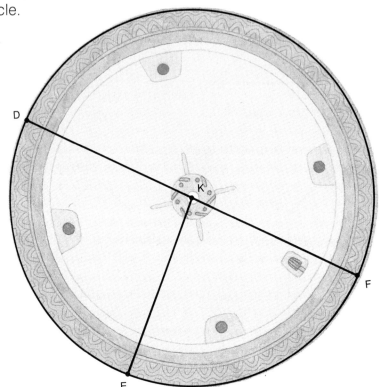

B. Work in groups. Use the circle that is drawn over the bicycle wheel.

Each of you name the center, a diameter, and a radius.

Compare answers. Are they the same? Should they be? Explain why or why not.

Which of the labeled points are part of the circle?

Try Use the circle below.

a. Sometimes the center is used to name the circle. Name this circle.

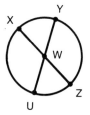

b. Name a diameter of the circle. How many diameters do you think there are in a circle?

c. Name a radius. How many radii do you think there are in a circle?

d. How many centers do you think a circle has?

Practice   Work in groups. Copy and complete the table. Use a centimeter ruler to measure.

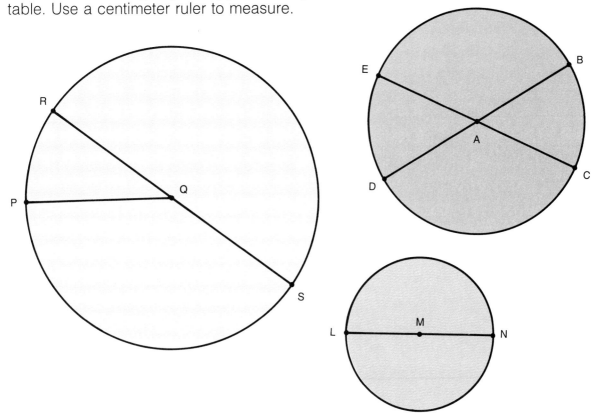

	Circle Q	Circle A	Circle M
Name a diameter	**1.**	**5.**	**9.**
Name a radius	**2.**	**6.**	**10.**
Length of the diameter	**3.** cm	**7.** cm	**11.** cm
Length of the radius	**4.** cm	**8.** cm	**12.** cm

13. For each circle, compare the measures of the diameter and the radius. Do you see a pattern? If you do, test it on Circle W and Circle K on page 200.

14. Write a sentence that compares the radius and the diameter of any circle.

Apply   Solve the problem.

15. Shawn has a letter with 73¢ postage. The postal rate was 22¢ for the first ounce and 17¢ for each additional ounce. How much did the letter weigh?

Discuss your strategy for solving the problem with your classmates.

Symmetry

A figure is symmetric if you can fold it and make the two parts match. The fold line is a *line of symmetry*.

A.

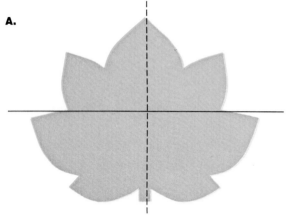

When the figure is folded on the broken line, the two parts match. The figure is symmetric, and the broken line is a line of symmetry.

When the figure is folded on the solid line, the two parts do not match. The solid line is not a line of symmetry.

B.

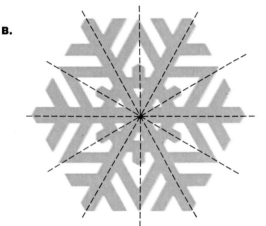

When the figure is folded on any of the broken lines, the two parts match. The figure has 6 lines of symmetry.

Try Trace each figure and cut it out.

a. Is the broken line a line of symmetry?

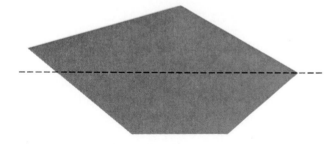

b. How many lines of symmetry does this figure have?

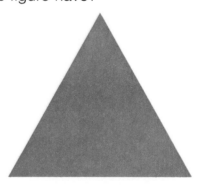

Practice Trace each figure and cut it out. Is the broken line a line of symmetry? Write *yes* or *no*.

1.

2.

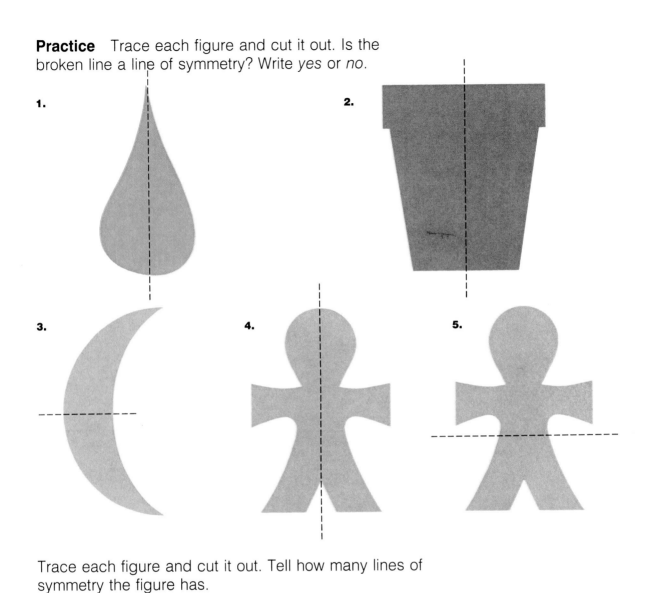

3.

4.

5.

Trace each figure and cut it out. Tell how many lines of symmetry the figure has.

6.

7.

8.

Three-Dimensional Figures

Many objects around you have the shape of a *rectangular prism*, a *cube*, a *cylinder*, a *cone*, or a *sphere.*

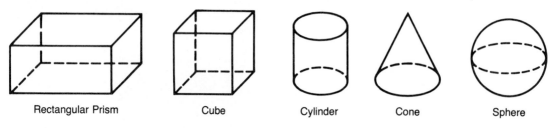

Rectangular Prism   Cube   Cylinder   Cone   Sphere

Try Name the shape of each object below. Use *rectangular prism, cube, cylinder, cone,* or *sphere.*

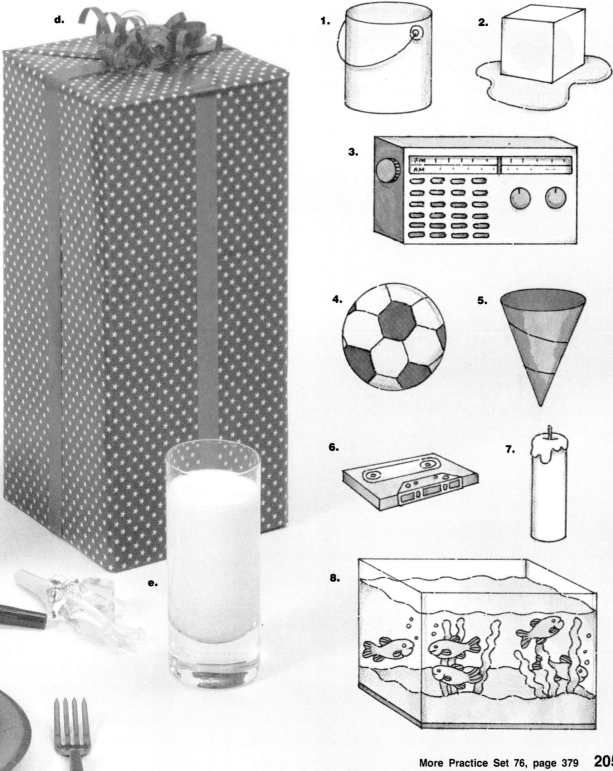

Practice Name the shape of each object. Use *rectangular prism, cube, cylinder, cone,* or *sphere.*

d.

e.

1.

2.

3.

4.

5.

6.

7.

8.

Volume

The *volume* of a three-dimensional figure is the number of cubic units inside the figure. The *cubic centimeter* is a unit of volume.

1 cubic centimeter

1 cm
1 cm
1 cm

This box is a rectangular prism. To find its volume, think of filling the box with cubes. It takes 24 cubes to fill it. Each cube is 1 cubic centimeter. So the volume of the box is 24 cubic centimeters.

Try Find the volume of each figure in cubic centimeters.

a.

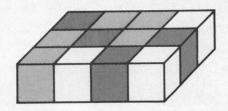

b.

Practice Find the volume of each figure in cubic centimeters.

1.

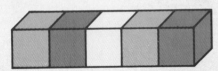

2.

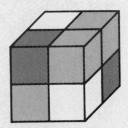

3.

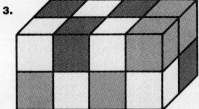

4.

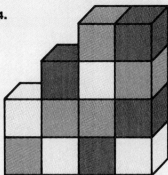

5.

6.

7.

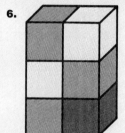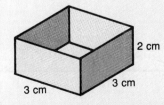

8.

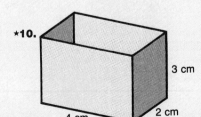

★9.

2 cm

3 cm   3 cm

★10.

3 cm

4 cm   2 cm

For each figure, use your calculator to find the length that is not given.

1. Perimeter: 1,028 ft.

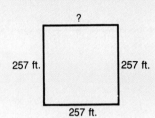

?

257 ft.   257 ft.

257 ft.

2. Perimeter: 922 ft.

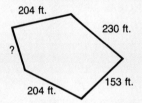

204 ft.

230 ft.

?

204 ft.   153 ft.

3. Perimeter: 1,757 in.

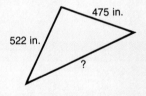

475 in.

522 in.

?

4. Perimeter: 997 in.

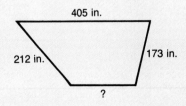

405 in.

212 in.   173 in.

?

Chapter 7 Test

1. Name the segment.

2. Are the lines parallel or intersecting?

3. Name the angle.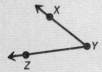

For Exercises 4–10, answer the question by writing *yes* or *no*.

4. Is the angle a right angle?

5. Is the figure a polygon?

6. Are the segments congruent?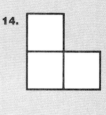

7. Are the polygons congruent?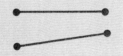

8. Is the polygon a parallelogram?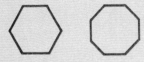

9. Is the polygon a rectangle?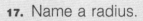

10. Is the broken line a line of symmetry?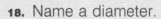

Find the perimeter of each figure.

11.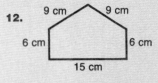

12.

Find the area of each figure in square centimeters.

13.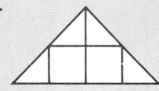

14.

15.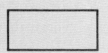

Use the circle for Exercises 16–18.

16. Name the center.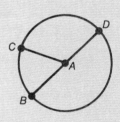

17. Name a radius.

18. Name a diameter.

19. Is the figure a sphere, cone, or cylinder?

20. Find the volume of this figure in cubic centimeters.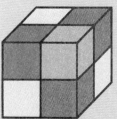

CHALLENGE

Drawing Similar Figures

Figures that have the same shape are *similar figures*.
Similar figures may differ in size. In the similar figures
shown below, each side of the large figure is twice as
long as the corresponding side of the small figure.

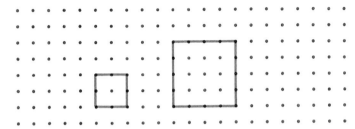

For each exercise, copy the figure. Then draw a
similar figure with sides twice as long.

For each exercise, copy the figure. Then draw a
similar figure with sides three times as long.

For each exercise, copy the figure. Then draw a
similar figure.

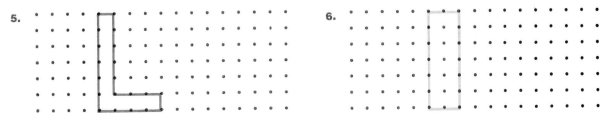

JENSEN'S FENCE

Mr. Jensen plans to fence in a rectangular barn lot for his cows. He plans to make a barbed-wire fence that has 3 strands of wire.

He has 3 partly-used rolls of barbed wire and plans to use all of the wire for his fence. He wants to fence in the largest lot possible.

One roll of wire has 112 feet. The second roll has 64 feet, and the third roll has 124 feet of wire.

1. What will be the perimeter of the barn lot?

2. If the lot is 20 feet wide, what will be

   its length?   its area?

3. If the lot is 40 feet long, what will be

   its width?   its area?

4. How should the lot be shaped to have as much room inside as possible?

PROBLEM-
SOLVING
STRATEGIES
• DRAW A
  PICTURE
• MAKE A TABLE
• FIND A PATTERN
• USE PHYSICAL
  MODELS
• USE LOGICAL
  REASONING
• WORK
  BACKWARD
• LIST ALL
  POSSIBILITIES
• TRY AND
  CHECK
• MAKE A GRAPH

Division Facts

$$3\overline{)9}{}^{\,3}$$

Meaning of Division

Work with another student.
Each of you will need your counters.

A. Ms. MacDonald is an art teacher. Each student in her class needs 3 crayons for an art project. How many students can do the project if she has 24 crayons?

Count out 24 counters to represent the crayons. Use them to show how many groups of 3 are in 24.

There are ▓ groups of 3 in 24.

▓ students can do the project.

B. Her 24 crayons fit into 3 boxes with the same number in each box. How many crayons are in each box?

Use your counters to show 24 separated into 3 equal groups. How many are in each group?

There are 3 groups of ▓ in 24.

There are ▓ crayons in each box.

Compare what you did in Example A with what you did in Example B. What does this show?

C. Each of you use 24 counters. One of you separate the counters into groups of 4, while the other separates his or her counters into 4 equal groups. Explain what this shows.

D. You can write a division sentence to show that 24 divided by 3 is 8.

24 ÷ 3 = 8
    ↑   ↑
Divisor   Quotient

Write a division sentence for Example C.

E. You can think of a multiplication fact to help you find a quotient.

For 24 ÷ 3 = ▓, think of 3 × ▓ = 24.

What multiplication facts can you use in Example C?

Try Use counters to complete each division sentence. Then make a sketch of your counters that shows the division sentence.

a. 12 in all
How many groups of 4?

$12 \div 4 =$ ▨    ▨ × 4 = 12

b. 18 in all
How many in each of 9 equal groups?

$18 \div 9 =$ ▨   9 × ▨ = 18

Practice Use counters to show how many groups. Then complete each division sentence.

1. 32 in all
Groups of 8

$32 \div 8 =$ ▨    ▨ × 8 = 32

2. 21 in all
Groups of 7

$21 \div 7 =$ ▨

3. 15 in all
Groups of 3

$15 \div 3 =$ ▨

Use counters to show how many in each group. Then complete each division sentence.

4. 20 in all
4 equal groups

$20 \div 4 =$ ▨   4 × ▨ = 20

5. 14 in all
2 equal groups

$14 \div 2 =$ ▨

6. 25 in all
5 equal groups

$25 \div 5 =$ ▨

Use counters to complete each division sentence.

7. $42 \div 3 =$ ▨

8. $48 \div 4 =$ ▨

9. $36 \div 18 =$ ▨

Apply Make a sketch and write a division sentence for each problem.

Mr. Reel went fishing with two friends. He bought a can of worms at a bait store. There were 63 worms in the can.

10. The fishermen shared the worms. Mr. Reel put the worms into 3 equal groups. How many worms were in each group?

11. One of the other fishermen wanted to put the worms into groups of 3. How do you think he planned to distribute the worms? Explain your thinking. How many worms would each fisherman get using this method?

Mr. Johanson plans to share a box of chalk equally with his art students. There are 36 pieces of chalk.

12. There are 12 students in class. How could he share the pieces of chalk?

13. Four pieces of chalk are needed for an art project. How many of his students can do the project?

Dividing by 2 and 3

There are 6 students in art class.

A. How many groups of 2 are there?

$$6 \div 2 = 3 \quad (3 \times 2 = 6)$$

There are 3 groups of 2 in 6.

B. How many students are in each of 2 equal groups?

$$6 \div 2 = 3 \quad (2 \times 3 = 6)$$

There are 3 students in each of 2 equal groups.

c. How many groups of 3 are in 12?

$12 \div 3 = 4$ $\quad$ $4 \times 3 = 12$

There are 4 groups of 3 in 12.

D. There are 12 dots. How many are there in each of 3 equal groups?

$12 \div 3 = 4$ $\quad$ $3 \times 4 = 12$

There are 4 in each of 3 equal groups.

Try Divide.

a. $18 \div 3$ $\quad$ **b.** $8 \div 2$ $\quad$ **c.** $27 \div 3$ $\quad$ **d.** $14 \div 2$ $\quad$ **e.** $15 \div 3$ $\quad$ **f.** $4 \div 2$

Practice Divide.

1. $4 \div 2$ $\quad$ **2.** $12 \div 3$ $\quad$ **3.** $16 \div 2$ $\quad$ **4.** $18 \div 3$ $\quad$ **5.** $24 \div 3$ $\quad$ **6.** $18 \div 2$

7. $6 \div 3$ $\quad$ **8.** $6 \div 2$ $\quad$ **9.** $15 \div 3$ $\quad$ **10.** $14 \div 2$ $\quad$ **11.** $10 \div 2$ $\quad$ **12.** $27 \div 3$

13. $12 \div 2$ $\quad$ **14.** $9 \div 3$ $\quad$ **15.** $8 \div 2$ $\quad$ **16.** $18 \div 2$ $\quad$ **17.** $21 \div 3$ $\quad$ **18.** $14 \div 2$

19. $24 \div 3$ $\quad$ **20.** $16 \div 2$ $\quad$ **21.** $12 \div 3$ $\quad$ **22.** $8 \div 2$ $\quad$ **23.** $27 \div 3$ $\quad$ **24.** $18 \div 3$

25. $4 \div 2$ $\quad$ **26.** $21 \div 3$ $\quad$ **27.** $15 \div 3$ $\quad$ **28.** $10 \div 2$ $\quad$ **29.** $12 \div 2$ $\quad$ **30.** $9 \div 3$

Apply Solve each problem.

31. If 15 students were separated into groups of 3, how many groups were there?

32. There were 16 students. Each student used 2 sheets of paper. How many sheets were used in all?

33. The teacher displayed 7 drawings on the wall, 6 on the door, and 10 along the board. How many drawings were displayed in all?

34. A box of paints has 18 colors. There are 3 rows of colors with the same number in each row. How many colors are in each row?

*35. Kiyoko shared 8 brushes with Marsha. Each girl got an equal number of brushes. How many brushes did each girl get?

36. *Thinking skills* Find all the numbers from 0 through 18 that can be divided by 2. What digits are in the ones place of numbers that can be divided by 2?

Dividing by 4 and 5

There are 20 jars of paint.

A. How many groups of 4 are there?

$$20 \div 4 = 5 \quad (5 \times 4 = 20)$$

There are 5 groups of 4.

C. How many are there in each of 4 equal groups?

$$20 \div 4 = 5 \quad (4 \times 5 = 20)$$

There are 5 in each of 4 equal groups.

B. How many groups of 5 are there?

$$20 \div 5 = 4 \quad (4 \times 5 = 20)$$

There are 4 groups of 5.

D. How many are there in each of 5 equal groups?

$$20 \div 5 = 4 \quad (5 \times 4 = 20)$$

There are 4 in each of 5 equal groups.

E. Division can be written in two ways.

Quotient

$$20 \div 4 = 5 \qquad 4\overline{)20}$$

Divisor

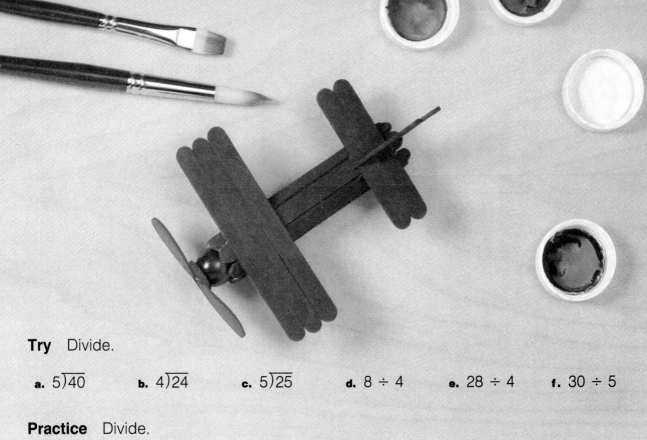

Try Divide.

a. $5\overline{)40}$ **b.** $4\overline{)24}$ **c.** $5\overline{)25}$ **d.** $8 \div 4$ **e.** $28 \div 4$ **f.** $30 \div 5$

Practice Divide.

1. $5\overline{)10}$ **2.** $4\overline{)12}$ **3.** $4\overline{)32}$ **4.** $4\overline{)24}$ **5.** $5\overline{)20}$ **6.** $4\overline{)28}$

7. $5\overline{)35}$ **8.** $5\overline{)30}$ **9.** $5\overline{)45}$ **10.** $4\overline{)20}$ **11.** $4\overline{)8}$ **12.** $5\overline{)15}$

13. $4\overline{)16}$ **14.** $5\overline{)40}$ **15.** $5\overline{)25}$ **16.** $4\overline{)36}$ **17.** $3\overline{)12}$ **18.** $2\overline{)8}$

19. $27 \div 3$ **20.** $15 \div 3$ **21.** $16 \div 2$ **22.** $6 \div 2$ **23.** $32 \div 4$ **24.** $16 \div 4$

25. $21 \div 3$ **26.** $9 \div 3$ **27.** $35 \div 5$ **28.** $20 \div 5$ **29.** $4 \div 2$ **30.** $18 \div 2$

Apply *Choosing a Computation Method* Calculator, Paper and Pencil, Mental Math, Estimation
Choose a method to solve each problem. Tell which method you used.

31. Large sheets of drawing paper cost 5 cents per sheet. How many sheets can you buy for 40 cents?

32. Mary has 32 jars of paint. Does she have enough paint to put 4 jars each in 10 project areas?

33. The school used 347 jars of paint one year, 629 jars the second year, and 705 jars the third. How many jars were used in all?

34. There were 5 boxes with 6 jars of paint in each. The students used 18 jars. Were there more or less than 10 jars of paint left?

1 and 0 in Division

A. There are 5 paintbrushes in the holder. How many groups of 5 are there?

$$5 \div 5 = 1 \quad \boxed{1 \times 5 = 5}$$

When any number is divided by itself, the answer is 1.

B. There are 5 paintbrushes in the holders. How many groups of 1 are there?

$$5 \div 1 = 5 \quad \boxed{5 \times 1 = 5}$$

When any number is divided by 1, the answer is that number.

C. There are no paintbrushes in the holder. How many groups of 5 are there?

$$0 \div 5 = 0 \quad \boxed{0 \times 5 = 0}$$

When 0 is divided by any number, the answer is 0.

D. There are 5 paintbrushes in the holder. How many groups of 0 are there?

That doesn't make sense!

Never divide by zero.

Try Divide.

a. $8 \div 1$ **b.** $0 \div 8$ **c.** $8 \div 8$ **d.** $1 \div 1$ **e.** $0 \div 1$ **f.** $0 \div 2$

Practice Divide.

1. $6 \div 1$ 2. $0 \div 3$ 3. $7 \div 7$

4. $0 \div 5$ 5. $9 \div 9$ 6. $4 \div 1$

7. $4 \div 4$ 8. $8 \div 1$ 9. $0 \div 7$

10. $0 \div 6$ 11. $2 \div 2$ 12. $9 \div 1$

13. $3 \div 3$ 14. $1 \div 1$ 15. $0 \div 9$

16. $6 \div 6$ 17. $2 \div 1$ 18. $0 \div 1$

19. $0 \div 4$ 20. $0 \div 8$ 21. $7 \div 1$

22. $3 \div 1$ 23. $0 \div 2$ 24. $8 \div 8$

Apply Solve each problem.

25. There are 7 easels divided equally among 7 students. How many easels will each student have?

26. Oscar had 8 feet of green yarn. How many 1-foot pieces can he cut from this?

27. Doris had 6 white sheets of paper and 1 blue sheet. How many sheets did she have in all?

28. Burt had 4 jars of paint on his tray. He spilled 4 of them. How many jars were not spilled?

29. There are 8 chalk boxes on the table. All of them are empty. How many pieces of chalk are there in the boxes?

30. **CALCULATOR** Make the display show 8. Use only these keys: 7, +, −, ×, ÷, =.

COMPUTER

BASIC: Division in PRINT Statements

In BASIC, the symbol / is used for division.

When this program is typed into a computer, the numbers are divided and only the answer is printed.

This is printed.

```
10 PRINT 45/5     9
20 PRINT 18/3     6
30 END
```

Tell what would be printed for each program. Watch for semicolons.

1.
```
10 PRINT 36/4
20 END
```

2.
```
10 PRINT 15/3;
20 PRINT 20/4
30 END
```

3.
```
10 PRINT 8/2
20 PRINT 8/4
30 PRINT 8/1
40 END
```

4.
```
10 PRINT 35/5;
20 PRINT 25/5;
30 PRINT 15/5
40 END
```

*5.
```
10 REM DIVISION
20 PRINT "27/3; ="
30 PRINT 27/3
40 END
```

*6.
```
20 PRINT 24+6
40 END
30 PRINT 24*6
10 PRINT 24-6
```

Deciding When an Estimate Is All You Need

A. You and your group are in charge of buying food and supplies for your class picnic. Everyone in the class will share the food expenses.

Meet with your group. Here are some things you must decide.

1. How much money will each person in your class contribute?

2. How many people are coming to the picnic?

3. What items do you want to buy?

4. How much of each item will you need?

Think of other things you need to decide. Talk about them with your group.

B. You go to the supermarket. You do not have a calculator to help you determine precisely what you are spending. You do not have the time to add with paper and pencil.

Below are the prices of some of the items you see.

paper plates (12 per box)	$1.35
apple juice (64 ounces)	1.59
orange juice (64 ounces)	1.39
yogurt (cup)	0.55
bread (24 slices a package)	0.99
peanut butter (2 pound jar)	2.49
tomatoes (pound)	1.29
paper cups (36 to a box)	0.89
cheese (12 slices a package)	1.89
turkey breast (1/4 pound)	1.19
apples (pound)	0.89
tunafish (6 ounce can)	0.49
roast beef (1/2 pound)	4.79
lettuce (1 head)	0.59

Select as many items from this list as you think you can afford. Record your choices. If some of the items you want are not on the list, decide how much money you think you need to put aside for them.

5. Talk about how you determined if you had enough money.

6. Did you need to know exactly how much money you were going to spend? Why or why not?

7. Would the way you decided you had enough money have changed if you had $5.00 less? $10.00 less? Talk about why or why not.

c. Assign someone to be the supermarket cashier. Go to the checkout counter with your shopping list. Find out exactly how much money you will need to pay for your choices.

8. How did the cashier figure out how much you owe? Can you think of a better way? Talk about it with your group.

9. Are you sure the cashier came up with the correct total? How did you check?

10. Did you have enough money? Talk about why or why not.

Think about other situations in which you need to know if you have about enough money and when you need to know if you have exactly enough money.

Dividing by 6

Settlers in the early American colonies often used beads made from shells as money. These beads were called wampum.

A. 6 white beads were worth one penny. How much were 18 white beads worth?

How many groups of 6 are in 18?

18 ÷ 6 = 3 ⟨3 × 6 = 18⟩

18 white beads were worth 3 pennies.

B. 24 beads were used in 6 necklaces. The same number of beads were used in each necklace. How many beads were used in each necklace?

How many are in each of 6 equal groups?

24 ÷ 6 = 4 ⟨6 × 4 = 24⟩

4 beads were used in each necklace.

Try Divide.

a. 6)‾30‾   **b.** 36 ÷ 6   **c.** 54 ÷ 6

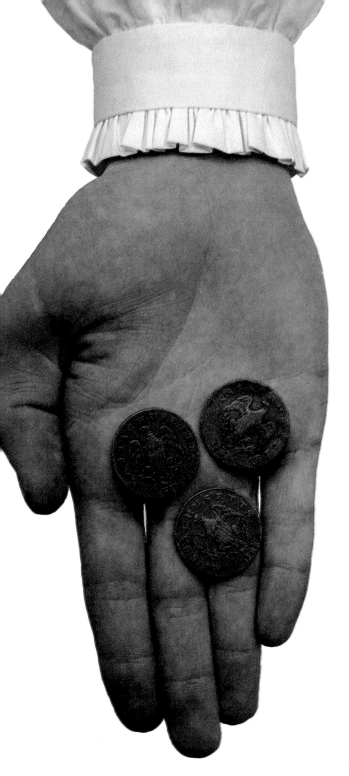

Practice Divide.

1. $6\overline{)12}$ 2. $6\overline{)48}$ 3. $6\overline{)6}$

4. $6\overline{)42}$ 5. $6\overline{)0}$ 6. $6\overline{)30}$

7. $6\overline{)18}$ 8. $6\overline{)12}$ 9. $6\overline{)54}$

10. $6\overline{)36}$ 11. $5\overline{)15}$ 12. $2\overline{)18}$

13. $3\overline{)21}$ 14. $4\overline{)32}$ 15. $1\overline{)6}$

16. $48 \div 6$ 17. $24 \div 4$ 18. $12 \div 2$

19. $9 \div 3$ 20. $45 \div 5$ 21. $6 \div 6$

22. $27 \div 3$ 23. $10 \div 2$ 24. $30 \div 5$

25. $16 \div 4$ 26. $42 \div 6$ 27. $18 \div 3$

Apply Solve each problem.

28. If 3 purple beads were worth one penny, how much were 24 purple beads worth?

29. If 6 beaver skins could be traded for 12 nails, how many nails could you get for one beaver skin?

30. To trade for one beaver skin, a person needed either 96 white beads or 48 purple beads. How many more white beads than purple beads were needed?

★31. Six white beads were worth a penny. A fathom of white beads was worth 60 pennies. How many white beads were in one fathom?

Dividing by 7

Merchant ships, like those above, carried food and other goods to trade in the American colonies.

There are 35 ships.
Think of 7 groups with 5 ships in each group. $7 \times 5 = 35$
Or, think of 7 ships in each of 5 equal groups. $5 \times 7 = 35$

$$35 \div 7 = 5 \quad \text{or} \quad 7\overline{)35} \; ^{5}$$

Try Divide.

a. $7\overline{)7}$ **b.** $7\overline{)42}$ **c.** $7\overline{)21}$ **d.** $63 \div 7$ **e.** $14 \div 7$ **f.** $49 \div 7$

Practice Divide.

1. $7\overline{)28}$ 2. $7\overline{)42}$ 3. $7\overline{)56}$ 4. $7\overline{)35}$ 5. $7\overline{)14}$ 6. $7\overline{)0}$

7. $7\overline{)21}$ 8. $7\overline{)7}$ 9. $7\overline{)49}$ 10. $7\overline{)63}$ 11. $3\overline{)12}$ 12. $5\overline{)25}$

13. $6\overline{)24}$ 14. $4\overline{)28}$ 15. $2\overline{)10}$ 16. $1\overline{)7}$ 17. $6\overline{)36}$ 18. $5\overline{)30}$

19. $3\overline{)21}$ 20. $2\overline{)6}$ 21. $4\overline{)20}$ 22. $1\overline{)1}$ 23. $2\overline{)14}$ 24. $6\overline{)54}$

25. $14 \div 7$ 26. $40 \div 5$ 27. $35 \div 7$ 28. $9 \div 1$ 29. $12 \div 4$ 30. $49 \div 7$

31. $2 \div 2$ 32. $0 \div 7$ 33. $6 \div 3$ 34. $42 \div 6$ 35. $28 \div 7$ 36. $2 \div 1$

37. $56 \div 7$ 38. $12 \div 2$ 39. $35 \div 5$ 40. $21 \div 7$ 41. $3 \div 3$ 42. $63 \div 7$

43. $30 \div 6$ 44. $8 \div 4$ 45. $7 \div 7$ 46. $18 \div 6$ 47. $20 \div 5$ 48. $42 \div 7$

Apply *Choosing a Computation Method* Calculator, Paper and Pencil, Mental Math, Estimation
Choose a method to solve each problem. Tell which method you used.

49. A large ship had 12 sails on 3 masts. The same number of sails were on each mast. How many sails were on each mast?

50. The length of a merchant ship was 90 feet. Its width was 26 feet. How much greater was its length than its width?

51. If one merchant ship weighed 175 tons, how many pounds would 35 merchant ships weigh?

52. In colonial times, it took a ship about 63 days to cross the Atlantic Ocean. Jason said it took about 2 months. Emily said it took about 9 weeks. Are the answers exact? Are they reasonable? Explain.

MAINTENANCE

Multiply.

1. 5×6 2. 3×4 3. 9×5 4. 8×6 5. 2×9 6. 7×4

7. 1×9 8. 7×8 9. 0×5 10. 3×7 11. 8×2 12. 2×6

13. 73×3 14. 28×9 15. 34×40 16. 87×50 17. 21×43

18. 22×14 19. 42×36 20. 67×63 21. 97×55 22. 46×58

Dividing by 8

Spanish gold coins were commonly used in the American colonies.

There are 48 coins.
Think of 8 groups with 6 coins in each group.
Or, think of 8 coins in each of 6 equal groups.

$8 \times 6 = 48$
$6 \times 8 = 48$

$$48 \div 8 = 6 \quad \text{or} \quad 8\overline{)48}^{\,6}$$

226

Try Divide.

a. $8\overline{)24}$ b. $8\overline{)56}$ c. $8\overline{)8}$ d. $64 \div 8$ e. $40 \div 8$ f. $16 \div 8$

Practice Divide.

1. $8\overline{)32}$ 2. $8\overline{)72}$ 3. $8\overline{)0}$ 4. $8\overline{)48}$ 5. $8\overline{)24}$ 6. $8\overline{)8}$

7. $8\overline{)40}$ 8. $8\overline{)56}$ 9. $8\overline{)64}$ 10. $8\overline{)16}$ 11. $7\overline{)14}$ 12. $4\overline{)36}$

13. $2\overline{)16}$ 14. $6\overline{)12}$ 15. $3\overline{)15}$ 16. $5\overline{)35}$ 17. $1\overline{)3}$ 18. $6\overline{)54}$

19. $4\overline{)32}$ 20. $7\overline{)49}$ 21. $3\overline{)24}$ 22. $1\overline{)8}$ 23. $5\overline{)10}$ 24. $2\overline{)14}$

25. $40 \div 8$ 26. $18 \div 3$ 27. $24 \div 8$ 28. $5 \div 5$ 29. $7 \div 1$ 30. $56 \div 8$

31. $21 \div 7$ 32. $8 \div 8$ 33. $48 \div 6$ 34. $72 \div 8$ 35. $4 \div 4$ 36. $16 \div 8$

37. $8 \div 2$ 38. $40 \div 5$ 39. $0 \div 8$ 40. $42 \div 7$ 41. $32 \div 8$ 42. $24 \div 6$

43. $64 \div 8$ 44. $16 \div 4$ 45. $4 \div 2$ 46. $6 \div 3$ 47. $48 \div 8$ 48. $56 \div 7$

Apply Solve each problem.

49. A storekeeper separated 64 Spanish gold coins equally among 8 pouches. How many coins did he put into each pouch?

50. A Spanish dollar was worth 8 *reales* or 72 English pennies. How many English pennies was each *real* worth?

51. A trapper brought in 27 beaver skins. He was paid one Spanish dollar for every 3 skins. How many Spanish dollars was he paid?

52. If 5 bolts of the same kind of cloth cost 10 Spanish dollars, how much did each bolt cost?

53. A Spanish dollar was also called a *piece of eight* because it could be cut into 8 equal pieces called *bits*. How many *bits* could be cut from 5 Spanish dollars?

★54. One English penny would buy 6 white beads. If 72 English pennies were worth the same as 1 Spanish dollar, how many white beads could be bought with one Spanish dollar?

Dividing by 9

A. There are 9 players on each baseball team.

There are 63 players.
Think of 9 players in each of 7 equal groups. $\boxed{7 \times 9 = 63}$

$$63 \div 9 = 7 \quad \text{or} \quad 9\overline{)63}^{\,7}$$

League
meet
today

B. These four number sentences make up a family of facts. The numbers used are 7, 9, and 63.

$7 \times 9 = 63 \quad 63 \div 7 = 9$
$9 \times 7 = 63 \quad 63 \div 9 = 7$

C. This family of facts has only two number sentences. It uses only two numbers, 9 and 3.

$3 \times 3 = 9$
$9 \div 3 = 3$

Try   Divide.

a. $9\overline{)9}$ **b.** $9\overline{)54}$ **c.** $9\overline{)27}$ **d.** $72 \div 9$ **e.** $18 \div 9$ **f.** $81 \div 9$

Write a family of facts using the given numbers.

g. 3, 6, 18   **h.** 9, 72, 8   **i.** 8, 4, 2   **j.** 25, 5   **k.** 1, 3

Practice   Divide.

1. $9\overline{)36}$ **2.** $9\overline{)0}$ **3.** $9\overline{)18}$ **4.** $9\overline{)27}$ **5.** $9\overline{)54}$ **6.** $9\overline{)72}$

7. $9\overline{)45}$ **8.** $9\overline{)81}$ **9.** $9\overline{)9}$ **10.** $9\overline{)63}$ **11.** $8\overline{)72}$ **12.** $5\overline{)15}$

13. $7\overline{)28}$ **14.** $4\overline{)36}$ **15.** $6\overline{)42}$ **16.** $1\overline{)9}$ **17.** $2\overline{)12}$ **18.** $3\overline{)9}$

19. $27 \div 9$ **20.** $24 \div 4$ **21.** $18 \div 9$ **22.** $49 \div 7$ **23.** $4 \div 2$ **24.** $40 \div 8$

25. $36 \div 6$ **26.** $63 \div 9$ **27.** $5 \div 1$ **28.** $9 \div 9$ **29.** $27 \div 3$ **30.** $45 \div 9$

31. $2 \div 2$ **32.** $81 \div 9$ **33.** $32 \div 8$ **34.** $54 \div 9$ **35.** $36 \div 9$ **36.** $35 \div 5$

37. Explain why you would or would not use a calculator to divide in Exercises 1–36.

Write a family of facts using the given numbers.

38. 2, 7, 14   **39.** 4, 16   **40.** 5, 6, 30   **41.** 8, 3, 24   **42.** 5, 9, 45

43. 64, 8   **44.** 8, 56, 7   **45.** 6, 2, 3   **46.** 4, 1   **47.** 9, 0

Apply   Solve each problem.

48. Over 100 players were in a baseball playoff. John said there were more than 9 teams. Is John's statement true? Explain why or why not.

49. How many basketball teams of 5 players each can be formed from 35 players?

Problem Solving | Multiple-Step Problems

In the game of marbles, the object is to knock marbles out
of the ring by hitting them with another marble.

Read   Myra and Thomas started a game with 16 marbles in the
ring. Myra knocked 5 marbles out. Thomas knocked
out 4 marbles. How many marbles were left in the ring?

Plan   First, add to find how many marbles in all were
knocked out. Then subtract the sum from the
number of marbles in the ring at the start of the
game to find how many marbles were left.

Solve

Number of marbles
knocked out

$$\begin{array}{r} 5 \\ + 4 \\ \hline 9 \end{array}$$

Number of
marbles left

$$\begin{array}{r} 16 \\ - 9 \\ \hline 7 \end{array}$$

Answer   There were 7 marbles left in the ring.

Look Back   Add the number of marbles left in the ring to the
number of marbles knocked out of the ring.

In   Out   Started with

7 + 4 + 5 = 16

The game started
with 16 marbles,
so the answer
checks.

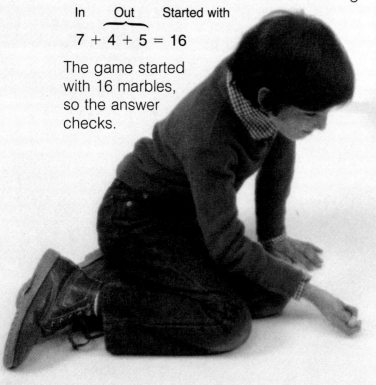

Try Solve each problem.

a. If 2 children each had 6 rainbow marbles and 3 cat's eye marbles, how many marbles did they have altogether?

b. There were 15 girls and 9 boys. They made 4 equal teams. How many children were on each team?

Apply Solve each problem.

1. Felipa put 10 jacks on the floor. She picked up 3 jacks on her first try and 3 more on the next. How many jacks were left on the floor?

2. Leona jumped rope 14 times. Mary jumped 5 times fewer than Leona. Nancy jumped 4 times fewer than Mary. How many times did Nancy jump?

3. There were 13 children playing *Tag* and 2 teams of 8 children each playing *Steal the Flag*. How many children were playing these two games?

4. Fred had 14 marbles. He put 2 of them into his pocket and then separated the remaining marbles into groups of 3. How many groups of 3 did Fred make?

5. There were 32 checkers on the playing board. If 7 red checkers and 8 black checkers were removed, how many checkers were left?

6. The Pirates had 6 runs, and the Indians had 7 runs. The Pirates then scored 3 more runs and won the game. By how many runs did the Pirates win?

7. On her first turn Maria went ahead 3 spaces from Start. On her next turns she went ahead 6 spaces, ahead 4 spaces, and back 5 spaces. Then how far was she from Start?

*8. There are 30 children to play basketball. Each team has 5 players. How many games will be played if each team plays only one game?

*9. There were 3 children riding bicycles and 5 children roller skating. How many wheels were there in all?

10. *Write a problem.* Write a problem that can be solved using addition and multiplication. Then solve the problem.

HOW MANY LEGS?

Lynn's father works in a carpenter shop. He makes only 3-legged stools and 4-legged tables. At the end of one day, he had used 31 legs. *How many stools and how many tables did he make?*

Think about the strategies you have used to solve problems. A strategy which you have used before may help you with solving this problem. Choose one of these strategies and try to use it with this problem. After you have tried to solve the problem, answer the questions below.

1. Could Lynn's father have made exactly 2 tables? Why or why not?

2. Could Lynn's father have made exactly 1 table? Why or why not?

3. Is there more than one solution to this problem?

4. What is the largest number of tables that Lynn's father could have made?

5. Look at your answer to Problem 4. What numbers less than that will not work for the number of tables?

6. How many tables and how many stools could Lynn's father have made?

7. If Lynn's father used 43 legs, how many tables and how many stools could he have made?

8. If Lynn's father used 44 legs, how many tables and how many stools could he have made?

9. How are the answers with 44 legs related to the answers with 43 legs?

Use the method that you used above to solve the following problem.

10. You work in a factory where you build bicycles and tricycles. Suddenly, the wheel-building machine shoots out 32 wheels. How many bicycles and tricycles can you build?

Find 24 ÷ 8.

Use repeated subtraction to find the quotient.

To find 24 ÷ 8, count how many 8s can be subtracted from 24.

Press	Display
24 $-$ 8 $=$	*16*
$-$ 8 $=$	*8*
$-$ 8 $=$	*0*

How many times did you subtract? *3*

Quotient

$$24 ÷ 8 = 3$$

Divide using repeated subtraction. Some quotients will have two digits.

1. 72 ÷ 9   **2.** 35 ÷ 5

3. 12 ÷ 6   **4.** 18 ÷ 2

5. 28 ÷ 4   **6.** 9 ÷ 3

7. 8 ÷ 1   **8.** 49 ÷ 7

9. 48 ÷ 8   **10.** 4 ÷ 4

11. 72 ÷ 6   **12.** 91 ÷ 7

13. 80 ÷ 8   **14.** 42 ÷ 3

15. 16 ÷ 1   **16.** 99 ÷ 9

17. 30 ÷ 2   **18.** 64 ÷ 4

19. 100 ÷ 5   **20.** 12 ÷ 12

Remainders

Work in groups. Use your counters.

A. Becky has 50 cents. Postcards cost 8 cents each. How many postcards can she buy? Will she have any money left over? If so, how much?

Find 50 ÷ 8.

Use 50 counters. Put them in groups of 8. What does each group of 8 represent? How many groups are there? How many counters are left over?

The number left over is called the *remainder*. The answer to 50 ÷ 8 is 6, remainder 2. This can be written 6 R2.

Quotient ⟶ **6 R2** ⟵ Remainder
Divisor ⟶ **8)͞50** ⟵ Dividend

Becky can buy ▒ postcards. She will have ▒ cents left over.

Dear Therese,
Hello! How are you?
I am fine. I saw a
bear, and it wasn't
in the zoo! Camping
is a lot of fun. I
will see you soon.
Your friend,
Jenny

B. Becky's father bought 36 stamps for postcards. He divided them evenly among his 5 children. How many stamps did each child get? How many stamps were left over?

Find 36 ÷ 5.

Use 36 counters and put them into 5 equal groups. Begin by taking 5 counters and putting one in each group. Then take 5 more and put one in each group. How many times can you do this? When must you stop?

How many counters are in each group? What does this number represent? How many counters are left over? What does this number represent?

C. You can check the reasonableness of your answer to a division problem by estimating a *range*. To find a range for the answer to 50 ÷ 8, recall that 48 ÷ 8 is 6 and 56 ÷ 8 is 7. Since 50 is between 48 and 56, you can say 50 ÷ 8 is between 6 and 7.

You found the answer to 50 ÷ 8 in Example A. Explain why it is reasonable.

Try Work in groups. Use counters to divide. Explain to another student why each answer is reasonable.

a. $3\overline{)16}$ **b.** $6\overline{)42}$ **c.** $47 \div 9$

Practice Work in groups. Use counters to divide.

1. $5\overline{)42}$ **2.** $2\overline{)11}$ **3.** $4\overline{)24}$ **4.** $8\overline{)46}$

5. $5\overline{)23}$ **6.** $6\overline{)39}$ **7.** $3\overline{)26}$ **8.** $2\overline{)17}$

9. $3\overline{)15}$ **10.** $8\overline{)56}$ **11.** $7\overline{)59}$ **12.** $9\overline{)75}$

13. $68 \div 8$ **14.** $33 \div 4$ **15.** $87 \div 9$ **16.** $39 \div 7$

17. $18 \div 5$ **18.** $23 \div 6$ **19.** $48 \div 7$ **20.** $57 \div 9$

21. $9 \div 2$ **22.** $63 \div 9$ **23.** $49 \div 6$ **24.** $10 \div 5$

Apply Solve each problem.

25. Sam bought a postcard for 21 cents. Then he decided to buy 5 more. How much did he spend for all the postcards?

26. Sam bought a 22-cent stamp for each postcard in Exercise 25. How much did he spend for the postcards and stamps?

27. If 25 people got on a sightseeing bus and 4 people sat in each row, how many rows were filled? How many people were in another row?

28. If postcards are on sale at 6 for 95 cents, what will you probably be charged if you buy only one postcard? Explain your answer.

29. **CALCULATOR** On your calculator, press 50 $\boxed{-}$ 8 $\boxed{=}$. Continue pressing $\boxed{=}$ until the display shows a number less than 8. How many times did you press $\boxed{=}$? Compare this with the answer in Example A. Work with other students to make a generalization. Then test your generalization, using some of the Practice exercises.

30. Explain to another student how to find $125 \div 13$ by using only the operation of subtraction.

Choose the Operation

The Andrews family brought 48 grapefruit home for their neighbors. They gave the same number of grapefruit to each of 8 neighbors. How many grapefruit did they give to each neighbor?

Read Facts: 48 grapefruit, same number to each of 8 neighbors

Find: Number given to each neighbor

Plan Since 48 grapefruit were separated into 8 equal groups, use division. Find $48 \div 8$.

Solve
$$8\overline{)48} \quad 6$$

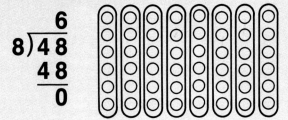

8 groups of 6

$$
\begin{array}{r}
6 \\
8\overline{)48} \\
48 \\
\hline
0
\end{array}
$$

Answer They gave each neighbor 6 grapefruit.

Look Back There were 8 groups with 6 grapefruit in each group. $8 \times 6 = 48$.

Try Tell whether you *add*, *subtract*, *multiply*, or *divide*. Then find the answer. Use place-value materials when you need them.

a. Philip bought 5 sets of coins with 6 coins in each set. What was the total number of coins?

b. The odometer on the Andrewses' car showed 4,965 before they left. Now it shows 8,213. How many miles did they travel?

Apply Tell whether you *add*, *subtract*, *multiply*, or *divide*. Then find the answer. Use place-value materials when you need them.

1. The Andrewses spent 28 days on vacation. How many 7-day weeks was that?

2. Jenny has collected 36 state flags. How many more of the 50 state flags does she need?

3. Jenny displayed 36 flags in rows with 5 flags in each row. How many rows were filled? How many flags were left over?

4. Philip counted 49 Texas license plates. Jenny counted 7 more Texas plates than Philip. How many Texas plates did she count?

5. William bought 6 travel booklets. Each booklet had 18 pages. How many pages were there in all?

6. William bought 32 drawings. The drawings came in sets of 4. How many sets did William buy?

7. The Andrewses spent $48.72 for gas the first week, $37.95 the second week, $57.03 the third week, and $51.18 the fourth week. What was the total cost of the gas?

8. The family used 8 rolls of film with 24 pictures on each roll. How many pictures did the family take?

9. Mr. Andrews brought 25 flower bulbs home. He planted an equal number of bulbs in each of 4 pots. How many bulbs did he plant in each pot? How many bulbs were left over?

10. Mr. Andrews drove the car 15 hours during the vacation. Mrs. Andrews drove the car 3 times as many hours as her husband. How many hours did they drive in all?

11. **CALCULATOR** The Andrews family also brought 72 oranges home. How many dozen oranges did they bring home?

Chapter 8 Test

Complete each division sentence.

1. 12 in all
How many groups of 3?

$12 \div 3 = $ ▨

2. 16 in all
8 equal groups
How many in each group?

$16 \div 8 = $ ▨

Divide.

3. $2\overline{)18}$ **4.** $3\overline{)15}$

5. $4\overline{)8}$ **6.** $5\overline{)20}$

7. $3\overline{)0}$ **8.** $1\overline{)6}$

9. $6\overline{)48}$ **10.** $7\overline{)49}$

11. $8\overline{)8}$ **12.** $9\overline{)27}$

13. $6 \div 2$ **14.** $21 \div 3$

15. $16 \div 4$ **16.** $5 \div 5$

17. $0 \div 9$ **18.** $2 \div 1$

19. $36 \div 6$ **20.** $56 \div 7$

21. $72 \div 8$ **22.** $45 \div 9$

Write a family of facts using the given numbers.

23. 5, 6, 30

Divide.

24. $9\overline{)70}$ **25.** $5\overline{)27}$ **26.** $4\overline{)31}$

Solve each problem.

27. Leslie had 17 pennies. She gave 5 pennies to her brother and 4 more to her sister. How many pennies did Leslie have left?

28. 11 children were playing. 3 children left. The remaining children made 2 equal teams. How many children were on each team?

Tell whether you *add, subtract, multiply,* or *divide.* Then find the answer.

29. Perry made a pattern with marbles. He put 4 marbles in each of 12 rows. How many marbles did he use in all?

30. A florist had 48 flowers. He put 6 flowers in each vase. How many vases did he use?

CHALLENGE

Missing Factors

A. The 18-foot Saguaro Cactus is 3 times as tall as the 6-foot Organ-Pipe Cactus.

$$3 \times 6 = 18$$

↑   ↑   ↑

Factor Factor Product

B. The 18-foot Saguaro Cactus is how many times as tall as the 2-foot Barrel Cactus?

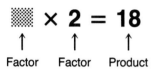 $\times 2 = 18$

↑   ↑   ↑

Factor Factor Product

To find the missing factor, divide the product by the given factor.

$$18 \div 2 = 9$$

9 is the missing factor.

The Saguaro Cactus is 9 times as tall as the Barrel Cactus.

Find each missing factor.

1. $4 \times$ ▨ $= 24$
2. ▨ $\times 6 = 36$
3. $3 \times$ ▨ $= 21$
4. ▨ $\times 2 = 14$

5. ▨ $\times 5 = 30$
6. $8 \times$ ▨ $= 16$
7. ▨ $\times 7 = 28$
8. $5 \times$ ▨ $= 20$

9. $8 \times$ ▨ $= 64$
10. ▨ $\times 6 = 42$
11. $9 \times$ ▨ $= 45$
12. ▨ $\times 7 = 49$

13. ▨ $\times 7 = 63$
14. $8 \times$ ▨ $= 72$
15. ▨ $\times 6 = 30$
16. $4 \times$ ▨ $= 36$

17. $3 \times$ ▨ $= 24$
18. ▨ $\times 9 = 0$
19. $7 \times$ ▨ $= 7$
20. ▨ $\times 9 = 36$

GRANDMA'S SUGAR BOWL

> Guess how much money I have in my sugar bowl.

There are 7 nickels, but that's not all.

There is less than a dollar.

I can separate it into 6 piles with the same amount in each pile.

I cannot make 7 piles with the same amount in each pile.

I could trade my money for dimes and have nothing left over.

If I had one more dime, I could then separate the money into 7 piles with the same amount in each pile.

1. How much money do I have in my sugar bowl?

My cream pitcher has less than a dollar in it including 6 dimes. I could make 3 equal piles of money but could not make 4, 5, or 6 equal piles.

2. What is the smallest amount of money that could be in the pitcher?

3. What is the greatest amount of money that could be in the pitcher?

Division

$$3\overline{)32}\,\,^{10\;R2}$$

One-Digit Divisors, Two-Digit Quotients

A. The Randalls collected 94 shells while on vacation. The shells were divided equally among their 4 children. How many shells did each child get? How many shells were left over?

Find 94 ÷ 4.

Work in groups of four. Use your place-value materials to show 9 tens and 4 ones.

Now pretend that each of you is one of the 4 Randall children and that your place-value materials are shells and groups of shells. Divide the 94 shells equally among the 4 of you. Do you have to exchange the 9 tens for 90 ones? How many tens do each of you have? What can you do with any of the tens that are left over?

How many shells did each of the Randall children get? How many shells were left over?

B. Find 80 ÷ 2.

Discuss in your group how to find this quotient mentally. Then give the quotient.

Try Work in groups. Use your place-value materials to divide.

a. $4\overline{)63}$ **b.** $2\overline{)98}$ **c.** $82 \div 7$

d. Find 60 ÷ 3 mentally.

Practice Use your place-value materials to divide.

1. $5\overline{)86}$ **2.** $3\overline{)96}$ **3.** $6\overline{)77}$

4. $2\overline{)51}$ **5.** $4\overline{)87}$ **6.** $9\overline{)99}$

7. $35 \div 2$ **8.** $46 \div 3$

9. $61 \div 5$ **10.** $88 \div 2$

Mental math Divide mentally. Write only the quotient.

11. $4\overline{)80}$ **12.** $3\overline{)90}$ **13.** $5\overline{)50}$

14. $2\overline{)60}$ **15.** $6\overline{)60}$ **16.** $2\overline{)40}$

17. Here's a way to record your work when you divide. Work in groups and use place-value materials to explain what is happening in each step.

Divide the tens into 4 equal groups.
How many tens in each group?
How many tens left over?

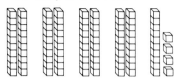

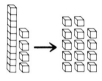

Divide.

Multiply. 2 × 4 = 8

Subtract and compare.

Is 1 less than 4?

Rename the left-over ten as ones. How many ones altogether?

2 3 R 2

4)**9** 4

8

1 4

1 2

2

Bring down.
The next digit is 4.

Divide.

Multiply. 3 × 4 = 12

Subtract and compare.

Is 2 less than 4?
Are there any more digits to bring down?
What is the remainder?

Divide the ones into 4 equal groups.
How many ones in each group?
How many ones left over?

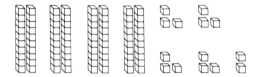

Check

2 3
× 4
_____

+ 2
_____

Multiply the quotient and the divisor.

Add the remainder.

The result should be the dividend.

What do you think happens when you check an answer with a remainder of 0?

Divide. Work in groups. Use your place-value materials as you record your work.

18. 4)56   **19.** 3)93   **20.** 5)70   **21.** 6)96   **22.** 2)56   **23.** 3)58

24. 62 ÷ 5   **25.** 95 ÷ 4   **26.** 75 ÷ 2   **27.** 90 ÷ 4   **28.** 84 ÷ 7

Apply   Solve each problem.

29. Mr. Randall packed 48 shells in 4 boxes. He put the same number of shells in each box. How many shells did he put in each box?

30. Barry got 14 shells last year and 23 shells this year. He chose 4 of the old shells and 16 new shells to divide equally among 5 friends. How many did he give to each friend?

Zeros in Two-Digit Quotients

Luisa wants to bring each of 8 friends the same souvenir from her vacation. She has 87 cents to spend. What is the greatest amount she can spend for each souvenir? How much will she have left?

Find 87 ÷ 8.

You can use *compatible numbers* to estimate this quotient. Find a number close to 87 that you can divide by 8 mentally. What is an estimate of the quotient?

Now divide. Use the pictures to help explain each step.

Divide the tens.

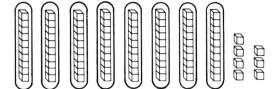

$$\begin{array}{r} 1 \\ 8\overline{)8\,7} \\ 8 \\ \hline 0 \end{array}$$

Divide.

Multiply.

Subtract and compare.

Divide the ones. Can you make 8 equal groups of ones?

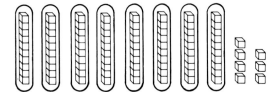

$$\begin{array}{r} 1\,0 \text{ R7} \\ 8\overline{)8\,7} \\ 8\downarrow \\ \hline 0\,7 \\ 0 \\ \hline 7 \end{array}$$

Bring down. The next digit is 7.

Divide. Each time you bring down a digit and divide, you must write a digit in the quotient. Sometimes this digit is zero.

Multiply.

Subtract and compare. The remainder is 7.

What is 87 ÷ 8? Is the answer close to your estimate? How much can Luisa spend for each souvenir? How much money will she have left over?

Try Divide. Explain orally why your answers are reasonable.

a. $5\overline{)54}$ **b.** $2\overline{)81}$ **c.** $76 \div 7$

d. Check the division. $6\overline{)94}$ with quotient 15 R4

Practice   Divide.

1. $4\overline{)40}$ 2. $2\overline{)20}$ 3. $3\overline{)90}$ 4. $2\overline{)40}$ 5. $4\overline{)42}$ 6. $6\overline{)72}$

7. $9\overline{)98}$ 8. $6\overline{)63}$ 9. $4\overline{)89}$ 10. $2\overline{)61}$ 11. $3\overline{)92}$ 12. $5\overline{)59}$

13. $62 \div 6$ 14. $83 \div 4$ 15. $95 \div 8$ 16. $71 \div 4$ 17. $62 \div 3$

18. $97 \div 9$ 19. $93 \div 3$ 20. $87 \div 8$ 21. $99 \div 7$ 22. $85 \div 3$

Check each division. If the answer is wrong, give the correct answer.

23. $2\overline{)80}$ (40)   24. $8\overline{)94}$ (11 R4)   25. $3\overline{)61}$ (20)   26. $3\overline{)49}$ (16 R1)   27. $2\overline{)97}$ (48)

Apply   *Choosing a Computation Method*   Calculator, Paper and Pencil, Mental Math, Estimation
Choose a method to solve Problems 28–31. Tell which method you used.

28. Luisa took 75 pictures while she was on vacation. She can put 8 pictures on each page of her album. Will she fill 10 pages?

29. Curt used 21 rolls of film on his vacation. Each roll has 12 pictures. Did he take more or less than 200 pictures?

30. Joan used 3 rolls of film to take 72 pictures. Each roll has the same number of pictures. How many pictures are on each roll?

31. Jan has 85 pictures. She can put 4 on each page of an album. She thinks 20 pages will be enough. Is she correct?

32. **⟨CALCULATOR⟩** Work in groups of 4 and use your calculator to find the answer to this problem.

It costs 8 cents to have a print made from a negative. How many prints can Brian have made for 75 cents? How much money will be left?

Which part of the calculator display tells how many prints Brian can have made? How can you use the display to find the number of cents left? Explain your reasoning.

33. **⟨CALCULATOR⟩** Use your calculator to solve Problem A on page 242.

What part of the display can be used to answer each question? Explain your answer.

One-Digit Divisors, Three-Digit Quotients

A. Paul Bunyan, the giant lumberman, climbed 984 feet to the top of a mountain in 6 equal strides. How long was each stride?

Work in groups of four. Use your place-value materials to find 984 ÷ 6.

Discuss how to find the answer without using 984 ones. Then share your method with the students in another group. If they used a different method, decide which method you like better.

How long was each of Paul Bunyan's strides?

B. Use the steps below to find 581 ÷ 2.

Step 1   Show 5 hundreds, 8 tens, and 1 one.

Step 2   Divide the hundreds into 2 equal groups.

Step 3   Regroup the hundreds that are left. Divide the tens into 2 equal groups.

Step 4   Regroup the tens that are left. Divide the ones into 2 equal groups.

Step 5   What is 581 ÷ 2?

Try Work in groups. Use your place-value materials to divide.

a. $2\overline{)246}$ **b.** $3\overline{)639}$ **c.** $978 \div 5$

Practice Work in groups. Use your place-value materials to divide.

1. $3\overline{)393}$ **2.** $4\overline{)485}$ **3.** $2\overline{)842}$

4. $3\overline{)935}$ **5.** $6\overline{)743}$ **6.** $5\overline{)942}$

7. $525 \div 4$ **8.** $388 \div 2$

9. $849 \div 7$ **10.** $983 \div 6$

Apply Use your place-value materials to solve each problem.

11. Paul Bunyan drank 424 quarts of milk. How many gallons is this? (4 quarts = 1 gallon)

12. Paul's cook used 955 eggs in 5 days. He used the same number of eggs each day. How many eggs did the cook use each day?

13. One day, Paul cut down 475 trees. He put them into 4 equal stacks of 117 trees and had 7 trees left over. Explain how you can use this information to find $475 \div 4$.

14. Another time Paul put the trees he cut into 3 stacks of 112. There were 2 trees left over. How many trees had Paul cut down?

Zeros in Three-Digit Quotients

A. Paul Bunyan once stopped a flooding river by freezing it and chopping it into 9 equal sections. If the river was 945 miles long, how long was each section?

Work with 3 other students. Use your place-value materials to find 945 ÷ 9.

How do you show 945 with your place-value materials? What do you divide first? What is the result?
What is the next step? What is the result? Continue until you find the answer to the problem.

How long was each section of river?

B. Find 802 ÷ 4.

Explain to the students in another group how you can use place-value materials to find the answer. What is 802 ÷ 4?

C. Find 600 ÷ 2.

Discuss how you can find this quotient mentally.

Try Work in groups. Use your place-value materials to divide.

a. 2)260  **b.** 3)603

c. 706 ÷ 7

d. Explain how you can find this quotient mentally.

600 ÷ 3

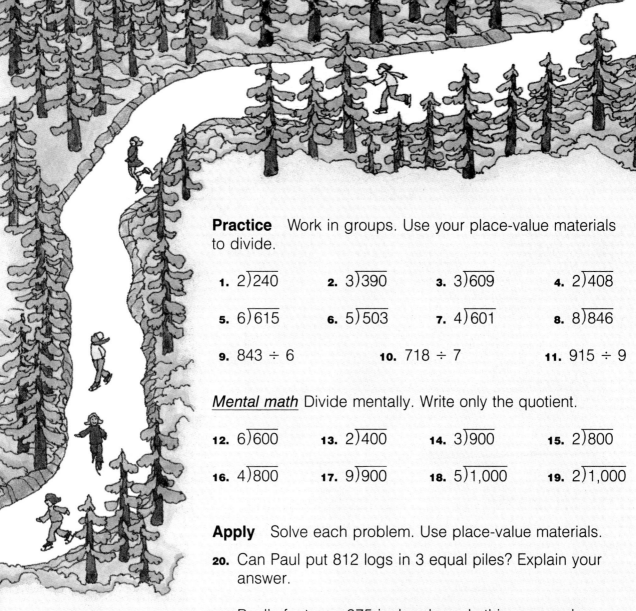

Practice Work in groups. Use your place-value materials to divide.

1. $2\overline{)240}$ 2. $3\overline{)390}$ 3. $3\overline{)609}$ 4. $2\overline{)408}$

5. $6\overline{)615}$ 6. $5\overline{)503}$ 7. $4\overline{)601}$ 8. $8\overline{)846}$

9. $843 \div 6$ 10. $718 \div 7$ 11. $915 \div 9$

Mental math Divide mentally. Write only the quotient.

12. $6\overline{)600}$ 13. $2\overline{)400}$ 14. $3\overline{)900}$ 15. $2\overline{)800}$

16. $4\overline{)800}$ 17. $9\overline{)900}$ 18. $5\overline{)1,000}$ 19. $2\overline{)1,000}$

Apply Solve each problem. Use place-value materials.

20. Can Paul put 812 logs in 3 equal piles? Explain your answer.

21. Paul's foot was 875 inches long. Is this more or less than 100 times the length of your foot? Explain your reasoning.

CALCULATOR

Use your calculator to find each mystery number.

1. This number is less than 30. When it is divided by 6, the remainder is 4. When it is divided by 5, the remainder is 3. What is the number?

2. This number is less than 50. When it is divided by 7, the remainder is 3. When it is divided by 8, the remainder is 5. What is the number?

Placing Digits in the Quotient

On pages 246–249 you divided 3-digit numbers using place-value materials. Here is a way to record your work. Work in groups of 4. For each example, use your place-value materials and discuss each step.

A. Find 984 ÷ 6.

> Estimate using compatible numbers: 1,000 ÷ 5 = 200

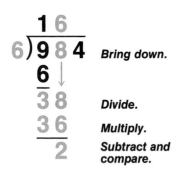

Divide.

Multiply.

Subtract and compare.

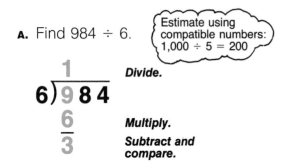

Bring down.

Divide.

Multiply.

Subtract and compare.

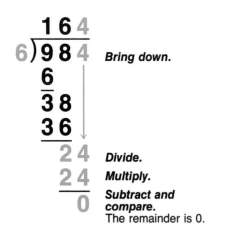

Bring down.

Divide.

Multiply.

Subtract and compare.
The remainder is 0.

What is the answer? Is it reasonable? How do you know? How can you check the answer?

B. Find 128 ÷ 7.

> Estimate using compatible numbers: 140 ÷ 7 = 20

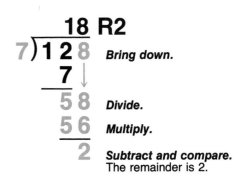

Divide.

Multiply.

Subtract and compare.

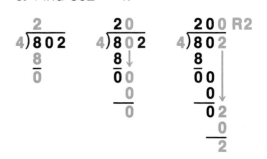

Bring down.

Divide.

Multiply.

Subtract and compare.
The remainder is 2.

What is the answer? Explain why it is reasonable.

c. Find 802 ÷ 4.

$$\begin{array}{r} 2 \\ 4\overline{)802} \\ 8 \\ \hline 0 \end{array} \qquad \begin{array}{r} 20 \\ 4\overline{)802} \\ 8\downarrow \\ \hline 00 \\ 0 \\ \hline 0 \end{array} \qquad \begin{array}{r} 200 \text{ R2} \\ 4\overline{)802} \\ 8\downarrow \\ \hline 00 \\ 0\downarrow \\ \hline 02 \\ 0 \\ \hline 2 \end{array}$$

d. How many digits will be in each quotient? Explain how you can tell.

$$5\overline{)630} \qquad 7\overline{)630} \qquad 8\overline{)63}$$

Try For each exercise, tell how many digits will be in the quotient. Then divide.

a. $5\overline{)650}$ **b.** $7\overline{)631}$ **c.** $8\overline{)70}$ **d.** $406 \div 3$ **e.** $803 \div 4$

Practice Tell how many digits will be in each quotient.

1. $4\overline{)48}$ **2.** $5\overline{)48}$ **3.** $4\overline{)480}$ **4.** $5\overline{)480}$ **5.** $8\overline{)400}$

Check each division. If the answer is wrong, give the correct answer.

6. $8\overline{)516}$ (64 R4)   **7.** $4\overline{)516}$ (104)   **8.** $3\overline{)650}$ (216 R2)   **9.** $7\overline{)714}$ (102)   **10.** $5\overline{)455}$ (90 R5)

Divide. Explain why your answer is reasonable.

11. $9\overline{)86}$ **12.** $2\overline{)609}$ **13.** $3\overline{)59}$ **14.** $8\overline{)875}$ **15.** $2\overline{)356}$

16. $4\overline{)536}$ **17.** $8\overline{)544}$ **18.** $7\overline{)623}$ **19.** $6\overline{)341}$ **20.** $9\overline{)915}$

21. $5\overline{)209}$ **22.** $3\overline{)407}$ **23.** $9\overline{)623}$ **24.** $8\overline{)783}$ **25.** $6\overline{)156}$

26. $198 \div 2$ **27.** $849 \div 7$ **28.** $721 \div 4$ **29.** $579 \div 9$ **30.** $435 \div 8$

31. $657 \div 2$ **32.** $589 \div 5$ **33.** $768 \div 4$ **34.** $777 \div 2$ **35.** $999 \div 5$

Apply Solve each problem.

36. Sara has 200 ounces of juice. How many 8-ounce glasses can she fill?

37. Can each of 235 students take a partner? Explain your answer.

38. *Thinking skills* In a division exercise, what numbers can be remainders if the divisor is 5?

39. **CALCULATOR** The $\div$ and $-$ keys are broken on your calculator. How can you use it to find $432 \div 27$?

Using Problem-Solving Strategies, page 426
More Practice Set 93, page 385

Dividing Money

A. Work with two other students in your class and use play money to explain how $7.35 can be divided among the three of you.

What coins and bills did you exchange for other coins and bills? What order did you follow when you were exchanging? Were you concerned with the decimal point in the process?

What is $7.35 ÷ 3?

B. Brian Whitewing bought 3 bags of oranges for $5.79. What was the cost of each bag?

Find $5.79 ÷ 3.

> Estimate using compatible numbers:
> $6.00 ÷ 3 = $2.00

Think of $5.79 as 579 cents. Divide. Then write the answer as dollars and cents.

```
     1 9 3      193 cents can be
  3)5 7 9        written as $1.93.
    3
    ‾‾
    2 7
    2 7
    ‾‾‾
      0 9
        9
      ‾‾‾
        0
```

The cost of each bag was $1.93.

c. Find $1.56 ÷ 4.

$$
\begin{array}{r}
3\,9 \rightarrow \mathbf{\$0.39} \\
4\overline{)1\,5\,6} \\
\underline{1\,2} \\
3\,6 \\
\underline{3\,6} \\
0
\end{array}
$$

Try Divide. Write each answer as dollars and cents. Explain to another student why your answers are reasonable.

a. $3.58 ÷ 2   **b.** $1.45 ÷ 5   **c.** $0.56 ÷ 4   **d.** $0.91 ÷ 7

e. Roxanne had $1.28 in her change purse. She had 8 coins altogether. None of them were dimes. What were the coins? Use play money to help you.

Practice Divide. Write each answer as dollars and cents.

1. $6.50 ÷ 5   **2.** $7.20 ÷ 6   **3.** $9.24 ÷ 3   **4.** $4.10 ÷ 2

5. $8.96 ÷ 8   **6.** $9.17 ÷ 7   **7.** $0.75 ÷ 5   **8.** $0.60 ÷ 4

Apply Solve each problem.

9. Soup is sold at 5 cans for $2.15. What is the cost per can?

10. Milk costs $1.49 per gallon. What is the cost of 2 gallons?

11. Three people divided a restaurant bill equally. The bill was $8.85. Is it reasonable to say that they each paid $5? Why or why not?

12. Joe counted the change in his pockets to be 58¢. Only three coins were pennies. What is the most number of coins he could have in his pockets? What is the least number of coins possible?

13. Brian bought 3 quarts of ice cream for $4.77. What was the cost per quart?

14. Brand A juice sells at 6 cans for $2.88. Brand B sells at 3 cans for $1.47. Which brand costs more per can?

Practice: Division

Divide.

1. $3\overline{)84}$
2. $6\overline{)90}$
3. $2\overline{)65}$
4. $5\overline{)77}$
5. $4\overline{)83}$

6. $7\overline{)75}$
7. $2\overline{)43}$
8. $3\overline{)77}$
9. $7\overline{)94}$
10. $4\overline{)67}$

11. $8\overline{)85}$
12. $3\overline{)93}$
13. $6\overline{)756}$
14. $5\overline{)927}$
15. $8\overline{)805}$

16. $3\overline{)622}$
17. $7\overline{)820}$
18. $4\overline{)754}$
19. $9\overline{)387}$
20. $6\overline{)189}$

21. $562 \div 8$
22. $389 \div 7$
23. $600 \div 5$
24. $480 \div 3$

25. $910 \div 6$
26. $463 \div 9$
27. $393 \div 6$
28. $973 \div 5$

29. $\$2.80 \div 4$
30. $\$7.86 \div 2$
31. $\$9.48 \div 6$
32. $\$0.92 \div 4$

Check each division. If the answer is wrong, give the correct answer.

33. $5\overline{)95}$ 19
34. $2\overline{)61}$ 31
35. $8\overline{)73}$ 90 R1
36. $6\overline{)85}$ 14 R1

37. $8\overline{)812}$ 11 R4
38. $3\overline{)601}$ 200 R1
39. $7\overline{)532}$ 76
40. $9\overline{)405}$ 40 R5

Apply   _Choosing a Computation Method_   Calculator, Paper and Pencil, Mental Math, Estimation
Choose a method to solve Problems 41–46. Tell which method you used.

41. Carl bought 3 notebooks for $4.47. All the notebooks cost the same. How much was each?

42. Juan has 4 shelves with 20 toy cars on each. How many toy cars are on the shelves?

43. An auditorium had 624 seats in 3 equal sections. How many seats were in each section?

44. Lucy has film for 12 pictures. She has taken 8 pictures. How many pictures are left to take?

45. Roberto and his brother bought 3 birthday cards that cost $0.90 each. They also bought a gift that cost $4.50. They split the total cost equally. How much did each boy pay?

46. Joan bought extra pages for her photo album. Each package of pages costs $3.79. She spent $18.95. How many packages of pages did she buy?

Wild animals three
Set off on a spree.
Across the big lake they were bound.
They didn't want to wade,
But the boat they had made
Would hold only eight hundred pounds.

Together their weight
Was two times as great
As the total their poor boat would hold.
So they sat down to think
How to sail and not sink,
But their answer has never been told.

47. Use the poem above to solve this problem.
Discuss your strategies with your classmates.

The bear weighed 500 pounds, the lion weighed
300 pounds, and the gorilla weighed 800 pounds.
How could the animals use the boat to get across
the lake?

When you use division to solve a problem, you may need to decide what the remainder means.

Mrs. Ching's class is making hats for a class play. They need 35 colored feathers. The feathers come in packages of 3 each. How many packages do they need to buy?

Read   Facts: 35 feathers needed, 3 in each package
Find: Number of packages to buy

Plan   Think of 35 separated into equal groups with 3 in each group. Use division. Find 35 ÷ 3.

Solve

$$\begin{array}{r} 11\ \text{R2} \\ 3\overline{)35} \\ 3 \\ \hline 05 \\ 3 \\ \hline 2 \end{array}$$

Estimate using compatible numbers: 30 ÷ 3 = 10

Answer   They need **11 packages plus 2 more feathers.**
To get 2 more feathers, they must buy 1 more package. 11 + 1 = 12
The class needs to buy 12 packages of feathers.

Look Back   Since 35 feathers are needed and 11 × 3 = 33, 11 packages would not be enough.
Since 12 × 3 = 36, 12 packages would be enough.

Try Solve each problem.

a. The class must sell $95 worth of tickets to cover costs. How many $2 tickets must they sell?

b. If 2 bows are needed for each hat, how many hats can be made with 57 bows?

Apply Solve each problem.

1. The students can make 6 tickets from each sheet of paper. How many sheets of paper are needed for 125 tickets?

2. There are 15 sheets of poster board for making signs. If 2 sheets are needed for each sign, how many signs can be made?

3. If 2 yards of fabric are needed for each costume, how many costumes can be made from 25 yards? How much fabric will be left over?

4. Diane has 108 inches of ribbon. If she cuts as many 8-inch pieces as possible, how much ribbon will be left over?

5. One group has 50 squares of green felt. They need 4 squares for each hat. How many green hats can they make?

6. The class needs 144 buttons for the costumes. If there are 5 buttons on a card, how many cards are needed?

7. Laura and Ben will set up chairs for the play. They have 75 chairs to put in rows of 8 each. How many chairs will be left over?

8. Dawn needs 38 gold stars for her costume. The stars come on sheets of 4 each. How many sheets does she need to buy?

Finding Averages

The 4 acts in the school play lasted 8 minutes, 10 minutes, 12 minutes, and 6 minutes. Suppose each act had lasted the same number of minutes. That number is the same as the *average* length of an act.

Use your counters and work in groups of 4. Each of you take enough counters to represent the number of minutes in one of the acts.

Put the counters together in one group. How many counters are in the group? How did you find the total number?

Now divide the counters so that each person has the same number. How many counters does each of you have?

What is the average length of an act?

Try Use your counters to find the average of each set of numbers.

a. 2, 6, 9, 3   b. 9, 7, 2

Practice Work in groups and use your counters to find the average of each set of numbers.

1. 1, 4, 7   2. 11, 9

3. 8, 12, 9, 3   4. 3, 8, 2, 5, 7

5. 3, 8, 2, 5, 1, 6, 3, 8, 0

6. Use these steps to find the average of 65, 67, and 72.

Step 1 Imagine putting this many counters together. How can you find the total number without counting?

Step 2 Now imagine dividing the total number into 3 equal groups. How can you find the number in each group? What is the average?

7. With other students, discuss a method for finding the average of a set of numbers. Without using counters, test your method on some of the exercises on page 258.

Find the average.

8. 17, 24, 19

9. 36, 48, 15, 13

10. 129, 132, 118, 100, 121, 42

11. 198, 204, 216, 187, 195

12. [CALCULATOR] Work in groups. Discuss how you can use a calculator to find an average. Then test your method on Exercises 10 and 11.

Apply Solve each problem.

13. Karen said that the average age of the students in her elementary school was 18. Was this reasonable? Explain why or why not.

14. Without computing, what do you think might be an average for this set of numbers?

5, 12, 17, 84, 88, 100

Explain your thinking to another student. Then compute the average.

15. [CALCULATOR] In the last 2 plays, there were a total of 49 people involved. Use your calculator to find the average number of people in each play. Could your answer be the actual number in each play? Explain your answer.

Multiples of 10 as Divisors

A. Jill has 150 boxes of T-shirts to distribute to 20 shops throughout Funland Amusement Park. If she gives each shop the same number of boxes, how many will each shop get? How many boxes will be left over?

Work with 3 other students. Use your place-value materials to find 150 ÷ 20. Try to do the work without using 150 ones.

Explain your method to other students. If they did the work differently, discuss both methods.

How many boxes of T-shirts will each shop get? How many boxes will be left over?

B. Find 271 ÷ 30.

Use place-value materials to find the answer. Explain your method to another student.

C. Find 360 ÷ 90 mentally.

Discuss with other students how you can use the basic fact 36 ÷ 9 to find this answer mentally.

Try

Work in groups. Use place-value materials to divide.

a. $40\overline{)241}$ **b.** $60\overline{)190}$ **c.** 526 ÷ 80

Divide mentally. Explain orally which basic fact you used to help.

d. $40\overline{)280}$ **e.** $20\overline{)120}$ **f.** $50\overline{)300}$

Practice Work in groups. Use place-value materials to divide.

1. $40\overline{)200}$ **2.** $60\overline{)420}$ **3.** $70\overline{)150}$ **4.** $50\overline{)280}$ **5.** $30\overline{)250}$

6. $80\overline{)407}$ **7.** $30\overline{)249}$ **8.** $50\overline{)435}$ **9.** $20\overline{)179}$ **10.** $90\overline{)685}$

11. $299 \div 30$ **12.** $391 \div 40$ **13.** $264 \div 70$ **14.** $568 \div 60$

Mental math Divide. Which basic fact helps you find the answer? Discuss this with another student in your group.

15. $50\overline{)250}$ **16.** $80\overline{)160}$ **17.** $20\overline{)140}$ **18.** $30\overline{)90}$ **19.** $70\overline{)420}$

20. $60\overline{)540}$ **21.** $40\overline{)320}$ **22.** $80\overline{)400}$ **23.** $90\overline{)270}$ **24.** $50\overline{)200}$

25. Demonstrate to another student in your group how you can use place-value materials to find $144 \div 48$. Discuss different ways to find the answer. What is $144 \div 48$?

Use your place-value materials to divide.

26. $18\overline{)126}$ **27.** $31\overline{)274}$ **28.** $26\overline{)192}$ **29.** $47\overline{)381}$ **30.** $83\overline{)642}$

Apply Use your place-value materials to solve each problem.

31. The Funland train holds 240 people. They ride in cars of 40 people each. How many cars are on the train?

32. Jill needs to order 132 straw hats for the souvenir store. The hats come in boxes of 12. How many boxes should she order?

MAINTENANCE

Divide.

1. $56 \div 7$ **2.** $18 \div 3$ **3.** $45 \div 5$ **4.** $32 \div 8$ **5.** $28 \div 4$ **6.** $10 \div 2$

7. $12 \div 4$ **8.** $27 \div 9$ **9.** $35 \div 5$ **10.** $8 \div 2$ **11.** $15 \div 3$ **12.** $36 \div 6$

13. $16 \div 4$ **14.** $63 \div 9$ **15.** $14 \div 2$ **16.** $30 \div 5$ **17.** $48 \div 6$ **18.** $54 \div 6$

19. $42 \div 7$ **20.** $81 \div 9$ **21.** $9 \div 3$ **22.** $64 \div 8$ **23.** $32 \div 4$ **24.** $72 \div 8$

25. $20 \div 5$ **26.** $28 \div 7$ **27.** $49 \div 7$ **28.** $54 \div 9$ **29.** $24 \div 3$ **30.** $36 \div 9$

31. $40 \div 8$ **32.** $18 \div 2$ **33.** $42 \div 6$ **34.** $36 \div 6$ **35.** $21 \div 3$ **36.** $24 \div 6$

Two-Digit Divisors, One-Digit Quotients

A. On page 260, you used place-value materials to divide 150 boxes of T-shirts equally among 20 shops. Here is a way to record your work.

Find 150 ÷ 20.

$$\begin{array}{r} 7 \\ 2\,0\,\overline{)1\,5\,0} \end{array}$$

Divide.
How many 20s in 150?
THINK How many 2s in 15?
Write 7 above the 0.

$$\begin{array}{r} 7\ \text{R}10 \\ 2\,0\,\overline{)1\,5\,0} \\ 1\,4\,0 \\ \hline 1\,0 \end{array}$$

Multiply.

Subtract and compare.

What is the answer? Explain to another student how you would check the answer.

B. Stan works in one of the Funland shops. One day he sold 48 key rings for a total of $144. How much did each key ring cost?

Find 144 ÷ 48.

$$\begin{array}{r} 3 \\ 4\,8\,\overline{)1\,4\,4} \end{array}$$

Divide.
How many 48s in 144?
THINK How many 4s in 14?
Write 3 above the 4.

$$\begin{array}{r} 3 \\ 4\,8\,\overline{)1\,4\,4} \\ 1\,4\,4 \\ \hline 0 \end{array}$$

Multiply.

Subtract and compare.
What is the remainder?

Each key ring cost $3. Does this seem reasonable for the cost of a key ring?

C. In each example, what is the first thing you think when you divide? Discuss this with another student.

$$\begin{array}{r} 4\ \text{R}1 \\ 6\,\overline{)2\,5} \\ 2\,4 \\ \hline 1 \end{array}$$

$$\begin{array}{r} 4\ \text{R}10 \\ 6\,0\,\overline{)2\,5\,0} \\ 2\,4\,0 \\ \hline 1\,0 \end{array}$$

$$\begin{array}{r} 4\ \text{R}2 \\ 6\,2\,\overline{)2\,5\,0} \\ 2\,4\,8 \\ \hline 2 \end{array}$$

$$\begin{array}{r} 4\ \text{R}9 \\ 6\,2\,\overline{)2\,5\,7} \\ 2\,4\,8 \\ \hline 9 \end{array}$$

Try Divide.

a. $30\,\overline{)274}$

b. $90\,\overline{)840}$

c. $25\,\overline{)75}$

d. $34\,\overline{)170}$

Practice Divide.

1. $40\overline{)206}$　　2. $60\overline{)425}$　　3. $70\overline{)143}$　　4. $50\overline{)256}$　　5. $90\overline{)275}$

6. $50\overline{)447}$　　7. $70\overline{)480}$　　8. $40\overline{)391}$　　9. $30\overline{)299}$　　10. $90\overline{)599}$

11. $67\overline{)80}$　　12. $33\overline{)78}$　　13. $24\overline{)58}$　　14. $23\overline{)115}$　　15. $32\overline{)290}$

16. $45\overline{)225}$　　17. $73\overline{)438}$　　18. $47\overline{)141}$　　19. $83\overline{)585}$　　20. $56\overline{)449}$

21. $84 \div 37$　　22. $810 \div 90$　　23. $105 \div 21$　　24. $387 \div 62$

25. $99 \div 43$　　26. $225 \div 75$　　27. $689 \div 82$　　28. $788 \div 91$

Mental math Divide mentally. Write only the quotient.

Mental
Math

29. $30\overline{)60}$　　30. $40\overline{)80}$　　31. $30\overline{)90}$　　32. $20\overline{)60}$　　33. $50\overline{)100}$

34. $80\overline{)320}$　　35. $70\overline{)560}$　　36. $60\overline{)300}$　　37. $20\overline{)180}$　　38. $90\overline{)360}$

Apply _Choosing a Computation Method_ Calculator, Paper and Pencil, Mental Math, Estimation
Choose a method to solve each problem. Tell which method you used.

39. Thirty-five students' tickets to Funland Park cost $175. How much does one student ticket cost?

40. One day Stan worked for 500 minutes. How many hours and minutes is this?

41. There are 57 Funland pennants in stock. A customer wants 3 boxes of 20 pennants. Are there enough pennants in stock to fill this order? Explain why or why not.

42. Kim Lee bought 3 T-shirts for $5.98 each. She gave the cashier a twenty dollar bill. Was this enough money? Explain why or why not.

43. The computer in the Funland storeroom shows that there are 108 key rings in stock. The key rings are in boxes of 36. How many boxes of key rings are in stock?

44. An average of 720 adults visit Funland Park each day. The park is open for 7 days a week. How many weeks will it take for 126,000 adults to visit Funland?

Correcting Estimates in One-Digit Quotients

On the moon an astronaut could walk 280 feet in 35 strides. What is the average length of each stride?

Find 280 ÷ 35.

$$35\overline{)280} \quad \begin{array}{l} 9 \end{array}$$

Divide.
How many 35s in 280?
THINK How many 3s in 28? 9

$$\begin{array}{r} 9 \\ 35\overline{)280} \\ 315 \end{array}$$

Multiply.
315 is greater than 280, so 9 is too big.

$$\begin{array}{r} 8 \\ 35\overline{)280} \\ 280 \\ \hline 0 \end{array}$$

Try 8.
Multiply.
Subtract and compare.
The remainder is 0.

The average length of each stride is 8 feet.

Check
$$\begin{array}{r} 35 \\ \times\ 8 \\ \hline 280 \end{array}$$

Try Divide.

a. $32\overline{)61}$ b. $25\overline{)175}$ c. $38\overline{)196}$

d. $63\overline{)241}$ e. $42\overline{)189}$

Practice Divide.

1. $25\overline{)72}$ **2.** $43\overline{)80}$ **3.** $53\overline{)251}$

4. $68\overline{)583}$ **5.** $47\overline{)165}$ **6.** $35\overline{)179}$

7. $21\overline{)106}$ **8.** $55\overline{)362}$ **9.** $49\overline{)208}$

10. $73\overline{)638}$ **11.** $85\overline{)320}$ **12.** $24\overline{)120}$

13. $96\overline{)273}$ **14.** $62\overline{)372}$ **15.** $34\overline{)265}$

16. $78\overline{)295}$ **17.** $31\overline{)249}$ **18.** $83\overline{)161}$

19. $181 \div 92$ **20.** $575 \div 72$

21. $543 \div 65$ **22.** $157 \div 52$

23. $98 \div 12$ **24.** $56 \div 14$

25. `CALCULATOR` **Press:** $84 \div 9 =$
What is the whole-number remainder?

Apply Solve each problem.

26. The first astronauts to orbit the moon were gone for 147 hours. How many days and hours is this?
(1 day = 24 hours)

27. Astronaut Neil Armstrong walked on the moon for 160 minutes. How many hours and minutes is this?
(1 hour = 60 minutes)

28. *Mental math* John Glenn made three orbits around the earth in about 300 minutes. How many hours was that?

29. *Write a problem.* Write a problem for which one of the numbers 5, 50, 500 would be a reasonable answer and for which the other two would not be reasonable.

Using Problem-Solving Strategies, page 427
More Practice Set 99, page 387

Two-Digit Divisors, Two-Digit Quotients

One of the Project Apollo space missions lasted about 295 hours. How many days and hours did it last? Remember, there are 24 hours in a day.

Find 295 ÷ 24. Estimate using compatible numbers. 295 is close to 300. 24 is close to 25. There are four 25s in every 100. So there are twelve 25s in 300. 295 ÷ 24 is about 12.

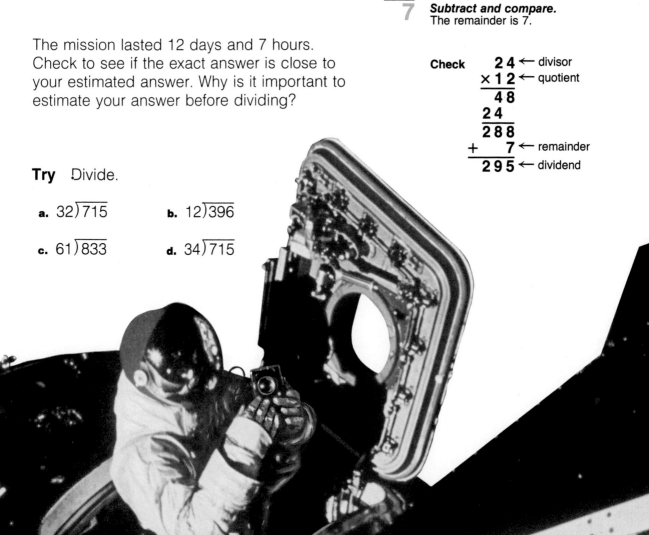

$$\begin{array}{r} 1 \\ 24\overline{\smash{)}295} \\ 24 \\ \hline 5 \end{array}$$

Divide.
How many 24s in 29? 1
Write 1 above the 9.

Multiply.

Subtract and compare.

$$\begin{array}{r} 12\ R7 \\ 24\overline{\smash{)}295} \\ 24\downarrow \\ \hline 55 \\ 48 \\ \hline 7 \end{array}$$

Bring down.

Divide.
How many 24s in 55?
THINK How many 2s in 5? 2

Multiply.

Subtract and compare.
The remainder is 7.

The mission lasted 12 days and 7 hours. Check to see if the exact answer is close to your estimated answer. Why is it important to estimate your answer before dividing?

Check
$$\begin{array}{r} 24 \leftarrow \text{divisor} \\ \times 12 \leftarrow \text{quotient} \\ \hline 48 \\ 24 \\ \hline 288 \\ +\quad 7 \leftarrow \text{remainder} \\ \hline 295 \leftarrow \text{dividend} \end{array}$$

Try Divide.

a. $32\overline{\smash{)}715}$ **b.** $12\overline{\smash{)}396}$

c. $61\overline{\smash{)}833}$ **d.** $34\overline{\smash{)}715}$

Practice Divide.

1. $23\overline{)496}$
2. $31\overline{)992}$
3. $68\overline{)789}$
4. $55\overline{)679}$
5. $47\overline{)991}$

6. $21\overline{)576}$
7. $58\overline{)754}$
8. $29\overline{)349}$
9. $72\overline{)976}$
10. $84\overline{)927}$

11. $30\overline{)742}$
12. $40\overline{)756}$
13. $75\overline{)900}$
14. $83\overline{)913}$
15. $12\overline{)498}$

16. $13\overline{)288}$
17. $65\overline{)780}$
18. $90\overline{)995}$
19. $24\overline{)538}$
20. $32\overline{)832}$

Apply _Use data from a table._ The table gives information about the Project Apollo missions. Solve each problem.

Mission	Length of mission
Apollo 7	260 hours
Apollo 8	147 hours
Apollo 9	241 hours
Apollo 10	192 hours
Apollo 11	195 hours
Apollo 12	245 hours
Apollo 13	143 hours
Apollo 14	216 hours
Apollo 15	295 hours
Apollo 16	266 hours
Apollo 17	302 hours

Find the length of each mission in days and hours. Remember, there are 24 hours in a day.

21. Apollo 15
22. Apollo 16

23. Apollo 8
24. Apollo 10

25. The Apollo 17 mission lasted how many hours longer than the Apollo 7 mission?

26. Astronaut Cernan was on Apollo 10 and Apollo 17. How many hours did he spend on these two missions?

27. Astronaut Lovell was on Apollo 8 and Apollo 13. How many hours did he spend on these two missions?

28. _Estimation_ About how many days long was the Apollo 9 mission? Choose the best estimate.

   1 day   10 days   100 days

29. _Find the facts._ Can the students in your class form teams with the same number on each team and no students left over? How many students might be on each team? How many teams would there be?

30. Let a be any number. Choose a number for b so that b is less than a. Put your numbers in the following sentences:

   $a \times b = b \times a$ $a \div b = b \div a$

   Are both of the sentences true? Explain why or why not.
   What happens in the sentences if b is zero?
   What can you say about the sentences when a and b are equal?

A PASSING PUZZLE

There are 6 members on the Madison School basketball team. During a practice exercise, the basketball was passed between each pair of team members once. *How many times was the basketball passed?*

Get into a group with 3 other students. In your group, discuss how you think that you might solve this problem. If you have more than one idea, try to solve the problem in more than one way.

1. How many times was the basketball passed?

2. How did you solve the problem? If other students in your group solved the problem in different ways, what methods did they use?

3. What methods did students in other groups use? Compare the methods that your group used with the methods that other groups used.

Try to use one or more methods to solve the following problems.

4. If there were 8 members on the basketball team, how many times would the basketball be passed?

5. If there were 12 members on the basketball team, how many times would the basketball be passed?

6. Suppose that a basketball was passed just once between every pair of students in your class. How many times would the basketball be passed?

7. Which method do you like the best? Why do you like this method the best?

8. When a basketball was passed once between every pair of players on the team, the ball was passed a total of 45 times. How many members were on the team?

9. A teacher divided his class of 20 students into 2 equal lines. Every student in class took a turn and passed the basketball to every student in the other line. How many times was the basketball passed after all the students had taken their turns passing?

COMPUTER

BASIC: INPUT Statements

In this program, an INPUT statement is used to enter the dividend (D). After the program is typed in, the computer reads it. When the computer reads INPUT, a ? appears on the screen and the computer waits for a number to be typed in.

When 12 is typed for D, this is printed.

```
10  INPUT D
20  PRINT D/3
30  END
```

```
?12
 4
```

When 30 is typed for D, this is printed.

```
?30
10
```

Tell what would be printed for the program above when each of the following is typed for D.

1. 42   2. 57   3. 96

4. Tell what would be printed for the following program when 184 is typed for D.

```
10  INPUT D
20  PRINT D/23
30  END
```

Tell what would be printed for the program in Exercise 4 when each of the following is typed for D.

5. 322   6. 782   7. 966

Problem Solving | Write an Equation

A. Charlie the cheetah ran 78 miles in 2 hours. What was his average speed in miles per hour?

Read Facts: 78 miles, 2 hours
Find: Average speed in miles per hour

Plan Think of Charlie running the same number of miles each hour. That number is the same as his average speed. Write an equation to show that the total number of miles separated into equal groups, one group for each hour, gives the average speed.

Number of miles	Number of hours	Number of miles per hour
78	÷ 2	= n

Solve

$$\begin{array}{r} 39 \\ 2\overline{)78} \\ \underline{6} \\ 18 \\ \underline{18} \\ 0 \end{array}$$

Estimate: 80 ÷ 2 = 40

$n = 39$

Answer Charlie's average speed was 39 miles per hour.

Look Back If Charlie ran 39 miles per hour for 2 hours, then his total distance could be found by multiplying 39 by 2. Since 2 × 39 = 78, the answer is correct.

B. Katy the kangaroo moves a distance of about 8 feet per hop. About how far does she move in 15 hops?

Distance per hop	Number of hops	Total distance
8	× 15	= n

$$\begin{array}{r} 15 \\ \times\ 8 \\ \hline 120 \end{array}$$

$n = 120$

Katy moves about 120 feet in 15 hops.

Try Write an equation. Then find the answer.

a. Bennie the butterfly can fly about 20 miles per hour. How far could he fly in 4 hours?

b. Hazel the honeybee flew 33 miles in 3 hours. What was her average speed in miles per hour?

Apply Write an equation. Then find the answer.

1. Tony the trout swam 30 miles in 2 hours. What was his average speed in miles per hour?

2. Dolly the dolphin can swim 37 miles per hour. How far could she swim in 5 hours?

3. Molly the mole spent almost 8 hours traveling 328 feet. What was her average speed in feet per hour?

4. Sonny the snail ran a race in 124 minutes. How many hours and minutes is this? (60 minutes = 1 hour)

5. Turk the tortoise can travel 15 feet per minute. Hattie the hare can travel 250 times as fast. How many feet per minute can Hattie travel?

6. Abbie the antelope runs at an average speed of 53 miles per hour. How far could she run in 8 hours?

7. Oscar the ostrich runs at an average speed of 27 miles per hour. How long would it take him to run 135 miles?

8. Cindy the centipede ran a race in 205 seconds. How many minutes and seconds is this? (60 seconds = 1 minute)

Chapter 9 Test

Divide.

1. $3\overline{)45}$ **2.** $8\overline{)93}$

3. $5\overline{)53}$ **4.** $2\overline{)81}$

5. $4\overline{)467}$ **6.** $6\overline{)996}$

7. $7\overline{)721}$ **8.** $3\overline{)601}$

9. $9\overline{)738}$ **10.** $5\overline{)49}$

11. $3.60 \div 2$ **12.** $0.48 \div 4$

Solve each problem.

13. Karen needs 64 beads to make a necklace. The beads come in packages of 5. How many packages should Karen buy?

14. A 7-inch piece of ribbon is needed to make a bow. How many bows can be made from 180 inches of ribbon?

Find the average of each group of numbers.

15. 2, 7, 9

16. 26, 37, 29, 42, 31

Divide.

17. $20\overline{)140}$ **18.** $30\overline{)275}$

19. $48\overline{)96}$ **20.** $51\overline{)115}$

21. $27\overline{)53}$ **22.** $74\overline{)568}$

23. $64\overline{)768}$ **24.** $32\overline{)845}$

Write an equation. Then find the answer.

25. A jackrabbit can run 45 miles per hour. At this rate, how far can he run in 2 hours?

26. A bus traveled 162 miles in 3 hours. What was its average speed in miles per hour?

CHALLENGE

Divisibility, Even Numbers, and Odd Numbers

One number is *divisible* by another number if the
remainder is zero when you divide.

Is 245 divisible by 5?

```
      4 9
5)2 4 5
  2 0
  ‾‾‾
    4 5
    4 5
    ‾‾‾
      0  ← Remainder is zero
```

245 is divisible by 5.

Is 245 divisible by 3?

```
      8 1 R2
3)2 4 5
  2 4
  ‾‾‾
    0 5
      3
    ‾‾‾
      2  ← Remainder is not zero
```

245 is not divisible by 3.

A number that is divisible by 2 is an *even number*.
Some even numbers are 0, 2, 4, 6, 8, 10.

A number that is not divisible by 2 is an *odd number*.
Some odd numbers are 1, 3, 5, 7, 9, 11.

Divide to find out if the first number is divisible by
the second number. Write *yes* or *no*.

1. 72; 4   **2.** 63; 2   **3.** 92; 3   **4.** 75; 5   **5.** 84; 7

6. 416; 3   **7.** 385; 5   **8.** 576; 6   **9.** 395; 9   **10.** 504; 8

Tell whether each number is even or odd.

11. 25   **12.** 86   **13.** 788   **14.** 151   **15.** 283

16. 472   **17.** 734   **18.** 187   **19.** 950   **20.** 429

21. If a number ends in 0, 2, 4, 6, or 8,
is the number even, or is it odd?

22. If a number ends in 1, 3, 5, 7, or 9,
is the number even, or is it odd?

DANNY'S DINER

Andy ate lunch four times at Danny's Diner.
He ordered the same meal for each of the
4 lunches, and he never ordered soup.
Andy spent a total of $7.20 for all the
lunches. What did he order for each lunch?

DANNY'S DINER MENU

Soup.....$0.60   Hamburgers:
Drinks: Jumbo..$1.50
   Milk...$0.50   Regular...0.80
   Juice...0.40   Ice Cream..$0.60

1. What was the average amount of money
   Andy spent for each lunch?

2. What did he order for lunch?

3. If Andy had ordered soup with 2 lunches,
   what would be the total amount spent
   for all the lunches?

4. How much would the daily average be
   for all the lunches if he ordered soup
   with 3 of his lunches?

PROBLEM-
SOLVING
STRATEGIES
• MAKE A
  TABLE
• USE
  LOGICAL
  REASONING
• TRY AND
  CHECK
• SOLVE A
  SIMPLER
  PROBLEM
• USE A
  FORMULA

Cumulative Test, Chapters 1–9

Give the letter for the correct answer.

1. Which number sentence is correct?

   A 45 > 39   **c** 45 > 52
   B 45 < 13   **D** 45 < 43

2. Add.

                A 19
                B 16
  4 + 6 + 8   **c** 18
                D 21

3. Tell whether you *add* or *subtract*. Solve the problem.

A bird laid 7 eggs. Only 5 eggs hatched. How many eggs did not hatch?

  A Add; 12 eggs
  B Add; 2 eggs
  c Subtract; 12 eggs
  D Subtract; 2 eggs

4. Give the standard form for five hundred thirty.

  A 530   **c** 503
  B 305   **D** 350

5. Round 248 to the nearest hundred.

  A 300   **c** 240
  B 200   **D** 250

6. Add.

              A 954
              B 934
   567   **c** 1,034
  + 487   **D** 1,054

7. Add.

          A 64
          B 84
   36   **c** 74
   18   **D** 73
 + 20

8. Subtract.

           A 559
           B 449
   734   **c** 549
 – 285   **D** 459

9. Subtract.

           A 545
           B 365
   800   **c** 355
 – 345   **D** 455

10. Choose the most sensible measure for the weight of a table.

  A 60 pounds   **c** 6 ounces
  B 60 tons   **D** 6,000 pounds

11. Multiply.

          A 11
          B 25
    5   **c** 30
  × 6   **D** 29

12. Multiply.

          A 459
          B 359
   153   **c** 360
 ×   3   **D** 460

13. Multiply.

$$\begin{array}{r} 209 \\ \times \quad 6 \\ \hline \end{array}$$

- **A** 1,704
- **B** 174
- **C** 215
- **D** 1,254

14. What is the perimeter of the rectangle below?

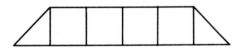

9 in.

2 in.

2 in.

9 in.

- **A** 18 in.
- **C** 11 in.
- **B** 22 in.
- **D** 36 in.

15. Find the area of this figure in square centimeters.

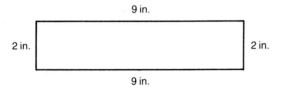

- **A** 4 square centimeters
- **B** 5 square centimeters
- **C** 10 square centimeters
- **D** 6 square centimeters

16. Which of the following is a diameter of the circle?

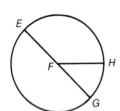

- **A** Segment EF
- **C** Segment EG
- **B** Segment GF
- **D** Segment HF

17. Divide.

$$0 \div 4$$

- **A** 1
- **B** 4
- **C** 2
- **D** 0

18. Divide.

$$9\overline{)72}$$

- **A** 17
- **B** 6
- **C** 8
- **D** 9

19. Divide.

$$6\overline{)58}$$

- **A** 9 R4
- **B** 8 R5
- **C** 10 R2
- **D** 9 R3

20. Tell whether you *add*, *subtract*, *multiply*, or *divide*. Solve the problem.

Sybil made a pattern with pebbles. She put 8 pebbles in each of 32 rows. How many pebbles did she use in all?

- **A** Divide; 4 pebbles
- **B** Add; 40 pebbles
- **C** Multiply; 256 pebbles
- **D** Subtract; 24 pebbles

21. Divide.

$$8\overline{)97}$$

- **A** 9 R3
- **B** 12 R1
- **C** 10 R2
- **D** 11 R3

22. Divide.

$$7\overline{)735}$$

- **A** 150 R2
- **B** 100 R5
- **C** 15
- **D** 105

23. Divide.

$$\$4.20 \div 6$$

- **A** $0.07
- **B** $7.00
- **C** $0.77
- **D** $0.70

24. Find the average of 7, 3, 6, and 8.

- **A** 6
- **B** 24
- **C** 18
- **D** 7

$$\begin{array}{r} 2.92 \\ -\ 0.45 \\ \hline 2.47 \end{array}$$

WEIGHT: 2.92 kg

WEIGHT: 0.45kg

Tenths

A. Turn over your hundred square so that the square is white. It represents 1 one.

Turn over your ten-sticks so that they look like white strips. Cover the square with the strips. How many strips cover the square?

This shows you that 1 can be divided into 10 equal parts. Each part is called a tenth.

You can use place value and write a decimal for one tenth.

ones	tenths
0	1

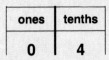

0.1

↑ Decimal point

A fraction with a denominator of 10 shows tenths. You can write this fraction for one tenth.

$$\frac{1}{10}$$ ← Denominator

B. The cyclometer shows that the bicycle has been ridden 0.4 miles. Four tenths is 4 out of 10 equal parts.

ones	tenths
0	4

Decimal   0.4

Fraction $\frac{4}{10}$

C. This figure shows two and three tenths.

ones	tenths
2	3

Decimal   2.3   Fraction $2\frac{3}{10}$

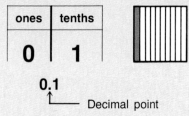

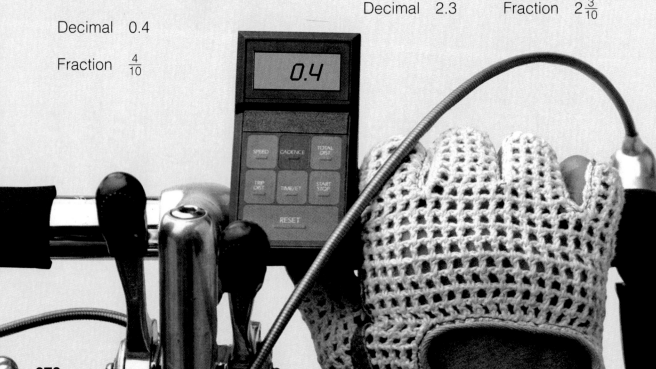

Try Work in groups. Write each number as a decimal and as a fraction. Show the numbers in Exercises c–e with your decimal models.

a.

b.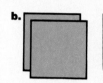

c. seven tenths

d. one and five tenths

e. three and one tenth

Write each number in words.

f. 0.3   **g.** 8.4   **h.** $2\frac{7}{10}$

Practice Write each number as a decimal and as a fraction. Show the numbers in Exercises 5–10 with your decimal models.

1.   **2.**   **3.**   **4.**

5. five tenths   **6.** eight tenths   **7.** zero tenths

8. four and one tenth   **9.** two and nine tenths   **10.** one and six tenths

Write each number in words.

11. 0.7   **12.** 5.2   **13.** 0.5   **14.** 3.9   **15.** 9.1

Apply Each cyclometer shows a decimal. Write the decimal in words.

16. 7.6

17. 2.9

18. 16.4

19. The odometer on a car shows the number of miles a car has been driven. The odometer on Mr. Davidson's car shows nine thousand two hundred thirteen and four tenths. Write the decimal for this number.

20. *Find the facts.* On most odometers, the digit at the right shows tenths. Find an odometer that shows tenths. Write the decimal for the number shown on this odometer.

Hundredths

A. Use a decimal model like this. The large square represents 1 one.

How many small squares make up the large square?

When 1 one is divided into 100 equal parts, each part is 1 hundredth. Show 1 hundredth on your decimal model.

You can use a decimal or a fraction to show one hundredth.

ones	tenths	hundredths
0	**0**	**1**

Decimal   0.01

Fraction $\frac{1}{100}$ A denominator of 100 shows hundredths.

B. After one minute of walking, Andrea's pedometer showed eight hundredths mile. At the end of the walk, it showed two and ten hundredths miles.

Work in groups. Show each of these numbers using your decimal models.

ones	tenths	hundredths
0	0	8

0.08 $\frac{8}{100}$

ones	tenths	hundredths
2	1	0

2.10 $2\frac{10}{100}$

C. Continue to work in groups. Cover 10 hundredths on your decimal model. How many tenths are covered? Explain to someone how you can regroup 10 hundredths. Explain how you can regroup 70 hundredths.

Try Work in groups. Write each number as a decimal and as a fraction.

a.   b.

c. thirty-six hundredths

d. forty-one hundredths

e. sixty-seven and four hundredths

f. Show forty hundredths with decimal models.

g. Write 5.26 in words.

Practice Write each number as a decimal and as a fraction. Show the numbers in Exercises 7–12 with decimal models.

1.   2.   3.

4. 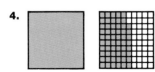   5. 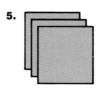   6.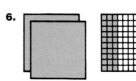

7. seventy-five hundredths

8. two and thirty-one hundredths

9. five hundredths

10. eighty-nine hundredths

11. four and four hundredths

12. twelve hundredths

Write each decimal in words.

13. 0.63   14. 0.02   15. 6.08   16. 0.29   17. 1.40

18. 7.13   19. 5.10   20. 0.18   21. 6.60   22. 0.07

Apply Solve each problem.

23. Rita's pedometer showed that she had walked two and fourteen hundredths miles. Write this number as a decimal and as a fraction.

24. Dan's pedometer showed 5.06. Write this number in words.

25. **CALCULATOR** Display 0.36 on your calculator. Can you do this without pressing the 0 key?

Place Value

A. *Career* Peter Harrison reads water meters for the city water department. When he read this meter, he reported a reading of 124.36 gallons.

hundreds	tens	ones	tenths	hundredths
1	2	4	3	6

124.36

one hundred twenty-four and thirty-six hundredths

B. What does each digit mean in 57.89?

5 7 . 8 9

5 tens — 7 ones — 8 tenths — 9 hundredths

Try Tell what the 6 means in each number.

a. 15.62   **b.** 461.78   **c.** 235.06   **d.** 96.20

e. Which decimals have 5 in the tenths place?

156.75   38.52   70.56

Write each decimal.

f. 2 hundreds 9 tens 7 ones 4 tenths 5 hundredths

g. 6 ones 3 hundredths   **h.** 7 tens 8 tenths

Practice Tell what the 7 means in each number.

1. 21.79   **2.** 6.07   **3.** 257.3   **4.** 76.94   **5.** 702.5

6. 8.67   **7.** 370.25   **8.** 741.9   **9.** 83.71   **10.** 17.43

Which decimals have

11. 3 in the tenths place?

73.05   4.3   146.32

12. 9 in the hundredths place?

1.09   946.27   38.95

13. 2 in the hundredths place?

15.72   236.48   3.92

14. 8 in the tenths place?

4.08   134.87   18.32

Write each decimal.

15. 8 ones 3 tenths 5 hundredths

16. 7 tens 6 ones 4 tenths

17. 4 hundreds 2 hundredths

18. 1 ten 6 tenths 8 hundredths

Apply Peter reported these water meter readings Write each decimal.

19. ninety-five and six hundredths gallons

20. five hundred twelve and thirty-four hundredths gallons

21. Write a decimal point, and the numbers 5, 2, and 6 on cards. How many different ways can the cards be arranged? Work with another student and list all the numbers.

22. Look at the list you wrote for Problem 21. Where is the decimal point when the numbers are greatest? Where is it when they are the least?

CALCULATOR

Pretend that the 4, 5, and 6 keys are broken on your calculator. Find the answers without using the 4, 5, and 6 keys. Write the keys you pressed.

734 + 608   **Press:**   732 `+` 2 `+` 308 `+` 300 `=`

Display: *1342*

1. 247 + 5,038   **2.** 8,407 + 263   **3.** 51 + 97,639

4. 6.1 + 925   **5.** 25.3 − 18.1   **★6.** 28 × 53

Money as Hundredths

Jim has 100 cents, or 1 dollar, to spend.

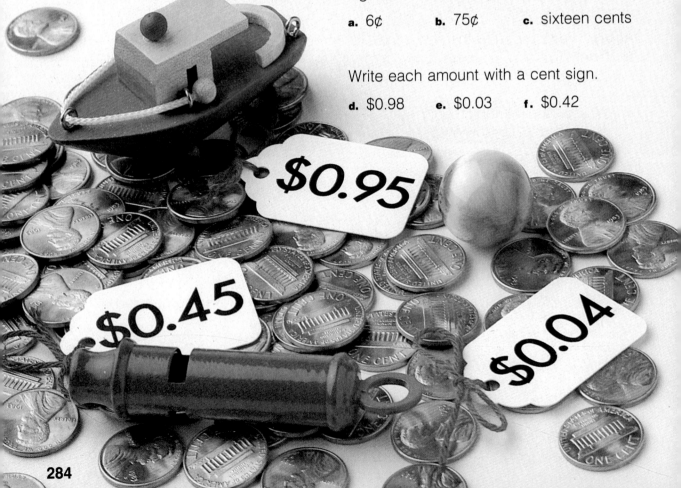

1 hundredth of a dollar	$0.01	**1¢**
5 hundredths of a dollar	$0.05	**5¢**
10 hundredths of a dollar	$0.10	**10¢**
25 hundredths of a dollar	$0.25	**25¢**
50 hundredths of a dollar	$0.50	**50¢**

Try Write each amount with a dollar sign and a decimal point.

a. 6¢   **b.** 75¢   **c.** sixteen cents

Write each amount with a cent sign.

d. $0.98   **e.** $0.03   **f.** $0.42

$0.95

$0.45

$0.04

Practice Write each amount with a dollar sign and a decimal point.

1. 8¢　　　　　　　**2.** 63¢　　　　　　　**3.** 14¢　　　　　　　**4.** 27¢

5. 56 cents　　　　**6.** 2 cents　　　　**7.** 12 cents　　　　**8.** 86 cents

9. forty cents　　**10.** fifteen cents　　**11.** nine cents　　**12.** sixty-two cents

Write each amount with a cent sign.

13. $0.79　　**14.** $0.20　　**15.** $0.07　　**16.** $0.81　　**17.** $0.99

Apply Solve each problem.

18. Jim received twenty-one cents in change. Write this amount with a dollar sign and a decimal point.

19. *Estimation* Carlotta spent $12.37 at the market. Tell whether you think this amount is exact or estimated.

Write each amount with a cent sign.

20. $0.95

21.  $0.04

22.  $0.45

MAINTENANCE

Find each answer.

1. 49 + 26

2. 386 + 129

3. 910 − 165

4. 8,319 − 2,576

5. 45 × 63

6. 304 × 75

7. 5,602 − 3,415

8. 4,612 + 1,835

9. 218 × 39

10. 462 × 47

Comparing Decimals

A. The number line shows some *equal decimals*.

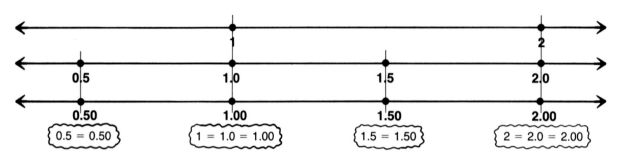

0.5 = 0.50

1 = 1.0 = 1.00

1.5 = 1.50

2 = 2.0 = 2.00

B. Write two number sentences to compare 0.07 and 0.05.

7 hundredths is greater than 5 hundredths.

0.07 > 0.05

5 hundredths is less than 7 hundredths.

0.05 < 0.07

C. Compare the decimals. Use <, >, or =.

26.3 ● 26.4

26.3 ● 26.4   The tens are the same.

26.3 ● 26.4   The ones are the same.

26.3 ● 26.4   3 tenths is less than 4 tenths.

26.3 is less than 26.4.

26.3 < 26.4

Try Write an equal decimal for

a. 0.6 in hundredths.   **b.** 3.90 in tenths.

Write two number sentences to compare the decimals. Use < and >.

c.   **d.**

Compare the decimals. Use <, >, or =.

e. 6.51 ● 6.38   **f.** 2.7 ● 2.70   **g.** 17.52 ● 18.25

Practice Write an equal decimal for

1. 1.3 in hundredths.

2. 0.20 in tenths.

3. 0.5 in hundredths.

4. 28.90 in tenths.

5. 14.7 in hundredths.

6. 10.60 in tenths.

Write two number sentences to compare the decimals. Use < and >.

7.

8.

9.

10.

11.

12.

Compare the decimals. Use <, >, or =.

13. 0.6 ● 0.7

14. 4.3 ● 4.5

15. 0.8 ● 0.80

16. 0.45 ● 0.29

17. 16.30 ● 16.3

18. 9.16 ● 9.19

19. 76.2 ● 74.2

20. 26.53 ● 26.51

21. 0.10 ● 0.01

22. 0.32 ● 0.23

23. 5.07 ● 5.70

24. 99.33 ● 96.36

25. 50.9 ● 50.50

26. 4.86 ● 4.80

27. 12.05 ● 21.50

Apply Solve each problem.

28. Miyoshi weighed 70.5 pounds. Aiko weighed 75.1 pounds. Who weighed less?

29. Lee spent $3.39 for tapes. Paul spent $3.43 for tapes. Who spent less?

30. [CALCULATOR] Find $4.50 + $8.70 on your calculator. What happens when you press [+] and [=]? How is the sum displayed?

31. I was a three-digit number with digits all the same. When multiplied by one of my digits 1,776 I became. What number was I?

Addition: Tenths and Hundredths

A. Meet Detective Daring Dartmouth. Della, of Della's Deli, found that some food was missing. Dartmouth searched and found a clue 0.6 mile from the Deli. He found the suspect 0.8 mile beyond that. How far was the suspect from the Deli?

Work in groups of four.
Use decimal models to find
$0.6 + 0.8$.

Shade 0.6 on a decimal model. Start where you left off and shade 0.8. How many tenths are there in all? How many ones and tenths is this? What is $0.6 + 0.8$?

B. Find $0.75 + 2$.

Discuss how to write 2 to show hundredths. Then use decimal models for hundredths and add.

C. Find $0.4 + 0.28$.

Discuss what decimal model to use. Then find the sum.

Try Work in groups of 4. Use decimal models to add.

a. 0.7
      $+ 0.9$

b. 2.4
      $+ 0.6$

c. $1 + 1.8 + 0.5$

Practice Use decimal models to add.

1. 0.3
       $+ 0.5$

2. 0.8
       $+ 0.7$

3. 1.2
       $+ 0.9$

4. 0.25
       $+ 0.46$

5. $0.83 + 0.17$

6. $2 + 0.6$

7. $0.3 + 0.9 + 0.7$

8. $0.64 + 2.13$

9. $1.7 + 0.64$

10. $0.4 + 0.37 + 1$

11. Find 3 + 1.25 + 0.7.

> Estimate using front-end digits:
> 3 + 1 + 0 = 4

Here is how you can record your work.

		Add the hundredths.	Add the tenths.	Add the ones.
3.00 1.25 + 0.47	Write 3 as 3.00. Line up the decimal points. Write the decimal point in the answer.	1 3.00 1.25 + 0.47 . 2	1 3.00 1.25 + 0.47 .72	1 3.00 1.25 + 0.47 4.72

Discuss how you write a whole number when you add it to a decimal. Why do you think you line up the decimal points? How is adding decimals like adding whole numbers?

Add.

12. 9.06
+ 0.35

13. 12.48
+ 8.04

14. 51.24
+ 8.39

15. 0.07
+ 16.07

16. 45.67
+ 60.88

17. 45.6 + 23.4

18. 7.19 + 6.34

19. 47 + 61.42

20. 25 + 4.8 + 3.5

21. 5 + 7.3 + 0.8

22. 2 + 0.37 + 0.45

23. 6 + 0.40 + 1.92

24. 0.25 + 0.56 + 7

25. 1.30 + 5 + 0.78

Apply *Choosing a Computation Method* Calculator, Paper and Pencil, Mental Math, Estimation
Choose a method to solve each problem. Tell which method you used.

26. Daring Dartmouth discovered that rolls costing $5.23 and rye bread costing $0.97 were missing. About how much did the rolls and rye bread cost together?

27. Della told Dartmouth that 39.4 pounds of food were taken on Monday, 25.8 pounds on Tuesday, 44.6 pounds on Wednesday, and 38.7 pounds on Thursday. How many pounds were taken in all?

Subtraction: Tenths and Hundredths

A. Daring Dartmouth was 3.2 kilometers from the treasure he was hired to find when he learned that Pirate Mean Moe was only 1.7 kilometers from the treasure. How much closer was Moe?

Find 3.2 − 1.7.

Work in groups of 4. Use decimal models to show 3.2. Discuss how you can remove 1.7. What must you do before you can remove 7 tenths? Remove 7 tenths. Then remove 1 one. What is 3.2 − 1.7?

Here is how you can record your work.

> Remember hundredths, tenths, and ones, and you'll understand how it's done.

Line up the decimal points. Write the decimal point in the answer.

$$\begin{array}{r} 3.2 \\ -\ 1.7 \\ \hline \end{array}$$

Rename to show 10 more tenths.

$$\begin{array}{r} \overset{2\ 12}{\cancel{3}.\cancel{2}} \\ -\ 1.7 \\ \hline \end{array}$$

Subtract the tenths.

$$\begin{array}{r} \overset{2\ 12}{\cancel{3}.\cancel{2}} \\ -\ 1.7 \\ \hline .5 \end{array}$$

Subtract the ones.

$$\begin{array}{r} \overset{2\ 12}{\cancel{3}.\cancel{2}} \\ -\ 1.7 \\ \hline 1.5 \end{array}$$

Moe was 1.5 kilometers closer to the treasure.

B. Find 18.37 − 6.

Discuss how you are going to write 6. Then subtract.

C. Find 7 − 2.38.

Discuss how to write 7. Then subtract.

Try Subtract. Use decimal models to subtract in Exercises a and b.

a. 2.5 − 1.2   **b.** 3 − 1.65   **c.** 6.74 − 3   **d.** 8.06 − 3.45

Practice _Choosing a Computation Method_ Calculator, Paper and Pencil, Mental Math
Choose a method to find each answer. Tell which method you used.

1.
$$\begin{array}{r} 9.7 \\ -\ 6.3 \\ \hline \end{array}$$

2.
$$\begin{array}{r} 8.2 \\ -\ 2.8 \\ \hline \end{array}$$

3.
$$\begin{array}{r} 15.8 \\ -\ 2.6 \\ \hline \end{array}$$

4.
$$\begin{array}{r} 2.43 \\ -\ 0.29 \\ \hline \end{array}$$

5.
$$\begin{array}{r} 2.68 \\ -\ 1.87 \\ \hline \end{array}$$

6.
$$\begin{array}{r} 19.21 \\ -\ 4.87 \\ \hline \end{array}$$

7.
$$\begin{array}{r} 37.58 \\ -\ 17.40 \\ \hline \end{array}$$

8.
$$\begin{array}{r} 9.06 \\ -\ 3.57 \\ \hline \end{array}$$

9.
$$\begin{array}{r} 14.15 \\ -\ 10.07 \\ \hline \end{array}$$

10.
$$\begin{array}{r} 80.91 \\ -\ 77.87 \\ \hline \end{array}$$

11. $7.4 - 5.9$ **12.** $13.06 - 9$ **13.** $2 - 0.25$

14. $8.03 - 6.17$ **15.** $67 - 5.81$ **16.** $9.68 - 4$

17. $27 - 13.81$ **18.** $41.33 - 12$ **19.** $50 - 6.01$

Apply   *Choosing a Computation Method*   Calculator, Paper and Pencil, Mental Math, Estimation
Choose a method to solve each problem. Tell which method you used.

20. Moe was now closer to the treasure than Dartmouth. So he changed the road sign to show 24.6 meters instead of 9.8 meters. By how many meters was the road sign changed?

21. To dig for treasure, Dartmouth bought a pick, a hoe, and a shovel. Each of the 3 items cost the same. The total cost was $9.78. What was the cost of each item?

22. Dartmouth's map showed that the buried treasure was 9.2 meters from Parrot Cove. Moe's map showed the treasure was 5.7 meters from Parrot Cove. How much less was the distance shown on Moe's map?

23. Dartmouth dug and found two treasure chests weighing 19.43 kilograms together. One chest weighed 5.08 kilograms. About how many kilograms did the second chest weigh?

24. Dartmouth's compass cost $2.60. His magnifying glass cost $8.40. What was the cost of both items?

25. *Write a problem.* Write a problem that will help Dartmouth find the treasure. Then solve the problem.

Problem Solving Choose the Operation

Marla and Brian attended the 4th Annual Model Airplane Competition. In the longest flight competition, Marla's plane flew a distance of 52.4 meters. Brian's plane flew 38.2 meters. How much farther did Marla's plane fly?

Read

Facts: Marla's plane—52.4 meters
Brian's plane—38.2 meters
Find: How many more meters did Marla's plane fly?

Plan

Use subtraction to compare the two distances. Find 52.4 − 38.2.

Solve

$$\begin{array}{r} 5\,2.4 \\ -\ 3\,8.2 \\ \hline 1\,4.2 \end{array}$$

Estimate:
50 − 40 = 10

Answer

Marla's plane flew 14.2 meters farther.

Look Back

Add your answer to the distance Brian's plane flew, to get the distance Marla's plane flew. 38.2 + 14.2 = 52.4

Try Tell whether you add or subtract. Then find the answer.

a. Simon's plane flew 43.6 meters on the first flight and 25.7 meters on the second flight. How far did his plane fly on both flights?

b. Deborah had two planes. One plane had a wingspan of 2.3 meters. The other plane had a wingspan of 1.9 meters. How much longer is the wingspan on the larger plane?

Apply Tell whether you add or subtract. Then find the answer.

1. To build her model airplane, Ellen spent $5.26 for wood, $2.73 for paint, and $1.40 for glue. How much did she spend in all?

2. John spent $11.00 for materials to build his model airplane. He then sold the plane for $16.85. How much money did he make on the sale?

3. During the first flight, Diane's glider stayed in the air for 20.14 seconds. On the second flight, it stayed up for 18.53 seconds. What was the total time Diane's glider stayed in the air?

4. Adam bought two stickers for his plane. One sticker cost $0.55. The other sticker cost $1.29. How much did the stickers cost together?

5. During two flights, Raul's glider stayed in the air for a total of 68.10 seconds. During the first flight, it stayed up for 29.63 seconds. How long did it stay up during the second flight?

6. Michelle's plane won first place for flying a distance of 63.8 meters. Kelly's plane flew a distance of 5.9 meters less than Michelle's. How many meters did Kelly's plane fly?

7. *Thinking skills* Use + and − to make this number sentence correct.

   4.08 ▨ 5.7 ▨ 3.9 ▨ 6.12 = 12.00

WHAT'S THE POINT?

During a football game last season, your favorite team scored 16 points. *What are the different ways that those 16 points could have been made?*

Points can be scored as follows:

Touchdown	6 points
Point after the touchdown	1 point
Field goal	3 points
Safety	2 points

Get into a group with 3 other students. In your group, try to find all the ways that 16 points could be scored in a football game. Make a list of all the ways that you find.

1. Could the team have scored 3 touchdowns?

2. Could the team have scored 2 touchdowns?

3. Could the team have scored 1 touchdown?

4. Could the team have scored no touchdowns?

Compare your list with those of other groups.

5. Does your list include any ways that other groups do not have?

6. Does any other group have ways listed that your group does not have?

It may be difficult to compare lists because the lists were written using different methods and in different orders. If you combine lists from each of the groups, you will probably get a complete list. However, you may have some ways listed twice and some ways not listed at all.

Therefore, if each group would write its list in the same order, it would be easier to compare lists.

7. Rewrite your list so that all ways with 2 touchdowns are listed first. Then list all ways with 1 touchdown. Finally, list all ways with no touchdowns. Use a chart like the one given below.

Touchdown	Point After	Field Goal	Safety
2	2	0	1
2	1	.	.
.	.	.	.
.	.	.	.

8. Now compare your list with those of other groups and try to complete your list. How many ways can 16 points be scored?

BASIC: GO TO Statements

This program uses GO TO statements. Ordinarily, the computer follows the instructions in a program in order of the line numbers. A GO TO statement sends the computer to the line number given in the statement.

```
10 PRINT "T";
20 GO TO 50
30 PRINT "O"
40 GO TO 70
50 PRINT "W";
60 GO TO 30
70 END
```

The computer is sent to line 50, and then goes to line 60.

This is printed.

T W O

For the program above, tell which line the computer will go to after completing

1. line 10.

2. line 20.

3. line 30.

4. line 40.

Tell what would be printed for each program.

5.
```
10 PRINT "0.3"
20 GO TO 40
30 PRINT "0.7"
40 END
```

6.
```
10 PRINT "0.02";
20 GO TO 70
30 PRINT "0.08"
40 GO TO 90
50 PRINT "0.06";
60 GO TO 30
70 PRINT "0.04";
80 GO TO 50
90 END
```

Too Much Information

On Tuesday, Danny walked 1.2 miles to the grocery store and spent $12.48 for food. Later that day, he walked 2.3 miles to the sports store and spent $2.75 for a baseball. How much money did Danny spend on Tuesday?

Read	Facts: 1.2 miles to grocery store, $12.48 for food 2.3 miles to sports store, $2.75 for baseball Find: Amount of money spent

Plan   To find the total amount of money spent, add the prices of the things Danny bought. The distances he walked are *extra information*. Do not use 1.2 miles and 2.3 miles.

Solve
$$\begin{array}{r} 1\,2.4\,8 \\ +\quad 2.7\,5 \\ \hline 1\,5.2\,3 \end{array}$$

Estimate:
$12 + $3 = $15

Answer   Danny spent $15.23 on Tuesday.

Look Back   The estimate of $15 is close to $15.23. The answer is reasonable.

296

Try Solve each problem.

a. Marco's store is open 12.5 hours each day. Sam's store is open 8 hours per day for 7 days each week. How many hours per week is Sam's store open?

b. Marco bought 18 feet of shelving and 6 gallons of paint. He used 12.5 feet of shelving. How many feet of shelving did he have left over?

Apply Solve each problem.

1. Julie bought 5.8 pounds of apples, 3.6 pounds of cheese, and 4.7 pounds of grapes. How many pounds of fruit did Julie buy?

2. Jack bought 2 pounds of onions at Sam's Foods for $0.29 per pound. At Marco's Food Store, onions cost $0.35 per pound. How much did Jack spend on onions?

3. Larry charges $12.80 to repair a radio, $34.50 to repair a T.V., $10.75 to repair a clock, and $9.35 to repair a toaster. How much did Sharon pay Larry to repair her toaster, radio, and clock?

4. Each day, Ramon walks 3.5 miles to work at Marco's Food Store. Last week, he worked 37.5 hours. This week, he worked 39 hours. How many hours did he work in those two weeks?

5. Nan sells roses for $0.98 each and a bunch of daisies for $1.56. Beth bought 14 roses. How much did the roses cost Beth?

⋆6. Beth gave Nan $20 for the roses. How much change did she receive?

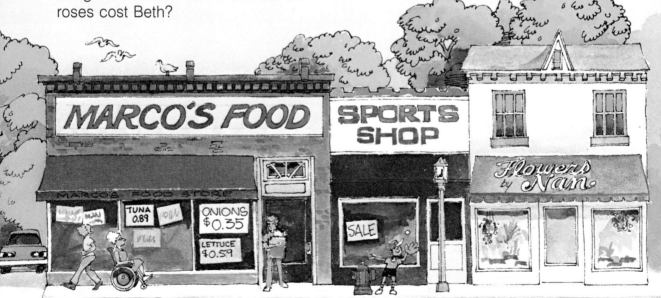

Chapter 10 Test

Write each decimal.

1.   **2.**

3. Four tenths

4. Seven and two tenths

5. Nine hundredths

6. One and forty-six hundredths

Tell what the 5 means in each number.

7. 31.05   **8.** 45.2   **9.** 6.58

Write each amount with a dollar sign and a decimal point.

10. 98¢   **11.** 16¢

12. Two cents   **13.** Sixty cents

Compare the decimals.
Use <, >, or =.

14. 2.73 ● 2.75

15. 28.30 ● 28.3

16. 99.4 ● 99.1

17. 5.7 ● 5.70

Add.

18. 5.2
      + 6.8

19. 47.07
      + 4.19

20. 3.6 + 5.8   **21.** 0.3 + 12 + 6.5

Subtract.

22. 43.2
      − 9.7

23. 4.04
      − 1.05

24. 72.6
      − 62.8

25. 58 − 17.31   **26.** 9.46 − 4

Tell whether you add or subtract. Then find the answer.

27. Mark spent $3.98 for tapes and $5.25 for a record. How much did he spend in all?

28. Jill ran 6 miles. Anita ran 3.7 miles. How many more miles did Jill run than Anita?

Solve each problem.

29. At Ben's hardware store, Al bought 3 gallons of paint, 8.5 feet of wide shelving, and 3.5 feet of narrow shelving. How many feet of shelving did he buy?

30. A rake weighs 1.8 pounds. A hose weighs 3.5 pounds. A sprinkler weighs 0.76 pounds. What is the difference in weight between a rake and a hose?

CHALLENGE

Rounding Decimals

Round these numbers to the nearest one.

7.32   7.9   7.54

In each number, the ones digit is 7, so
each number is between 7 and 8.

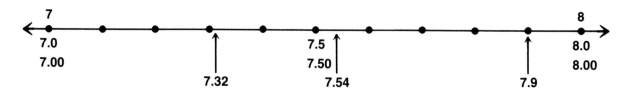

To round to the nearest one, first look at the
tenths digit.

7.32	**7.9**	**7.54**
The tenths digit is less than 5.	The tenths digit is greater than 5.	The tenths digit is 5.
The ones digit stays the same.	Add 1 to the ones digit.	Add 1 to the ones digit.
7	**8**	**8**

Round each decimal to the nearest one.

1. 6.1   **2.** 6.12   **3.** 6.56   **4.** 6.07   **5.** 6.8

6. 12.05   **7.** 12.5   **8.** 12.3   **9.** 12.39   **10.** 12.72

11. 9.6   **12.** 9.45   **13.** 9.83   **14.** 9.1   **15.** 9.5

16. 30.08   **17.** 30.8   **18.** 30.25   **19.** 30.17   **20.** 30.71

SATURDAY SHOPPING

One Saturday, Mark went shopping with some friends. He rode the bus to the shopping center for 75¢.

Mark bought a miniature race car for $1.12 and 3 puzzle books for 75¢ each.

He found a quarter outside one of the stores.

The boys ate lunch while they were out. Mark bought a sandwich for $1.25 and milk for 40¢.

Mark's friend, Denny, talked him into selling his pen. Denny paid Mark $1.50 for it.

After lunch, Mark rode back home on the bus. The ride cost 75¢.

After Mark got home, he counted his money. He had $4.43 left. How much money did he start out with?

Fractions

$$\frac{3}{4} + \frac{1}{4} = \frac{4}{4}$$

Fractions: Part of a Whole

At Perry's Pizza Place you can buy rectangular shaped pizzas
that measure 30 inches by 20 inches. Perry cuts the pizzas into
equal parts.

A. Work in groups of 4. Each of you cut out a piece of grid paper
that is 30 units by 20 units to represent one of Perry's Pizzas.
Fold it into equal parts. Open the paper and shade some of the
parts. What fraction of your pizza is shaded?

Look at this pizza model.
You can write a fraction to show that
5 of the 8 equal parts are shaded.

$\frac{5}{8}$ ← The number of shaded parts is written in the numerator.
   ← The number of equal parts is written in the denominator.

Now look at your pizza model. How many equal parts are there?
How many parts are shaded? What fraction of your pizza is shaded?

Look at your pizza model. What would you write if you shaded
all the equal parts?

B. Fold another grid paper into ten equal parts. Shade two
of the tenths. Write two tenths in two ways.

Save your models to use with other lessons in this chapter.

Practice   Work in groups of 4. Each of you will need 9 sheets of grid
paper that are 30 units long and 20 units wide. Each sheet of grid
paper represents a whole pizza. For each exercise, you are to fold a
new sheet of grid paper into the number of equal pieces indicated.

As you work each exercise, discuss how each person folded his or her
paper. Did all of you fold your papers the same way? Could they be
folded differently and still show equal parts? How can you be sure
that the parts are equal? For each pizza, color one of the equal
parts. Then label the shaded part.

1. 2 equal pieces   **2.** 3 equal pieces   **3.** 4 equal pieces

4. 5 equal pieces   **5.** 6 equal pieces   **6.** 8 equal pieces

7. 9 equal pieces   **8.** 10 equal pieces   **9.** 12 equal pieces

Save your models to use with other lessons in this chapter.

10. Use a circular model to draw a circle. Cut it out. Fold the circle in half. Shade one half of it.

11. Draw a triangle with two equal sides. Fold the triangle in half. Shade one half of it.

12. Compare your models for Exercises 1, 10, and 11. What did you do to each model? Did the shaded parts look the same? Explain.

Write a fraction and a decimal to show how much of the figure is shaded.

13.

14.

15.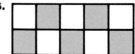

16.

Give the number of equal parts and tell what they are called.

17.

18.

Does the figure show

19. sixths?

20. fourths?

Apply Work in groups of 4. Each of you will need several sheets of grid paper that measure 30 units by 20 units.

21. How many different ways can your group fold the grid paper to show four equal parts? Each person in the group should try to fold his or her sheet of grid paper to show fourths in a way that is different from the others. Count the unit squares in one fourth. Compare your count with others in your group. Are they the same? Why or why not?

22. Repeat Problem 21 with each of you folding a paper into ten equal parts.

23. Using the information from Problems 21 and 22, make a generalization about the number of unit squares you could expect to find in each part if you fold one of the grid papers in 12 equal parts. Then check your generalization by folding the grid paper and counting the unit squares in one twelfth.

Fractions: Part of a Set

A. Work with another student. You will each need your "pizzas" from Perry's that you made for the previous lesson.

Place all of the pizzas in front of you. Turn the pizzas over so that there are no shaded parts showing. On some of the pizzas write the word *cheese*. On the rest of them, write the word *sausage*. Take some of each kind of pizza. What fraction of the pizzas that you took are cheese?

▨ ⟵ Number of cheese pizzas
▨ ⟵ Number of pizzas

Take some more of each kind of pizza. Put them with the other pizzas you took. What fraction of these pizzas are cheese?

Take all of the pizzas that both of you have. What fraction of them are cheese?

How is what you have just done different from what you did with the pizzas in the previous lesson?

B. Give an example that shows a fraction of a whole.
Give an example that shows a fraction of a set.
Show and explain your examples to another student.

Try What fraction of the
a. fruit are apples?

b. letters are *A*s?

For Exercises c–g, tell if the items are a fraction of a set or a fraction of a whole.

c. A piece of cake   **d.** Six apples out of twelve apples   **e.** Half a fish

f. Two cans from a six-pack of apple juice   **g.** Three red squares on a checkerboard

h. Perry had an order for 5 pepperoni pizzas. What fraction of the pizzas were pepperoni pizzas? sausage pizzas?

304

Practice   What fraction of the

1. books are closed?

2. balls are basketballs?

3. crayons are blue?

4. coins are pennies?

For Exercises 5–10, tell if the fraction is a fraction of a set or a fraction of a whole.

5. One fourth of an apple

6. Two thirds of the records in a collection

7. Four fifths of the pennies in a bank

8. Four tenths of a lawn mowed

9. Three fourths of the checkers in a game

10. Half of a carton of milk

Apply   Solve each problem.

11. What fraction of the letters in the word CALIFORNIA are As?

12. What two letters are each $\frac{4}{11}$ of the letters in the word MISSISSIPPI?

13. Perry cut a pizza into ten equal slices. Nine of them were eaten. What fraction of the pizza was not eaten? Write your answers as a fraction and as a decimal.

14. One night Perry delivered a total of 15 cheese pizzas, 34 sausage pizzas, 48 pepperoni pizzas, and 23 other kinds. What fraction of the delivered pizzas were cheese?

15. Take a survey in your class. Have everyone name his or her favorite kind of pizza. Picture this information and write the fractions that are used.

Comparing Fractions

A. In a timed run, Gwen ran $\frac{7}{8}$ mile and Leon ran $\frac{5}{8}$ mile.
Who ran farther, Gwen or Leon?

Compare $\frac{5}{8}$ and $\frac{7}{8}$.

Look at the number line above. $\frac{7}{8}$ is to the right of $\frac{5}{8}$, so $\frac{7}{8}$ is greater than $\frac{5}{8}$.

Now look at the fractions. The denominators are the same.
To compare fractions with the same denominator, you only
need to compare their numerators.

$$\frac{5}{8} < \frac{7}{8}$$ 5 is less than 7.
$\frac{5}{8}$ is less than $\frac{7}{8}$.

$$\frac{7}{8} > \frac{5}{8}$$ 7 is greater than 5.
$\frac{7}{8}$ is greater than $\frac{5}{8}$.

Gwen ran the farthest.

B. Using number lines, you can compare fractions that have
different denominators. You can also compare a fraction with 1.

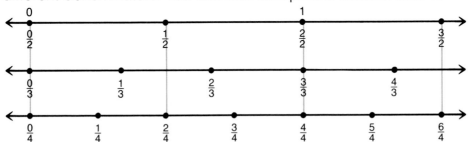

To compare	Locate	Think	Write
$\frac{1}{3}$ and $\frac{1}{2}$	$\frac{1}{3}$ is to the left of $\frac{1}{2}$.	$\frac{1}{3}$ is less than $\frac{1}{2}$.	$\frac{1}{3} < \frac{1}{2}$
$\frac{3}{4}$ and $\frac{2}{3}$	$\frac{3}{4}$ is to the right of $\frac{2}{3}$.	$\frac{3}{4}$ is greater than $\frac{2}{3}$.	$\frac{3}{4} > \frac{2}{3}$
$\frac{1}{2}$ and $\frac{2}{4}$	$\frac{1}{2}$ lines up with $\frac{2}{4}$.	$\frac{1}{2}$ is equal to $\frac{2}{4}$.	$\frac{1}{2} = \frac{2}{4}$
$\frac{5}{4}$ and 1	$\frac{5}{4}$ is to the right of 1.	$\frac{5}{4}$ is greater than 1.	$\frac{5}{4} > 1$

Try Compare the fractions. Use < or >.

a. $\frac{3}{4}$ ● $\frac{5}{4}$
b. $\frac{1}{2}$ ● $\frac{0}{2}$
c. $\frac{7}{12}$ ● $\frac{10}{12}$
d. $\frac{8}{7}$ ● $\frac{10}{7}$

Use the number lines in Example B to compare the fractions. Use <, >, or =.

e. $\frac{2}{3}$ ● $\frac{1}{2}$
f. $\frac{6}{4}$ ● $\frac{3}{2}$
g. 1 ● $\frac{4}{3}$
h. $\frac{3}{4}$ ● $\frac{4}{3}$
i. $\frac{3}{3}$ ● $\frac{4}{4}$

Practice Compare the fractions. Use < or >.

1. $\frac{5}{6}$ ● $\frac{3}{6}$
2. $\frac{1}{4}$ ● $\frac{0}{4}$
3. $\frac{2}{6}$ ● $\frac{4}{6}$
4. $\frac{7}{10}$ ● $\frac{9}{10}$
5. $\frac{5}{2}$ ● $\frac{2}{2}$

6. $\frac{0}{8}$ ● $\frac{5}{8}$
7. $\frac{6}{3}$ ● $\frac{3}{3}$
8. $\frac{4}{4}$ ● $\frac{3}{4}$
9. $\frac{11}{12}$ ● $\frac{14}{12}$
10. $\frac{6}{5}$ ● $\frac{3}{5}$

Use the number lines to compare the fractions. Use <, >, or =.

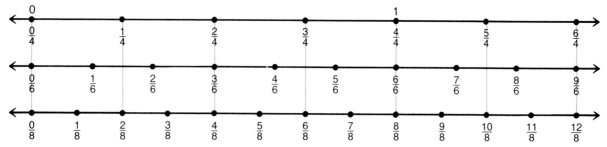

11. $\frac{0}{4}$ ● $\frac{1}{8}$
12. $\frac{3}{6}$ ● $\frac{2}{4}$
13. $\frac{7}{8}$ ● $\frac{3}{4}$
14. $\frac{2}{6}$ ● $\frac{3}{4}$
15. $\frac{0}{4}$ ● $\frac{0}{8}$

16. $\frac{1}{4}$ ● $\frac{1}{6}$
17. $\frac{7}{6}$ ● $\frac{8}{8}$
18. $\frac{4}{8}$ ● $\frac{3}{6}$
19. $\frac{5}{8}$ ● $\frac{5}{4}$
20. $\frac{4}{4}$ ● $\frac{6}{6}$

Compare each fraction with 1. Use <, >, or =.

21. $\frac{5}{4}$ ● 1
22. $\frac{3}{3}$ ● 1
23. $\frac{2}{5}$ ● 1
24. $\frac{0}{6}$ ● 1
25. $\frac{7}{2}$ ● 1

Work with another student. Study your answers to Exercises 21–25.
By just looking at a fraction, how can you tell if it is

26. less than 1?
27. equal to 1?
28. greater than 1?
29. equal to 0?

Apply Solve each problem.

30. Todd ran $\frac{2}{3}$ mile and Jason ran $\frac{3}{4}$ mile. Who ran the farthest?

★31. Alice ran $\frac{3}{4}$ mile. Martha ran $\frac{5}{6}$ mile. Sandy ran $\frac{5}{8}$ mile. Who ran the farthest? Who was second?

Mixed Numbers

A. Mr. and Mrs. Sengle walk $1\frac{3}{4}$ miles every day. How many fourths is this?

Work with two other students. Use your punchout fraction models and take turns working steps 1–4.

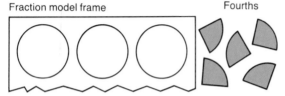

Fraction model frame   Fourths

Step 1 Fill in one circle of the fraction model frame with 4 of the fourths.

Step 2 Fill in another circle with 3 of the fourths.

$1\frac{3}{4}$ circles are filled in the frame.

Step 3 Remove the frame and separate the parts that formed $1\frac{3}{4}$ circles.

Step 4 Count the number of fourths. How many fourths were used in all?

Write a number sentence that relates Steps 1 and 2 with Steps 3 and 4.

B. Numbers like $1\frac{3}{4}$ are *mixed numbers.*

A mixed number is made up of a whole number and a fraction.

$$1\frac{3}{4}$$

whole number —⤴ ⤴— fraction

one and three fourths

C.

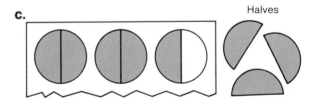

Halves

In this model, two and one half circles are filled in. The circles are divided into halves. Five halves are used in all.

$$2\frac{1}{2} = \frac{5}{2}$$

Try

a. Use your punchout fraction models to show three and one fourth as a mixed number. Write the mixed number.

b. Write a fraction and a
mixed number for the model.

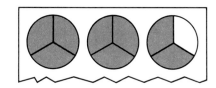

Practice Work in groups for all of the exercises. Write each mixed number.
Show the mixed numbers in Exercises 1–3 in your punchout fraction models.

1. Three and five tenths

2. two and five sixths

3. one and three fifths

4. four and one fourth

5. seven and one half

6. six and five eighths

7. For Exercises 4–6, *sketch* figures other than
circles to show the mixed numbers.

Write a fraction and a mixed number for each picture.

8.

9.

10.

11.

Complete the number lines using mixed numbers or whole numbers.

12.

$$\frac{0}{4} \quad \frac{1}{4} \quad \frac{2}{4} \quad \frac{3}{4} \quad \frac{4}{4} \quad \frac{5}{4} \quad \frac{6}{4} \quad \frac{7}{4} \quad \frac{8}{4}$$

13.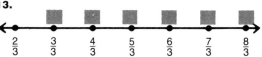

$$\frac{2}{3} \quad \frac{3}{3} \quad \frac{4}{3} \quad \frac{5}{3} \quad \frac{6}{3} \quad \frac{7}{3} \quad \frac{8}{3}$$

CALCULATOR

You can use your calculator to show a fraction as a decimal.

Show $\frac{7}{20}$ as a decimal.   **Press:**   7 $\div$ 20   **Display:** *0.35*

Show each fraction as a decimal.

1. $\frac{3}{4}$ **2.** $\frac{5}{8}$ **3.** $\frac{17}{85}$ **4.** $\frac{41}{50}$ **5.** $\frac{13}{20}$ **6.** $\frac{52}{65}$ **7.** $\frac{60}{96}$ **8.** $\frac{24}{32}$ **9.** $\frac{39}{60}$

What do you notice about the fractions in

10. 1 and 8?   **11.** 2 and 7?   **12.** 5 and 9?

Fractions in Measurement

A. When an inch is separated into two equal parts, you can measure in half inches.

This calculator is $3\frac{1}{2}$ inches long.

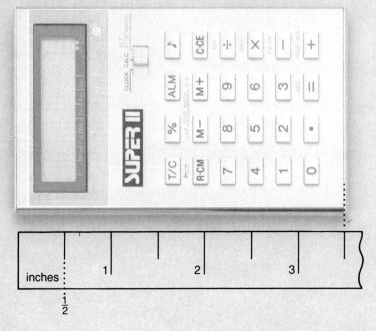

B. When an inch is separated into four equal parts, you can measure in fourth inches.

The width of this battery is $\frac{1}{4}$ inch.

Notice that the same mark on this ruler shows either $\frac{2}{4}$ inch or $\frac{1}{2}$ inch.

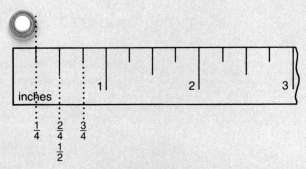

Try Give the length of each segment.

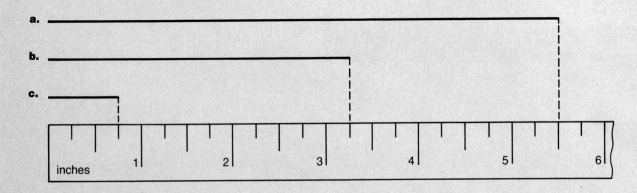

Practice   Give the length of each segment or object.

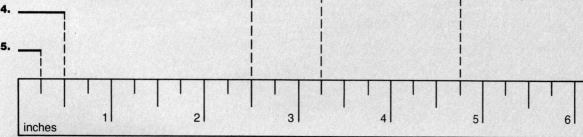

1.

2.

3.

4.

5.

inches   1   2   3   4   5   6

6.

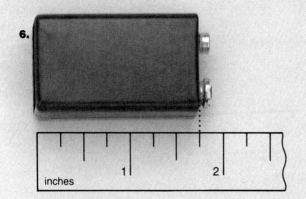

inches   1   2

7.

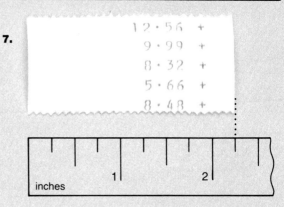

12·56 +
9·99 +
8·32 +
5·66 +
8·48 +

inches   1   2

Use a ruler to measure each segment.

8. _____

9. _____

10. _____

11. _____

Apply

12. Use a ruler to measure the width of the battery in Exercise 6.

13. Use a ruler to draw a segment that is $2\frac{3}{4}$ inches long.

14. **CALCULATOR** Is $\frac{125}{16}$ inches more or less than 8 inches? Check your answer by changing the fraction to a decimal. **Press:** 125 ÷ 16 =.

Finding Fractional Parts

Dawn and Nancy Redbird played a game. Each player had 20 game marbles. Dawn lost $\frac{1}{4}$ of her game marbles to Nancy. How many game marbles did she lose to Nancy?

Find $\frac{1}{4}$ of 20.

You can put the 20 marbles into 4 equal groups.

Each group is $\frac{1}{4}$ of 20.

There are 5 marbles in each group.

$\frac{1}{4}$ of 20 is 5.

You can also divide 20 by 4 to find $\frac{1}{4}$ of 20.

$20 \div 4 = 5$

Dawn lost 5 game marbles to Nancy.

Try Find each answer.

a. $\frac{1}{3}$ of 9

$9 \div 3 = $ ▦

b. $\frac{1}{5}$ of 20

$20 \div 5 = $ ▦

Practice Find each answer.

1. ● ● ● ●
   ● ● ● ●

   $\frac{1}{2}$ of 8

2. ● ● ●
   ● ● ●

   $\frac{1}{3}$ of 6

3. $\frac{1}{4}$ of 4

4. $\frac{1}{5}$ of 10

5. $\frac{1}{2}$ of 16

6. $\frac{1}{3}$ of 33

7. $\frac{1}{4}$ of 28

8. $\frac{1}{5}$ of 25

9. $\frac{1}{6}$ of 42

10. $\frac{1}{8}$ of 72

11. $\frac{1}{2}$ of 38

12. $\frac{1}{4}$ of 56

13. $\frac{1}{5}$ of 60

14. $\frac{1}{3}$ of 93

Apply Solve each problem.

15. Mr. Garcia bought 24 poster boards. He used $\frac{1}{2}$ of them to make games. How many poster boards did he use to make games?

16. A game board had 50 squares. $\frac{1}{10}$ of them were blue. How many squares were blue?

Add or subtract.

1. 46 + 84

2. 52 + 79

3. 74 − 57

4. 63 − 36

5. 356 + 473

6. 265 + 383

7. 456 − 228

8. 368 − 175

9. 1.58 + 2.83

10. 3.74 + 1.48

11. 2.83 − 1.58

12. 7.61 − 3.05

13. 21.4 + 68.6

14. 43.7 + 36.3

15. 68.6 − 57.8

16. 35.1 − 19.2

17. 33.78 + 26.81

18. 50.26 + 18.97

19. 53.21 − 24.06

20. 75.39 − 4.57

Problem Solving Use a Picture

Read

There are 15 students in Mr. Reed's class. If $\frac{2}{3}$ of them ride the school bus each day, how many of the students ride the school bus each day?

Plan

In $\frac{2}{3}$, the 3 means 3 equal groups, and the 2 means 2 of the groups. To draw a picture showing the 15 students separated into 3 equal groups, place an *x* in each group until you have made 15 *x*s. Then count the number of *x*s in 2 groups.

Solve

Group 1	Group 2	Group 3
X	X	X
X	X	X
X	X	X
X	X	X
X	X	X

There are 10 *x*s in 2 groups.

Answer

There are 10 students from Mr. Reed's class who ride the school bus each day.

Look Back

$\frac{2}{3}$ of the students would be twice as many as $\frac{1}{3}$.

$\frac{1}{3}$ of 15 = 5   ($15 \div 3 = 5$)

$2 \times 5 = 10$

The answer is reasonable.

Try Solve each problem. Draw a picture to help you.

a. A reading class has 20 students. If $\frac{7}{10}$ of the class went to the library, how many students went to the library?

b. If $\frac{3}{4}$ of the 28 members of Shelley's swimming team are girls, how many members are girls?

Apply Solve each problem. Draw a picture to help you.

1. The art class has 36 projects for the art fair. If $\frac{5}{6}$ of the projects are drawings, how many drawings are there?

2. Mitch's science class had 15 chicken eggs. If $\frac{3}{5}$ of the eggs hatched, how many eggs hatched?

3. If $\frac{5}{8}$ of the 40 students in gym class have new shoes, how many students have new shoes?

4. Ken has finished working $\frac{2}{5}$ of 25 math problems. How many problems has he finished?

5. Miss Rako's class has 30 students. If $\frac{3}{10}$ of the students are absent, how many students are absent?

6. The Wilson School football team won $\frac{4}{5}$ of its 20 games. How many games did they win?

7. Maria used $\frac{7}{8}$ of her 8 crayons to color a picture. How many crayons did she use?

8. After class, $\frac{9}{10}$ of the 50 students had boarded the bus. How many students had boarded the bus?

★9. If $\frac{3}{8}$ of the 32 desks in Mr. Clark's room are new, how many desks are old?

10. **CALCULATOR** Find $\frac{3}{4}$ of 20 with paper and pencil. Then use a calculator. **Press:** 20 $\boxed{\div}$ 4 $\boxed{\times}$ 3 $\boxed{=}$. Is the answer the same using either method?

Addition: Same Denominator

For this lesson you need to work with another student.
Both of you will use your punchout fraction models.

A. At the community art fair, Charles Wilson used
$\frac{1}{5}$ of his booth to display puppets and $\frac{3}{5}$ of his
booth for wood carvings. What fraction of
the booth was used for displaying puppets
or wood carvings?

Find $\frac{1}{5} + \frac{3}{5}$.

Use your punchout models to add.

Fraction model frame

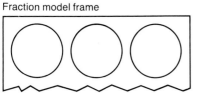

Fifths

Place one of the fifths in a circle.
Place three more of the fifths in the same circle.
How many fifths are in the circle?

What fraction of the booth was used for displaying
puppets or wood carvings?

B. Find $\frac{7}{8} + \frac{3}{8}$.

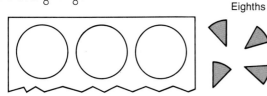

Eighths

Discuss how to find the sum. Use your models to
find the sum. Is it less than 1, greater than 1,
or equal to 1? How do you know?

Try   Use your punchout fraction models to add.

a. $\frac{1}{3} + \frac{1}{3}$ **b.** $\frac{3}{4} + \frac{2}{4}$ **c.** $\frac{7}{10} + \frac{3}{10}$

316

Practice Use your punchout fraction models to add.

1. $\frac{1}{4} + \frac{1}{4}$ 2. $\frac{2}{6} + \frac{1}{6}$ 3. $\frac{3}{5} + \frac{2}{5}$

4. $\frac{1}{7} + \frac{5}{7}$ 5. $\frac{0}{2} + \frac{1}{2}$ 6. $\frac{4}{8} + \frac{3}{8}$

7. $\frac{4}{9} + \frac{5}{9}$ 8. $\frac{2}{5} + \frac{4}{5}$ 9. $\frac{4}{2} + \frac{3}{2}$

10. $\frac{3}{6} + \frac{2}{6}$ 11. $\frac{2}{8} + \frac{3}{8}$ 12. $\frac{3}{6} + \frac{5}{6}$

13. $\frac{2}{3} + \frac{0}{3}$ 14. $\frac{2}{5} + \frac{2}{5}$ 15. $\frac{5}{4} + \frac{4}{4}$

16. $\frac{1}{3} + \frac{2}{3}$ 17. $\frac{3}{10} + \frac{4}{10}$ 18. $\frac{3}{4} + \frac{2}{4}$

19. $\frac{6}{10} + \frac{7}{10}$ 20. $\frac{4}{12} + \frac{7}{12}$ 21. $\frac{5}{8} + \frac{9}{8}$

Apply Solve each problem.

22. At a county fair, $\frac{1}{10}$ of the art was jewelry and $\frac{2}{10}$ was woodcraft. What fraction of the art was jewelry or woodcraft?

23. One eighth of the 40 artists at the fair received prize ribbons. How many of the artists received ribbons?

24. At the art guild fair, $\frac{4}{6}$ of the art is paintings done with oils or water colors and $\frac{2}{6}$ of the art is sketches done with pastels, charcoal, pen or pencil. What fraction of the fair is paintings or sketches?

25. _Find the facts._ What fraction of the students in your class are boys? What fraction are girls? What is the sum of these two fractions?

BASIC: INPUT Statements

Some fractions can be written as whole numbers. The program below changes these fractions to whole numbers.

INPUT statements are used to enter the numerator (N) and the denominator (D).

```
10 PRINT "ENTER NUMERATOR"
20 INPUT N
30 PRINT "ENTER DENOMINATOR"
40 INPUT D
50 PRINT N/D
60 END
```

When the fraction is $\frac{6}{2}$, 6 is typed for N, 2 is typed for D, and this is printed.

```
ENTER NUMERATOR
?6
ENTER DENOMINATOR
?2
3
```

What number should be typed for N for each of the following?

1. $\frac{4}{2}$ 2. $\frac{9}{3}$ 3. $\frac{10}{2}$

What number should be typed for D for each of the following?

4. $\frac{8}{4}$ 5. $\frac{12}{3}$ 6. $\frac{15}{3}$

For the program above, tell what would be printed using the fraction given in

7. Exercise 1. 8. Exercise 2.

9. Exercise 3. 10. Exercise 4.

11. Exercise 5. 12. Exercise 6.

Equal Fractions

Work in groups of 4.

A. Mrs. Renner had two mini-loaves of French bread. She cut them into pieces for her family. Each person got the same amount of the bread with none left over. Mr. and Mrs. Renner each had 1 piece, Amanda had 2 equal pieces, and David had 4 equal pieces. How can this be?

Discuss this situation in your group. Be prepared to show how this can be and explain your thinking to the class.

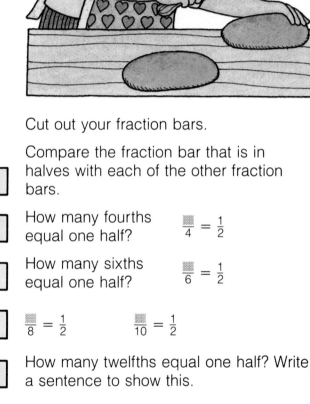

B. You can use fraction bars to show that two fractions are equal.

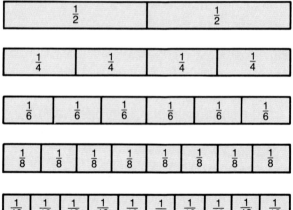

Cut out your fraction bars.

Compare the fraction bar that is in halves with each of the other fraction bars.

How many fourths equal one half? $\frac{\blacksquare}{4} = \frac{1}{2}$

How many sixths equal one half? $\frac{\blacksquare}{6} = \frac{1}{2}$

$\frac{\blacksquare}{8} = \frac{1}{2}$ $\frac{\blacksquare}{10} = \frac{1}{2}$

How many twelfths equal one half? Write a sentence to show this.

C. Use fraction bars to find some fractions equal to $\frac{1}{3}$.

Try   Use fraction bars to find the equal fractions.

a. $\frac{1}{5} = \frac{\blacksquare}{10}$ **b.** $\frac{\blacksquare}{4} = \frac{4}{8}$ **c.** $\frac{\blacksquare}{9} = \frac{3}{3}$ **d.** $\frac{2}{3} = \frac{\blacksquare}{6}$

e. Make a fraction bar that is marked in twelfths to go with your set of fraction bars. One sixth and two twelfths are equal fractions. How does this help you make the fraction bar?

f. Use equal fractions to explain how each of the Renners got the same amount of French bread.

Practice   Use fraction bars to find the equal fractions.

1. $\frac{3}{4} = \frac{\blacksquare}{8}$

2. $\frac{2}{3} = \frac{\blacksquare}{6}$

3. $\frac{4}{5} = \frac{\blacksquare}{10}$

4. $\frac{3}{9} = \frac{\blacksquare}{3}$

5. $\frac{\blacksquare}{9} = \frac{2}{3}$

6. $\frac{\blacksquare}{4} = \frac{8}{8}$

7. $\frac{\blacksquare}{5} = \frac{4}{10}$

8. $\frac{\blacksquare}{8} = \frac{1}{4}$

9. $\frac{1}{3} = \frac{\blacksquare}{6}$

10. $\frac{8}{10} = \frac{\blacksquare}{5}$

11. $\frac{\blacksquare}{3} = \frac{8}{12}$

12. $\frac{\blacksquare}{6} = \frac{10}{12}$

You can use fraction bars to draw number lines. Draw a line.
Mark off a segment that is the length of the bar marked in halves.
Locate and label the points that correspond to $\frac{0}{2}$, $\frac{1}{2}$, and $\frac{2}{2}$.

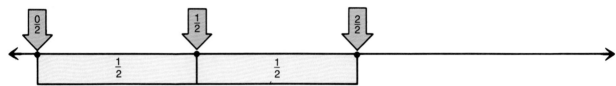

Draw another number line below the first. Mark off a segment that
is the length of the bar marked in thirds. Locate and label the
points that correspond to $\frac{0}{3}$, $\frac{1}{3}$, $\frac{2}{3}$, and $\frac{3}{3}$. Be sure the points that
correspond to 0 line up directly beneath one another. You might use
a colored pencil to draw a vertical line through the points.

Continue drawing number lines, one below another.
Mark the lines successively in fourths, fifths, sixths, eighths,
ninths, tenths, and twelfths.

How can you use number lines to find equal fractions?

Use your number lines to find the equal fractions.

13. $\frac{3}{4} = \frac{\blacksquare}{12}$

14. $\frac{2}{3} = \frac{\blacksquare}{12}$

15. $\frac{\blacksquare}{10} = \frac{3}{5}$

16. $\frac{\blacksquare}{6} = \frac{4}{8}$

17. $\frac{3}{9} = \frac{\blacksquare}{12}$

18. $\frac{1}{4} = \frac{\blacksquare}{8}$

19. $\frac{\blacksquare}{16} = \frac{1}{2}$

20. $\frac{\blacksquare}{20} = \frac{4}{10}$

Apply   Solve each problem.

21. Explain why seven days in February
(not a leap year) can be called one
fourth of a month.

22. David said he slept for 8 hours.
Amanda said, "You slept a third of a
day." Explain.

CALCULATOR   You can compare fractions by changing
them to decimals. **Press:** numerator $\boxed{\div}$ denominator $\boxed{=}$.

23. Which is smaller $\frac{45}{75}$ or $\frac{95}{125}$?

24. Which is larger $\frac{128}{160}$ or $\frac{112}{128}$?

Addition: Different Denominators

A. At an art fair, $\frac{2}{8}$ of the space was used to display wax or wood carvings and $\frac{3}{8}$ of the space was used to display paintings. What fraction of the space was used for carvings or paintings?

Find $\frac{2}{8} + \frac{3}{8}$.

On pages 316–317 you used models to add fractions. Use your punchout fraction models to add the fractions.

$\frac{5}{8}$ of the tables were used for wax or wood carvings.

Here is a way to record your work.

$$\frac{2}{8} + \frac{3}{8} = \frac{5}{8}$$

The denominators of the two fractions are the same. What do you notice about the denominator of the sum? What can you say about the numerator of the sum? Write a rule for adding fractions with the same denominator.

B. To find the sum of two fractions with different denominators, it is helpful to use number lines.

Use number lines to find $\frac{3}{4} + \frac{1}{2}$.

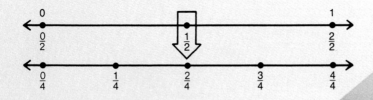

$$\frac{3}{4} = \frac{3}{4}$$

$$+\frac{1}{2} = \frac{2}{4} \qquad \scriptstyle \frac{1}{2} = \frac{2}{4}$$

$$\overline{\frac{5}{4}}$$

Add the numerators.
Use the same denominator.

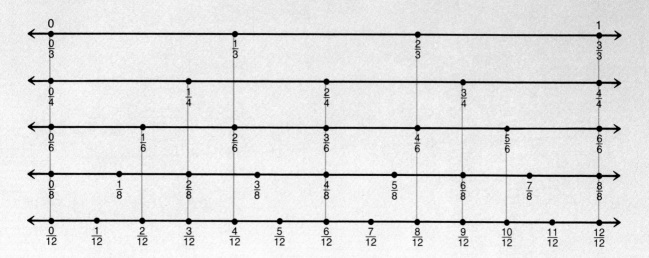

Try Add. Use the number lines above.

a. $\frac{1}{4} + \frac{5}{8}$

b. $\frac{5}{6} + \frac{3}{6}$

c. $\begin{array}{r} \frac{1}{3} \\ + \frac{5}{12} \\ \hline \end{array}$

d. $\begin{array}{r} \frac{3}{4} \\ + \frac{1}{12} \\ \hline \end{array}$

Practice Add. Use the number lines above.

1. $\frac{2}{3} + \frac{1}{6}$

2. $\frac{2}{3} + \frac{1}{12}$

3. $\frac{3}{4} + \frac{3}{8}$

4. $\frac{5}{6} + \frac{1}{3}$

5. $\frac{1}{8} + \frac{7}{8}$

6. $\frac{5}{6} + \frac{5}{12}$

7. $\frac{2}{4} + \frac{5}{6}$

8. $\frac{7}{12} + \frac{1}{4}$

9. $\begin{array}{r} \frac{1}{4} \\ + \frac{6}{8} \\ \hline \end{array}$

10. $\begin{array}{r} \frac{1}{3} \\ + \frac{7}{12} \\ \hline \end{array}$

11. $\begin{array}{r} \frac{2}{6} \\ + \frac{2}{6} \\ \hline \end{array}$

12. $\begin{array}{r} \frac{6}{8} \\ + \frac{7}{12} \\ \hline \end{array}$

13. $\begin{array}{r} \frac{2}{6} \\ + \frac{7}{12} \\ \hline \end{array}$

★14. $\begin{array}{r} \frac{1}{4} \\ + \frac{1}{6} \\ \hline \end{array}$

Apply Work these problems with 3 other students.

15. Celia used $\frac{3}{4}$ yard of blue ribbon and $\frac{5}{8}$ yard of red ribbon. Explain how you can tell that she used less than 2 yards of ribbon without adding.

16. How many yards of ribbon did Celia actually use?

17. *Thinking skills* A fraction that is less than 1 is a proper fraction. What is true about the sum of any 2 proper fractions? About the sum of any 3 proper fractions?

18. *Write a problem.* Write a problem about fractional parts of the day. Have someone solve the problem.

Subtraction: Same Denominator

Toby and Remlar live on the planet Zyp. Toby lives $\frac{4}{5}$ zeptron from school. Remlar lives $\frac{3}{5}$ zeptron from school. How much farther from school does Toby live?

Find $\frac{4}{5} - \frac{3}{5}$.

Use your punchout fraction models.

Frame   Fifths

Place four fifths in a circle.
Take three of the fifths away.
What fraction of the whole is left?

How much farther from school does Toby live?

Here is a way to record your work.

$$\frac{4}{5} - \frac{3}{5} = \frac{1}{5}$$

What do you notice about the denominator of the difference? What can you say about the numerator of the difference?

Write a rule for subtracting fractions that have the same denominator.

Here is another way to write $\frac{4}{5} - \frac{3}{5}$.

$$\begin{array}{r} \frac{4}{5} \\ - \frac{3}{5} \\ \hline \frac{1}{5} \end{array}$$

Try Subtract. Use your punchout fraction models.

a. $\dfrac{7}{6} - \dfrac{2}{6}$

b. $\dfrac{9}{12} - \dfrac{4}{12}$

c. $\dfrac{5}{5} - \dfrac{4}{5}$

d. $\dfrac{14}{8} - \dfrac{7}{8}$

Practice Subtract. Use your punchout fraction models if you need them.

1. $\dfrac{4}{8} - \dfrac{3}{8}$

2. $\dfrac{5}{7} - \dfrac{2}{7}$

3. $\dfrac{2}{3} - \dfrac{2}{3}$

4. $\dfrac{3}{5} - \dfrac{1}{5}$

5. $\dfrac{1}{2} - \dfrac{0}{2}$

6. $\dfrac{2}{4} - \dfrac{1}{4}$

7. $\dfrac{5}{3} - \dfrac{2}{3}$

8. $\dfrac{4}{5} - \dfrac{1}{5}$

9. $\dfrac{3}{9} - \dfrac{2}{9}$

10. $\dfrac{9}{6} - \dfrac{4}{6}$

11. $\dfrac{6}{8} - \dfrac{3}{8}$

12. $\dfrac{10}{12} - \dfrac{6}{12}$

13. $\dfrac{3}{4} - \dfrac{3}{4}$

14. $\dfrac{2}{3} - \dfrac{0}{3}$

15. $\dfrac{9}{10} - \dfrac{3}{10}$

16. $\dfrac{8}{6} - \dfrac{5}{6}$

Apply Solve each problem.

17. The distance from Toby's house to the spaceport is $\dfrac{3}{4}$ zeptron. Toby has walked $\dfrac{1}{4}$ zeptron towards the spaceport. How much farther does he have to walk?

18. At the spaceport, $\dfrac{1}{6}$ of the 36 spaceships were being refueled. How many spaceships were being refueled?

19. Toby used $\dfrac{2}{3}$ of the fuel in his power pack. He had $\dfrac{2}{3}$ vallow left. How many vallows of fuel did he start with?

20. In Toby's class, $\dfrac{5}{8}$ of the students have spaceships. What fraction of the students do not have spaceships?

Subtraction: Different Denominators

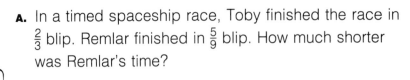

A. In a timed spaceship race, Toby finished the race in $\frac{2}{3}$ blip. Remlar finished in $\frac{5}{9}$ blip. How much shorter was Remlar's time?

Find $\frac{2}{3} - \frac{5}{9}$.

The greater denominator is 9. Using the number lines, you can see that $\frac{2}{3}$ can be written with a denominator of 9.

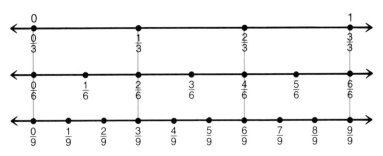

$$\frac{2}{3} - \frac{5}{9} \quad \left(\frac{2}{3} = \frac{6}{9} \right)$$

$$\downarrow \qquad \downarrow$$

$$\frac{6}{9} - \frac{5}{9} = \frac{6 - 5}{9} = \frac{1}{9}$$

Subtract the numerators.
Use the same denominator.

Remlar's time was $\frac{1}{9}$ blip shorter than Toby's.

B. Find $\frac{5}{6} - \frac{1}{3}$.

$$\frac{5}{6} = \frac{5}{6}$$

The greater denominator is 6.
Look at the number lines.

$$-\frac{1}{3} = \frac{2}{6}$$

$\frac{1}{3}$ can be written with a denominator of 6.

$$\frac{3}{6} \quad \left(5 - 2 = 3 \right)$$

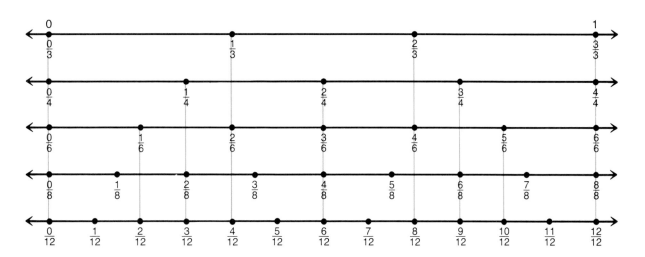

Try Subtract. Use the number lines above.

a. $\frac{4}{6} - \frac{7}{12}$

b. $\frac{5}{6} - \frac{2}{4}$

c. $\begin{array}{r} \frac{2}{3} \\ -\frac{5}{12} \\ \hline \end{array}$

d. $\begin{array}{r} \frac{1}{3} \\ -\frac{1}{6} \\ \hline \end{array}$

Practice Subtract. Use the number lines above.

1. $\frac{1}{3} - \frac{2}{12}$

2. $\frac{3}{4} - \frac{3}{12}$

3. $\frac{5}{8} - \frac{1}{4}$

4. $\frac{8}{12} - \frac{2}{3}$

5. $\frac{3}{4} - \frac{1}{8}$

6. $\frac{1}{4} - \frac{1}{8}$

7. $\frac{5}{6} - \frac{2}{3}$

8. $\frac{3}{6} - \frac{1}{8}$

9. $\frac{1}{8} - \frac{0}{4}$

10. $\frac{4}{4} - \frac{4}{12}$

11. $\begin{array}{r} \frac{7}{12} \\ -\frac{2}{6} \\ \hline \end{array}$

12. $\begin{array}{r} \frac{10}{12} \\ -\frac{1}{4} \\ \hline \end{array}$

13. $\begin{array}{r} \frac{4}{6} \\ -\frac{2}{3} \\ \hline \end{array}$

14. $\begin{array}{r} \frac{11}{12} \\ -\frac{5}{6} \\ \hline \end{array}$

15. $\begin{array}{r} \frac{6}{8} \\ -\frac{5}{12} \\ \hline \end{array}$

★16. $\begin{array}{r} \frac{1}{3} \\ -\frac{1}{4} \\ \hline \end{array}$

Apply Solve each problem.

17. The power pack on a spaceship has been recharging for $\frac{1}{4}$ blip. It takes $\frac{11}{12}$ blip to fully recharge. How much longer does the power pack need to recharge? Use the number lines above.

18. Remlar's spaceship flew 348 zeptrons in 12 blips. How many zeptrons per blip did it travel?

19. **CALCULATOR** A calculator's display will *overflow* when an answer has too many digits for the display.
Press: 99 999 999 $\boxed{+}$ 9 $\boxed{=}$. How does your calculator show an overflow?

PLAY BALL

Work in a group with three other students. Choose two of the following problems to solve in your group. Discuss with your group why each problem was chosen, how you plan to solve each problem, why your method will work, and if the same method can be used for both of the problems. When the problems have been solved, present your work to the rest of the class. If another group has solved the same problem, compare the problem-solving methods used.

1. A baseball team has six pitchers and two catchers. How many different pairs of pitchers and catchers can be chosen?

2. Someday Scott is going to be a great basketball player. On Saturday, he made 20 baskets. Each day he makes 10 more baskets than the day before. On which day did he make 100 baskets?

3. Fred gave one half of his baseball cards to Sally. Sally gave Jeff half of the cards that she got from Fred. Jeff gave Allen half of the cards that he got from Sally. Allen got 6 cards. How many cards did Fred originally have?

4. The Panther team has a set of twins, Patty and Penny. The Hawks also have a set of twins, Harry and Hank. The girls are 2 years older than the boys. The sum of all their ages is 40. How old are the girls? How old are the boys?

5. Tickets for a football game cost $2.75. If you give the ticket seller $3.00, how many different combinations of coins might you get in change?

6. There are 10 players entered in a ping-pong tournament. If losing one game eliminates a player from the tournament, how many games have to be played to determine the winner?

7. A basketball team scored 65 points in one game. They made twice as many field goals as free throws. Each field goal scores 2 points, and each free throw scores 1 point. How many field goals and free throws did they make?

8. The Hornets, Bulldogs, Falcons, and Raiders played in a local soccer tournament. There were 2 games played in the first round. In the second round the winners of the first-round games played for the championship. The Hornets defeated the Bulldogs in the first round. The Falcons played the Hornets in the second round. The Hornets won 1 game and lost 1 game in the tournament. Which team won the championship?

9. Mrs. Cohen was selling tickets for a hockey game. The tickets were 50 cents each. Mrs. Cohen had dimes, quarters, dollar bills, and a ten-dollar bill, but she could not give change to the first person who wanted to buy a ticket. What did this person give to Mrs. Cohen?

Chapter 11 Test

Write a fraction to show how much of the figure is shaded.

1.

2.

3. What fraction of the letters are *B*s?

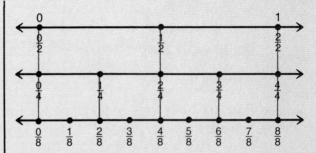

Write each mixed number.

4. six and three fourths

5. ten and two thirds

Give the length of this segment.

6.

Find each answer.

7. $\frac{1}{2}$ of 18

8. $\frac{1}{6}$ of 42

Add.

9. $\frac{2}{7} + \frac{4}{7}$

10. $\frac{2}{3} + \frac{1}{3}$

Subtract.

11. $\frac{5}{6} - \frac{1}{6}$

12. $\frac{4}{5} - \frac{3}{5}$

Compare the fractions. Use <, >, or =. Use the number lines above for Exercise 14.

13. $\frac{1}{3}$ ● $\frac{2}{3}$

14. $\frac{3}{4}$ ● $\frac{5}{8}$

Use the number lines above to help you find equal fractions.

15. $\frac{1}{2} = \frac{▧}{8}$

16. $\frac{3}{4} = \frac{▧}{8}$

Add. Use the number lines above.

17. $\frac{5}{8} + \frac{1}{4}$

18. $\frac{3}{4} + \frac{1}{2}$

Subtract. Use the number lines above.

19. $\frac{3}{4} - \frac{1}{8}$

20. $\frac{7}{8} - \frac{1}{2}$

Solve each problem. Draw a picture to help you.

21. A store had 24 kites. $\frac{3}{8}$ of the kites were sold. How many kites were sold?

22. Patty had 12 stickers. She used $\frac{2}{3}$ of them. How many stickers did she use?

CHALLENGE

Probability: Listing Possible Outcomes

Ms. Lee will choose a boy and a girl as ushers for the school play. The boy chosen will be Bob or Guy. The girl chosen will be Amy, May, or Joy.

This tree diagram shows the possible outcomes of Ms. Lee's choices.

Boy	Girl	Possible Outcomes
	Amy	Bob - Amy
Bob	May	Bob - May
	Joy	Bob - Joy
	Amy	Guy - Amy
Guy	May	Guy - May
	Joy	Guy - Joy

Find each answer.

1. What fraction of times might Bob be an usher? $\frac{\text{Choice of Bob} \quad ▨}{\text{Possible outcomes} \quad 6}$

2. What fraction of times might May be an usher? $\frac{\text{Choice of May} \quad ▨}{\text{Possible outcomes} \quad ▨}$

3. Draw a tree diagram to list the possible outcomes if the choices are among Amy, May, or Joy, and Bob, Guy, or Sam.

4. What fraction of times might Sam be an usher? $\frac{\text{Choice of Sam} \quad ▨}{\text{Possible outcomes} \quad 9}$

5. What fraction of times might Joy be an usher? $\frac{\text{Choice of Joy} \quad ▨}{\text{Possible outcomes} \quad ▨}$

6. Draw a tree diagram to list the possible outcomes if the choices are among Rita, Beth, or Dee, and Ken, Van, Ted, or Bill.

7. What fraction of times might Van be an usher?

8. What fraction of times might Dee be an usher?

9. In Exercises 3 and 6, is it true that the number of girls times the number of boys equals the number of possible outcomes?

329

GASOLINE GAUGE

The gasoline tank in Mr. Barrio's car holds 16 gallons. The pictures show the gasoline gauge at various times during a trip. *How many gallons of gasoline did Mr. Barrio use on this trip?*

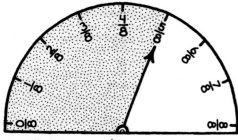

7:00 **A.M.** (Start of trip)

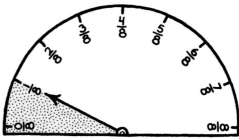

12:00 noon (Before adding gas)

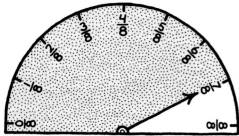

12:00 noon (After adding gas)

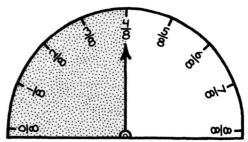

3:30 **P.M.** (End of trip)

Use the gasoline gauges for Problems 1 and 2.

1. What fraction of a tank of gasoline did Mr. Barrio use from 7:00 A.M. to 12:00 noon?

2. What fraction of a tank did he use from 12 noon to 3:30 P.M.?

3. What fraction of a tank of gasoline did Mr. Barrio use on the entire trip?

4. How many gallons of gasoline did Mr. Barrio use? Draw a picture to help you.

YOU CAN DO IT. HERE'S THE KEY. USE PROBLEM-SOLVING STRATEGIES.

PROBLEM-SOLVING STRATEGIES
- DRAW A PICTURE
- MAKE A TABLE
- FIND A PATTERN
- USE PHYSICAL MODELS
- USE LOGICAL REASONING
- WORK BACKWARD
- LIST ALL POSSIBILITIES
- TRY AND CHECK
- MAKE A GRAPH

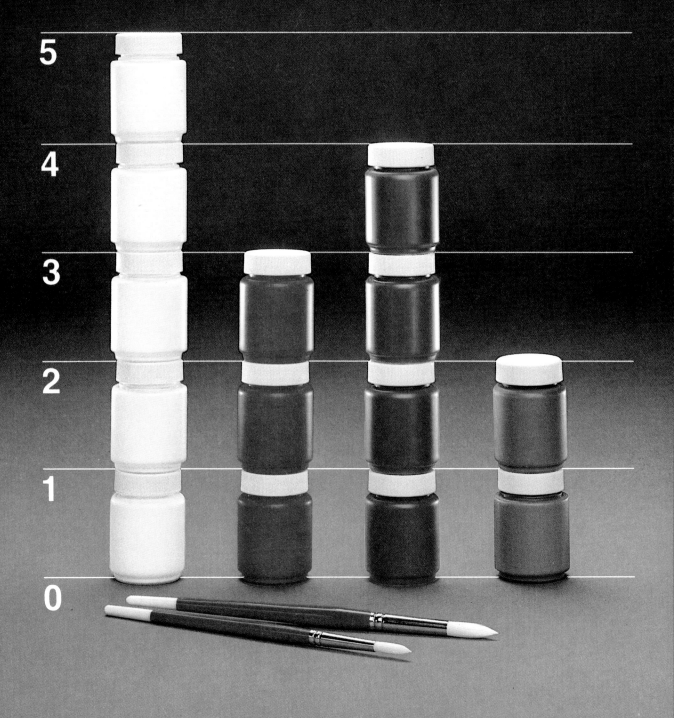

Pictographs

This *pictograph* shows the number of students at Harris School who belong to each club.

Number of Students in Clubs

Reading Club	🧍🧍🧍🧍🧍🧍
Computer Club	🧍🧍🧍🧍🧍
Bicycle Club	🧍🧍🧍🧍🧍🧍🧍🧍🧍🧍🧍
Swimming Club	🧍
Art Club	🧍🧍

Each 🧍 means 3 students.

A. How many students at Harris School belong to the computer club?

There are 5 🧍 after *computer club*; each 🧍 means 3 students.

15 students belong to the computer club.

B. Which club at Harris School has the fewest students?

There is only 1 🧍 after *swimming club*. The other clubs have more.

The swimming club has the fewest students.

Try Use the pictograph above to find each answer.

a. How many students belong to the reading club?

b. How many students belong to the art club?

c. Does the computer club or the reading club have more members?

d. Which club has the greatest number of students?

Practice The pictograph below shows the number of students in each grade who are members of the bicycle club at Harris School.

Number of Bicycle Club Members

First Grade	🚲
Second Grade	🚲 🚲
Third Grade	🚲 🚲
Fourth Grade	🚲 🚲 🚲 🚲 🚲
Fifth Grade	🚲 🚲 🚲 🚲 🚲 🚲
Sixth Grade	🚲 🚲

Each 🚲 means 2 students.

How many members of the bicycle club are in

1. first grade?
2. second grade?
3. third grade?

4. fourth grade?
5. fifth grade?
6. sixth grade?

7. Which grade has the most students who belong to the bicycle club?

8. Which grade has the fewest students who belong to the bicycle club?

9. Does first grade or fifth grade have more students who belong to the bicycle club?

10. Which three grades have the same number of students who belong to the bicycle club?

Apply Solve each problem.
Use data from a pictograph. Use the pictograph above for Problems 11–13.

11. How many fewer members of the bicycle club are from second grade than from fifth grade?

12. How many more members of the bicycle club are from fifth grade than from sixth grade?

13. All of the bicycle-club members who are in the fourth, fifth, and sixth grades went on a field trip. How many members went?

14. *Thinking skills* Lorie is making a pictograph. She will use one circle to mean 2 students. How many circles will she use to show 4 students? 1 student? 15 students?

15. Using each of the digits 0 through 9 once, write two 5-digit numbers that have a sum of 90,000.

Bar Graphs

This *bar graph* shows the number of students in each grade at Fisher School who took a 6-week computer course.

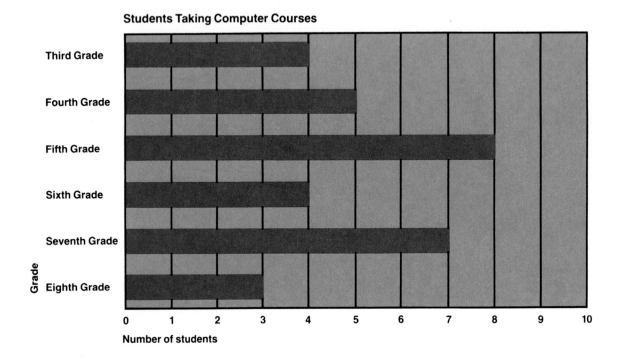

Students Taking Computer Courses

Number of students

Grade

A. How many third-grade students took the computer course?

The bar for third grade stops at 4.

4 third-grade students took the course.

B. Which grade had the greatest number of students who took the computer course?

The bar for fifth grade stops at 8. For each of the other grades, the bar stops before 8.

Fifth grade had the most students who took the computer course.

Try Use the bar graph above to find each answer.

a. How many seventh-grade students at Fisher School took the computer course?

b. How many sixth-grade students at Fisher School took the 6-week computer course?

c. Which grade has the least number of students who took the computer course?

d. Does third grade or fourth grade have more students who took the computer course?

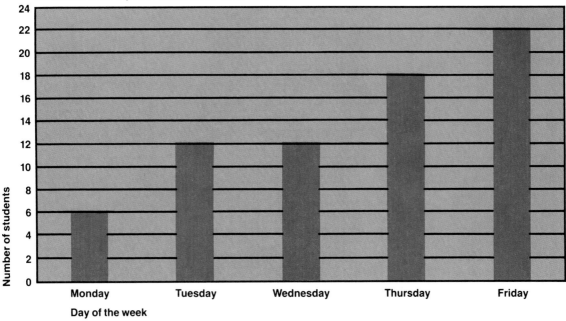

Students in Computer Class at Johnson School

Number of students (y-axis: 0, 2, 4, 6, 8, 10, 12, 14, 16, 18, 20, 22, 24)

Monday, Tuesday, Wednesday, Thursday, Friday

Day of the week

Practice Use the bar graph above to find each answer.

How many students at Johnson School have computer class on

1. Monday?   **2.** Tuesday?   **3.** Wednesday?   **4.** Thursday?   **5.** Friday?

On which day does the class have

6. the greatest number of students?   **7.** the least number of students?

8. more than 20 students?   **9.** fewer than 10 students?

Apply *Use data from a bar graph.* Solve each problem.

10. How many more students have computer class on Friday than on Monday? Use the bar graph above.

11. What is the total number of students who have computer class? Use the bar graph above.

12. *Find the facts.* Work with 3 other students. Select a topic for which you can make a bar graph. Have your teacher approve your topic. Then collect the data and make a bar graph. Discuss your graph with the class.

13. **CALCULATOR** A computer club bought 18 program packages. Each package cost $34.95. What was the total cost?

Broken-Line Graphs

The computer-club teacher at Frost School kept a record of the number of computer programs written by students during the school year. This *broken-line graph* shows the results.

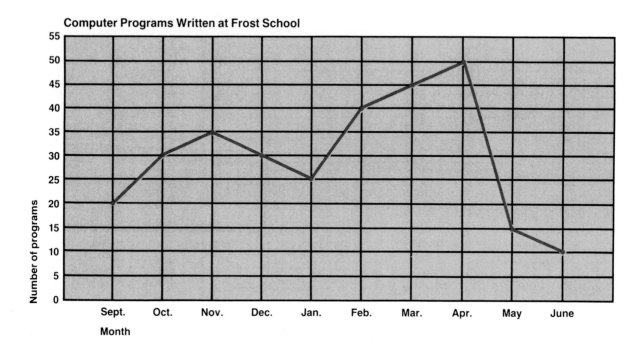

Computer Programs Written at Frost School

A. How many computer programs were written in May?

The months are named at the bottom of the grid. Find *May* and follow the grid line straight up to the graph point. Then follow the grid line straight to the left where the number of programs is shown as 15.

15 programs were written in May.

B. In which month were 25 computer programs written?

The numbers of programs are given on the left side of the grid. Find 25 programs and follow the grid line straight to the right where there is a graph point. Then follow the grid line straight down to the bottom where the month is shown as January.

January is the month in which 25 programs were written.

Try Use the broken-line graph above to find each answer.

a. How many programs were written in September?

b. In which month were 45 programs written?

336

Practice Use the broken-line graph on page 336 to find each answer.

How many programs were written in

1. October?
2. November?

3. February?
4. March?

In which month were

5. 10 programs written?
6. 35 programs written?

In which month was

7. the greatest number of programs written?

8. the least number of programs written?

9. the same number of programs written as in October?

Were there any months in which

10. exactly 5 programs were written?

11. exactly 40 programs were written?

Apply *Use data from a broken-line graph.* Solve each problem.

What was the total number of programs written in

12. September through December?

*13. the entire school year?

*14. What was the average number of programs written in a month?

15. **CALCULATOR** Find the average number of lines in the programs given in the computer sections of this book.

BASIC: LET Statements

A LET statement puts a number into a storage location until it is used later in the program.

In line 10 of this program, 5 is put into a storage location labeled *N*. In line 20, 5 is taken out of the storage location and used for *N*.

This is printed.

```
10 LET N=5
20 PRINT N*9
30 END
```

45

Tell what would be printed for each program.

1.
```
10 LET N=7
20 PRINT 42/N
30 END
```

2.
```
10 LET X=7
20 LET Y=9
30 PRINT X+Y
40 END
```

3. 8 is typed for X.
```
10 INPUT X
20 LET Y=20
30 PRINT Y-X
40 END
```

4. 12 is typed for N.
```
10 INPUT N
20 LET P=7
30 PRINT N+P;
40 PRINT N-P
50 END
```

The Coin Experiment

When two coins are tossed, one of three possibilities will occur. Both coins will fall heads; both coins will fall tails; or one coin will fall heads and the other coin will fall tails.

1. If you toss two coins 1,000 times, how many times would you expect both coins to fall heads? Write your prediction and give reasons for your guess.

Perform an experiment with two coins. Work with a partner. One of you tosses the two coins while the other records the result.

Tossing two coins 1,000 times would take a long time. So, consider the results of tossing two coins 100 times. You might divide the work between you and your partner. But you could also just toss two coins 10 times and combine your results with the results of 9 other pairs of students. Then all of you will have the results for 100 tosses.

2. Toss two coins 10 times and record the results. How many times did both coins fall heads?

Now combine your results with those of 9 other pairs of students. This will give you the results for 100 tosses.

3. How many times out of 100 tosses did both coins fall heads?

4. Would you get the same answer to Problem 3 if you used the results of a different group of 10 pairs of students?

Perform the experiment again. This time make a list of the results for each of the 10 pairs of students.

5. Find out which pair of students has the least number of tosses in which both coins fall heads. What is the least number of times that both coins fall heads?

6. What is the greatest number of times that a pair of students tossed two coins that both fell heads?

7. What is the average of the least number and greatest number of tosses in which both coins fall heads?

8. About what fraction of all the tosses is the average number of tosses in which both coins fall heads?

9. Look at your answer to Problem 3. What fraction of the tosses did both coins fall heads?

10. If you were to perform the experiment again, about how many times out of 100 tosses would you expect both coins to fall heads? tails? one head and one tail?

11. Use the average to predict the number of times that both coins will fall heads when the coins are tossed 1,000 times. Explain how you used the average to get your prediction.

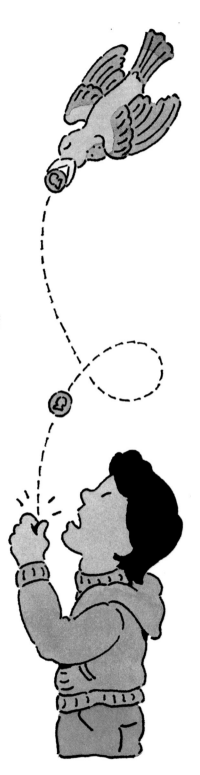

Points on a Grid

A *number pair* like (3, 5) tells where a point is located on a grid.

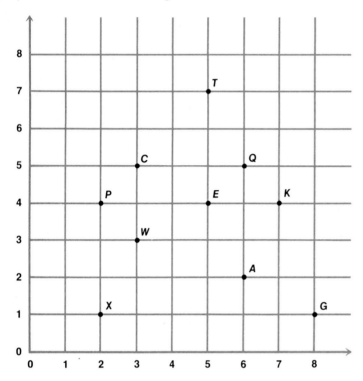

A. Which letter names the point located by the number pair (3, 5)?

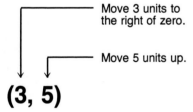

Move 3 units to the right of zero.

Move 5 units up.

(3, 5)

The letter *C* names the point located by the number pair (3, 5).

B. What number pair gives the location of the point named by the letter *T*?

T is 5 units to the right of 0, and 7 units up from 0.

The number pair (5, 7) gives the location of point *T*.

Try

a. Which letter names the point located by the number pair (7, 4)?

b. What number pair gives the location of the point named by the letter *P*?

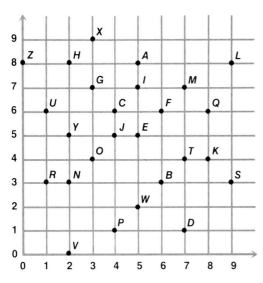

Practice Write the letter that names the point located by each number pair.

1. (7, 4)   **2.** (9, 3)   **3.** (2, 8)

4. (1, 6)   **5.** (5, 5)   **6.** (3, 9)

Write the number pair that gives the location named by each letter.

7. M   **8.** R   **9.** D

10. W   **11.** Q   **12.** B

Apply To find each answer, write the letter that names each point.

13. What state is high in the middle?

(3, 4), (2, 8), (5, 7), (3, 4)

14. Spell hard water in 3 letters.

(5, 7), (4, 6), (5, 5)

15. _Write a problem._ Write a question that can be answered with a word. Then write the ordered pairs for each letter in the word.

Rick's teacher gave 7 extra points if a student finished a project in 4 days or less. The teacher also subtracted 5 points if a student took 8 days or more to finish a project. The broken-line graph below shows Rick's work for one month.

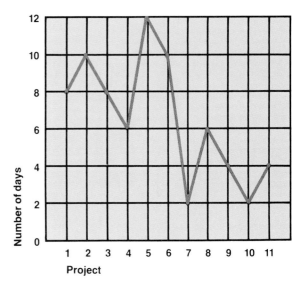

1. How many times did Rick receive extra points?

2. How many extra points did he receive?

3. How many times did Rick lose points?

4. How many points did he lose?

5. How many total points did Rick gain or lose?

Graphing Number Pairs

Alicia made a picture of the constellation, *Big Dipper*, by graphing number pairs.

She numbered a grid, and used the following number pairs. She located the points, labeled them, and connected them in order.

A (1, 3)

C (3, 5)
Connect *A* and *C*.

E (5, 5)
Connect *C* and *E*.

G (7, 5)
Connect *E* and *G*.

I (8, 4)
Connect *G* and *I*.

K (11, 5)
Connect *I* and *K*.

M (11, 7)
Connect *K* and *M*.

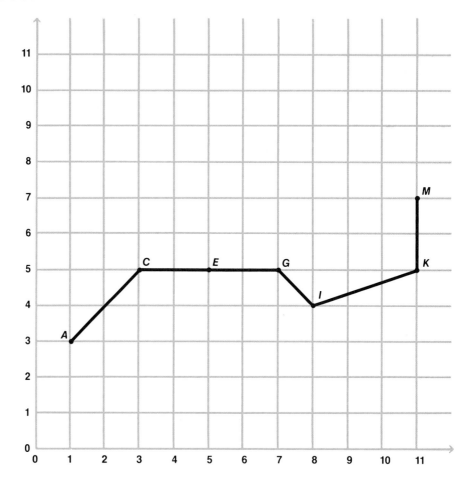

Try Number a grid. Then graph and label the points located by the number pairs given. Connect the points as directed, to make a letter of the alphabet.

a. *B* (1, 5) **b.** *D* (5, 5) **c.** *E* (3, 5) **d.** *G* (3, 1)
  Connect *B* and *D*.   Connect *E* and *G*.

Practice Number a grid for Exercises 1–5. Then graph and label the points located by the number pairs given. Connect the points as directed, to make a 5-pointed star.

1. V (1, 8)

2. W (11, 8)
Connect V and W.

3. X (1, 1)
Connect W and X.

4. Y (6, 11)
Connect X and Y.

5. Z (11, 1)
Connect Y and Z.
Connect V and Z.

Add.

1. $\frac{1}{5}$
$+\frac{2}{5}$

2. $\frac{1}{6}$
$+\frac{2}{6}$

3. $\frac{1}{7}$
$+\frac{1}{7}$

4. $\frac{2}{4} + \frac{3}{4}$

5. $\frac{3}{8} + \frac{1}{8}$

6. $\frac{1}{6} + \frac{4}{6}$

Subtract.

7. $\frac{4}{5}$
$-\frac{2}{5}$

8. $\frac{7}{8}$
$-\frac{3}{8}$

9. $\frac{3}{4}$
$-\frac{1}{4}$

10. $\frac{2}{3} - \frac{1}{3}$

11. $\frac{4}{5} - \frac{1}{5}$

12. $\frac{5}{7} - \frac{3}{7}$

Apply Number a grid and graph these number pairs to make a picture of the constellation, *the Dragon*. Locate the points, label them, and connect them in alphabetical order.

6. A (15, 1)   **7.** B (13, 2)

8. C (9, 3)   **9.** D (5, 5)

10. E (5, 7)   **11.** F (6, 8)

12. G (8, 10)   **13.** H (11, 12)

14. I (11, 14)   **15.** J (10, 15)

16. K (8, 14)   **17.** L (4, 14)

18. M (3, 13)   **19.** N (1, 13)

20. O (1, 11)   **21.** P (3, 11)

22. Connect P and M.

Add.

13. 8.3
$+ 5.6$

14. 4.5
$+ 7.2$

15. 25.04
$+ 36.18$

16. 17.63 + 31.12   **17.** 45 + 36.73

18. 3 + 5.6 + 2.7   **19.** 13 + 4.9

Subtract.

20. 8.6
$- 3.5$

21. 24.3
$- 7.6$

22. 68.73
$- 39.59$

23. 67.89 − 49.93   **24.** 38 − 17.55

25. 18.7 − 6.8   **26.** 0.15 − 0.06

Problem Solving | Use a Graph

Read Jennie works in a craft store that sells packages of pre-cut rug yarn. The price of the yarn is $1.20 for 2 packages. How much should she charge for 20 packages of yarn?

Plan Make a graph to show the prices for different numbers of packages of yarn. Count by 2s to label the bottom of a grid with the number of packages. Label the left side with the prices. Since the price goes up $1.20 for each additional 2 packages, keep adding $1.20 to get the next price.

Solve Locate the points for 0 packages at $0.00, 2 packages at $1.20, and 4 packages at $2.40. Connect the points and extend the graph to the grid line for 20 packages.

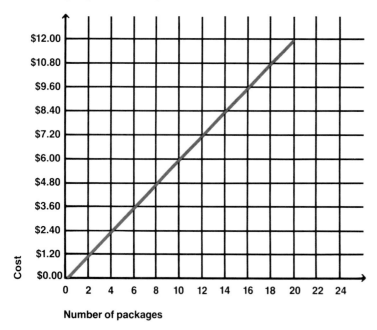

Read across on the grid line to find the price for 20 packages.

Answer Jennie should charge the customer $12.00.

Look Back Since 20 packages is 10 times as many as 2 packages, and $12.00 is 10 times $1.20, the answer checks.

344

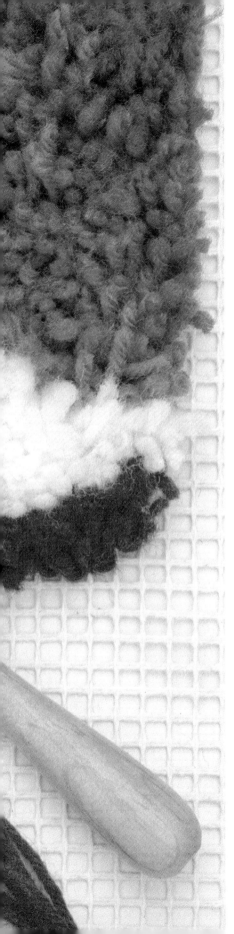

Try Use the graph on page 344. Solve each problem.

a. Kimiko has $6.00. How many packages of rug yarn can she buy?

b. Denny bought 18 packages of rug yarn. How much change did he receive from $15.00?

Apply Use the graph on page 344. Solve each problem.

1. Margo bought 12 packages of rug yarn. How much did she spend on the yarn?

2. Cary spent $3.60 for rug yarn. How many packages did he buy?

3. Chuck has $6.00. What is the greatest number of packages of rug yarn that he can buy?

4. Mateo bought 16 packages of rug yarn. How much change did he receive from $10.00?

5. Teresa bought 14 packages of rug yarn, rug backing for $3.70, and rug hook for $1.25. Find the total cost.

6. Emily bought materials to make 3 wall hangings. Each wall hanging required 12 packages of pre-cut rug yarn. How much did Emily spend on the yarn?

7. Renee bought 20 packages of rug yarn on sale for $8.95. How much less was this than the regular price?

8. Hans bought 14 packages of rug yarn. Roy bought 8 packages. How much more did Hans spend for yarn than Roy?

⋆9. How much will it cost if Tashi buys 5 packages of pre-cut rug yarn?

⋆10. **CALCULATOR** Kay bought packages of different colors of yarn. Find the total cost of 20 packages of red, 15 of yellow, 9 of green, and 17 of blue.

Chapter 12 Test

Piano Practice Hours

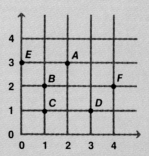

Steve	🕐 🕐 🕐
Shirley	🕐 🕐
Roger	🕐 🕐 🕐 🕐

Each 🕐 means 1 hour.

1. How many hours did Steve practice?

2. Who practiced the most hours?

3. Who practiced the fewest hours?

Favorite Exercise

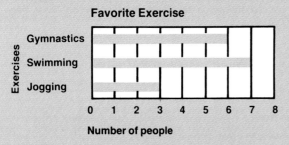

Exercises: Gymnastics, Swimming, Jogging

Number of people

4. How many people chose jogging as their favorite exercise?

5. Which exercise did 6 people choose as their favorite?

6. Which exercise was chosen by the most people?

Rainy Days Each Month

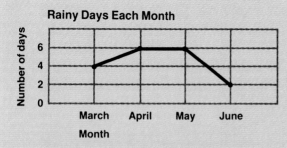

Number of days — March, April, May, June
Month

7. How many rainy days were in May?

8. Which month had 4 rainy days?

9. Which month had 2 rainy days?

10. Which letter names the point located by (4, 2)?

11. Which letter names the point located by (3, 1)?

What number pair gives the location of each point?

12. A   **13.** B   **14.** C

Number a grid. Then graph and label the points located by the number pairs given.

15. W (4, 1)   **16.** X (2, 4)

17. Y (3, 2)   **18.** Z (5, 3)

Cost of Tickets

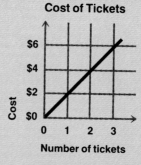

Cost — Number of tickets

19. What is the cost of 3 tickets?

20. Lea bought 1 ticket. How much change did she get from $5.00?

Making a Bar Graph

Some computers read digits by using light beams. Each digit may be printed in a square that has 9 regions. The regions are numbered as shown in the square at the right.

Region 1	Region 2	Region 3
Region 4	Region 9	Region 5
Region 6	Region 7	Region 8

The computer reads a digit by the reflection of segments in the region. The squares below show the position of segments that form each of the digits 0–9.

Regions Used	Regions Used	Regions Used	Regions Used	Regions Used	Regions Used	Regions Used	Regions Used	Regions Used	Regions Used
1, 2, 3, 4, 5, 6, 7, 8	2, 7, 9	2, 3, 4, 5, 6, 7, 8, 9	1, 2, 3, 5, 6, 7, 8, 9	1, 2, 4, 5, 7, 9	1, 2, 4, 5, 6, 7, 8, 9	1, 4, 5, 6, 7, 8, 9	1, 2, 3, 5, 8	1, 2, 3, 4, 5, 6, 7, 8, 9	1, 2, 3, 4, 5, 8, 9

Complete this table to show the number of times each region is used when forming the digits 0–9.

Region	Number of Times Used
1	8
2	1.
3	2.
4	3.
5	4.
6	5.
7	6.
8	7.
9	8.

9. Make a bar graph using the information in the table at the left. Start your graph like the one below.

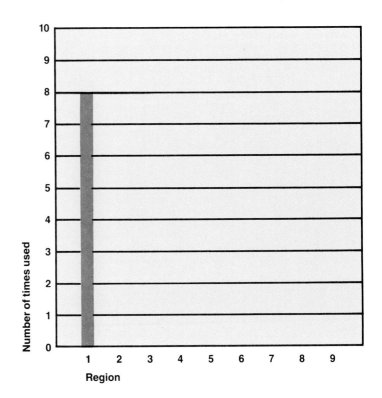

Number of times used

Region

THE MEETING PLACE

Pete is to meet his friends out in the country.
He drew a grid on the map of the area. *Find the
location where they are to meet.* He knows that
the bridge is at point B(0, 0), and that the
fence is at point C(1, 2).

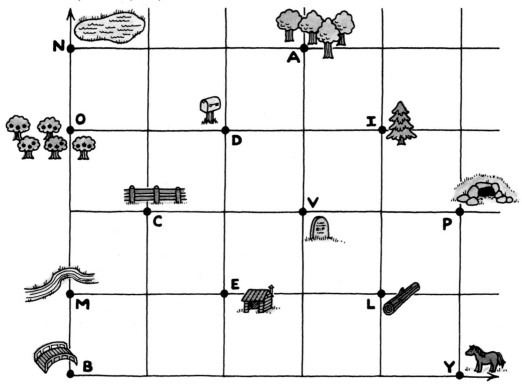

1. Write the letter of the point which has the
   number pair (4, 3).

2. Write the number pair of the point which
   has letter name M.

3. The following number pairs name points on the
   map. Write the letters of the number pairs, in
   order, to spell out the location where Pete is to
   meet his friends.

   (5, 2)   (0, 3)   (0, 4)   (2, 3)

   ____   ____   ____   ____

Cumulative Test, Chapters 1–12

Give the letter for the correct answer.

1. Round 643 to the nearest ten.

   A 640   **c** 650
   B 600   **D** 700

2. What does the 8 mean in 18,306?

   A 8 thousands
   B 8 ten-thousands
   c 8 hundreds
   D 8 ones

3. Add.

     476
   + 585

   A 1,051
   B 961
   c 951
   D 1,061

4. Subtract.

   6,284
  − 2,476

   A 4,818
   B 4,808
   c 3,818
   D 3,808

5. What time is shown on this clock?

   A 7:17   **c** 8:22
   B 4:43   **D** 5:43

6. Multiply.

   4,009
  ×   6

   A 24,054
   B 28,004
   c 2,804
   D 2,454

7. Multiply.

    26
  × 53

   A 910
   B 1,310
   c 1,378
   D 978

8. Tell whether you *add*, *subtract*, or *multiply*. Solve the problem.

Diego bought a book that costs $2. He paid with a $10 bill. How much change did he get?

   A Add; $12   **c** Subtract; $8
   B Multiply; $20   **D** Add; $8

9. How many sides does this figure have?

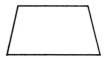

   A 3   **B** 5   **c** 6   **D** 4

10. In which figure is the broken line a line of symmetry?

11. Divide.

   7)32

   A 5 R3
   B 4 R4
   c 3 R6
   D 4 R5

12. Divide.

$4\overline{)83}$

A 18 R1
B 18 R3
C 20 R1
D 20 R3

13. What is four and sixteen hundredths written as a decimal?

A 4.16
B 160.4
C 4.016
D 16.04

14. Which decimal has a 4 in the tenths place?

A 2.41
B 4.07
C 3.04
D 0.54

15. Which number sentence is correct?

A 7.11 > 7.21
B 7.11 < 7.11
C 7.11 > 7.01
D 7.11 < 7.10

16. Add.

$\begin{array}{r} 4.3 \\ + 3.5 \\ \hline \end{array}$

A 9.6
B 78
C .78
D 7.8

17. Subtract.

$\begin{array}{r} 9.6 \\ - 2.4 \\ \hline \end{array}$

A 7.2
B 5.4
C 2.7
D 4.5

18. What fraction is shaded?

A $\frac{5}{8}$
C $\frac{3}{6}$
B $\frac{3}{8}$
D $\frac{5}{6}$

19. What fraction is shaded?

A $\frac{3}{4}$
C $\frac{3}{5}$
B $\frac{2}{5}$
D $\frac{2}{3}$

20. Add.

$\frac{2}{7} + \frac{3}{7}$

A $\frac{5}{14}$
B $\frac{9}{10}$
C $\frac{5}{7}$
D $\frac{4}{5}$

21. Subtract.

$\frac{4}{5} - \frac{2}{5}$

A $\frac{6}{10}$
B $\frac{2}{10}$
C $\frac{1}{5}$
D $\frac{2}{5}$

Use this bar graph for Exercise 22.

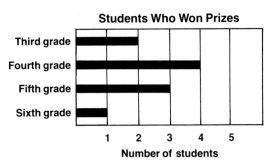

22. How many fifth-grade students won prizes?

A 4 **B** 3 **C** 2 **D** 1

Contents/Pages 352–433

MORE PRACTICE

Set 1 *pages 2–3* For each picture, tell if the number is used to count, to measure, to order, or to label.

1.

2.

3.

4.

5.

6.

7.

8.

9.

Set 2 *pages 4–5* Write two number sentences to compare each pair of numbers. Use < and >

1. 8 and 17	**2.** 26 and 45	**3.** 19 and 11	**4.** 83 and 76	**5.** 33 and 42
6. 24 and 42	**7.** 91 and 6	**8.** 82 and 81	**9.** 39 and 64	**10.** 21 and 49
11. 52 and 37	**12.** 12 and 16	**13.** 30 and 40	**14.** 62 and 59	**15.** 86 and 53

Write the numbers in order from least to greatest.

16. 26　12　13

17. 7　3　9

18. 32　76　48

19. 49　72　53

20. 18　6　24

21. 96　64　35

22. 61　40　26　3

23. 13　44　29　72

24. 81　66　25　14

25. 43　37　51　49

26. 21　16　36　32

27. 34　27　53　51

Set 3 *pages 6-7*

1.	2.	3.	4.	5.	6.	7.	8.	9.
6 + 2	2 + 3	1 + 5	2 + 2	4 + 5	3 + 6	2 + 9	3 + 0	5 + 5

10.	11.	12.	13.	14.	15.	16.	17.	18.
5 + 6	8 + 7	3 + 3	1 + 4	8 + 2	2 + 4	6 + 8	7 + 6	3 + 5

19.	20.	21.	22.	23.	24.	25.	26.	27.
7 + 3	1 + 8	4 + 3	5 + 7	9 + 1	8 + 5	9 + 7	7 + 3	4 + 6

28. 1 + 1 **29.** 0 + 9 **30.** 8 + 6 **31.** 9 + 7 **32.** 2 + 6 **33.** 4 + 8 **34.** 8 + 3

35. 6 + 5 **36.** 9 + 8 **37.** 5 + 2 **38.** 3 + 9 **39.** 0 + 4 **40.** 6 + 9 **41.** 9 + 6

Set 4 *pages 8-9*

1.	2.	3.	4.	5.	6.	7.	8.
9 − 5	7 − 2	4 − 0	11 − 7	9 − 9	5 − 3	13 − 5	8 − 7

9.	10.	11.	12.	13.	14.	15.	16.
8 − 6	6 − 1	11 − 4	9 − 6	16 − 7	10 − 5	3 − 1	9 − 0

17.	18.	19.	20.	21.	22.	23.	24.
12 − 8	15 − 9	9 − 3	8 − 4	6 − 0	12 − 5	10 − 2	8 − 2

25. 15 − 8 **26.** 14 − 6 **27.** 7 − 5 **28.** 5 − 1 **29.** 17 − 9 **30.** 11 − 8 **31.** 12 − 9

Set 5 *pages 12-13* Tell which fact does not belong to each family.

1.	2.	3.	4.	5.
9 − 2 = 7	4 − 1 = 3	6 + 8 = 14	3 + 6 = 9	5 + 2 = 7
2 + 7 = 9	3 + 1 = 4	14 − 6 = 8	3 + 3 = 6	5 + 7 = 12
9 − 2 = 7	3 − 1 = 2	8 + 6 = 14	9 − 3 = 6	12 − 7 = 5
7 + 2 = 9	1 + 3 = 4	8 − 6 = 2	9 − 6 = 3	7 + 5 = 12
9 + 2 = 11	4 − 3 = 1	14 − 8 = 6	6 + 3 = 9	12 − 5 = 7

Write a family of facts using the given numbers.

6. 10   4   6   **7.** 9   8   1   **8.** 4   8   **9.** 6   7   13   **10.** 6   15   9

11. 2   7   9   **12.** 3   4   1   **13.** 13   9   4   **14.** 5   3   8   **15.** 14   7

MORE PRACTICE

Set 6 *pages 14–15*

1. 6 5 +3	2. 2 8 +7	3. 1 4 +2	4. 9 1 +5	5. 6 6 +2	6. 3 5 +2	7. 4 8 +5	8. 1 3 +9	9. 7 5 +4

10. 9 2 3 +4	11. 4 3 7 +2	12. 6 1 5 +1	13. 2 9 3 +2	14. 6 1 5 +5	15. 3 2 7 +4	16. 5 4 3 +8	17. 6 3 5 1 +4	18. 7 5 2 3 +1

19. 6 + 3 + 7   **20.** 3 + 3 + 4 + 4   **21.** 1 + 7 + 2 + 4 + 5   **22.** 7 + 6 + 4 + 1 + 1

Set 7 *pages 16–17*   Tell whether you would *add* or *subtract*. Then find the answer.

1. Peter has 2 basketballs and 9 tennis balls. How many fewer basketballs than tennis balls does he have?

2. Katie swam 6 laps in her swimming pool in the morning and 5 laps in the afternoon. How many laps did Katie swim in all?

3. Lou has 3 brothers. Lisa has 2 more brothers than Lou. How many brothers does Lisa have?

4. Mrs. Estrella had 13 empty flowerpots. She put flowers in 4 of them. How many empty flowerpots did she have left?

5. Tony had 14 coins in his pocket. 8 of the coins were dimes. How many coins were not dimes?

6. Jason went to the library. He checked out 4 books about animals, 2 books about rocks and 1 book about trees. How many books did he check out in all?

Set 8 *pages 18–19*   Give each missing addend.

1. $n + 6 = 10$ **2.** $3 + n = 7$ **3.** $n + 7 = 13$ **4.** $5 + n = 8$ **5.** $2 + n = 10$

6. $4 + n = 12$ **7.** $n + 8 = 9$ **8.** $1 + n = 3$ **9.** $6 + n = 6$ **10.** $4 + n = 11$

11. $n + 2 = 9$ **12.** $3 + n = 8$ **13.** $8 + n = 9$ **14.** $n + 9 = 16$ **15.** $n + 0 = 5$

16. $8 + n = 11$ **17.** $6 + n = 12$ **18.** $4 + n = 13$ **19.** $7 + n = 15$ **20.** $n + 8 = 8$

21. $9 + n = 13$ **22.** $n + 5 = 6$ **23.** $0 + n = 3$ **24.** $n + 7 = 10$ **25.** $7 + n = 9$

26. $n + 4 = 5$ **27.** $n + 8 = 15$ **28.** $6 + n = 14$ **29.** $9 + n = 9$ **30.** $9 + n = 17$

Set 9 *pages 24–25*   Use digits to write each number.

1. ⑆⑆⑆⑆⑆ ⁄   **2.** nineteen   **3.** fifty-nine   **4.** seventy-six   **5.** eighty-four

What is the ones digit in each number?

6. 63   **7.** 49   **8.** 78   **9.** 21   **10.** 29   **11.** 52   **12.** 86   **13.** 10   **14.** 96

What is the tens digit in each number?

15. 52   **16.** 36   **17.** 45   **18.** 93   **19.** 71   **20.** 16   **21.** 89   **22.** 30   **23.** 58

Using the given digits, write as many two-digit numbers
as you can. Do not repeat a digit in a number.

24. 6 and 2   **25.** 3 and 7   **26.** 9 and 1   **27.** 5 and 4   **28.** 2 and 8   **29.** 7 and 2

Set 10 *pages 26–27*   Write each number in standard form.

1. 6 hundreds 8 tens   **2.** 9 hundreds 3 ones   **3.** 4 hundreds 5 ones

4. twenty-seven   **5.** forty-three   **6.** eight hundred eleven

7. four hundred twenty   **8.** five hundred fifty   **9.** six hundred forty-one

Tell what the 6 means in each number.

10. 46   **11.** 61   **12.** 65   **13.** 267   **14.** 536   **15.** 604   **16.** 96   **17.** 687   **18.** 160

Write each number in words.

19. 23   **20.** 67   **21.** 501   **22.** 209   **23.** 740   **24.** 320   **25.** 905   **26.** 413

Set 11 *pages 28–29*   Write each number in standard form.

1. 8,000 + 200 + 30 + 1   **2.** 6,000 + 100 + 3   **3.** 6,000 + 50 + 4

4. four thousand, two hundred thirty-seven   **5.** nine thousand, six hundred forty-nine

6. three thousand, two hundred five   **7.** six thousand, seven

For each number, tell what digit is in the given place.

8. 5,419 (ones)   **9.** 2,892 (hundreds)   **10.** 8,625 (thousands)

Write each number in words.

11. 270   **12.** 902   **13.** 384   **14.** 625   **15.** 8,307   **16.** 2,000   **17.** 4,560   **18.** 3,649

Write each number in expanded form.

19. 238   **20.** 960   **21.** 720   **22.** 3,476   **23.** 8,621   **24.** 2,098   **25.** 5,601

MORE PRACTICE

Set 12 *pages 30–31*   Compare the numbers. Use < or >

1. 634 ● 597   **2.** 324 ● 416   **3.** 283 ● 277   **4.** 537 ● 541

5. 707 ● 712   **6.** 938 ● 944   **7.** 652 ● 651   **8.** 123 ● 125

9. 6,407 ● 5,436   **10.** 2,468 ● 1,934   **11.** 5,021 ● 4,899   **12.** 3,632 ● 4,617

13. 7,412 ● 7,365   **14.** 3,681 ● 3,826   **15.** 4,213 ● 4,308   **16.** 5,964 ● 5,896

17. 9,135 ● 9,162   **18.** 8,627 ● 8,613   **19.** 2,534 ● 2,597   **20.** 1,367 ● 1,359

21. 6,431 ● 6,428   **22.** 1,576 ● 1,579   **23.** 4,638 ● 4,632   **24.** 2,492 ● 2,495

Set 13 *pages 32–33*   Write the numbers in order from least to greatest.

1. 743   522   659   **2.** 5,324   5,497   5,236

3. 256   235   241   213   **4.** 826   804   813   821

5. 2,403   2,386   2,471   2,316   **6.** 9,543   9,547   9,426   9,572

Write the numbers in order from greatest to least.

7. 317   282   465   **8.** 516   497   522

9. 7,652   8,316   7,813   **10.** 826   804   813   821

11. 3,814   3,739   3,823   3,904   **12.** 5,364   5,386   5,283   5,394

Write the number that is 1,000 greater.

13. 3,654   **14.** 7,321   **15.** 5,016   **16.** 2,317   **17.** 4,396   **18.** 720   **19.** 6,043

Write the number that is 100 greater.

20. 592   **21.** 230   **22.** 1,346   **23.** 4,825   **24.** 3,154   **25.** 6,597   **26.** 2,034

Write the number that is 10 greater.

27. 417   **28.** 560   **29.** 2,835   **30.** 9,631   **31.** 1,203   **32.** 6,907   **33.** 5,696

Set 14 *pages 34–35*   Round each number to the nearest ten.

1. 27   **2.** 86   **3.** 51   **4.** 35   **5.** 18   **6.** 73   **7.** 32   **8.** 65

9. 66   **10.** 92   **11.** 45   **12.** 352   **13.** 798   **14.** 345   **15.** 116   **16.** 349

17. 364   **18.** 543   **19.** 867   **20.** 716   **21.** 265   **22.** 654   **23.** 981   **24.** 425

Round each number to the nearest hundred.

25. 627   **26.** 437   **27.** 264   **28.** 103   **29.** 356   **30.** 931   **31.** 545   **32.** 879

33. 760   **34.** 523   **35.** 379   **36.** 450   **37.** 262   **38.** 830   **39.** 176   **40.** 650

41. 684   **42.** 263   **43.** 935   **44.** 197   **45.** 723   **46.** 650   **47.** 349   **48.** 603

Set 15 *pages 36–37* Round each number to the nearest thousand.

1. 2,347   **2.** 1,845   **3.** 8,501   **4.** 6,916   **5.** 3,624   **6.** 5,039   **7.** 2,395

8. 1,193   **9.** 6,500   **10.** 9,296   **11.** 4,902   **12.** 2,499   **13.** 4,628   **14.** 8,146

15. 6,381   **16.** 3,746   **17.** 1,250   **18.** 7,695   **19.** 8,500   **20.** 2,503   **21.** 3,555

Round each number to the nearest hundred.

22. 823   **23.** 564   **24.** 872   **25.** 649   **26.** 750   **27.** 125   **28.** 906

29. 7,842   **30.** 1,450   **31.** 2,923   **32.** 6,365   **33.** 9,489   **34.** 4,648   **35.** 7,009

36. 5,492   **37.** 3,602   **38.** 8,172   **39.** 2,043   **40.** 3,050   **41.** 1,111   **42.** 8,555

Set 16 *pages 40–41* Solve each problem. Use the table below.

Westdale Mayoral Election Results

Polling Place	Ann Thompson	Mike Sanchez
Jefferson School	2,014	3,938
Grant Junior High School	2,392	5,947
Jackson School	597	1,155
Hamilton School	4,056	893
Westdale High School	6,544	3,928

1. Find the vote total for Mike Sanchez at Jackson School to the nearest thousand.

2. Find the vote total for Ann Thompson at Hamilton School to the nearest hundred.

3. List the vote totals for Ann Thompson in order from least to greatest.

4. List the vote totals for Mike Sanchez in order from greatest to least.

5. At which polling places did Ann Thompson have more votes than Mike Sanchez?

MORE PRACTICE

Set 17 *pages 42–43*   Write each number in standard form.

1. 70,000 + 2,000 + 100 + 90 + 2

2. 600,000 + 20,000 + 3,000

3. 400,000 + 30,000 + 7,000 + 60

4. 70,000 + 900

5. two hundred sixty thousand, eight hundred seventy-six

6. thirty-four thousand, nine hundred twenty-seven

7. six hundred thirty-four thousand

8. one hundred fifty-two thousand, six

Tell what the 7 means in each number.

9. 73,042   **10.** 134,728   **11.** 97,438   **12.** 739,461   **13.** 64,397   **14.** 764,398

15. 637,941   **16.** 368,574   **17.** 796,545   **18.** 396,674   **19.** 476,300   **20.** 26,742

Set 18 *pages 44–45*   Write each number in standard form.

1. four hundred ninety six million, three hundred twenty-five thousand, six hundred seventeen

2. thirty-nine million, two hundred nine thousand, three hundred forty-eight

3. six million, five hundred twelve thousand, forty-three

4. sixteen million, forty thousand, fifteen

Tell what the 2 means in each number.

5. 3,235,006   **6.** 87,392,513   **7.** 342,839,117   **8.** 83,297,693   **9.** 32,076,964

10. 26,398,015   **11.** 503,263,061   **12.** 8,374,265   **13.** 2,397,614   **14.** 65,394,267

15. 620,845,366   **16.** 6,346,524   **17.** 23,074,698   **18.** 694,327,059   **19.** 8,021,985

Set 19 *pages 46–47*   Choose the most sensible answer.

1. How many students are in Mary's gym class?

    3   30   300

2. John's scout troop went on a hike for 2 hours. How many miles did they hike?

    6   60   600

3. How much did Jim charge to mow his neighbor's lawn?

    $5 $50 $5,000

4. How much will it cost to buy 10 new swingsets for the parks in Brookdale?

    $7 $70 $7,000

5. How many minutes does it take Mrs. Patel to prepare dinner?

    4   40   400

6. How many gallons of water does it take to fill a swimming pool?

    8   80   8,000

Set 20 *pages 52–53* Estimate each sum.

First round both numbers to the nearest ten.

1. 29 + 11 **2.** 56 + 39 **3.** 42 + 21 **4.** 263 + 17 **5.** 447 + 28 **6.** 45 + 231

First round both numbers to the nearest hundred.

7. 523 + 274 **8.** 264 + 309 **9.** 705 + 236 **10.** 3,183 + 595 **11.** 1,431 + 362

First round both numbers to the nearest thousand.

12. 5,638 + 1,247 **13.** 3,057 + 2,595 **14.** 2,500 + 3,483 **15.** 5,460 + 2,803

Set 21 *pages 54–55* Rename. Write the standard form.

1.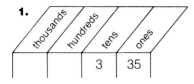

2.

3.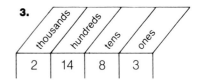

4.

5.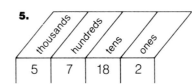

6.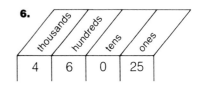

7.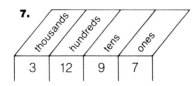

8.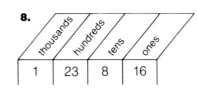

9.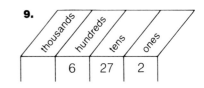

Set 22 *pages 56–57*

1. 57 + 24	**2.** 36 + 47	**3.** 79 + 16	**4.** 64 + 18	**5.** 526 + 155	**6.** 372 + 154	**7.** 293 + 264

8. 413 + 195	**9.** 3,628 + 1,851	**10.** 5,042 + 2,374	**11.** 4,246 + 3,952	**12.** 573 + 64	**13.** 695 + 83	**14.** 6,453 + 626

15. 58 + 28 **16.** 783 + 46 **17.** 334 + 275 **18.** 6,847 + 137 **19.** 3,041 + 5,639

MORE PRACTICE

Set 23 *pages 58-59*

1. 364
+ 278

2. 693
+ 138

3. 245
+ 376

4. 563
+ 338

5. 373
+ 259

6. 454
+ 267

7. 5,386
+ 2,437

8. 2,726
+ 1,435

9. 4,536
+ 476

10. 2,794
+ 5,407

11. 3,842
+ 4,683

12. 297
+ 16

13. 583
+ 48

14. 7,365
+ 758

15. 6,528 + 5,683   **16.** 3,635 + 7,395   **17.** 2,936 + 657   **18.** 564 + 859

Set 24 *pages 60-61*

1. 3
8
+ 25

2. 16
37
+ 5

3. 85
21
+ 36

4. 43
54
+ 28

5. 261
107
+ 324

6. 116
231
+ 522

7. 352
416
+ 283

8. 1,872
3,410
+ 2,016

9. 3,651
1,342
+ 4,465

10. 23
12
46
+ 34

11. 38
51
19
+ 72

12. 317
103
232
+ 116

13. 406
231
152
+ 115

14. 2,318
1,726
1,452
+ 2,564

15. 48 + 78 + 51   **16.** 61 + 253 + 647   **17.** 306 + 224 + 152

18. 16 + 23 + 15 + 34   **19.** 42 + 325 + 18 + 241   **20.** 223 + 145 + 509 + 372

Set 25 *pages 64-65* Estimate each difference.

First round both numbers to the nearest ten.

1. 23 − 14   **2.** 88 − 26   **3.** 91 − 38   **4.** 56 − 31   **5.** 71 − 47   **6.** 52 − 39

7. 65 − 29   **8.** 164 − 73   **9.** 175 − 46   **10.** 152 − 29   **11.** 117 − 36   **12.** 132 − 28

First round both numbers to the nearest hundred.

13. 735 − 316   **14.** 812 − 263   **15.** 524 − 303   **16.** 465 − 207   **17.** 677 − 214

18. 1,382 − 304   **19.** 1,627 − 287   **20.** 1,816 − 504   **21.** 1,553 − 496   **22.** 1,907 − 878

First round both numbers to the nearest thousand.

23. 1,724 − 1,046   **24.** 6,070 − 1,663   **25.** 7,542 − 2,700   **26.** 3,097 − 1,020

27. 4,238 − 2,106   **28.** 5,876 − 2,245   **29.** 8,082 − 5,703   **30.** 6,500 − 1,500

Set 26 *pages 66-67*   Rename to show 10 more ones.

1.

2.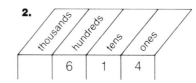

3.

Rename to show 10 more tens.

4.

5.

6.

7.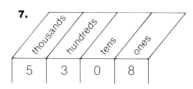

8.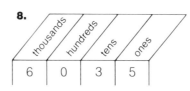

9.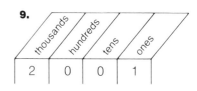

Rename to show 10 more hundreds.

10.

11.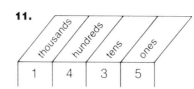

12.

Set 27 *pages 68-69*

1. 35 − 16

2. 83 − 49

3. 64 − 37

4. 50 − 24

5. 346 − 175

6. 263 − 126

7. 819 − 247

8. 4,583 − 1,741

9. 3,528 − 2,463

10. 9,627 − 4,208

11. 297 − 38

12. 527 − 73

13. 2,651 − 471

14. 3,176 − 452

15. 6,425 − 1,274

16. 418 − 263

17. 4,835 − 681

18. 7,631 − 4,215

19. 5,387 − 626

20. 9,465 − 6,274

21. 623 − 82

22. 9,246 − 85

MORE PRACTICE

Set 28 *pages 70-71*

1.	312 − 46	**2.**	645 − 76	**3.**	320 − 35	**4.**	532 − 186	**5.**	411 − 243	**6.**	760 − 286	**7.**	963 − 268

8.	2,846 − 379	**9.**	7,652 − 847	**10.**	5,764 − 2,697	**11.**	6,283 − 3,791	**12.**	656 − 68	**13.**	2,346 − 678	**14.**	4,356 − 1,478

15. 560 − 74   **16.** 4,265 − 1,572   **17.** 8,174 − 3,259   **18.** 6,271 − 652

Set 29 *pages 72-73*

1.	700 − 324	**2.**	402 − 159	**3.**	807 − 588	**4.**	500 − 236	**5.**	900 − 761	**6.**	304 − 175	**7.**	806 − 98

8.	401 − 73	**9.**	705 − 49	**10.**	600 − 53	**11.**	3,500 − 1,385	**12.**	7,804 − 5,687	**13.**	6,301 − 2,182	**14.**	9,700 − 7,418

15. 3,023 − 74   **16.** 6,040 − 756   **17.** 5,006 − 412   **18.** 8,000 − 2,342

Set 30 *pages 76-77*   Check each answer. Tell whether it is right or wrong. If it is wrong, give the correct answer.

1.	23 + 97 120	**2.**	56 + 89 145	**3.**	564 + 227 801	**4.**	691 + 286 877	**5.**	3,436 + 5,921 9,357	**6.**	1,267 + 2,185 3,442	**7.**	3,848 + 3,361 7,209

8.	53 − 27 36	**9.**	286 − 58 228	**10.**	726 − 64 662	**11.**	513 − 197 316	**12.**	8,647 − 928 8,719	**13.**	5,006 − 2,741 2,265	**14.**	9,084 − 1,293 8,211

Watch the signs. Check each answer.

15.	374 + 563	**16.**	807 − 234	**17.**	618 − 249	**18.**	288 + 437	**19.**	700 − 231	**20.**	403 + 298

21.	6,073 − 425	**22.**	4,265 + 354	**23.**	2,685 + 6,256	**24.**	8,264 − 3,381	**25.**	7,002 − 3,849	**26.**	2,525 + 3,475

Set 31 *pages 78–79*

1.	2.	3.	4.	5.	6.
$6.37 + 0.71	$2.56 + 3.89	$0.73 + 0.76	$7.58 + 0.98	$13.84 + 7.63	$53.98 + 15.26

7.	8.	9.	10.	11.	12.
$6.45 − 3.82	$7.00 − 4.25	$9.50 − 3.99	$22.87 − 9.68	$16.05 − 8.40	$95.36 − 76.29

Set 32 *pages 82–83*   Write an equation. Then give the answer.

1. On Friday, 316 people attended the play at Nole School. On Saturday, 83 more people attended the play than on Friday. How many people attended the play on Saturday?

2. Tanya's family traveled 923 miles on their vacation. Sam's family traveled 268 miles less than Tanya's family. How many miles did Sam's family travel?

3. Colin counted 46 cars, 12 vans, 23 trucks, and 4 buses on his way home from school. How many vehicles did he count in all?

4. The total for Mr. Murphy's paint supplies was $12.73. He paid for them with a $20.00 bill. How much money did Mr. Murphy get back?

5. Jill read 45 pages of her book. Yoshio read 16 pages less than Jill. How many pages did Yoshio read?

6. Tina delivered 193 newspapers. Tom delivered 184 newspapers. How many newspapers did they deliver in all?

7. Tim weighs 84 pounds. Lee weighs 78 pounds. Tarik weighs 81 pounds. What is their total weight?

8. Rita bought a pair of shoes on sale for $16.99. Before the sale the shoes cost $24.00. How much did Rita save?

Set 33 *pages 90–91*   Write the time shown. Then write the time indicated under the clock.

1.

3 hours later

2.

6 hours later

3.

25 minutes later

4.

10 minutes later

5.

50 minutes later

6.

6:13
27 minutes later

7.

7:56
6 minutes later

8.

2:07
34 minutes later

MORE PRACTICE

Set 34 *pages 92–93*   Use the calendar on page 92 for each exercise. Name the day of the week for each date.

1. July 27   **2.** September 26   **3.** March 20   **4.** November 11   **5.** August 10   **6.** May 26

Name the date for each day.

7. Third Saturday in April

8. Three weeks from February 2

9. Fifth Wednesday in May

10. Second Friday in October

11. One week from December 6

12. First Sunday in June

Choose the most sensible answer.

13. Jane spends 7 (minutes, hours, days) in school each day.

14. There are about 30 (hours, days, weeks) in a month.

Set 35 *pages 94–95*   Estimate each length to the nearest centimeter. Then measure it.

1. _____

2. _____

3. _____

Tell if the measure is sensible. Write *yes* or *no*.

4. A pencil is about 17 cm long.

5. An album cover is about 3 cm wide.

6. A door is about 9 dm wide.

7. A tennis racket is about 7 dm long.

8. A baby is about 4 cm long.

9. A paper clip is about 4 cm long.

Set 36 *pages 96–97*   Would you use centimeters, meters, or kilometers to measure

1. the distance a ball can be thrown?

2. the width of a piece of notebook paper?

3. the length of a swimming pool?

4. the distance from Chicago to Atlanta?

5. the length of a pen?

6. the distance you can walk in 3 hours?

Choose the most sensible measure.

7. Height of a pineapple

2 cm   2 dm   2 km

8. Distance run in a race

5 cm   5 m   5 km

9. Height of the mailman

2 cm   2 m   2 km

10. Thickness of a magazine

1 cm   1 m   1 km

Set 37 *pages 98-99* Would you use grams or kilograms to measure the weight of

1. a lawn mower?

2. a car?

3. a pocket calculator?

4. a postcard?

5. a tomato?

6. a bookcase?

Choose the more sensible measure.

7. Baseball bat

850 g   850 kg

8. Flashlight

200 g   200 kg

9. Dictionary

2 g   2 kg

10. Sunglasses

65 g   65 kg

Set 38 *pages 100-101* Would you use milliliters or liters to measure the amount of liquid in

1. a cereal bowl?

2. a test tube?

3. a horse trough?

4. an eye dropper?

5. a sponge?

6. a sink?

Choose the more sensible measure.

7. Baby bottle

200 mL   200 L

8. Soup ladle

125 mL   125 L

9. Washing machine

60 mL   60 L

10. Watering can

4 mL   4 L

Set 39 *pages 104-105* Solve each problem. Use the map on page 104.

1. Is the actual distance from the lookout point to the pond less than or greater than the actual distance from the landing to the pond?

2. Is the actual distance from the snake pit to the quicksand less than or greater than the actual distance from the quicksand to the buried treasure?

3. Choose the most sensible estimate for the actual distance from the snake pit to the landing.

8 km   12 km   20 km

4. Choose the most sensible estimate for the actual distance from the quicksand to the cave.

15 km   30 km   40 km

MORE PRACTICE

Set 40 *pages 106–107* Estimate each length to the nearest inch. Then measure it.

1. _____

2. _____

3. _____

Tell if each measure is sensible. Write *yes* or *no*.

4. A fishing pole is about 4 feet long.

5. A key is about 2 inches long.

6. A bedroom is about 13 feet wide.

7. A table is about 30 feet tall.

Set 41 *pages 108–109* Which unit would you use to measure the

1. height of a fence?

   (feet or miles)

2. length of a garden?

   (yards or miles)

3. distance of a bicycle race?

   (inches or miles)

4. width of a photograph?

   (inches or yards)

Choose the most sensible measure.

5. Length of your little finger

   2 in.   2 ft.   2 mi.

6. Length of a swimming pool

   25 in.   25 yd.   25 mi.

7. Height of a door

   7 in.   7 ft.   7 yd.

8. Width of a newspaper

   14 in.   14 ft.   14 yd.

Set 42 *pages 110–111* Would you use ounces, pounds, or tons to measure the weight of

1. a turkey?

2. a van?

3. a tomato?

4. a necklace?

5. a bowling ball?

6. an ocean liner?

Choose the most sensible measure.

7. Toaster

   4 ounces   4 pounds   4 tons

8. Piano

   1 ounce   1 pound   1 ton

9. Bicycle

   30 ounces   30 pounds   30 tons

10. Lightbulb

   2 ounces   2 pounds   2 tons

Set 43 *pages 112–113* Choose the unit you would use to measure the amount of liquid in

1. a soup ladle.

(cup or quart)

2. a fish tank.

(pint or gallon)

3. a teapot.

(pint or gallon)

Choose the more sensible measure.

4. Birdbath

3 cups   3 gallons

5. Bucket

6 cups   6 quarts

6. Bathtub

15 cups   15 gallons

Set 44 *pages 116–117* Choose the more sensible measure. Use the thermometers on page 116 to help you.

1. Temperature inside a refrigerator

45°F   100°F

2. Temperature during a heat wave

40°F   98°F

3. Temperature of warm bathtub water

40°C   90°C

4. Picnic weather

−10°C   25°C

Give the more sensible measure. Use C (Celsius) or F (Fahrenheit).

5. Jason is raking leaves. The temperature is 10°▨.

6. Kristen is swimming in her pool. The temperature of the water is 72°▨.

7. Zachary went to the shopping mall. The temperature in the mall is 20°▨.

8. Beatrice is skiing. The temperature is 20°▨.

Set 45 *pages 122–123* Copy and complete each sentence.

1.

$3 + 3 + 3 + 3 =$ ▨

$4 \times 3 =$ ▨

2.

$2 + 2 + 2 + 2 + 2 =$ ▨

$5 \times 2 =$ ▨

3.

$3 + 3 =$ ▨

$2 \times 3 =$ ▨

4.

$4 + 4 =$ ▨

$2 \times 4 =$ ▨

5.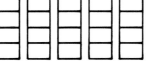

$4 + 4 + 4 + 4 + 4 =$ ▨

$5 \times 4 =$ ▨

6.

$2 + 2 =$ ▨

$2 \times 2 =$ ▨

MORE PRACTICE

Set 46 *pages 124–125*   Copy and complete the multiplication sentence for each picture.

1.

2.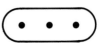

$2 \times 3 = $ ▨

$3 \times 5 = $ ▨

3. 3×2 **4.** 6×2 **5.** 2×9 **6.** 7×3 **7.** 3×6 **8.** 5×2 **9.** 3×8

10. 3×4 **11.** 7×2 **12.** 6×3 **13.** 3×5 **14.** 2×2 **15.** 2×4 **16.** 4×3

17. 3×3 **18.** 8×2 **19.** 2×6 **20.** 9×2 **21.** 3×9 **22.** 4×2 **23.** 8×3

Set 47 *pages 126–127*

1. $\begin{array}{r}3\\ \times 4\\\hline\end{array}$ **2.** $\begin{array}{r}9\\ \times 4\\\hline\end{array}$ **3.** $\begin{array}{r}6\\ \times 5\\\hline\end{array}$ **4.** $\begin{array}{r}5\\ \times 4\\\hline\end{array}$ **5.** $\begin{array}{r}7\\ \times 5\\\hline\end{array}$ **6.** $\begin{array}{r}4\\ \times 3\\\hline\end{array}$ **7.** $\begin{array}{r}3\\ \times 9\\\hline\end{array}$ **8.** $\begin{array}{r}5\\ \times 5\\\hline\end{array}$ **9.** $\begin{array}{r}4\\ \times 7\\\hline\end{array}$

10. $\begin{array}{r}4\\ \times 4\\\hline\end{array}$ **11.** $\begin{array}{r}5\\ \times 8\\\hline\end{array}$ **12.** $\begin{array}{r}2\\ \times 8\\\hline\end{array}$ **13.** $\begin{array}{r}8\\ \times 4\\\hline\end{array}$ **14.** $\begin{array}{r}5\\ \times 6\\\hline\end{array}$ **15.** $\begin{array}{r}4\\ \times 9\\\hline\end{array}$ **16.** $\begin{array}{r}7\\ \times 4\\\hline\end{array}$ **17.** $\begin{array}{r}5\\ \times 2\\\hline\end{array}$ **18.** $\begin{array}{r}9\\ \times 5\\\hline\end{array}$

19. $\begin{array}{r}3\\ \times 5\\\hline\end{array}$ **20.** $\begin{array}{r}4\\ \times 6\\\hline\end{array}$ **21.** $\begin{array}{r}4\\ \times 5\\\hline\end{array}$ **22.** $\begin{array}{r}5\\ \times 3\\\hline\end{array}$ **23.** $\begin{array}{r}5\\ \times 9\\\hline\end{array}$ **24.** $\begin{array}{r}6\\ \times 4\\\hline\end{array}$ **25.** $\begin{array}{r}4\\ \times 5\\\hline\end{array}$ **26.** $\begin{array}{r}2\\ \times 4\\\hline\end{array}$ **27.** $\begin{array}{r}5\\ \times 7\\\hline\end{array}$

28. 4×2 **29.** 2×5 **30.** 8×5 **31.** 2×7 **32.** 4×8 **33.** 2×6 **34.** 8×3

Set 48 *pages 128–129*

1. $\begin{array}{r}6\\ \times 3\\\hline\end{array}$ **2.** $\begin{array}{r}7\\ \times 6\\\hline\end{array}$ **3.** $\begin{array}{r}2\\ \times 6\\\hline\end{array}$ **4.** $\begin{array}{r}6\\ \times 4\\\hline\end{array}$ **5.** $\begin{array}{r}6\\ \times 9\\\hline\end{array}$ **6.** $\begin{array}{r}4\\ \times 5\\\hline\end{array}$ **7.** $\begin{array}{r}6\\ \times 6\\\hline\end{array}$ **8.** $\begin{array}{r}5\\ \times 6\\\hline\end{array}$ **9.** $\begin{array}{r}9\\ \times 6\\\hline\end{array}$

10. $\begin{array}{r}6\\ \times 7\\\hline\end{array}$ **11.** $\begin{array}{r}8\\ \times 6\\\hline\end{array}$ **12.** $\begin{array}{r}8\\ \times 4\\\hline\end{array}$ **13.** $\begin{array}{r}6\\ \times 2\\\hline\end{array}$ **14.** $\begin{array}{r}4\\ \times 6\\\hline\end{array}$ **15.** $\begin{array}{r}6\\ \times 5\\\hline\end{array}$ **16.** $\begin{array}{r}6\\ \times 8\\\hline\end{array}$ **17.** $\begin{array}{r}2\\ \times 7\\\hline\end{array}$ **18.** $\begin{array}{r}6\\ \times 4\\\hline\end{array}$

19. $\begin{array}{r}6\\ \times 9\\\hline\end{array}$ **20.** $\begin{array}{r}3\\ \times 7\\\hline\end{array}$ **21.** $\begin{array}{r}6\\ \times 6\\\hline\end{array}$ **22.** $\begin{array}{r}6\\ \times 3\\\hline\end{array}$ **23.** $\begin{array}{r}2\\ \times 8\\\hline\end{array}$ **24.** $\begin{array}{r}6\\ \times 8\\\hline\end{array}$ **25.** $\begin{array}{r}7\\ \times 5\\\hline\end{array}$ **26.** $\begin{array}{r}8\\ \times 6\\\hline\end{array}$ **27.** $\begin{array}{r}3\\ \times 9\\\hline\end{array}$

28. 8×3 **29.** 2×6 **30.** 4×9 **31.** 7×6 **32.** 9×6 **33.** 4×8 **34.** 6×5

Set 49 *pages 132–133*

| 1. 6 ×0 | 2. 1 ×5 | 3. 4 ×0 | 4. 7 ×1 | 5. 1 ×1 | 6. 0 ×3 | 7. 9 ×0 | 8. 0 ×7 | 9. 0 ×1 |

| 10. 1 ×4 | 11. 3 ×0 | 12. 8 ×1 | 13. 0 ×6 | 14. 0 ×0 | 15. 6 ×1 | 16. 1 ×2 | 17. 4 ×1 | 18. 8 ×0 |

19. 1×3 20. 7×0 21. 1×0 22. 9×1 23. 5×0 24. 0×2 25. 5×1

Set 50 *pages 134–135*

| 1. 7 ×4 | 2. 6 ×3 | 3. 9 ×7 | 4. 5 ×9 | 5. 7 ×1 | 6. 8 ×7 | 7. 4 ×7 | 8. 7 ×6 | 9. 7 ×7 |

| 10. 2 ×7 | 11. 4 ×7 | 12. 7 ×0 | 13. 6 ×6 | 14. 5 ×7 | 15. 7 ×8 | 16. 8 ×4 | 17. 7 ×2 | 18. 7 ×9 |

| 19. 7 ×5 | 20. 3 ×7 | 21. 6 ×7 | 22. 7 ×3 | 23. 6 ×4 | 24. 5 ×8 | 25. 7 ×7 | 26. 7 ×0 | 27. 1 ×7 |

28. 7×8 29. 0×4 30. 7×9 31. 8×6 32. 7×5 33. 0×7 34. 9×1

35. 2×7 36. 3×7 37. 4×9 38. 5×7 39. 8×7 40. 0×1 41. 6×7

Set 51 *pages 136–137*

| 1. 8 ×3 | 2. 8 ×9 | 3. 5 ×8 | 4. 8 ×8 | 5. 1 ×8 | 6. 9 ×6 | 7. 2 ×8 | 8. 8 ×5 | 9. 0 ×8 |

| 10. 4 ×8 | 11. 6 ×4 | 12. 8 ×1 | 13. 9 ×8 | 14. 5 ×6 | 15. 7 ×8 | 16. 8 ×0 | 17. 3 ×4 | 18. 8 ×4 |

| 19. 7 ×8 | 20. 8 ×6 | 21. 3 ×8 | 22. 8 ×2 | 23. 8 ×5 | 24. 9 ×7 | 25. 8 ×3 | 26. 6 ×8 | 27. 7 ×5 |

28. 8×7 29. 2×6 30. 0×8 31. 2×8 32. 4×8 33. 8×8 34. 8×1

35. 0×1 36. 6×8 37. 9×8 38. 5×6 39. 8×7 40. 6×3 41. 8×9

MORE PRACTICE

Set 52 *pages 138–139*

1. 9
    ×2

2. 5
    ×9

3. 9
    ×8

4. 4
    ×5

5. 2
    ×7

6. 9
    ×0

7. 3
    ×9

8. 9
    ×5

9. 0
    ×1

10. 4
    ×7

11. 8
    ×9

12. 9
    ×3

13. 6
    ×3

14. 2
    ×9

15. 7
    ×1

16. 9
    ×6

17. 5
    ×7

18. 9
    ×1

19. 9
    ×7

20. 8
    ×6

21. 1
    ×9

22. 6
    ×9

23. 9
    ×4

24. 0
    ×9

25. 3
    ×4

26. 9
    ×9

27. 7
    ×9

28. 9 × 4
29. 3 × 7
30. 7 × 9
31. 5 × 8
32. 2 × 9
33. 7 × 8
34. 9 × 9

35. 9 × 1
36. 8 × 9
37. 9 × 5
38. 6 × 4
39. 9 × 6
40. 6 × 6
41. 3 × 9

Set 53 *pages 142–143*

Write a problem about

1. buying 2 boxes of pencils.

2. buying a box of pens and a notebook.

3. the change received from $10 when buying 2 notebooks.

4. how much more one item costs than another.

5. which of two items costs more.

6. the sale price of an item when it is $0.50 off the regular price.

Set 54 *pages 148–149*

1. 6 × 1
2. 6 × 10
3. 6 × 100
4. 6 × 1,000
5. 9 × 1,000

6. 4 × 100
7. 3 × 10
8. 5 × 10
9. 5 × 100
10. 5 × 1,000

11. 4 × 6
12. 4 × 60
13. 4 × 600
14. 4 × 6,000
15. 24 × 10

16. 7 × 10
17. 7 × 20
18. 7 × 30
19. 7 × 200
20. 7 × 3,000

21. 3 × 200
22. 3 × 300
23. 3 × 4,000
24. 3 × 500
25. 3 × 2,000

26. 4,000 × 8
27. 10 × 100
28. 14 × 1,000
29. 7 × 100
30. 200 × 6

31. 100 × 100
32. 5,000 × 6
33. 36 × 10
34. 16 × 100
35. 7 × 8,000

Set 55 *pages 150–151*

1. 43 × 2	**2.** 21 × 4	**3.** 33 × 3	**4.** 13 × 2	**5.** 70 × 3	**6.** 61 × 4
7. 51 × 8	**8.** 90 × 6	**9.** 214 × 2	**10.** 322 × 3	**11.** 121 × 3	**12.** 104 × 2
13. 403 × 2	**14.** 501 × 6	**15.** 210 × 9	**16.** 823 × 3	**17.** 411 × 8	**18.** 603 × 3
19. 2,102 × 4	**20.** 5,233 × 3	**21.** 6,203 × 3	**22.** 8,434 × 2	**23.** 7,021 × 4	**24.** 6,224 × 2
25. 4,323 × 3	**26.** 9,114 × 2	**27.** 5,214 × 2	**28.** 8,003 × 3	**29.** 7,022 × 4	**30.** 6,324 × 2

Set 56 *pages 152–153*

1. 16 × 7	**2.** 48 × 3	**3.** 45 × 2	**4.** 26 × 8	**5.** 73 × 6	**6.** 54 × 4
7. 59 × 3	**8.** 63 × 7	**9.** 28 × 3	**10.** 78 × 5	**11.** 34 × 7	**12.** 66 × 9
13. 472 × 4	**14.** 326 × 3	**15.** 164 × 2	**16.** 371 × 5	**17.** 517 × 5	**18.** 214 × 5
19. 151 × 6	**20.** 238 × 2	**21.** 960 × 8	**22.** 417 × 5	**23.** 831 × 8	**24.** 919 × 3
25. 3,602 × 4	**26.** 5,117 × 5	**27.** 3,016 × 4	**28.** 4,421 × 4	**29.** 7,392 × 2	**30.** 1,019 × 4

31. 37×5 **32.** 74×3 **33.** 9×65 **34.** 872×2 **35.** 551×6

36. 4×419 **37.** 325×2 **38.** $5,160 \times 3$ **39.** $7 \times 6,012$ **40.** $2,352 \times 2$

41. 85×7 **42.** 29×6 **43.** 617×4 **44.** 572×4 **45.** $8,411 \times 8$

MORE PRACTICE

Set 57 *pages 154–155* Solve each problem.

In the products for the factor 6, what pattern is made by

1. the ones digit?

2. the sums of the digits? If there is a 2-digit sum, add again to get a 1-digit sum.

In the products for the factor 8, what pattern is made by

3. the ones digit?

4. the sums of the digits? If there is a 2-digit sum, add again to get a 1-digit sum.

Set 58 *pages 156–157*

1. 164 × 3	**2.** 287 × 3	**3.** 294 × 5	**4.** 526 × 8	**5.** 718 × 9	**6.** 443 × 6
7. 652 × 7	**8.** 356 × 4	**9.** 789 × 2	**10.** 486 × 3	**11.** 2,184 × 4	**12.** 1,316 × 5
13. 3,761 × 2	**14.** 4,123 × 7	**15.** 1,615 × 4	**16.** 1,827 × 2	**17.** 2,360 × 4	**18.** 1,918 × 3

19. 354 × 6 **20.** 572 × 5 **21.** 168 × 3 **22.** 227 × 7 **23.** 418 × 9

24. 7 × 1,371 **25.** 2,154 × 6 **26.** 3,264 × 3 **27.** 5 × 1,716 **28.** 3 × 3,460

Set 59 *pages 158–159*

1. 703 × 3	**2.** 450 × 5	**3.** 602 × 7	**4.** 104 × 9	**5.** 230 × 6	**6.** 405 × 6
7. 500 × 4	**8.** 301 × 9	**9.** 270 × 2	**10.** 603 × 4	**11.** 7,080 × 6	**12.** 2,008 × 4
13. 4,042 × 6	**14.** 1,034 × 5	**15.** 2,602 × 6	**16.** 3,120 × 6	**17.** 5,009 × 9	**18.** 8,012 × 9
19. 5,063 × 4	**20.** 3,402 × 6	**21.** 1,090 × 2	**22.** 2,009 × 5	**23.** 4,013 × 4	**24.** 6,070 × 7

Set 60 *pages 162–163*

1. 4×70
2. 20×80
3. 400×30
4. 20×600
5. 60×600
6. 300×70

7. 3×20
8. 30×30
9. 600×40
10. 4×500
11. 5×700
12. $6 \times 9,000$

13. 60×5
14. 70×40
15. 900×70
16. 2×900
17. 30×600
18. 40×80

19. 90×7
20. 50×10
21. 300×50
22. 7×600
23. 9×400
24. 700×4

25. 50×2
26. 90×30
27. 6×900
28. 20×800
29. 50×50
30. 300×30

31. 70×6
32. 20×80
33. $30 \times 2,000$
34. 40×200
35. 300×90
36. 70×700

Set 61 *pages 164–165*   Estimate each product.

1. 71×3
2. 8×38
3. 9×22
4. 18×84
5. 46×29
6. 28×59

7. 64×6
8. 19×3
9. 4×87
10. 39×43
11. 31×81
12. 52×64

13. 92×4
14. 6×42
15. 62×2
16. 42×91
17. 16×61
18. 68×38

19. 8×26
20. 9×51
21. 3×16
22. 61×35
23. 58×45
24. 12×76

25. 7×32
26. 29×4
27. 34×6
28. 23×32
29. 33×96
30. 71×23

31. 5×16
32. 63×2
33. 56×7
34. 74×22
35. 85×56
36. 49×78

Set 62 *pages 166–167*

1. $\begin{array}{r} 24 \\ \times 30 \\ \hline \end{array}$
2. $\begin{array}{r} 46 \\ \times 20 \\ \hline \end{array}$
3. $\begin{array}{r} 53 \\ \times 60 \\ \hline \end{array}$
4. $\begin{array}{r} 16 \\ \times 90 \\ \hline \end{array}$
5. $\begin{array}{r} 82 \\ \times 20 \\ \hline \end{array}$
6. $\begin{array}{r} 73 \\ \times 40 \\ \hline \end{array}$
7. $\begin{array}{r} 29 \\ \times 20 \\ \hline \end{array}$
8. $\begin{array}{r} 67 \\ \times 70 \\ \hline \end{array}$

9. $\begin{array}{r} 35 \\ \times 50 \\ \hline \end{array}$
10. $\begin{array}{r} 72 \\ \times 40 \\ \hline \end{array}$
11. $\begin{array}{r} 63 \\ \times 20 \\ \hline \end{array}$
12. $\begin{array}{r} 63 \\ \times 24 \\ \hline \end{array}$
13. $\begin{array}{r} 24 \\ \times 40 \\ \hline \end{array}$
14. $\begin{array}{r} 24 \\ \times 48 \\ \hline \end{array}$
15. $\begin{array}{r} 52 \\ \times 30 \\ \hline \end{array}$
16. $\begin{array}{r} 52 \\ \times 33 \\ \hline \end{array}$

17. $\begin{array}{r} 42 \\ \times 16 \\ \hline \end{array}$
18. $\begin{array}{r} 23 \\ \times 36 \\ \hline \end{array}$
19. $\begin{array}{r} 41 \\ \times 64 \\ \hline \end{array}$
20. $\begin{array}{r} 27 \\ \times 81 \\ \hline \end{array}$
21. $\begin{array}{r} 35 \\ \times 22 \\ \hline \end{array}$
22. $\begin{array}{r} 83 \\ \times 19 \\ \hline \end{array}$
23. $\begin{array}{r} 47 \\ \times 34 \\ \hline \end{array}$
24. $\begin{array}{r} 82 \\ \times 96 \\ \hline \end{array}$

25. 34×12
26. 42×46
27. 61×35
28. 83×24
29. 92×38
30. 67×62

31. 27×19
32. 49×26
33. 54×31
34. 74×53
35. 81×94
36. 29×68

MORE PRACTICE

Set 63 *pages 168–169*

1. 200 × 26	**2.** 600 × 45	**3.** 900 × 18	**4.** 316 × 30	**5.** 442 × 60	**6.** 571 × 20	**7.** 207 × 38	**8.** 603 × 57
9. 290 × 79	**10.** 410 × 32	**11.** 368 × 28	**12.** 219 × 33	**13.** 487 × 61	**14.** 703 × 89	**15.** 521 × 25	**16.** 839 × 32
17. 706 × 34	**18.** 139 × 45	**19.** 427 × 51	**20.** 818 × 26	**21.** 622 × 52	**22.** 574 × 43	**23.** 334 × 12	**24.** 901 × 29

Set 64 *pages 172–173*

1. $0.06 × 7	**2.** $0.09 × 3	**3.** $0.06 × 8	**4.** $0.34 × 4	**5.** $0.23 × 5	**6.** $0.75 × 6
7. $1.55 × 3	**8.** $7.60 × 5	**9.** $8.35 × 4	**10.** $2.98 × 7	**11.** $4.00 × 6	**12.** $5.79 × 2
13. $0.29 × 15	**14.** $0.98 × 22	**15.** $0.45 × 42	**16.** $0.80 × 36	**17.** $2.95 × 21	**18.** $6.03 × 34

19. 24 × $0.72   **20.** 40 × $0.96   **21.** 12 × $1.59   **22.** 65 × $2.10   **23.** 32 × $4.65

24. $0.62 × 2   **25.** $3.50 × 8   **26.** $4.38 × 12   **27.** $7.14 × 18   **28.** $1.98 × 32

Set 65 *pages 174–175* Tell whether you *add*, *subtract*, or *multiply*. Then find the answer.

1. Michiko practiced playing her clarinet 45 minutes each day. How many minutes did she practice in 5 days?

2. Jack was born in 1974. Jack's brother is 6 years older. In what year was Jack's brother born?

3. Scott sold 263 tickets to the school play. Aurelio sold 174 tickets. How many tickets did they sell in all?

4. Tracy bought 3 balloons at the circus. The cost of each balloon was $1.25. How much did she spend for the balloons?

5. Erin bought two birthday presents. One present cost $8.75. The other present cost $7.50. How much did the presents cost in all?

6. Last week 47 people bought bicycle tags. Each tag cost $3.75. How much was spent on tags in all?

Set 66 *pages 182–183*   Name each segment or line.

1.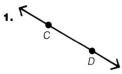

2.

3.

For each exercise, tell whether the lines are intersecting lines or parallel lines.

4.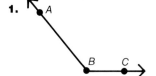

5.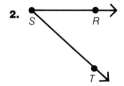

6.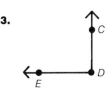

Set 67 *pages 184–185*   Give two names for each angle.

1.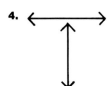

2.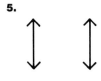

3.

Is each angle a right angle? Use a card to help you decide. Write *yes* or *no*.

4.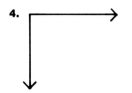

5.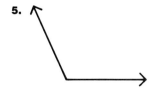

6.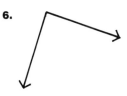

Set 68 *pages 186–187*   Tell whether each figure is a polygon. Write *yes* or *no*.

1.

2.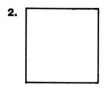

3.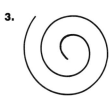

For each polygon, write the number of sides and the number of angles.

4.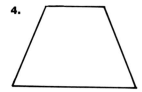

5.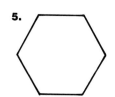

6.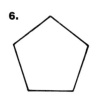

MORE PRACTICE

Set 69 *pages 188–189*   Tell whether the segments or polygons are congruent. Write *yes* or *no*.

1.

2.

3.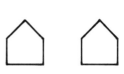

4.

5.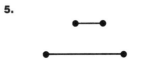

6.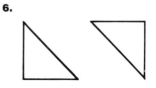

Set 70 *pages 190–191*   Is each figure a parallelogram? Write *yes* or *no*.

1.

2.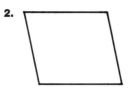

3.

4.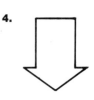

5.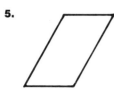

6.

7.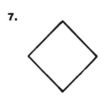

8.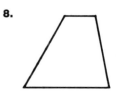

Is each figure a rectangle? Write *yes* or *no*.

9.

10.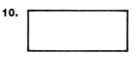

11.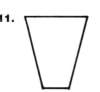

12.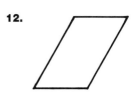

13.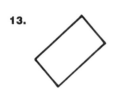

14.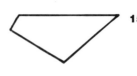

15.

16.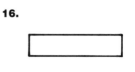

Is each figure a square? Write *yes* or *no*.

17.

18.

19.

20.

Set 71 *pages 192–193* Find the perimeter of each figure.

1.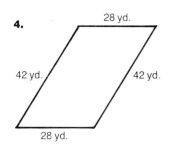

25 in.
16 in. 16 in.
25 in.

2.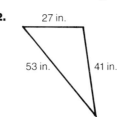

27 in.
53 in. 41 in.

3.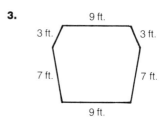

9 ft.
3 ft. 3 ft.
7 ft. 7 ft.
9 ft.

4.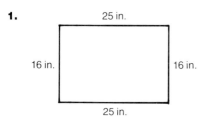

28 yd.
42 yd. 42 yd.
28 yd.

5.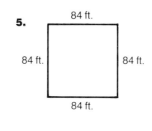

84 ft.
84 ft. 84 ft.
84 ft.

6.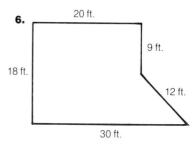

20 ft.
9 ft.
18 ft.
12 ft.
30 ft.

Set 72 *pages 194–195* Find the area of each figure in square centimeters.

1.   **2.**   **3.**

4.   **5.**   **6.**

7.   **8.**   **9.**

377

MORE PRACTICE

Set 73 *pages 198–199*   Find the area of each figure.

1.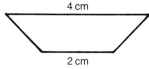

2.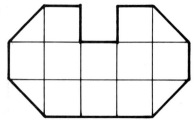

3.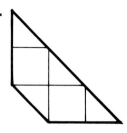

Trace each figure on centimeter grid paper. Then find the area.

4.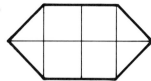
4 cm
2 cm

5.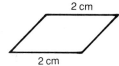
2 cm
2 cm

6.
2 cm
2 cm

Set 74 *pages 200–201*   For each circle, name the center, a radius, and a diameter.

1. Center

2. Radius

3. Diameter

4. Center

5. Radius

6. Diameter

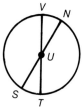

7. Center

8. Radius

9. Diameter

10. Center

11. Radius

12. Diameter

Set 75 *pages 202–203*   Trace each figure and cut it out.
Is the broken line a line of symmetry? Write *yes* or *no*.

1.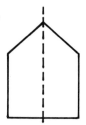

2.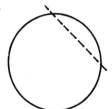

3.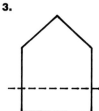

4.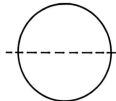

Trace each figure and cut it out. Tell how many lines of symmetry the figure has.

5.

6.

7.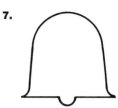

Set 76 *pages 204–205*   Name the shape of each object. Use rectangular prism, cube, cylinder, cone, and sphere.

1.

2.

3.

4.

5.

6.

Set 77 *pages 206–207*   Find the volume of each figure in cubic centimeters.

1.

2.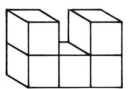

3.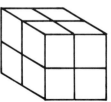

4.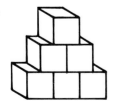

5.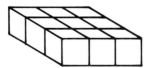

6.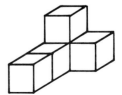

379

MORE PRACTICE

Set 78 *pages 212-213*   Find how many groups. Then complete each division sentence.

1. 15 in all
Groups of 3

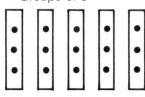

15 ÷ 3 = ▧

2. 16 in all
Groups of 8

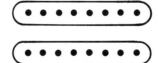

16 ÷ 8 = ▧

3. 16 in all
Groups of 4

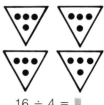

16 ÷ 4 = ▧

Find how many in each group. Then complete each division sentence.

4. 12 in all
2 equal groups

12 ÷ 2 = ▧

5. 30 in all
6 equal groups

30 ÷ 6 = ▧

6. 9 in all
3 equal groups

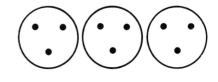

9 ÷ 3 = ▧

Set 79 *pages 214-215*

1. 8 ÷ 2	**2.** 9 ÷ 3	**3.** 18 ÷ 3	**4.** 4 ÷ 2	**5.** 10 ÷ 2	**6.** 6 ÷ 3
7. 12 ÷ 2	**8.** 24 ÷ 3	**9.** 18 ÷ 2	**10.** 21 ÷ 3	**11.** 14 ÷ 2	**12.** 15 ÷ 3
13. 12 ÷ 3	**14.** 16 ÷ 2	**15.** 9 ÷ 3	**16.** 27 ÷ 3	**17.** 16 ÷ 2	**18.** 8 ÷ 2
19. 6 ÷ 2	**20.** 4 ÷ 2	**21.** 14 ÷ 2	**22.** 12 ÷ 3	**23.** 18 ÷ 2	**24.** 18 ÷ 3
25. 15 ÷ 3	**26.** 12 ÷ 2	**27.** 10 ÷ 2	**28.** 24 ÷ 3	**29.** 21 ÷ 3	**30.** 27 ÷ 3

Set 80 *pages 216-217*

1. 5)15	**2.** 4)32	**3.** 5)25	**4.** 4)8	**5.** 4)28	**6.** 5)20
7. 5)40	**8.** 4)20	**9.** 5)10	**10.** 4)36	**11.** 4)16	**12.** 5)45
13. 4)12	**14.** 5)35	**15.** 3)18	**16.** 4)24	**17.** 5)30	**18.** 2)16
19. 10 ÷ 2	**20.** 24 ÷ 4	**21.** 24 ÷ 3	**22.** 25 ÷ 5	**23.** 28 ÷ 4	**24.** 14 ÷ 2
25. 6 ÷ 3	**26.** 15 ÷ 5	**27.** 40 ÷ 5	**28.** 8 ÷ 2	**29.** 45 ÷ 5	**30.** 36 ÷ 4

Set 81 *pages 218-219*

1. $2 \div 1$
2. $2 \div 2$
3. $8 \div 1$
4. $0 \div 2$
5. $4 \div 1$
6. $0 \div 9$
7. $3 \div 3$

8. $0 \div 7$
9. $6 \div 6$
10. $7 \div 1$
11. $6 \div 1$
12. $0 \div 4$
13. $0 \div 1$
14. $8 \div 8$

15. $0 \div 1$
16. $5 \div 1$
17. $0 \div 8$
18. $7 \div 7$
19. $9 \div 1$
20. $1 \div 1$
21. $4 \div 4$

22. $0 \div 5$
23. $1 \div 1$
24. $6 \div 1$
25. $0 \div 6$
26. $0 \div 8$
27. $3 \div 1$
28. $9 \div 9$

29. $0 \div 3$
30. $5 \div 5$
31. $0 \div 4$
32. $3 \div 3$
33. $5 \div 1$
34. $0 \div 2$
35. $0 \div 7$

Set 82 *pages 222-223*

1. $6\overline{)18}$
2. $2\overline{)8}$
3. $3\overline{)24}$
4. $6\overline{)48}$
5. $6\overline{)30}$
6. $6\overline{)6}$

7. $5\overline{)15}$
8. $4\overline{)8}$
9. $6\overline{)0}$
10. $2\overline{)18}$
11. $4\overline{)20}$
12. $1\overline{)6}$

13. $4\overline{)16}$
14. $6\overline{)42}$
15. $3\overline{)21}$
16. $6\overline{)54}$
17. $5\overline{)35}$
18. $6\overline{)24}$

19. $6\overline{)12}$
20. $5\overline{)30}$
21. $3\overline{)27}$
22. $6\overline{)36}$
23. $4\overline{)36}$
24. $2\overline{)12}$

25. $6 \div 6$
26. $20 \div 5$
27. $42 \div 6$
28. $12 \div 6$
29. $25 \div 5$
30. $30 \div 6$

31. $24 \div 4$
32. $0 \div 6$
33. $48 \div 6$
34. $9 \div 3$
35. $18 \div 6$
36. $54 \div 6$

37. $36 \div 6$
38. $6 \div 1$
39. $15 \div 3$
40. $24 \div 6$
41. $16 \div 2$
42. $21 \div 3$

Set 83 *pages 224-225*

1. $7\overline{)28}$
2. $7\overline{)56}$
3. $7\overline{)0}$
4. $7\overline{)21}$
5. $2\overline{)10}$
6. $7\overline{)35}$

7. $7\overline{)42}$
8. $7\overline{)7}$
9. $2\overline{)18}$
10. $3\overline{)27}$
11. $7\overline{)63}$
12. $4\overline{)16}$

13. $4\overline{)20}$
14. $5\overline{)15}$
15. $2\overline{)6}$
16. $7\overline{)14}$
17. $7\overline{)49}$
18. $6\overline{)36}$

19. $3\overline{)12}$
20. $5\overline{)45}$
21. $3\overline{)21}$
22. $4\overline{)28}$
23. $4\overline{)36}$
24. $6\overline{)54}$

25. $0 \div 7$
26. $24 \div 3$
27. $42 \div 7$
28. $4 \div 1$
29. $28 \div 7$
30. $1 \div 1$

31. $4 \div 2$
32. $21 \div 7$
33. $45 \div 5$
34. $15 \div 3$
35. $63 \div 7$
36. $7 \div 7$

37. $56 \div 7$
38. $10 \div 5$
39. $49 \div 7$
40. $14 \div 7$
41. $24 \div 4$
42. $16 \div 2$

43. $48 \div 6$
44. $1 \div 1$
45. $32 \div 4$
46. $18 \div 6$
47. $35 \div 7$
48. $25 \div 5$

MORE PRACTICE

Set 84 *pages 226–227*

1. $8\overline{)8}$
2. $8\overline{)56}$
3. $5\overline{)20}$
4. $8\overline{)24}$
5. $6\overline{)42}$
6. $8\overline{)72}$

7. $4\overline{)12}$
8. $8\overline{)48}$
9. $3\overline{)21}$
10. $6\overline{)54}$
11. $8\overline{)32}$
12. $8\overline{)0}$

13. $8\overline{)40}$
14. $7\overline{)56}$
15. $8\overline{)16}$
16. $8\overline{)64}$
17. $1\overline{)4}$
18. $8\overline{)32}$

19. $48 \div 8$
20. $0 \div 2$
21. $8 \div 8$
22. $36 \div 4$
23. $72 \div 8$
24. $24 \div 8$

25. $0 \div 8$
26. $40 \div 8$
27. $64 \div 8$
28. $3 \div 3$
29. $16 \div 8$
30. $56 \div 8$

Set 85 *pages 228–229*

1. $9\overline{)45}$
2. $6\overline{)36}$
3. $9\overline{)72}$
4. $9\overline{)0}$
5. $5\overline{)40}$
6. $9\overline{)54}$

7. $8\overline{)56}$
8. $9\overline{)9}$
9. $7\overline{)42}$
10. $4\overline{)28}$
11. $9\overline{)18}$
12. $5\overline{)5}$

13. $9\overline{)63}$
14. $7\overline{)0}$
15. $9\overline{)81}$
16. $9\overline{)27}$
17. $5\overline{)35}$
18. $9\overline{)36}$

19. $18 \div 9$
20. $54 \div 6$
21. $72 \div 9$
22. $36 \div 9$
23. $9 \div 9$
24. $63 \div 9$

25. $81 \div 9$
26. $27 \div 9$
27. $54 \div 9$
28. $0 \div 9$
29. $27 \div 3$
30. $45 \div 9$

Write a family of facts using the given numbers.

31. 3, 4, 12
32. 6, 30, 5
33. 9, 81
34. 4, 5, 20
35. 72, 8, 9
36. 8, 4, 32

37. 6, 1
38. 3, 5, 15
39. 21, 3, 7
40. 16, 8, 2
41. 6, 36
42. 6, 9, 54

Set 86 *pages 230–231*   Solve each problem.

1. Jan had 30 papers to deliver. She delivered 12 papers on Elm Street and 9 papers on Oak Avenue. How many papers did she have left to deliver on Forest Road?

2. Chuck had 4 bags of groceries with 5 items in each bag. He wanted to put all of his groceries in 2 bags. If he put the same number of items in each of the 2 bags, how many items would he have in each bag?

3. Eric picked 16 tomatoes and Anne picked 11 tomatoes. They separated the tomatoes into groups of 3. How many tomatoes were in each group?

4. There were 17 girls and 12 boys at the park. 4 more boys came to the park to play tennis. How many more girls than boys were at the park?

5. In art class, there were 16 children painting pictures and 3 groups of 4 children each putting models together. How many children were in art class?

6. Theresa has 11 cousins. Haruo has 3 fewer cousins than Theresa. Susan has 4 fewer cousins than Haruo. How many cousins does Susan have?

1. $3\overline{)14}$
2. $4\overline{)26}$
3. $6\overline{)16}$
4. $8\overline{)58}$
5. $2\overline{)15}$
6. $7\overline{)16}$

7. $4\overline{)35}$
8. $9\overline{)16}$
9. $3\overline{)19}$
10. $8\overline{)19}$
11. $9\overline{)38}$
12. $5\overline{)12}$

13. $7\overline{)62}$
14. $2\overline{)13}$
15. $6\overline{)34}$
16. $4\overline{)22}$
17. $3\overline{)23}$
18. $6\overline{)42}$

19. $7\overline{)48}$
20. $8\overline{)42}$
21. $5\overline{)40}$
22. $7\overline{)24}$
23. $8\overline{)23}$
24. $2\overline{)10}$

25. $5\overline{)11}$
26. $3\overline{)21}$
27. $9\overline{)44}$
28. $6\overline{)52}$
29. $5\overline{)36}$
30. $7\overline{)33}$

31. $17 \div 2$
32. $31 \div 4$
33. $43 \div 5$
34. $25 \div 7$
35. $62 \div 9$
36. $21 \div 6$

37. $15 \div 4$
38. $52 \div 7$
39. $75 \div 8$
40. $58 \div 6$
41. $17 \div 3$
42. $27 \div 5$

43. $27 \div 7$
44. $10 \div 3$
45. $11 \div 2$
46. $12 \div 8$
47. $24 \div 4$
48. $16 \div 3$

49. $36 \div 8$
50. $28 \div 6$
51. $57 \div 9$
52. $28 \div 5$
53. $19 \div 2$
54. $64 \div 8$

55. $72 \div 9$
56. $19 \div 5$
57. $56 \div 7$
58. $37 \div 4$
59. $29 \div 9$
60. $43 \div 6$

Set 88 *pages 236–237*   Tell whether you *add, subtract, multiply,* or *divide*. Then find the answer.

1. There are 18 boats in the harbor with yellow sails and 33 boats in the harbor with white sails. How many more boats have white sails than yellow sails?

2. During a one-hour period, 9 airplanes took off from Parker Field. If the same number of planes took off each hour, how many planes took off in 8 hours?

3. Dan ran 30 laps on the running track. How many miles did Dan run if 5 laps equal one mile?

4. At the school fair, 7 students sold 8 balloons each. How many balloons did they sell in all?

5. Mrs. Chong spent $43.10 at the butcher, $26.37 at the grocery store, and $11.54 at the fruit and vegetable stand. What was the total cost of her purchases?

6. Laura put 26 pictures in her album with 4 pictures on each page. How many pages did she fill? How many pictures were left over?

7. Kelly has 23 children in her classroom. Sally has 5 more children in her classroom than Kelly. How many children are in Sally's classroom?

8. Donato has saved $6.45. The game he wants to buy costs $9.99. How much more money does he need to save before he can buy the game?

9. At the local radio station there are 5 minutes of news, 2 minutes of sports, and 14 minutes for commercials each hour. How many minutes of each hour are used for these items?

10. Katie put 34 candles on her mother's birthday cake in rows with 8 candles in each row. How many rows were filled? How many candles were left over?

MORE PRACTICE

Set 89 *pages 242–243* Check each division. If the answer is wrong, give the correct answer.

11 R2	13	15 R1	25	11 R2	17 R5	18
1. 7)79	**2.** 5)65	**3.** 6)92	**4.** 3)74	**5.** 4)46	**6.** 3)56	**7.** 2)36

Divide.

8. 2)26   **9.** 4)47   **10.** 7)83   **11.** 3)56   **12.** 4)51   **13.** 5)75   **14.** 8)89   **15.** 5)62

16. 7)81   **17.** 2)93   **18.** 5)71   **19.** 8)96   **20.** 6)74   **21.** 2)37   **22.** 7)82   **23.** 4)58

24. 4)86   **25.** 2)29   **26.** 3)43   **27.** 5)64   **28.** 6)71   **29.** 7)99   **30.** 2)32   **31.** 6)68

32. 3)39   **33.** 3)94   **34.** 6)76   **35.** 2)87   **36.** 3)65   **37.** 5)63   **38.** 2)57   **39.** 5)94

40. 8)91   **41.** 5)83   **42.** 7)98   **43.** 4)92   **44.** 6)79   **45.** 4)51   **46.** 3)82   **47.** 8)98

48. 3)74   **49.** 4)59   **50.** 6)73   **51.** 3)65   **52.** 7)87   **53.** 8)93   **54.** 3)97   **55.** 5)86

Set 90 *pages 244–245*

1. 3)60   **2.** 4)80   **3.** 6)60   **4.** 2)60   **5.** 9)90   **6.** 2)80   **7.** 4)40   **8.** 5)50

9. 8)82   **10.** 3)31   **11.** 4)43   **12.** 3)32   **13.** 6)65   **14.** 4)41   **15.** 2)41   **16.** 3)30

17. 3)92   **18.** 6)64   **19.** 4)81   **20.** 5)54   **21.** 8)86   **22.** 9)96   **23.** 7)76   **24.** 4)83

25. 3)61   **26.** 2)21   **27.** 6)61   **28.** 5)51   **29.** 3)91   **30.** 4)82   **31.** 9)97   **32.** 8)82

33. 8)85   **34.** 7)72   **35.** 4)42   **36.** 2)61   **37.** 2)81   **38.** 5)52   **39.** 6)65   **40.** 7)74

41. 6)63   **42.** 9)92   **43.** 7)73   **44.** 6)62   **45.** 3)62   **46.** 5)53   **47.** 8)83   **48.** 9)98

Set 91 *pages 246–247*

1. 2)284   **2.** 7)791   **3.** 5)565   **4.** 3)642   **5.** 2)836   **6.** 4)848   **7.** 5)595

8. 2)626   **9.** 4)476   **10.** 6)684   **11.** 2)492   **12.** 5)570   **13.** 7)784   **14.** 8)896

15. 6)672   **16.** 5)593   **17.** 8)892   **18.** 4)465   **19.** 2)346   **20.** 3)567   **21.** 6)673

22. 4)532   **23.** 3)725   **24.** 3)486   **25.** 8)992   **26.** 2)471   **27.** 3)397   **28.** 5)662

29. 3)852   **30.** 6)715   **31.** 5)823   **32.** 3)381   **33.** 7)824   **34.** 8)915   **35.** 4)628

36. 7)937   **37.** 4)913   **38.** 3)823   **39.** 2)263   **40.** 8)888   **41.** 4)460   **42.** 8)924

43. 5)745   **44.** 3)492   **45.** 7)938   **46.** 6)995   **47.** 7)867   **48.** 4)746   **49.** 5)962

Set 92 *pages 248-249*

1. 2)460   **2.** 6)600   **3.** 3)930   **4.** 4)804   **5.** 8)824   **6.** 4)420

7. 5)603   **8.** 3)902   **9.** 2)611   **10.** 5)545   **11.** 9)928   **12.** 7)735

13. 3)511   **14.** 2)208   **15.** 7)986   **16.** 6)642   **17.** 8)840   **18.** 5)850

19. 728 ÷ 7   **20.** 408 ÷ 4   **21.** 631 ÷ 3   **22.** 864 ÷ 8   **23.** 515 ÷ 5   **24.** 806 ÷ 2

25. 900 ÷ 3   **26.** 705 ÷ 7   **27.** 807 ÷ 2   **28.** 775 ÷ 7   **29.** 636 ÷ 6   **30.** 860 ÷ 8

31. 714 ÷ 7   **32.** 481 ÷ 4   **33.** 750 ÷ 5   **34.** 413 ÷ 2   **35.** 921 ÷ 3   **36.** 612 ÷ 6

Set 93 *pages 250-251*   Tell how many digits will be in each quotient.

1. 4)35   **2.** 7)58   **3.** 3)21   **4.** 4)93   **5.** 6)72   **6.** 5)638   **7.** 7)227

8. 8)910   **9.** 5)696   **10.** 4)537   **11.** 5)322   **12.** 4)916   **13.** 3)416   **14.** 2)163

Divide.

15. 2)64   **16.** 5)48   **17.** 3)23   **18.** 7)86   **19.** 9)73   **20.** 4)57

21. 7)764   **22.** 6)596   **23.** 4)216   **24.** 5)735   **25.** 3)619   **26.** 9)823

27. 6)719   **28.** 8)283   **29.** 9)819   **30.** 4)352   **31.** 7)637   **32.** 2)156

33. 837 ÷ 9   **34.** 694 ÷ 2   **35.** 255 ÷ 3   **36.** 288 ÷ 9   **37.** 373 ÷ 4   **38.** 623 ÷ 7

39. 245 ÷ 5   **40.** 742 ÷ 7   **41.** 320 ÷ 4   **42.** 432 ÷ 6   **43.** 119 ÷ 2   **44.** 291 ÷ 3

45. 512 ÷ 8   **46.** 156 ÷ 6   **47.** 324 ÷ 5   **48.** 387 ÷ 4   **49.** 613 ÷ 8   **50.** 607 ÷ 5

Set 94 *pages 252-253*   Divide. Write each answer as dollars and cents.

1. $3.20 ÷ 2   **2.** $0.96 ÷ 4   **3.** $6.36 ÷ 6   **4.** $9.68 ÷ 8   **5.** $3.42 ÷ 6

6. $4.86 ÷ 3   **7.** $8.82 ÷ 7   **8.** $9.92 ÷ 8   **9.** $9.87 ÷ 3   **10.** $7.92 ÷ 6

11. $8.96 ÷ 2   **12.** $7.53 ÷ 3   **13.** $9.87 ÷ 7   **14.** $6.05 ÷ 5   **15.** $7.48 ÷ 4

16. $2.96 ÷ 8   **17.** $9.42 ÷ 3   **18.** $7.74 ÷ 6   **19.** $8.94 ÷ 3   **20.** $6.15 ÷ 5

21. $8.13 ÷ 3   **22.** $8.12 ÷ 7   **23.** $8.48 ÷ 8   **24.** $7.62 ÷ 6   **25.** $8.68 ÷ 4

26. $1.80 ÷ 5   **27.** $8.72 ÷ 4   **28.** $9.24 ÷ 7   **29.** $9.00 ÷ 9   **30.** $7.38 ÷ 2

31. $7.50 ÷ 5   **32.** $9.54 ÷ 9   **33.** $8.70 ÷ 5   **34.** $9.24 ÷ 6   **35.** $8.76 ÷ 6

MORE PRACTICE

Set 95 *pages 256–257*   Solve each problem.

1. Mr. Pucci is planting flowers in his garden. He has 48 plants to put in rows of 5 each. How many plants will he have left over?

2. Ramona has 35 pictures to put in her photo album. If she puts 4 pictures on each page, how many pictures will be left over?

3. Jerry needs to buy 74 stamps. The stamps are sold in packets of 8 each. How many packets does he need to buy?

4. Heidi must sell $25 worth of cards to go on her band trip. How many boxes of cards must she sell if each box costs $2?

5. If 3 party favors are put in each child's party bag, how many party bags can be made with 37 favors? How many party favors will be left over?

6. Vicente has 113 inches of string. How many 9-inch pieces of string can he make if he uses the entire string?

Set 96 *pages 258–259*   Find the average of each group of numbers.

1. 3, 8, 4
2. 7, 6, 8
3. 5, 6, 16
4. 2, 6, 8, 8
5. 4, 3, 1, 4
6. 2, 9, 9, 8
7. 6, 5, 18, 11
8. 8, 14, 19, 11
9. 36, 22, 17, 25
10. 216, 104, 97
11. 92, 34, 16, 56, 87
12. 177, 224, 196, 203
13. 112, 116, 111
14. 84, 26, 37
15. 31, 92, 75
16. 2, 4, 6, 8, 10
17. 3, 9, 17, 14, 2
18. 100, 200, 100, 200
19. 112, 134, 126, 103, 115
20. 184, 153, 124, 201, 213
21. 206, 196, 172, 235, 101

Set 97 *pages 260–261*

1. $20\overline{)80}$
2. $30\overline{)60}$
3. $40\overline{)80}$
4. $30\overline{)120}$
5. $20\overline{)160}$
6. $50\overline{)150}$
7. $90\overline{)450}$
8. $20\overline{)180}$
9. $60\overline{)360}$
10. $70\overline{)210}$
11. $80\overline{)640}$
12. $40\overline{)320}$
13. $60\overline{)486}$
14. $70\overline{)563}$
15. $50\overline{)359}$
16. $80\overline{)325}$
17. $70\overline{)289}$
18. $50\overline{)206}$
19. $30\overline{)276}$
20. $40\overline{)362}$
21. $90\overline{)723}$
22. $20\overline{)184}$
23. $80\overline{)403}$
24. $60\overline{)546}$
25. $80\overline{)486}$
26. $40\overline{)261}$
27. $70\overline{)583}$
28. $90\overline{)642}$
29. $30\overline{)236}$
30. $90\overline{)557}$
31. $90\overline{)834}$
32. $20\overline{)116}$
33. $40\overline{)248}$
34. $60\overline{)372}$
35. $50\overline{)417}$
36. $80\overline{)552}$
37. $30\overline{)247}$
38. $30\overline{)112}$
39. $20\overline{)145}$
40. $70\overline{)363}$
41. $40\overline{)294}$
42. $50\overline{)467}$

Set 98 *pages 262-263*

1. $43\overline{)86}$ **2.** $21\overline{)147}$ **3.** $23\overline{)138}$ **4.** $34\overline{)102}$ **5.** $52\overline{)107}$ **6.** $25\overline{)77}$

7. $34\overline{)78}$ **8.** $45\overline{)97}$ **9.** $57\overline{)63}$ **10.** $76\overline{)84}$ **11.** $48\overline{)99}$ **12.** $62\overline{)86}$

13. $22\overline{)179}$ **14.** $72\overline{)347}$ **15.** $32\overline{)136}$ **16.** $84\overline{)431}$ **17.** $45\overline{)228}$ **18.** $37\overline{)149}$

19. $68\overline{)418}$ **20.** $42\overline{)129}$ **21.** $97\overline{)613}$ **22.** $59\overline{)297}$ **23.** $93\overline{)846}$ **24.** $63\overline{)516}$

25. $56 \div 28$ **26.** $490 \div 70$ **27.** $528 \div 66$ **28.** $111 \div 37$ **29.** $308 \div 44$ **30.** $265 \div 53$

31. $84 \div 41$ **32.** $268 \div 32$ **33.** $197 \div 47$ **34.** $487 \div 51$ **35.** $689 \div 75$ **36.** $229 \div 54$

37. $99 \div 31$ **38.** $419 \div 62$ **39.** $256 \div 83$ **40.** $895 \div 98$ **41.** $846 \div 92$ **42.** $374 \div 49$

Set 99 *pages 264-265*

1. $21\overline{)40}$ **2.** $12\overline{)46}$ **3.** $67\overline{)253}$ **4.** $24\overline{)178}$ **5.** $72\overline{)286}$ **6.** $87\overline{)681}$

7. $56\overline{)326}$ **8.** $24\overline{)110}$ **9.** $51\overline{)202}$ **10.** $45\overline{)293}$ **11.** $36\overline{)102}$ **12.** $96\overline{)549}$

13. $24\overline{)86}$ **14.** $63\overline{)362}$ **15.** $72\overline{)502}$ **16.** $48\overline{)254}$ **17.** $59\overline{)339}$ **18.** $56\overline{)159}$

19. $34\overline{)198}$ **20.** $92\overline{)364}$ **21.** $73\overline{)572}$ **22.** $23\overline{)194}$ **23.** $75\overline{)361}$ **24.** $24\overline{)216}$

25. $146 \div 37$ **26.** $182 \div 48$ **27.** $368 \div 42$ **28.** $183 \div 31$ **29.** $296 \div 43$ **30.** $572 \div 83$

31. $452 \div 51$ **32.** $284 \div 29$ **33.** $309 \div 63$ **34.** $254 \div 86$ **35.** $211 \div 71$ **36.** $162 \div 59$

37. $173 \div 44$ **38.** $359 \div 52$ **39.** $284 \div 33$ **40.** $487 \div 62$ **41.** $404 \div 84$ **42.** $236 \div 37$

Set 100 *pages 266-267*

1. $24\overline{)286}$ **2.** $36\overline{)772}$ **3.** $66\overline{)793}$ **4.** $73\overline{)861}$ **5.** $41\overline{)565}$ **6.** $23\overline{)487}$

7. $65\overline{)723}$ **8.** $82\overline{)976}$ **9.** $74\overline{)819}$ **10.** $31\overline{)993}$ **11.** $59\overline{)727}$ **12.** $45\overline{)966}$

13. $43\overline{)992}$ **14.** $22\overline{)484}$ **15.** $21\overline{)259}$ **16.** $42\overline{)759}$ **17.** $77\overline{)893}$ **18.** $32\overline{)687}$

19. $31\overline{)716}$ **20.** $47\overline{)989}$ **21.** $56\overline{)734}$ **22.** $33\overline{)528}$ **23.** $22\overline{)693}$ **24.** $90\overline{)997}$

25. $58\overline{)649}$ **26.** $75\overline{)923}$ **27.** $37\overline{)782}$ **28.** $75\overline{)993}$ **29.** $67\overline{)816}$ **30.** $28\overline{)598}$

31. $64\overline{)876}$ **32.** $36\overline{)793}$ **33.** $72\overline{)864}$ **34.** $25\overline{)785}$ **35.** $76\overline{)862}$ **36.** $39\overline{)823}$

37. $28\overline{)596}$ **38.** $57\overline{)712}$ **39.** $87\overline{)983}$ **40.** $38\overline{)874}$ **41.** $79\overline{)956}$ **42.** $68\overline{)825}$

MORE PRACTICE

Set 101 *pages 270–271*   Write an equation. Then find the answer.

1. Mr. Hale drove his car 212 miles in 4 hours. What was his average speed in miles per hour?

2. Michele played tennis for 137 minutes. How many hours and minutes is this? (60 minutes = 1 hour)

3. 34 buses left the bus terminal each hour. How many buses left the bus terminal in 5 hours?

4. The movie showing at the Sunshine Theater ran for 202 minutes. How many hours and minutes is this?

Set 102 *pages 278–279*   Write each decimal.

1. 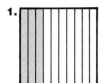   **2.** 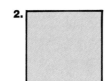   **3.**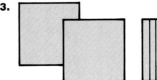

4. three tenths

5. one and two tenths

6. two and nine tenths

7. six tenths

8. four and one tenth

9. three and eight tenths

10. seven tenths

11. eight and four tenths

12. five and seven tenths

Write each decimal in words.

13. 6.7   **14.** 8.2   **15.** 0.3   **16.** 1.4   **17.** 9.8   **18.** 0.6   **19.** 2.5   **20.** 1.9

21. 5.3   **22.** 9.1   **23.** 3.6   **24.** 0.1   **25.** 7.2   **26.** 2.8   **27.** 3.7   **28.** 8.6

Set 103 *pages 280–281*   Write each decimal.

1. 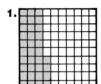   **2.** 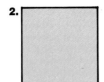   **3.**

4. thirty-nine hundredths

5. fifteen hundredths

6. one and forty-seven hundredths

7. three hundredths

8. fifty-one hundredths

9. six and two hundredths

Write each decimal in words.

10. 0.46   **11.** 0.07   **12.** 5.03   **13.** 8.36   **14.** 0.81   **15.** 1.20   **16.** 3.16

17. 2.54   **18.** 0.36   **19.** 1.08   **20.** 3.33   **21.** 7.40   **22.** 2.85   **23.** 4.06

Set 104 *pages 282-283* Tell what the 4 means in each number.

1. 34.07 **2.** 7.45 **3.** 49.62 **4.** 92.14 **5.** 452.7 **6.** 9.84 **7.** 16.40 **8.** 724.02

Which decimals have

9. 6 in the hundredths place?

211.76   643.8   2.63

10. 7 in the tenths place?

72.06   4.73   223.07

11. 1 in the tenths place?

37.13   26.51   410.62

12. 5 in the hundredths place?

516.72   24.35   259.02

Write each decimal.

13. 2 tens 3 ones 9 tenths

14. 6 ones 1 tenth 8 hundredths

15. 7 ones 2 hundredths

16. 5 hundreds 2 ones 4 hundredths

Set 105 *pages 284-285* Write each amount with a dollar sign and a decimal point.

1. 6¢ **2.** 72¢ **3.** 16¢ **4.** 39¢

5. 27 cents **6.** 94 cents **7.** 50 cents **8.** 8 cents

9. nineteen cents **10.** three cents **11.** thirty cents **12.** seventy-five cents

Write each amount with a cent sign.

13. $0.05 **14.** $0.80 **15.** $0.44 **16.** $0.71 **17.** $0.16 **18.** $0.23 **19.** $0.09

Set 106 *pages 286-287* Write an equal decimal for

1. 0.70 in tenths **2.** 3.6 in hundredths **3.** 6.80 in tenths **4.** 9.1 in hundredths

Write two number sentences to compare each decimal. Use < and >.

5. 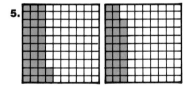 **6.** 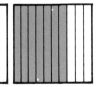 **7.**

Compare the decimals. Use <, >, or =.

8. 0.4 ● 0.2 **9.** 7.6 ● 7.2 **10.** 2.6 ● 2.60 **11.** 0.37 ● 0.61

12. 0.62 ● 0.58 **13.** 1.34 ● 0.34 **14.** 35.62 ● 35.66 **15.** 32.20 ● 32.02

16. 38.6 ● 36.8 **17.** 45.16 ● 44.61 **18.** 16.4 ● 16.42 **19.** 10.1 ● 10.10

20. 21.60 ● 21.7 **21.** 63.60 ● 36.06 **22.** 23.02 ● 21.03 **23.** 52.9 ● 52.89

389

MORE PRACTICE

Set 107 *pages 288–289*

1.　0.2
　＋ 0.3

2.　7.3
　＋ 5.6

3.　2.7
　＋ 9.6

4.　46.3
　＋ 24.2

5.　56.7
　＋ 52.9

6.　0.29
　＋ 0.18

7.　0.61
　＋ 0.49

8.　2.48
　＋ 6.31

9.　5.87
　＋ 6.14

10.　3.62
　＋ 5.99

11.　12.46
　＋ 16.32

12.　82.13
　＋ 17.89

13.　7.26
　＋ 0.47

14.　10.73
　＋ 6.43

15.　62.03
　＋ 24.98

16.　0.02
　＋ 25.09

17.　70.27
　＋ 28.75

18.　36.84
　＋ 75.57

19. 38 + 12.93

20. 0.38 + 19.54

21. 9 + 34.06

22. 0.6 + 4.7 + 7

23. 2 + 1.36 + 0.70

24. 0.46 + 1.13 + 4

25. 0.98 + 0.24 + 8

26. 0.58 + 1.43 + 0.72

Set 108 *pages 290–291*

1.　8.8
　− 4.7

2.　6.3
　− 2.1

3.　9.4
　− 7.3

4.　6.4
　− 2.7

5.　8.3
　− 6.8

6.　5.7
　− 3.9

7.　18.3
　− 5.6

8.　16.1
　− 0.8

9.　3.62
　− 0.38

10.　9.17
　− 2.93

11.　6.02
　− 1.84

12.　8.22
　− 4.86

13.　23.72
　− 2.61

14.　38.17
　− 5.64

15.　53.92
　− 7.87

16.　20.32
　− 11.94

17.　34.12
　− 10.05

18.　29.36
　− 12.07

19. 8.3 − 4.7

20. 36.13 − 8

21. 4.82 − 0.93

22. 6 − 3.26

23. 9 − 0.87

24. 46 − 2.82

25. 58 − 14.92

26. 26 − 23.45

27. 41.29 − 28

28. 24.17 − 18.96

Set 109 *pages 292–293*　Tell whether you would *add* or *subtract*. Then find the answer.

1. Claudia bought a basketball on sale for $8.99. The basketball sold for $12.00 before the sale. How much money did Claudia save at the sale?

2. Sandy babysat 23.5 hours in March and 19 hours in April. How many more hours did she babysit in March than in April?

3. Takashi weighs 35.6 kilograms. His dog weighs 12.8 kilograms. How much more does Takashi weigh than his dog?

4. Lucy bought 3 hair ribbons. One ribbon cost $0.98, one ribbon cost $1.29, and one ribbon cost $1.09. How much did the ribbons cost altogether?

Set 110 *pages 296–297*   Solve each problem.

1. Roberto bicycled 6.8 miles in 1.75 hours on Monday. He bicycled 4.6 miles in 1 hour on Tuesday. How many miles did he bicycle in all.

2. Vicky bought 9 yards of red fabric and 6 yards of green fabric. She used 2.6 yards of green fabric. How much green fabric did she have left?

3. Everett spent $7.50 for an album, $16.34 for a sweater, and $12.98 for a shirt. How much did he spend for the shirt and sweater?

4. Nate collected cans weighing 3.5 kilograms on Monday, 1 kilogram on Tuesday, and 1.7 kilograms on Wednesday. How many more kilograms did he collect on Monday than on Wednesday?

Set 111 *pages 302–303*   Write a fraction to show how much of the figure is shaded.

1.   2.   3. 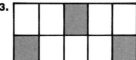   4.

Write each fraction.

5. three fourths   6. one seventh   7. two thirds   8. four fourths   9. six tenths

Write each fraction in words.

10. $\frac{1}{3}$ 11. $\frac{3}{5}$ 12. $\frac{2}{6}$ 13. $\frac{5}{6}$ 14. $\frac{6}{8}$ 15. $\frac{1}{5}$ 16. $\frac{3}{4}$ 17. $\frac{7}{9}$ 18. $\frac{5}{8}$ 19. $\frac{4}{7}$

Set 112 *pages 304–305*   What fraction of the

1. animals are ducks?

2. doors are open?

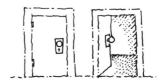

3. letters are *r*s?

4. shapes are square?

5. balloons are red?

6. cups are full?

MORE PRACTICE

Set 113 *pages 306–307*   Compare the fractions. Use < or >.

1. $\frac{3}{4}$ ⬤ $\frac{1}{4}$ **2.** $\frac{7}{9}$ ⬤ $\frac{6}{9}$ **3.** $\frac{2}{6}$ ⬤ $\frac{4}{6}$ **4.** $\frac{5}{3}$ ⬤ $\frac{1}{3}$ **5.** $\frac{6}{8}$ ⬤ $\frac{7}{8}$ **6.** $\frac{14}{15}$ ⬤ $\frac{12}{15}$ **7.** $\frac{13}{14}$ ⬤ $\frac{14}{14}$

8. $\frac{7}{2}$ ⬤ $\frac{3}{2}$ **9.** $\frac{0}{5}$ ⬤ $\frac{4}{5}$ **10.** $\frac{1}{7}$ ⬤ $\frac{3}{7}$ **11.** $\frac{2}{9}$ ⬤ $\frac{8}{9}$ **12.** $\frac{0}{4}$ ⬤ $\frac{1}{4}$ **13.** $\frac{7}{11}$ ⬤ $\frac{17}{11}$ **14.** $\frac{6}{10}$ ⬤ $\frac{8}{10}$

Use the number lines to compare the fractions. Use <, >, or =.

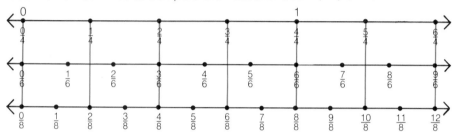

15. $\frac{4}{4}$ ⬤ $\frac{8}{8}$ **16.** $\frac{1}{4}$ ⬤ $\frac{4}{8}$ **17.** $\frac{1}{6}$ ⬤ $\frac{3}{8}$ **18.** $\frac{5}{6}$ ⬤ $\frac{6}{8}$ **19.** $\frac{6}{6}$ ⬤ $\frac{7}{8}$ **20.** $\frac{0}{8}$ ⬤ $\frac{1}{6}$ **21.** $\frac{5}{4}$ ⬤ $\frac{10}{8}$

22. $\frac{3}{4}$ ⬤ $\frac{5}{6}$ **23.** $\frac{3}{6}$ ⬤ $\frac{2}{4}$ **24.** $\frac{1}{4}$ ⬤ $\frac{1}{8}$ **25.** $\frac{7}{6}$ ⬤ $\frac{7}{8}$ **26.** $\frac{2}{6}$ ⬤ $\frac{5}{8}$ **27.** $\frac{0}{6}$ ⬤ $\frac{0}{4}$ **28.** $\frac{11}{8}$ ⬤ $\frac{6}{4}$

Compare each fraction with 1. Use <, >, or =.

29. $\frac{2}{4}$ ⬤ 1   **30.** $\frac{6}{6}$ ⬤ 1   **31.** $\frac{5}{8}$ ⬤ 1   **32.** $\frac{7}{6}$ ⬤ 1   **33.** $\frac{0}{8}$ ⬤ 1   **34.** $\frac{6}{4}$ ⬤ 1   **35.** $\frac{3}{8}$ ⬤ 1

Set 114 *pages 308–309*   Write each mixed number.

1. one and two fifths   **2.** seven and one third   **3.** four and three eighths

4. six and four sixths   **5.** five and two fourths   **6.** eight and four fifths

Write a fraction and a mixed number for each picture.

7.   **8.**

9.   **10.**

11.    **12.**

Set 115 *pages 310–311* Give the length of each segment.

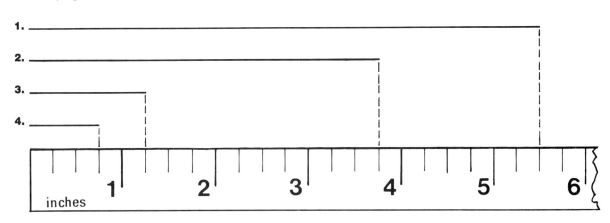

Use a ruler to measure each segment.

5. _____

6. _____

7. _____

8. _____

Set 116 *pages 312–313* Find each answer.

1. $\frac{1}{3}$ of 27 **2.** $\frac{1}{2}$ of 12 **3.** $\frac{1}{5}$ of 25 **4.** $\frac{1}{8}$ of 40 **5.** $\frac{1}{4}$ of 36 **6.** $\frac{1}{3}$ of 6

7. $\frac{1}{5}$ of 20 **8.** $\frac{1}{6}$ of 30 **9.** $\frac{1}{2}$ of 42 **10.** $\frac{1}{4}$ of 12 **11.** $\frac{1}{8}$ of 64 **12.** $\frac{1}{3}$ of 21

13. $\frac{1}{2}$ of 52 **14.** $\frac{1}{3}$ of 90 **15.** $\frac{1}{8}$ of 56 **16.** $\frac{1}{5}$ of 75 **17.** $\frac{1}{4}$ of 96 **18.** $\frac{1}{6}$ of 78

Set 117 *pages 314–315* Solve each problem. Draw a picture to help you.

1. In Jody's garden, $\frac{2}{3}$ of the 18 flowers are roses. How many of the flowers are roses?

2. It rained on $\frac{3}{5}$ of the 30 days in April. How many days did it rain in April?

3. On Hickory Road, $\frac{5}{6}$ of the 36 parked cars were yellow. How many of the parked cars were yellow?

4. Dr. Zabin examined 32 pets on Saturday. If $\frac{3}{4}$ of the pets were dogs, how many of the pets were dogs?

5. Don made $\frac{4}{5}$ of his 10 free throws. How many free throws did he make?

6. If $\frac{1}{6}$ of the 6 musicians in the band played drums, how many musicians played drums?

MORE PRACTICE

Set 118 *pages 316–317*

1. $\frac{1}{7} + \frac{2}{7}$
2. $\frac{1}{3} + \frac{2}{3}$
3. $\frac{2}{8} + \frac{2}{8}$
4. $\frac{4}{6} + \frac{1}{6}$
5. $\frac{3}{5} + \frac{2}{5}$
6. $\frac{0}{2} + \frac{1}{2}$
7. $\frac{3}{4} + \frac{2}{4}$

8. $\frac{3}{9} + \frac{5}{9}$
9. $\frac{0}{6} + \frac{2}{6}$
10. $\frac{5}{2} + \frac{3}{2}$
11. $\frac{4}{3} + \frac{3}{3}$
12. $\frac{5}{6} + \frac{5}{6}$
13. $\frac{1}{7} + \frac{4}{7}$
14. $\frac{6}{9} + \frac{7}{9}$

15. $\frac{7}{8} + \frac{2}{8}$
16. $\frac{2}{6} + \frac{4}{6}$
17. $\frac{0}{3} + \frac{2}{3}$
18. $\frac{2}{5} + \frac{4}{5}$
19. $\frac{4}{9} + \frac{4}{9}$
20. $\frac{6}{8} + \frac{5}{8}$
21. $\frac{8}{2} + \frac{9}{2}$

22. $\frac{3}{10}$ $+ \frac{8}{10}$
23. $\frac{7}{8}$ $+ \frac{8}{8}$
24. $\frac{9}{12}$ $+ \frac{6}{12}$
25. $\frac{3}{6}$ $+ \frac{4}{6}$
26. $\frac{5}{10}$ $+ \frac{9}{10}$
27. $\frac{3}{5}$ $+ \frac{6}{5}$
28. $\frac{4}{12}$ $+ \frac{7}{12}$

Set 119 *pages 318–319*   Use the number lines to help you find equal fractions.

1. $\frac{4}{8} = \frac{}{2}$
2. $\frac{4}{4} = \frac{}{2}$

3. $\frac{1}{2} = \frac{}{4}$
4. $\frac{2}{4} = \frac{}{8}$

5. $\frac{1}{4} = \frac{}{8}$
6. $\frac{0}{2} = \frac{}{8}$

7. $\frac{8}{8} = \frac{}{4}$
8. $\frac{6}{8} = \frac{}{4}$

9. $\frac{2}{3} = \frac{}{12}$
10. $\frac{6}{12} = \frac{}{4}$

11. $\frac{3}{4} = \frac{}{12}$
12. $\frac{0}{4} = \frac{}{3}$

13. $\frac{4}{12} = \frac{}{3}$
14. $\frac{3}{3} = \frac{}{12}$

15. $\frac{3}{12} = \frac{}{4}$
16. $\frac{12}{12} = \frac{}{4}$

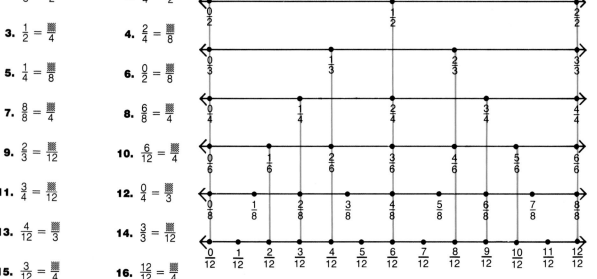

Set 120 *pages 320–321*   Add. Use the number lines above.

1. $\frac{1}{3} + \frac{5}{12}$
2. $\frac{2}{3} + \frac{2}{12}$
3. $\frac{1}{8} + \frac{1}{4}$
4. $\frac{0}{6} + \frac{5}{12}$
5. $\frac{5}{6} + \frac{2}{12}$
6. $\frac{2}{3} + \frac{4}{6}$

7. $\frac{1}{6} + \frac{9}{12}$
8. $\frac{2}{8} + \frac{5}{12}$
9. $\frac{3}{4} + \frac{7}{8}$
10. $\frac{4}{4} + \frac{3}{12}$
11. $\frac{4}{6} + \frac{7}{12}$
12. $\frac{3}{8} + \frac{2}{4}$

13. $\frac{2}{3}$ $+ \frac{2}{12}$
14. $\frac{1}{8}$ $+ \frac{3}{4}$
15. $\frac{6}{8}$ $+ \frac{1}{4}$
16. $\frac{3}{12}$ $+ \frac{4}{8}$
17. $\frac{1}{8}$ $+ \frac{3}{6}$
18. $\frac{6}{8}$ $+ \frac{2}{12}$

Set 121 *pages 322–323*

1. $\frac{3}{4} - \frac{1}{4}$ 2. $\frac{7}{9} - \frac{2}{9}$ 3. $\frac{6}{8} - \frac{2}{8}$ 4. $\frac{4}{5} - \frac{3}{5}$ 5. $\frac{1}{6} - \frac{0}{6}$ 6. $\frac{2}{3} - \frac{2}{3}$ 7. $\frac{9}{10} - \frac{5}{10}$

8. $\frac{3}{6} - \frac{1}{6}$ 9. $\frac{6}{7} - \frac{5}{7}$ 10. $\frac{8}{5} - \frac{3}{5}$ 11. $\frac{3}{2} - \frac{2}{2}$ 12. $\frac{8}{9} - \frac{6}{9}$ 13. $\frac{5}{4} - \frac{2}{4}$ 14. $\frac{11}{12} - \frac{5}{12}$

15. $\frac{7}{8}$ $-\frac{4}{8}$ 16. $\frac{10}{12}$ $-\frac{3}{12}$ 17. $\frac{7}{8}$ $-\frac{3}{8}$ 18. $\frac{6}{5}$ $-\frac{2}{5}$ 19. $\frac{4}{7}$ $-\frac{4}{7}$ 20. $\frac{8}{10}$ $-\frac{0}{10}$ 21. $\frac{2}{4}$ $-\frac{1}{4}$

Set 122 *pages 324–325*   Subtract. Use the number lines on page 394.

1. $\frac{2}{4} - \frac{2}{8}$ 2. $\frac{6}{8} - \frac{1}{4}$ 3. $\frac{9}{12} - \frac{2}{6}$ 4. $\frac{3}{6} - \frac{1}{3}$ 5. $\frac{1}{4} - \frac{1}{12}$ 6. $\frac{8}{12} - \frac{3}{6}$ 7. $\frac{2}{4} - \frac{3}{8}$

8. $\frac{5}{8} - \frac{1}{4}$ 9. $\frac{7}{8} - \frac{2}{4}$ 10. $\frac{4}{6} - \frac{5}{12}$ 11. $\frac{8}{8} - \frac{3}{4}$ 12. $\frac{5}{12} - \frac{2}{6}$ 13. $\frac{11}{12} - \frac{0}{6}$ 14. $\frac{4}{6} - \frac{1}{3}$

15. $\frac{8}{12}$ $-\frac{3}{6}$ 16. $\frac{3}{8}$ $-\frac{1}{4}$ 17. $\frac{11}{12}$ $-\frac{2}{3}$ 18. $\frac{6}{12}$ $-\frac{2}{4}$ 19. $\frac{7}{8}$ $-\frac{3}{4}$ 20. $\frac{5}{6}$ $-\frac{5}{12}$ 21. $\frac{2}{4}$ $-\frac{1}{8}$

Set 123 *pages 332–333*   This pictograph shows the number of balloons sold at the zoo.

Number of Balloons Sold at the Zoo

Monday	〇〇〇〇〇〇〇
Tuesday	〇〇〇〇〇
Wednesday	〇〇〇〇
Thursday	〇〇〇〇〇〇〇
Friday	〇〇〇〇〇〇〇〇〇〇〇〇

Each 〇 means 8 balloons.

How many balloons were sold on

1. Monday?   2. Tuesday?   3. Wednesday?   4. Thursday?   5. Friday?

6. On which day were the most balloons sold?   7. On which day were the least balloons sold?

8. On which days were the same number of balloons sold?   9. How many balloons were sold on Tuesday and Wednesday?

MORE PRACTICE

Set 124 *pages 334–335*   Use the bar graph below to find each answer.

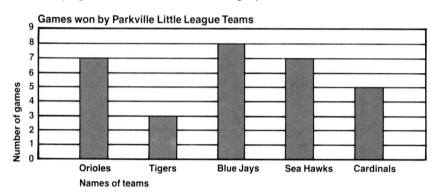

How many games were won by the

1. Orioles?   **2.** Tigers?   **3.** Blue Jays?   **4.** Sea Hawks?   **5.** Cardinals?

6. Which teams won more than 6 games?

7. Which teams won the same number of games?

8. Which team won fewer than 4 games?

9. Which team won the most games?

Set 125 *pages 336–337*   Use the broken-line graph below to answer each question.

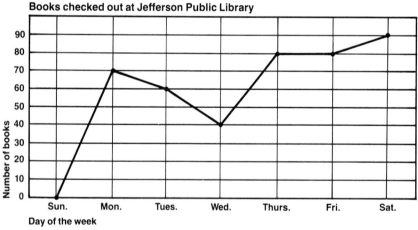

How many books were checked out on

1. Sunday?   **2.** Monday?   **3.** Tuesday?   **4.** Wednesday?   **5.** Thursday?   **6.** Friday?

7. On which day was the greatest number of books checked out?

8. On which days was the same number of books checked out?

9. On which day were 40 books checked out?

10. On which day was the least number of books checked out?

Set 126 *pages 340–341* Write the letter that names the point located by each number pair. Use the grid below.

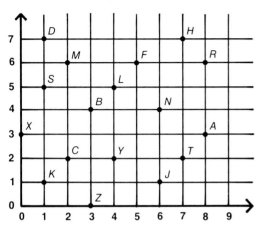

1. (6, 4)   **2.** (2, 2)   **3.** (0, 3)   **4.** (1, 7)   **5.** (5, 6)   **6.** (4, 2)   **7.** (7, 7)

Write the number pair that gives the location named by each letter. Use the grid above.

8. *B*   **9.** *R*   **10.** *T*   **11.** *Z*   **12.** *K*   **13.** *L*   **14.** *J*   **15.** *M*   **16.** *A*   **17.** *S*

Set 127 *pages 342–343* Number a grid for Exercises 1–8. Then graph and label the points located by the number pairs given. Connect the points as directed.

1. *D* (2, 4)

2. *E* (2, 6)
Connect *D* and *E*

3. *F* (4, 8)
Connect *E* and *F*

4. *G* (6, 8)
Connect *F* and *G*

5. *H* (8, 6)
Connect *G* and *H*

6. *I* (8, 4)
Connect *H* and *I*

7. *J* (6, 2)
Connect *I* and *J*

8. *K* (4, 2)
Connect *J* and *K*
Connect *D* and *K*

Set 128 *pages 344–345* Use the graph below to solve each problem.

1. Carl spent $3.75 for folders. How many folders did he buy?

2. Beth bought 25 folders. How much did she spend on folders?

3. Casey bought 5 folders. How much change did he receive from $5.00?

4. Gail bought 15 folders. Georgina bought 25 folders. How much more did Georgina spend for folders than Gail?

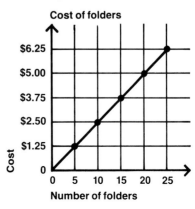

Cost of folders

MAINTENANCE

Add or subtract.

1. 15 − 7	**2.** 3 − 3	**3.** 7 + 8	**4.** 5 + 9	**5.** 10 − 6	**6.** 8 − 1	**7.** 4 + 3
8. 7 + 2	**9.** 8 + 5	**10.** 9 + 9	**11.** 17 − 8	**12.** 15 − 9	**13.** 11 − 8	**14.** 5 − 0
15. 4 + 7	**16.** 5 + 5	**17.** 8 − 5	**18.** 13 − 8	**19.** 2 + 2	**20.** 6 + 5	**21.** 9 − 3
22. 6 − 4	**23.** 3 + 8	**24.** 6 + 7	**25.** 7 + 7	**26.** 0 + 4	**27.** 12 − 7	**28.** 11 − 2

29. 6 + 6   **30.** 2 + 9   **31.** 3 + 6   **32.** 5 + 2   **33.** 8 − 4   **34.** 12 − 4

35. 16 − 7   **36.** 14 − 9   **37.** 5 + 4   **38.** 7 + 5   **39.** 9 + 8   **40.** 9 + 1

41. 11 − 4   **42.** 10 − 2   **43.** 1 + 5   **44.** 9 + 3   **45.** 8 + 0   **46.** 9 − 9

47. 14 − 5   **48.** 13 − 7   **49.** 9 + 7   **50.** 16 − 8   **51.** 6 + 8   **52.** 9 + 6

Choosing a Computation Method
Calculator, Paper and Pencil, Mental Math

Use the best method to solve each problem. Tell which method you used.

53. Carl ate 11 carrot sticks. Ann ate 6 carrot sticks. How many more did Carl eat than Ann?

54. The family ate 5 oranges, 4 apples and 7 bananas at the picnic. How many pieces of fruit did they eat?

55. Carl collected 16 wildflowers. Sue collected 24 wildflowers. Who collected the greatest number of wildflowers?

56. The Roberts family brought 12 sandwiches to the picnic. They ate 8 of the sandwiches. How many were left?

57. The Roberts family drove 48 miles to the picnic. The Martinez family drove 29 miles. How much farther did the Roberts family drive?

58. Friday, 83 children came to the park. Saturday, 99 children came. Sunday, 121 children came. How many children came to the park in all?

MAINTENANCE

Add or subtract.

1. $8 + 7$ **2.** $4 + 5$ **3.** $17 - 8$ **4.** $16 - 9$ **5.** $6 + 9$ **6.** $4 + 7$

7. $14 - 6$ **8.** $12 - 3$ **9.** $9 + 7$ **10.** $11 - 4$ **11.** $12 - 7$ **12.** $9 + 3$

13. $11 - 8$ **14.** $9 + 9$ **15.** $6 + 7$ **16.** $15 - 7$ **17.** $9 - 3$ **18.** $7 + 7$

19. $5 + 5$ **20.** $17 - 9$ **21.** $8 + 8$ **22.** $10 - 3$ **23.** $11 - 5$ **24.** $4 + 9$

Compare the numbers. Use $<$ or $>$.

25. 35 ● 29 **26.** 64 ● 67 **27.** 329 ● 327

28. 584 ● 482 **29.** 4,638 ● 4,724 **30.** 7,372 ● 7,360

Write the numbers in order from least to greatest.

31. 56 47 39 **32.** 84 93 81 **33.** 30 39 35 32

34. 354 362 360 **35.** 746 731 738 **36.** 1,473 1,186 1,452

Choosing a Computation Method
Calculator, Paper and Pencil, Mental Math,

Use the best method to solve each problem. Tell which method you used.

37. Michelle had 45 dollars before she went shopping. She spent 18 dollars. How much money did she have left after shopping?

38. There were 8 puppies in Jerry's Pet Shop. The shop received 9 more puppies. How many puppies were in the shop then?

39. Mary Kay has 235 stamps in her collection. Susanne has 342 stamps in her collection. Which girl has more stamps?

40. Janet had 59 marbles. Sam gave her some more. Now she has 115 marbles. How many marbles did Sam give her?

41. Andrea made 6 posters for the fair. Rich made 5 posters. How many posters did Andrea and Rich make in all?

42. On his vacation, Craig spent 3 days traveling, 6 days camping, and 7 days at a lake resort. How many days was he on vacation?

MAINTENANCE

Tell what the 4 means in each number.

1. 154,112   **2.** 407,286   **3.** 27,481   **4.** 4,579,301

Write the standard form.

5. nine thousand, nine hundred nine

6. six hundred-thousand, thirty-five

7. five million, sixteen thousand, four hundred twenty-three

8. seventy-one thousand, six hundred thirteen

Round each number to the nearest ten.

9. 57   **10.** 25   **11.** 82   **12.** 178   **13.** 314   **14.** 735

Round each number to the nearest hundred.

15. 829   **16.** 352   **17.** 462   **18.** 7,346   **19.** 1,092   **20.** 2,957

Round each number to the nearest thousand.

21. 2,502   **22.** 8,143   **23.** 6,489   **24.** 5,924   **25.** 7,084

Choosing a Computation Method   Calculator, Paper and Pencil, Mental Math, Estimation

Use the best method to solve each problem. Tell which method you used.

26. There were 13 beavers in the pond. Then 5 beavers moved to another pond. How many were left?

27. There are 85 turtles in the pond, 27 on the bank and 36 in the sand. How many turtles are there in all?

28. There were 31 birds in the yard. Of these, 17 birds were cardinals. How many of the birds were not cardinals?

29. Pat must identify 50 birds to earn a merit badge. She saw 24 wrens, 13 robins, and 18 crows. Did she earn her badge?

30. There were 29 frogs on the bank, and 12 frogs on the log. About how many frogs were there in all?

31. There were 53 squirrels and 19 chipmunks in the field. How many more squirrels were there than chipmunks?

MAINTENANCE

Add or subtract.

1. $\begin{array}{r} 36 \\ +23 \\ \hline \end{array}$	2. $\begin{array}{r} 42 \\ +59 \\ \hline \end{array}$	3. $\begin{array}{r} 85 \\ -41 \\ \hline \end{array}$	4. $\begin{array}{r} 635 \\ -27 \\ \hline \end{array}$	5. $\begin{array}{r} 984 \\ +420 \\ \hline \end{array}$
6. $\begin{array}{r} 537 \\ +68 \\ \hline \end{array}$	7. $\begin{array}{r} 265 \\ +847 \\ \hline \end{array}$	8. $\begin{array}{r} 4,035 \\ -676 \\ \hline \end{array}$	9. $\begin{array}{r} 8,671 \\ +5,493 \\ \hline \end{array}$	10. $\begin{array}{r} 5,000 \\ -2,368 \\ \hline \end{array}$
11. $\begin{array}{r} 71 \\ 46 \\ +23 \\ \hline \end{array}$	12. $\begin{array}{r} 19 \\ 34 \\ +87 \\ \hline \end{array}$	13. $\begin{array}{r} 206 \\ 741 \\ +384 \\ \hline \end{array}$	14. $\begin{array}{r} 2,376 \\ 178 \\ +3,626 \\ \hline \end{array}$	15. $\begin{array}{r} 1,307 \\ 4,528 \\ +3,064 \\ \hline \end{array}$

16. $63 - 22$

17. $80 - 54$

18. $527 + 35$

19. $435 - 19$

20. $353 + 483$

21. $4,753 + 208$

22. $6,000 - 2,143$

23. $4,376 + 890 + 1,468$

24. $5,748 + 455 + 1,849$

Choosing a Computation Method

Calculator, Paper and Pencil, Mental Math, Estimation

Use the best method to solve each problem. Tell which method you used.

25. Henry had $20.00. He bought a hat for $5.73. Did he have enough change to buy a tie for $15.00?

26. Helen saw a skirt for $9.47 and a blouse for $8.39. Could she buy both with $20.00?

27. There were 15,743 tickets sold for a baseball game. Of these, 859 tickets were not used. How many tickets were used?

28. Yoshio collected 17 stamps this week. He now has 234 stamps in his collection. How many stamps did Yoshio have last week?

29. When an airplane landed in El Paso, 147 people remained on board and 58 more people got on the plane. How many people were then on the plane?

30. The library now has 673 books. There were 289 new books ordered. The library has space for 950 books. Will there be enough space for the new books?

31. Kelly jogged for 45 minutes. Ann jogged for 10 minutes longer than Kelly. How long did Ann jog?

32. A card store sold 163 birthday cards, 89 get-well cards, and 318 note cards. How many cards were sold in all?

MAINTENANCE

Add or subtract.

1. 8
   +7

2. 13
   − 6

3. 17
   − 9

4. 9
   +8

5. 15
   − 6

6. 7
   +6

7. 23
   − 9

8. 54
   − 8

9. 67
   + 7

10. 43
    + 8

11. 87
    − 54

12. 41
    + 58

13. 81
    − 42

14. 34
    − 27

15. 98
    + 87

16. 205
    + 75

17. 608
    − 76

18. 491
    + 27

19. 741 − 286

20. 594 + 307

21. 921 − 448

22. 671 + 893

23. 4,235 + 136

24. 2,671 − 480

25. 7,021 + 998

26. 5,000 − 2,139

Choosing a Computation Method
Calculator, Paper and Pencil, Mental Math, Estimation

Use the best method to solve each problem. Tell which method you used.

27. In one season, a football team scored 28, 34, 17, 24, 37, 45, and 26 points. How many points in all did the team score?

28. Hank Aaron hit 733 home runs in the National League and 22 more in the American League. He hit how many home runs in all?

29. Tony read 3 books. One book had 327 pages. The others had 265 pages, and 235 pages. About how many pages did Tony read in all?

30. A garden has 7 rows of corn with 8 plants in each row. How many corn plants are in the garden?

31. The Nile River is 6,632 kilometers long. The Amazon River is 6,400 kilometers long. How much longer is the Nile River?

32. A quarter has the same value as 5 nickels. Beth saved 65 quarters. How many nickels can she get for these quarters?

33. Martin Luther King, Jr. was born in 1929. He was awarded the Nobel Peace Prize 35 years later. In what year did he receive this prize?

34. Clara Barton founded the American Red Cross and became its president in 1881. She remained its president until 1904. How many years was she president?

MAINTENANCE

Find each answer.

1. $\begin{array}{r} 3 \\ \times 9 \\ \hline \end{array}$ 2. $\begin{array}{r} 15 \\ -\ 6 \\ \hline \end{array}$ 3. $\begin{array}{r} 7 \\ +7 \\ \hline \end{array}$ 4. $\begin{array}{r} 0 \\ \times 9 \\ \hline \end{array}$ 5. $\begin{array}{r} 6 \\ \times 6 \\ \hline \end{array}$ 6. $\begin{array}{r} 13 \\ -\ 9 \\ \hline \end{array}$ 7. $\begin{array}{r} 4 \\ +7 \\ \hline \end{array}$

8. $\begin{array}{r} 7 \\ +8 \\ \hline \end{array}$ 9. $\begin{array}{r} 16 \\ -\ 8 \\ \hline \end{array}$ 10. $\begin{array}{r} 9 \\ \times 9 \\ \hline \end{array}$ 11. $\begin{array}{r} 12 \\ -\ 7 \\ \hline \end{array}$ 12. $\begin{array}{r} 5 \\ \times 8 \\ \hline \end{array}$ 13. $\begin{array}{r} 6 \\ \times 7 \\ \hline \end{array}$ 14. $\begin{array}{r} 9 \\ -0 \\ \hline \end{array}$

15. $\begin{array}{r} 7 \\ \times 7 \\ \hline \end{array}$ 16. $\begin{array}{r} 9 \\ +0 \\ \hline \end{array}$ 17. $\begin{array}{r} 14 \\ -\ 8 \\ \hline \end{array}$ 18. $\begin{array}{r} 5 \\ \times 9 \\ \hline \end{array}$ 19. $\begin{array}{r} 8 \\ \times 7 \\ \hline \end{array}$ 20. $\begin{array}{r} 9 \\ -9 \\ \hline \end{array}$ 21. $\begin{array}{r} 13 \\ -\ 8 \\ \hline \end{array}$

22. $\begin{array}{r} 8 \\ +9 \\ \hline \end{array}$ 23. $\begin{array}{r} 9 \\ +7 \\ \hline \end{array}$ 24. $\begin{array}{r} 18 \\ -\ 9 \\ \hline \end{array}$ 25. $\begin{array}{r} 7 \\ +6 \\ \hline \end{array}$ 26. $\begin{array}{r} 7 \\ \times 1 \\ \hline \end{array}$ 27. $\begin{array}{r} 8 \\ -7 \\ \hline \end{array}$ 28. $\begin{array}{r} 14 \\ -\ 8 \\ \hline \end{array}$

29. $\begin{array}{r} 8 \\ \times 5 \\ \hline \end{array}$ 30. $\begin{array}{r} 13 \\ -\ 7 \\ \hline \end{array}$ 31. $\begin{array}{r} 8 \\ \times 8 \\ \hline \end{array}$ 32. $\begin{array}{r} 11 \\ -\ 6 \\ \hline \end{array}$ 33. $\begin{array}{r} 5 \\ +8 \\ \hline \end{array}$ 34. $\begin{array}{r} 6 \\ +6 \\ \hline \end{array}$ 35. $\begin{array}{r} 9 \\ \times 6 \\ \hline \end{array}$

Choosing a Computation Method
Calculator, Paper and Pencil, Mental Math, Estimation

Use the best method to solve each problem. Tell which method you used.

36. Mr. Johnson rides the train 21 miles to and from work each day. How far does he ride if he goes to work 250 days in one year?

37. One year a news magazine sold 4,615,594 copies, a sports magazine sold 2,448,486 copies, and a childrens magazine sold 1,452,201 copies. Find the total number of copies sold.

38. Betty rides the bus to school for 16 blocks and then walks the remaining 7 blocks. How many more blocks does she ride than walk?

39. Sharda rides her bicycle 3 miles each day going to school and back. How far does she ride her bicycle in 5 days?

40. One day, George took a taxi to school. It cost $3.00. He had $1.95 in his bookbag and $1.35 in his pocket. Did he have enough money?

41. Mrs. White put 13 gallons of gas in her car. The car can go 21 miles on each gallon of gas. About how many miles can she drive on this gas?

MAINTENANCE

Find each answer.

1. $\begin{array}{r} 17 \\ + \ 6 \\ \hline \end{array}$

2. $\begin{array}{r} 69 \\ + \ 4 \\ \hline \end{array}$

3. $\begin{array}{r} 135 \\ + \ 77 \\ \hline \end{array}$

4. $\begin{array}{r} 25 \\ - \ 16 \\ \hline \end{array}$

5. $\begin{array}{r} 37 \\ - \ 28 \\ \hline \end{array}$

6. $\begin{array}{r} 618 \\ - \ 136 \\ \hline \end{array}$

7. $\begin{array}{r} 291 \\ + \ 359 \\ \hline \end{array}$

8. $\begin{array}{r} 7,986 \\ - \ 6,361 \\ \hline \end{array}$

9. $\begin{array}{r} 728 \\ + \ 39 \\ \hline \end{array}$

10. $\begin{array}{r} 376 \\ + \ 158 \\ \hline \end{array}$

11. $953 - 85$

12. $5,148 + 263$

13. $800 - 175$

14. $7,737 + 1,642$

15. $647 - 392$

16. $6,982 + 3,845$

17. $600 - 283$

18. $2,337 + 2,493$

19. $\begin{array}{r} 29 \\ \times \ 4 \\ \hline \end{array}$

20. $\begin{array}{r} 215 \\ \times \ 7 \\ \hline \end{array}$

21. $\begin{array}{r} 348 \\ \times \ 9 \\ \hline \end{array}$

22. $\begin{array}{r} 406 \\ \times \ 6 \\ \hline \end{array}$

23. $\begin{array}{r} 22 \\ \times \ 5 \\ \hline \end{array}$

24. $\begin{array}{r} 875 \\ \times \ 4 \\ \hline \end{array}$

25. $\begin{array}{r} 195 \\ \times \ 9 \\ \hline \end{array}$

26. $\begin{array}{r} 300 \\ \times \ 6 \\ \hline \end{array}$

27. $\begin{array}{r} 1,049 \\ \times \ 7 \\ \hline \end{array}$

28. $\begin{array}{r} 3,610 \\ \times \ 2 \\ \hline \end{array}$

Choosing a Computation Method
Calculator, Paper and Pencil, Mental Math, Estimation

Use the best method to solve each problem. Tell which method you used.

29. Kim traveled 237 miles on Saturday, 374 miles on Sunday, 218 miles on Monday, 288 miles on Tuesday, and 347 miles on Wednesday. How many miles did she travel in all?

30. Mr. Taft offered to give the students at Mills School a ride in his airplane. He can take 18 students at one time. If he makes 23 trips, about how many students can he take for a ride in all?

31. Ed traveled 364 miles on his vacation last year. This year he traveled 492 miles farther than last year. How many miles did Ed travel on his vacation this year?

32. To raise money for their school, a parent's club sold calendars for $2.25 each. They sold 189 calendars. How much money did they raise?

33. A swimming pool is 50 yards long. Ruth swam 3 lengths of the pool. How many yards did she swim?

34. Glenbrook has a population of 72,430 people. In the last election 39,537 people voted. How many people did not vote?

MAINTENANCE

Give each answer. Watch the signs.

1. $4 + 3$ **2.** $5 - 3$ **3.** 6×4 **4.** 8×2 **5.** $14 - 7$ **6.** $7 - 1$

7. $6 + 6$ **8.** $14 - 9$ **9.** 9×8 **10.** $81 \div 9$ **11.** $6 + 9$ **12.** $13 - 8$

13. 8×4 **14.** $2 + 7$ **15.** 5×7 **16.** $10 - 7$ **17.** $4 + 6$ **18.** 6×1

19. $2 + 4$ **20.** $36 \div 9$ **21.** 6×8 **22.** $5 + 3$ **23.** $12 - 3$ **24.** $9 + 8$

25. 3×9 **26.** $7 + 4$ **27.** $11 - 3$ **28.** 3×7 **29.** $2 + 8$ **30.** $40 \div 5$

31. $8 + 8$ **32.** $9 - 3$ **33.** 9×7 **34.** $10 - 5$ **35.** $6 + 7$ **36.** $18 - 9$

37. $56 \div 8$ **38.** $8 + 4$ **39.** 3×6 **40.** $11 - 6$ **41.** $3 + 3$ **42.** 6×9

43. 0×7 **44.** $9 - 8$ **45.** $6 + 2$ **46.** $15 - 7$ **47.** $42 \div 6$ **48.** 6×6

49. 7×4 **50.** $9 + 4$ **51.** $12 - 5$ **52.** $0 + 7$ **53.** $2 + 9$ **54.** $18 \div 2$

55. 3×8 **56.** $4 - 2$ **57.** 7×2 **58.** 4×3 **59.** $7 - 2$ **60.** $14 - 8$

Choosing a Computation Method
Calculator, Paper and Pencil, Mental Math, Estimation

Use the best method to solve each problem. Tell which method you used.

61. A baby blue whale gains about 96 kilograms per day. About how many kilograms would the whale gain in one week?

62. A citrus orchard has room for 27 rows of orange trees. If Mr. Wayne plants about 39 trees in each row, will he have room for 850 trees?

63. An African elephant weighed 7,025 kilograms. An Asian elephant weighed 4,890 kilograms. How much more did the African elephant weigh than the Asian elephant?

64. Mr. Fry traveled 963 miles from Boston to Chicago, 1,067 miles from Chicago to Houston and 1,804 miles from Houston to Boston. How many miles did he travel in all?

65. The school bus left school carrying 52 students. At the first stop, 12 students got off. How many students were left on bus?

66. A chicken egg takes 21 days to hatch. How many weeks is this? (7 days = 1 week)

MAINTENANCE

Find each answer.

1. $\begin{array}{r} 45 \\ + 56 \\ \hline \end{array}$

2. $\begin{array}{r} 87 \\ - 49 \\ \hline \end{array}$

3. $\begin{array}{r} 31 \\ \times\ 5 \\ \hline \end{array}$

4. $\begin{array}{r} 386 \\ + 457 \\ \hline \end{array}$

5. $\begin{array}{r} 749 \\ - 386 \\ \hline \end{array}$

6. $\begin{array}{r} 349 \\ \times\ \ 2 \\ \hline \end{array}$

7. $\begin{array}{r} 923 \\ - 819 \\ \hline \end{array}$

8. $\begin{array}{r} 486 \\ + 375 \\ \hline \end{array}$

9. $\begin{array}{r} 9{,}562 \\ \times\ \ \ \ \ 3 \\ \hline \end{array}$

10. $\begin{array}{r} 3{,}927 \\ + 1{,}516 \\ \hline \end{array}$

11. $\begin{array}{r} 7{,}890 \\ - 1{,}682 \\ \hline \end{array}$

12. $\begin{array}{r} 485 \\ +\ \ 49 \\ \hline \end{array}$

13. $\begin{array}{r} 208 \\ \times\ \ \ 5 \\ \hline \end{array}$

14. $\begin{array}{r} 9{,}005 \\ - 1{,}287 \\ \hline \end{array}$

15. $\begin{array}{r} 3{,}219 \\ +\ \ \ 486 \\ \hline \end{array}$

16. $7 \times 6{,}003$

17. $4{,}860 + 853$

18. $2{,}850 - 634$

19. $5 \times 1{,}020$

20. $800 - 57$

21. $98 + 526$

22. 32×593

23. $8{,}068 - 989$

24. 38×73

25. $675 + 36$

26. $8{,}309 - 657$

27. 231×6

Choosing a Computation Method
Calculator, Paper and Pencil, Mental Math, Estimation

Use the best method to solve each problem. Tell which method you used.

28. A student ticket to a play is $1.75. Would $50.00 be enough to buy tickets for 38 students?

29. At noon the temperature was 57°. By evening it had dropped 12°. What was the evening temperature?

30. Don had $10.00. He spent $0.79 for a pen, $1.45 for lunch, and $2.89 for a book. How much money did he have left?

31. Anita has 3 shelves with 17 books on each. How many books are on the shelves?

32. There were 49 students on Bus A and 54 students on Bus B. How many more students were on Bus B than on Bus A?

33. The Corrins drove 385 miles in the morning and 147 miles later. Their car will go 500 miles on a tank of gas. Did they need to stop for gas?

34. Connie has 436 coins in her collection. Of these, 152 are American coins. The rest are foreign coins. How many are foreign coins?

35. Jose practiced piano 35 minutes on Monday, 55 minutes on Tuesday, and 75 minutes on Wednesday. Find the average number of minutes he practiced per day.

MAINTENANCE

Find each answer.

1. $\begin{array}{r} 47 \\ + 51 \\ \hline \end{array}$

2. $\begin{array}{r} 68 \\ + 95 \\ \hline \end{array}$

3. $\begin{array}{r} 307 \\ + 89 \\ \hline \end{array}$

4. $\begin{array}{r} 277 \\ + 384 \\ \hline \end{array}$

5. $\begin{array}{r} 4,063 \\ + 512 \\ \hline \end{array}$

6. $\begin{array}{r} 57 \\ - 32 \\ \hline \end{array}$

7. $\begin{array}{r} 603 \\ - 158 \\ \hline \end{array}$

8. $\begin{array}{r} 917 \\ - 635 \\ \hline \end{array}$

9. $\begin{array}{r} 2,482 \\ - 937 \\ \hline \end{array}$

10. $\begin{array}{r} 7,001 \\ - 2,589 \\ \hline \end{array}$

11. $\begin{array}{r} 84 \\ \times 2 \\ \hline \end{array}$

12. $\begin{array}{r} 703 \\ \times 6 \\ \hline \end{array}$

13. $\begin{array}{r} 8,045 \\ \times 4 \\ \hline \end{array}$

14. $\begin{array}{r} 215 \\ \times 74 \\ \hline \end{array}$

15. $\begin{array}{r} 389 \\ \times 32 \\ \hline \end{array}$

16. $4\overline{)96}$

17. $3\overline{)925}$

18. $70\overline{)264}$

19. $29\overline{)149}$

20. $42\overline{)517}$

21. $38 + 9$

22. $74 + 26$

23. $385 + 76$

24. $8,205 + 156$

25. $91 - 50$

26. $433 - 78$

27. $200 - 138$

28. $6,002 - 473$

29. 26×8

30. 340×3

31. $1,204 \times 7$

32. 105×25

33. $53 \div 4$

34. $613 \div 2$

35. $75 \div 21$

36. $482 \div 64$

Choosing a Computation Method
Calculator, Paper and Pencil, Mental Math, Estimation

Use the best method to solve each problem. Tell which method you used.

37. A gallon of paint costs $14.95. Is $150 enough money to buy 9 gallons of paint?

38. There are 43 passengers on each of 5 buses. About how many passengers are there in all?

39. An airplane flew 1,200 miles in 3 hours. What was the average speed in miles per hour?

40. A human body has 68 bones in the hands and face. There are 138 bones in the rest of the body. What is the total number of bones?

41. The 83 fourth graders sold 996 tickets to the school fair. What was the average number of tickets sold per student?

42. A bakery bakes an average of 1,875 loaves of bread each day. How many days will it take to bake 15,000 loaves of bread?

MAINTENANCE

Tell what the 7 means in each number.

1. 71
2. 17
3. 724
4. 372

5. 6,762
6. 7,330
7. 3,072
8. 7,043

9. 6.7
10. 7.3
11. 17.4
12. 29.7

13. 50.67
14. 19.75
15. 10.79
16. 58.07

Add or subtract.

17. $9.08 + 3.96$
18. $4.87 + 1.18$
19. $267 - 88$
20. $345 - 189$

21. $5.78 - 3.87$
22. $4.56 - 2.89$
23. $519 + 283$
24. $437 + 274$

25. $4.2 + 3.9$
26. $2.7 + 4.6$
27. $865 - 568$
28. $642 - 246$

29. $156 + 287$
30. $265 + 378$
31. $5.42 - 2.45$
32. $83.21 - 1.23$

Choosing a Computation Method   Calculator, Paper and Pencil, Mental Math, Estimation

Use the best method to solve each problem. Tell which method you used.

33. Tim has $8.67. Lisa has $5.83 more than Tim. Does Lisa have enough to buy a sweatshirt for $15.00?

34. Ben has $26.37. Joe has $9.89 less than Ben. Ty has $7.59 less than Joe. How much money does Ty have?

35. Cory skated 20 minutes each day for 12 days. How many minutes did he skate in all?

36. Machiko made 25 packets from 600 sheets of paper. How many sheets were in each packet?

37. The Reading Club bought 34 books. Each book costs $1.76. About how much did they pay for all the books?

38. Ms. Green divided 56 sheets of paper equally among 8 people. How many sheets did each person get?

39. The Burke family drove 689 miles on Friday and 1,045 miles on Saturday. How much farther did they drive on Saturday?

40. During one month a veterinarian treated 19 birds, 36 cats, 29 dogs, and 17 other animals. How many animals did he treat that month?

MAINTENANCE

Add or subtract.

1. $\frac{5}{7}$
   $+\frac{1}{7}$

2. $\frac{4}{7}$
   $-\frac{3}{7}$

3. $\frac{4}{5}$
   $-\frac{1}{5}$

4. $\frac{4}{6}$
   $+\frac{1}{6}$

5. $\frac{8}{10}$
   $-\frac{5}{10}$

6. $\frac{2}{8}$
   $+\frac{2}{8}$

7. $\frac{5}{6}$
   $-\frac{4}{6}$

8. $\frac{7}{8} - \frac{1}{8}$

9. $\frac{2}{3} + \frac{1}{3}$

10. $\frac{3}{7} + \frac{2}{7}$

11. $\frac{0}{3} + \frac{1}{3}$

12. $\frac{11}{12} - \frac{3}{12}$

13. $\frac{2}{4} + \frac{2}{4}$

14. 9.6
    $+4.3$

15. 2.6
    $+5.2$

16. 7.8
    -6.5

17. 35.63
    -19.72

18. 48.64
    -11.09

19. 47.96
    $+21.38$

20. 36.8
    $+9.7$

21. 57.3
    -8.5

22. 24.05
    -16.56

23. 3.04
    $+7.99$

24. $32.47 - 20.81$

25. $8.6 - 4.5$

26. $14.08 + 25.62$

27. $6 - 4.02$

28. $8.4 + 6.2$

29. $15 + 8.07$

30. $8.07 - 4.32$

31. $90 - 40.38$

Choosing a Computation Method

Calculator, Paper and Pencil, Mental Math, Estimation

Use the best method to solve each problem. Tell which method you used.

32. David weighs 44.6 kilograms. Sue weighs 25.9 kilograms. How much heavier is David than Sue?

33. Fred's bike cost $98.95. Elena's bike cost $79.87. What is the total cost of the two bikes?

34. Jack scored 9,476 points on a computer game. Tim scored 16,785 points. Ken scored 22,359 points. How many points did they score in all?

35. Alex and Anthony worked on a science project together. Alex spent $4.69 and Anthony spent $5.78. Did they spend more or less than $10.00?

36. Mandy spent $2\frac{1}{2}$ days reading a mystery book. She then spent $6\frac{1}{2}$ days reading a biography. How much longer did Mandy spend reading the biography?

37. Loretta used $\frac{1}{3}$ cup of water and $\frac{2}{3}$ cup of milk in a recipe for bread. How much liquid did she use in all?

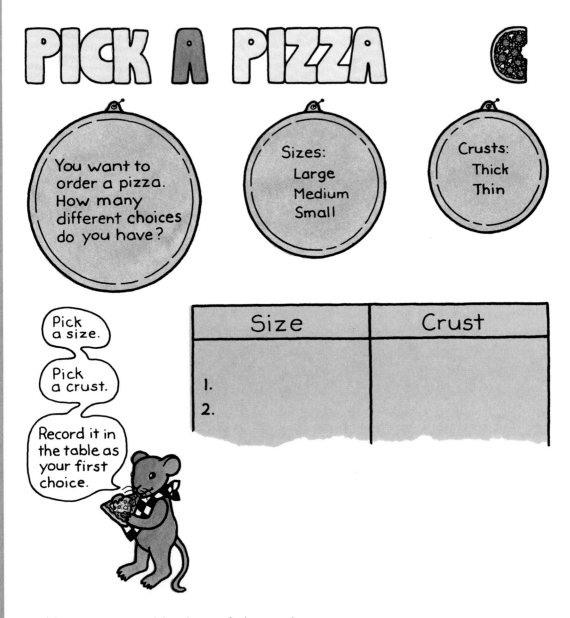

PICK A PIZZA

You want to order a pizza. How many different choices do you have?

Sizes:
Large
Medium
Small

Crusts:
Thick
Thin

Pick a size.

Pick a crust.

Record it in the table as your first choice.

Size	Crust
1.	
2.	

1. How many combinations of size and crust are there? Make a table like the one shown. Complete the table to show all the possibilities.

2. If you could choose from toppings of mushroom, onion, or green pepper, how many choices would you have? (Make a list on another piece of paper.)

burp!

410

PLAY THE BUTTON GAME

Play this game with a friend.

Place 15 buttons on a table and decide who goes first. Take turns picking up either 1 or 2 buttons. You are not allowed to skip your turn. You lose if you pick up the last button.

1. If there's 1 button left on the table and it's your turn, who wins?

2. If it's your turn and there are 2 buttons left, how many buttons should you pick up?

3. If there are 4 buttons left, how many buttons should you pick up?

4. Describe a winning strategy for this game.

5. How does your strategy change if the winner is the player who picks up the last button?

YOU CAN DO IT. HERE'S THE KEY. USE PROBLEM-SOLVING STRATEGIES.

PROBLEM-SOLVING STRATEGIES
- MAKE A TABLE
- FIND A PATTERN
- USE PHYSICAL MODELS
- USE LOGICAL REASONING
- WORK BACKWARD
- LIST ALL POSSIBILITIES
- TRY AND CHECK
- DRAW A DIAGRAM
- MAKE A GRAPH

Using Problem-Solving Strategies

BIRTHDAY CLUES

On a piece of paper, number the months in order from 1 to 12, beginning with January. Now use the clues to answer the questions.

Clue: I am alive now and was born in a month whose number has 0 in the ones place.

1. In what month was I born?

Clue: The date of my birthday has 2 digits. The difference of those digits is 7. One of those digits is also the hundreds digit of the year I was born.

2. On what day of the month was I born?

Clue: If you add the thousands digit of the year of my birth to the hundreds digit, the sum is the same as when you add the tens digit to the ones digit. The ones digit of that year is less than the tens digit.

Clue: All the digits in the year of my birth are odd.

3. When was I born?

4. How old am I?

Guess my birthday.

WHO AM I?

A two-digit number, that's me
I'm even, not odd, you see
    Add my digits and get five
    Oh my goodness, sakes alive,
There's not just one answer—there are three!

Leaf us alone!

Is that a poet-tree?

1. Name a pair of digits whose sum is 5.

2. Name five 2-digit numbers whose digits add to 5.

3. Answer the limerick above by finding the three 2-digit numbers that are even numbers. (Hint: Even numbers end in 0, 2, 4, 6, or 8.)

4. Who am I? Use the clues below to find out.

The sum of my two digits is eight.
I'm odd, and I'll tell you straight.
    Round me to the nearest ten
    And you'll get forty then.
Find out who I am—don't wait!

PAM'S PATH PUZZLE

Pam drew a map to help her find the different paths she could take from her house to school. *How many different paths could she take?*

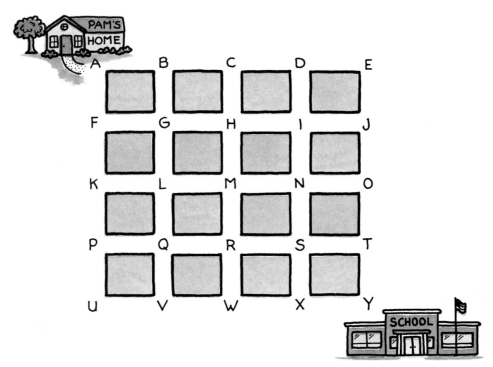

There are two different paths Pam can walk from her home to the intersection at **G.**

Pam walks directly to an intersection. She would not backtrack or walk to intersections **A, B, C, H,** and **G** to reach intersection **G.**

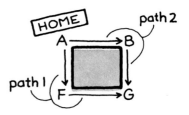

1. How many different paths can she take to **H?**

2. How many different paths can she take to **L?**

3. How many paths are there to intersection **M?**

4. How many paths are there to school?

THE CARRS GO DRIVING

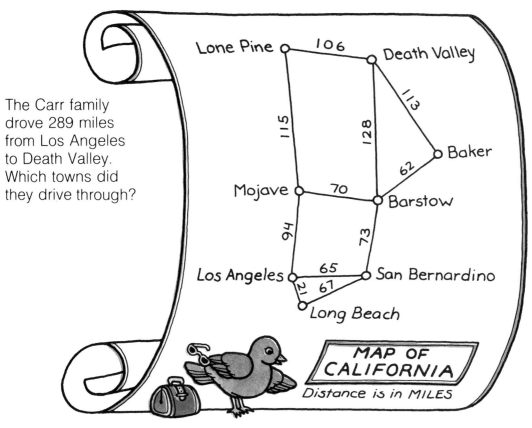

The Carr family drove 289 miles from Los Angeles to Death Valley. Which towns did they drive through?

Lone Pine — 106 — Death Valley

115 · 128 · 113

Baker

62

Mojave — 70 — Barstow

94 · 73

Los Angeles — 65 — San Bernardino

21 · 67

Long Beach

MAP OF CALIFORNIA

Distance is in MILES

1. How many miles is it from Los Angeles to Death Valley if you drive through Mojave and Lone Pine?

2. Is this more or less than the number of miles driven by the Carr family?

3. Which towns did the Carr family drive through on the 289 mile trip from Los Angeles to Death Valley?

4. On the return trip, the Carr family drove 339 miles. Through which towns did they drive?

GOING SOUTH
San Bernardino
Long Beach
Bird Sanctuary

415

Using Problem-Solving Strategies

TIME FOR THE NEWS

If it is 12:00 noon, Monday, April 6, in Chicago, what time and date will each clock show if:

San Francisco is 2 hours behind,
London   is 6 hours ahead,
Tokyo   is 15 hours ahead,
Honolulu   is 4 hours behind,
Moscow   is 9 hours ahead.

Chicago
Mon.
12:00 noon
Apr. 6

San Francisco
10:00 A.M.
Apr.

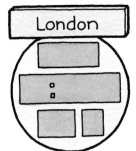

London

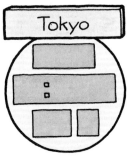

Tokyo

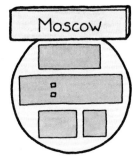

Honolulu

It's 12 noon, Monday, April 6th. And now the world news...

Moscow

1. Draw 5 clocks like the ones shown here. Fill in each clock with the correct day, time, and date.

2. After 12 hours have passed, which clocks will still show the SAME day and date?

3. After 8 hours have passed, which clocks will show a different date?

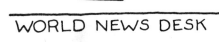

WORLD NEWS DESK

416

HAPPY BIRTHDAY

A group of students in Michael's class were talking about birthdays.

They discovered that Michael's birthday is exactly 2 weeks before Andy's.

Andy's birthday is 2 days after Sandra's.

Sandra has her birthday on the same day of the month as Jimmy, but her birthday is 3 months earlier than his.

Darla's birthday is 3 days after Jimmy's and 6 days after Betty's.

Betty's birthday is on the 4th of July.

1. When is Darla's birthday?

2. When is Jimmy's birthday?

3. When is Michael's birthday?

THE ORDERLY BAND

While watching a parade, Joe noticed that all the members of one band had 2 numbers on their hats. He noticed that the first number told what row that person was in, and the second number told how far to the left the person was.

The band member wearing hat number 2,6 was in the second row and was the sixth person in the row.

3,1 meant the band member was in the third row and was the first person in the row.

The band had 14 rows of players. There were 7 players in each row.

A player had 8,5 on his hat.

1. How many band members were in rows ahead of him?

2. How many band members were behind him?

If you were a band member and had hat number 6,4,

3. how many players would be in rows behind you?

4. how many players would be in rows ahead of you?

5. how many players would be in front of you and to your right?

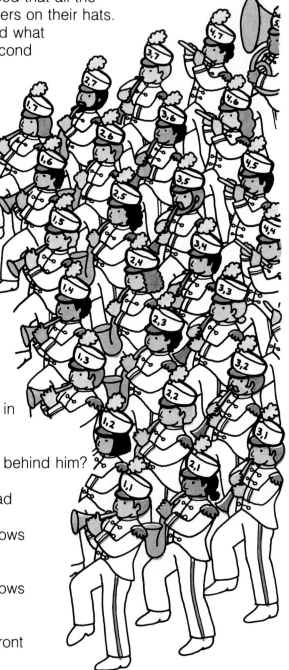

418

BANANAS, APPLES,  NUTS

Jane bought only apples and nuts for a salad.
Harold bought only apples and bananas.
Jane spent 31¢ and Harold spent 75¢.
What did each one buy?

BANANAS
9¢ each

APPLES
7¢ each

NUTS
5¢ per handful

1. How much would it cost Jane to buy 4 apples?

2. If Jane bought 4 apples and 2 handfuls of nuts,
   how much would she spend?
   Is this more or less than 31¢?

3. What did Jane buy for 31¢?

4. What did Harold buy for 75¢?

PROBLEM-
SOLVING
STRATEGIES
• MAKE A
  TABLE
• WORK
  BACKWARD
• LIST ALL
  POSSIBILITIES
• TRY AND
  CHECK
• DRAW A
  DIAGRAM
• MAKE A
  GRAPH

DRINK JUICE FOR A CHANGE

What coins can you use to buy a
cup of juice from this machine?

I used two quarters.

JUICE MACHINE

APPLE ORANGE

CARROT KUMQUAT

50¢

Exact
change
only

Use only
quarters,
dimes,
& nickels.

Coin
return

1. Give another example of coins you could
   use to buy a cup of juice.

2. Find eight more ways. Make a chart like
   the one below for your answers.

Quarters	Dimes	Nickels
2	0	0

WALTER'S ACCOUNT

Walter's Aunt Betty decided to start a savings account for him.

She said she would put 1¢ in the account on the first day, 2¢ on the second day, 3¢ on the third day, and 4¢ on the fourth day. She would continue this pattern for 100 days.

Aunt Betty told Walter, "If you can tell me the total amount of money in your account after 100 days, I will double the total on the 101st day."
How much money will Aunt Betty be giving Walter?

1. How much money would Walter have after 4 days?

2. How much money would he have after 10 days?

3. How much money would he have after 100 days?

4. If Aunt Betty doubles the total amount of money, after 100 days how much will Walter have in the savings account?

PROBLEM-
SOLVING
STRATEGIES
• USE
  PHYSICAL
  MODELS
• LIST ALL
  POSSIBILITIES
• TRY AND
  CHECK
• FIND A
  PATTERN
• SOLVE A
  SIMPLER
  PROBLEM

LOTS OF FENCE

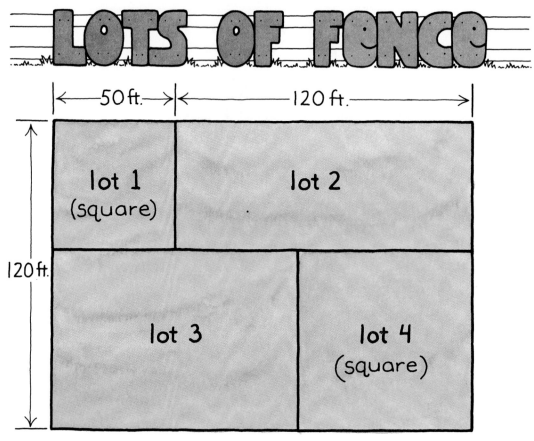

Anita's family has divided their property into 4 rectangular lots as pictured above. They plan to put a fence around each rectangle. Anita's mother asked her to figure out how many feet of fence they should buy.

1. Copy the lots above on grid paper. Label the lengths of all the sides of all the rectangles.

2. How much fence is needed?

Anita's brother also wants to put a fence from one corner of lot 2 to the opposite (diagonal) corner of lot 2.

3. About how many extra feet of fence would Anita's brother need?

When learning about area, Lucita's class cut rectangles out of grid paper, then compared the dimensions of the rectangles to their areas.

Lucita's twin sister, Rita, cut out a rectangle that was twice as long as it was wide. Rita's rectangle had an area of 18 square units.

Bill's rectangle was also twice as long as it was wide, but the width of his rectangle was exactly the same as the length of Rita's.

The rectangle that Ronald cut out was just as long as Bill's. Ronald's rectangle was 4 times as long as it was wide.

Lucita's rectangle was just as wide as Ronald's and twice as long as it was wide.

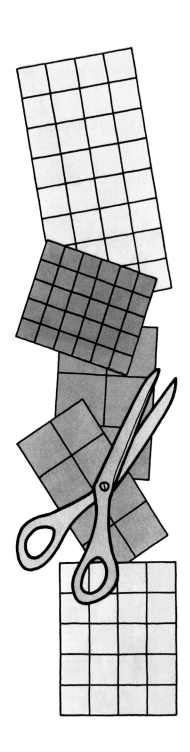

1. What were the dimensions of Rita's rectangle?

2. What were the dimensions of Bill's rectangle?

   What was its area?

3. What was the area of Ronald's rectangle?

4. What was the area of Lucita's rectangle?

SONNY'S HONEY

After school, Sonny helps in the food mart. For the honey sale, Sonny has to make up 2-pound jars of honey from larger containers of honey. Sonny can only find an empty 3-pound can and an empty 4-pound can. *How can he measure out 2 pounds at a time?*

1. Using only the 3-pound can and the 4-pound can, how can Sonny get 1 pound?

2. Using the same containers as in Problem 1, how can Sonny get 2 pounds?

3. If Sonny had only a 5-pound and a 3-pound can, how could he measure out 4 pounds?

INK SPOTS

Darlisa's parents own a company that builds patios out of square paving blocks. The patios are separated into rectangular sections with redwood boards.

Darlisa spilled ink on several of the patio plans, covering up some of the patio measurements. She had to figure out what numbers were covered by ink.
Find the missing numbers for each patio plan.

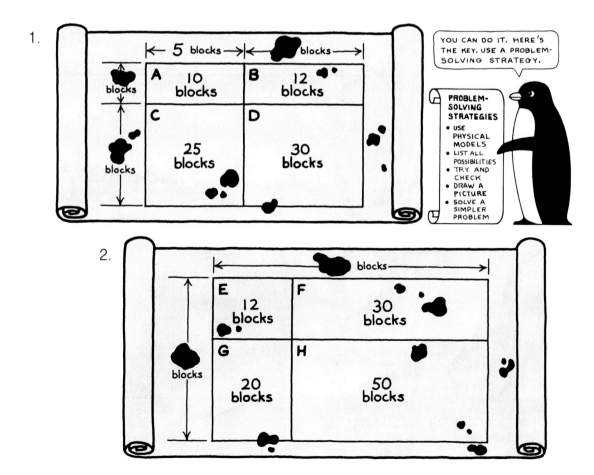

1.

← 5 blocks → ← ▓ blocks →

▓ blocks	A 10 blocks	B 12 blocks
▓ blocks	C 25 blocks	D 30 blocks

YOU CAN DO IT. HERE'S THE KEY. USE A PROBLEM-SOLVING STRATEGY.

PROBLEM-SOLVING STRATEGIES
• USE PHYSICAL MODELS
• LIST ALL POSSIBILITIES
• TRY AND CHECK
• DRAW A PICTURE
• SOLVE A SIMPLER PROBLEM

2.

← ▓ blocks →

E 12 blocks	F 30 blocks
G 20 blocks	H 50 blocks

▓ blocks

MR. PENN'S PENCILS

Mr. Penn wants to buy pencils for each of the 25 students in his fourth-grade class. *How many different ways can he buy them?*

Make a table showing all of his choices.

PENCIL SALE

The most boxes of BLUE he can buy is 6.

Then he'd have 24 (6×4) BLUE pencils.

He should buy 1 RED to total 25 pencils.

Here's how to write it in the chart.

DO NOT OPEN BOXES

RED PENCILS Buy 1 or more

4 in a box

Boxes of 4 blue pencils	Red Single pencils
6	1
5	

1. If he buys 5 boxes of blue pencils, how many red pencils should he buy?

2. Complete the table. How many choices does he have?

3. If blue pencils came 3 to a box, how many choices would he have?

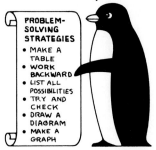

YOU CAN DO IT. HERE'S THE KEY. USE PROBLEM-SOLVING STRATEGIES.

PROBLEM-SOLVING STRATEGIES
• MAKE A TABLE
• WORK BACKWARD
• LIST ALL POSSIBILITIES
• TRY AND CHECK
• DRAW A DIAGRAM
• MAKE A GRAPH

CHECKERS, ANYONE?

Cindy organized a checker tournament for her class.

Each player was to play one game against every other player. 8 students signed up to play. *How many games did Cindy need to schedule?*

SIGN UP TO PLAY CHECKERS

1. Alice Green
2. Bill Ellis
3. Cary Simms
4. Denise Brown
5. Willy Wallace
6. Earl Young
7. Francie Smith
8. Cindy H

Since each person had to play 7 others, Willy thought there would be 8 × 7 games. Cindy thought Willy was wrong. She thought the tournament would be easier to schedule if she started with fewer players.

1. How many games would be needed for

   3 players?   4 players?   5 players?

2. Was Willy's method right?

3. How many games will be scheduled for 8 players?

YOU CAN DO IT. HERE'S THE KEY. USE PROBLEM-SOLVING STRATEGIES.

PROBLEM-SOLVING STRATEGIES
- MAKE A TABLE
- FIND A PATTERN
- USE LOGICAL REASONING
- WORK BACKWARD
- LIST ALL POSSIBILITIES
- TRY AND CHECK
- DRAW A PICTURE
- SOLVE A SIMPLER PROBLEM

POLYGON PUZZLE

Trace, and then cut out these four patterns. Fold along the dotted lines and use clear tape to make them into cubes.

The object of the puzzle is to place the cubes next to each other in a row so that along the top, bottom, front, and back there is a different polygon.

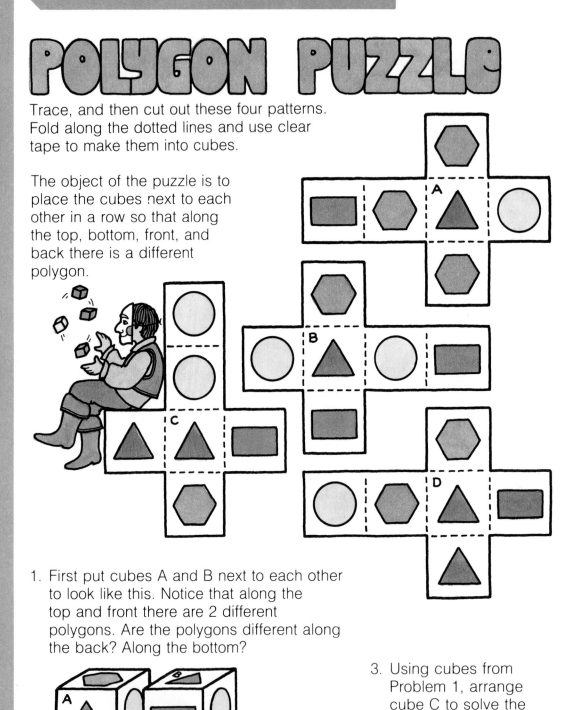

1. First put cubes A and B next to each other to look like this. Notice that along the top and front there are 2 different polygons. Are the polygons different along the back? Along the bottom?

2. Use cubes C and D to solve the puzzle.

3. Using cubes from Problem 1, arrange cube C to solve the puzzle.

4. Use all four cubes.

Using Problem-Solving Strategies

KAREN GOES THE DISTANCE

From Karen's house, it is 2.3 km to school and 1.4 km to the library. It's 3.2 km from school to the library.

If Karen biked from home to school, back home, and then to the library, how far did she bike?

1. Below is a diagram showing Karen's home, the school, and library. Copy the diagram. Then, complete the diagram by labeling all the distances.

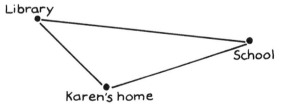

Library

School

Karen's home

2. How far did Karen bike?

3. Zal's home is 1.8 km from school. It is on the opposite side of the school from Karen's. He walked from his home to school, to the library, and then to Karen's home. How far did he walk?

THUMBTACKING A RIDE

The 20 students in Ms. Paul's fourth-grade class each drew a picture of a vehicle in which they would like to ride to school. What is the fewest number of thumbtacks she would need to attach the pictures in a line around the room.

Each corner must have a tack in it.

1. How many thumbtacks are needed to attach two pictures separately?

2. How many tacks are needed to attach 2 pictures if the corners overlap?

3. What is the fewest number of tacks needed to attach the 20 pictures in a line?

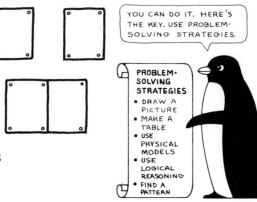

YOU CAN DO IT. HERE'S THE KEY. USE PROBLEM-SOLVING STRATEGIES.

PROBLEM-SOLVING STRATEGIES
• DRAW A PICTURE
• MAKE A TABLE
• USE PHYSICAL MODELS
• USE LOGICAL REASONING
• FIND A PATTERN

430

GENEROUS JENNIFER JUDSON

Jennifer Judson brought some peanuts
with her to school one day.

She asked Billy Baxter if he would like
some peanuts. He said, "Yes, give me 8."
So that's what Jennifer did.

She asked Patsy Purdy how many she
would like. Patsy said, "Give me $\frac{1}{2}$ of
what you have plus 1 more."
So that's what Jennifer did.

Then Cindy Simpson said, "Give 3 to
me." So that's what Jennifer did.

Donnie Davis wanted $\frac{1}{2}$ of what was
left. So, Jennifer gave him half.

Katie Kirk said, "I want $\frac{1}{2}$ of what's
left plus 1 more." So, that's what
Jennifer gave her.

When Jennifer saw that she only had
2 peanuts left, she thought, "I'm sure
glad that I don't like peanuts."

How many peanuts did Jennifer start with?

ON THE TRAIL

At 1:00 this afternoon, some hikers started walking on the trail from Pinewood Camp to Timberline Camp which is 12 miles away. They walked 2 miles each hour.

At 4:00 P.M., Rick started from Pinewood Camp and followed the same trail as the hikers. He was on horseback and rode 6 miles each hour.

At what time did Rick overtake the hikers?

1. The hikers started at 1:00. How many miles had they walked by 2:00? by 3:00? by 4:00? by 5:00? by 6:00?

2. Rick started at 4:00. How many miles had he ridden by 5:00? by 6:00?

3. Did Rick catch up to the hikers by 5:00? by 6:00?

4. At what time did Rick overtake the hikers?

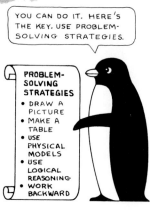

YOU CAN DO IT. HERE'S THE KEY. USE PROBLEM-SOLVING STRATEGIES.

PROBLEM-SOLVING STRATEGIES
• DRAW A PICTURE
• MAKE A TABLE
• USE PHYSICAL MODELS
• USE LOGICAL REASONING
• WORK BACKWARD

BIRTHDAY BAR GRAPH

Which month of the year has the most birthdays?

1. Ask each of 30 people what his or her birth month is. Make a table of the months of the year, and list the 30 replies.

2. Use the information in your table to complete a bar graph like the one below.

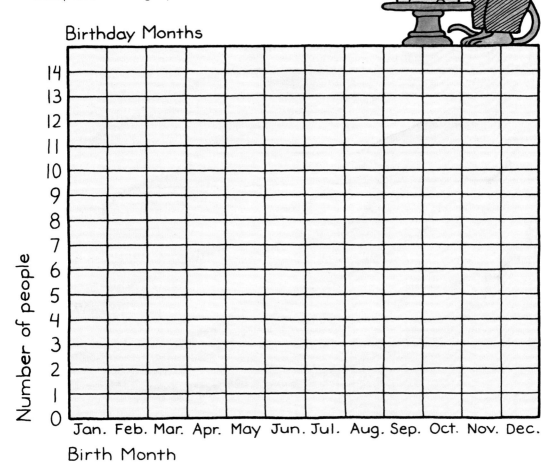

Birthday Months

Number of people

14
13
12
11
10
9
8
7
6
5
4
3
2
1
0

Jan. Feb. Mar. Apr. May Jun. Jul. Aug. Sep. Oct. Nov. Dec.

Birth Month

3. In which month were the most people born?

4. Compare your graph with the graphs of your classmates. Were the results the same?

Tables

Metric System

Length

$$10 \text{ millimeters (mm)} = 1 \text{ centimeter (cm)}$$

$$\left.\begin{array}{r} 10 \text{ centimeters} \\ 100 \text{ millimeters} \end{array}\right\} = 1 \text{ decimeter (dm)}$$

$$\left.\begin{array}{r} 10 \text{ decimeters} \\ 100 \text{ centimeters} \end{array}\right\} = 1 \text{ meter (m)}$$

$$1{,}000 \text{ meters} = 1 \text{ kilometer (km)}$$

Area

$$100 \text{ square millimeters (mm}^2) = 1 \text{ square centimeter (cm}^2)$$
$$10{,}000 \text{ square centimeters} = 1 \text{ square meter (m}^2)$$
$$100 \text{ square meters} = 1 \text{ are (a)}$$
$$10{,}000 \text{ square meters} = 1 \text{ hectare (ha)}$$

Volume

$$1{,}000 \text{ cubic millimeters (mm}^3) = 1 \text{ cubic centimeter (cm}^3)$$
$$1{,}000 \text{ cubic centimeters} = 1 \text{ cubic decimeter (dm}^3)$$
$$1{,}000{,}000 \text{ cubic centimeters} = 1 \text{ cubic meter (m}^3)$$

Mass (weight)

$$1{,}000 \text{ milligrams (mg)} = 1 \text{ gram (g)}$$
$$1{,}000 \text{ grams} = 1 \text{ kilogram (kg)}$$
$$1{,}000 \text{ kilograms} = 1 \text{ metric ton (t)}$$

Capacity

$$1{,}000 \text{ milliliters (mL)} = 1 \text{ liter (L)}$$

Customary System

Length

$$12 \text{ inches (in.)} = 1 \text{ foot (ft.)}$$

$$\left.\begin{array}{r} 3 \text{ feet} \\ 36 \text{ inches} \end{array}\right\} = 1 \text{ yard (yd.)}$$

$$\left.\begin{array}{r} 1{,}760 \text{ yards} \\ 5{,}280 \text{ feet} \end{array}\right\} = 1 \text{ mile (mi.)}$$

$$6{,}076 \text{ feet} = 1 \text{ nautical mile}$$

Area

$$144 \text{ square inches (sq. in.)} = 1 \text{ square foot (sq. ft.)}$$
$$9 \text{ square feet} = 1 \text{ square yard (sq. yd.)}$$
$$4{,}840 \text{ square yards} = 1 \text{ acre (A.)}$$

Volume

$$1{,}728 \text{ cubic inches (cu. in.)} = 1 \text{ cubic foot (cu. ft.)}$$
$$27 \text{ cubic feet} = 1 \text{ cubic yard (cu. yd.)}$$

Weight

$$16 \text{ ounces (oz.)} = 1 \text{ pound (lb.)}$$
$$2{,}000 \text{ pounds} = 1 \text{ ton (T.)}$$

Capacity

$$8 \text{ fluid ounces (fl. oz.)} = 1 \text{ cup (c.)}$$
$$2 \text{ cups} = 1 \text{ pint (pt.)}$$
$$2 \text{ pints} = 1 \text{ quart (qt.)}$$
$$4 \text{ quarts} = 1 \text{ gallon (gal.)}$$

Time

$$60 \text{ seconds} = 1 \text{ minute}$$
$$60 \text{ minutes} = 1 \text{ hour}$$
$$24 \text{ hours} = 1 \text{ day}$$
$$7 \text{ days} = 1 \text{ week}$$

$$\left.\begin{array}{r} 365 \text{ days} \\ 52 \text{ weeks} \\ 12 \text{ months} \end{array}\right\} = 1 \text{ year}$$

$$366 \text{ days} = 1 \text{ leap year}$$

Addition-Subtraction Table

+	0	1	2	3	4	5	6	7	8	9
0	0	1	2	3	4	5	6	7	8	9
1	1	2	3	4	5	6	7	8	9	10
2	2	3	4	5	6	7	8	9	10	11
3	3	4	5	6	7	8	9	10	11	12
4	4	5	6	7	8	9	10	11	12	13
5	5	6	7	8	9	10	11	12	13	14
6	6	7	8	9	10	11	12	13	14	15
7	7	8	9	10	11	12	13	14	15	16
8	8	9	10	11	12	13	14	15	16	17
9	9	10	11	12	13	14	15	16	17	18

Multiplication-Division Table

×	1	2	3	4	5	6	7	8	9
1	1	2	3	4	5	6	7	8	9
2	2	4	6	8	10	12	14	16	18
3	3	6	9	12	15	18	21	24	27
4	4	8	12	16	20	24	28	32	36
5	5	10	15	20	25	30	35	40	45
6	6	12	18	24	30	36	42	48	54
7	7	14	21	28	35	42	49	56	63
8	8	16	24	32	40	48	56	64	72
9	9	18	27	36	45	54	63	72	81

Glossary

Acute angle   An angle that has a measure less than 90°.

Addend   A number that is added. In 8 + 4 = 12, the addends are 8 and 4.

Angle (∠)   The figure formed by two rays with the same endpoint.

Area   A number indicating the size of the inside of a plane figure. The area of this figure is 8 square units.

Associative property of addition   The way in which addends are grouped does not affect the sum. Also called the grouping property of addition. For example,
$(7 + 2) + 5 = 7 + (2 + 5)$

Associative property of multiplication   The way in which factors are grouped does not affect the product. Also called the grouping property of multiplication. For example,
$(7 \times 2) \times 5 = 7 \times (2 \times 5)$

Average   A number obtained by dividing the sum of two or more addends by the number of addends.

BASIC   A simple language used to give instructions to computers.

Basic fact   A number sentence that has at least two one-digit numbers. The sentences below are examples of basic facts.
$7 + 2 = 9$ $16 - 7 = 9$
$5 \times 3 = 15$ $8 \div 4 = 2$

Cardinal number   A number, such as *three*, used to count or to tell how many.

Central angle   An angle with its vertex at the center of a circle.

Circle   A plane figure with all of its points the same distance from a given point called the *center*.

Circumference   The distance around a circle.

Common denominator   A common multiple of two or more denominators. A common denominator for $\frac{1}{6}$ and $\frac{3}{8}$ is 48.

Common factor   A number that is a factor of two or more numbers. A common factor of 6 and 12 is 3.

Common multiple   A number that is a multiple of two or more numbers. A common multiple of 4 and 6 is 12.

Commutative property of addition   The order in which numbers are added does not affect the sum. Also called the order property of addition. For example,
$4 + 6 = 6 + 4$

Commutative property of multiplication   The order in which numbers are multiplied does not affect the product. Also called the order property of multiplication. For example,
$4 \times 6 = 6 \times 4$

Composite number   A whole number, greater than 0, that has more than two factors. 12 is a composite number because it has more than two factors: 1, 2, 3, 4, 6, and 12.

Computer program   A set of instructions that tells the computer how to do a certain job.

Cone   A space figure formed by connecting a circle to a point not in the plane of the circle.

Congruent   Having the same size and the same shape.

Cross-products   For the ratios $\frac{3}{4}$ and $\frac{9}{12}$, the cross-products are 3×12 and 4×9.

Cube   A prism with all square faces.

Cylinder   A space figure shaped like this.

Decimal   A number that is written using place value and a decimal point.   3.84   0.076

Degree (of an angle)   A unit for measuring angles.

Diagonal   In a polygon, a segment that connects one vertex to another vertex but is not a side of the polygon.

Diameter   In a circle, a segment that passes through the center and has its endpoints on the circle.

Difference   The answer to a subtraction problem. In 95 − 68 = 27, the difference is 27.

Digit   Any of the single symbols used to write numbers. In the base-ten system, the digits are 0, 1, 2, 3, 4, 5, 6, 7, 8, and 9.

Distributive property   The general pattern of numbers of which the following is an example.
$4 \times (7 + 3) = (4 \times 7) + (4 \times 3)$

Dividend   A number that is divided by another number. In 48 ÷ 6 = 8, the dividend is 48.

Divisor   A number that divides another number. In 48 ÷ 6 = 8, the divisor is 6.

Edge   In a space figure, a segment where two faces meet.

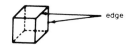

END   The last line in a BASIC computer program.

Endpoint   The point at the end of a segment or a ray.

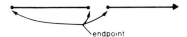

Equal fractions   Fractions that name the same number. $\frac{2}{3}$ and $\frac{8}{12}$ are equal fractions.

Equal ratios   Ratios indicating the same rate or comparison, such as $\frac{3}{4}$ and $\frac{9}{12}$. Cross-products of equal ratios are equal. $3 \times 12 = 4 \times 9$

Equation A mathematical sentence that uses the = symbol. $14 - 7 = 7$

Equilateral triangle A triangle with all three sides congruent.

Even number A whole number with a factor of 2.

Expanded form The expanded form for 5,176 is $5,000 + 100 + 70 + 6$.

Exponent In 4^3, the exponent is 3. It tells that 4 is to be used as a factor three times.
$$4^3 = 4 \times 4 \times 4$$

Face A flat surface that is part of a polyhedron.

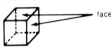

Factor (1) A number to be multiplied. (2) A number that divides evenly into a given second number is a factor of that number.

Family of facts The related number sentences for addition and subtraction (or multiplication and division) that contain all the same numbers.
$$5 + 3 = 8 \quad 8 - 3 = 5$$
$$3 + 5 = 8 \quad 8 - 5 = 3$$

Flow chart A diagram illustrating the steps used to solve a problem.

FOR . . . NEXT BASIC statements in a computer program that tell the computer to do something a certain number of times.

FORWARD (FD) A LOGO command that tells the turtle to move forward a certain number of steps.

Fraction A number written in the form $\frac{a}{b}$, such as $\frac{2}{3}$, or $\frac{11}{5}$, or $\frac{4}{1}$.

GO TO A BASIC statement in a computer program that tells the computer to go to another line in the program.

Graph (1) A picture used to show data. Some types of graphs are bar graphs, circle graphs, line graphs, pictographs and coordinate graphs.

Greater than (>) A relation between two numbers with the greater number given first.
$$8 > 5 \quad 9 > 1.4 \quad \frac{1}{3} > \frac{1}{4}$$

Greatest common factor The greatest number that is a factor of two or more numbers. The greatest common factor of 8 and 12 is 4.

Grouping property See Associative property of addition and Associative property of multiplication.

Hexagon A six-sided polygon.

IF . . . THEN A BASIC statement used to test certain conditions and to act on the results of the test.

Improper fraction A fraction that names a whole number or a mixed number, such as $\frac{15}{2}$ and $\frac{2}{1}$.

INPUT A BASIC statement in a computer program that allows information to be entered into the program by the program user.

Integers The whole numbers and their opposites. Some integers are $+2$, -2, $+75$, and -75.

Intersecting lines Two lines that meet at exactly one point.

Isosceles triangle A triangle with at least two sides congruent.

Least common multiple The smallest number that is a common multiple of two given numbers. The least common multiple of 6 and 8 is 24.

Less than (<) A relation between two numbers with the lesser number given first.
$$5 < 8 \quad 1.4 < 9 \quad \frac{1}{4} < \frac{1}{3}$$

LET A BASIC statement that allows a value to be assigned to a memory location named by a letter.

Line of symmetry A fold line of a figure that makes the two parts of the figure match exactly.

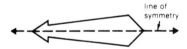

line of symmetry

LOGO A simple language used to give instructions to a computer.

Lowest terms A fraction is in lowest terms if 1 is the only number that will divide both the numerator and the denominator.

Minuend A number from which another number is subtracted. In $95 - 68 = 27$, the minuend is 95.

Mixed number A number that has a whole number part and a fraction part, such as $3\frac{1}{4}$ and $6\frac{7}{8}$.

Multiple A multiple of a number is the product of that number and a whole number. Some multiples of 3 are 3, 6, and 9.

Multiplicand A number that is multiplied by another number.
$$\begin{array}{r} 7 \\ \times\, 3 \\ \hline 21 \end{array}$$ The multiplicand is 7.

Multiplier A number that multiplies another number.
$$\begin{array}{r} 7 \\ \times\, 3 \\ \hline 21 \end{array}$$ The multiplier is 3.

Negative integer An integer less than 0, such as -1, -5, -7, or -10.

Number pair See Ordered pair.

Number sentence An equation or an inequality.
$$3 + 5 = 8 \quad 4 < 7 \quad 9 > 6$$

Obtuse angle An angle that has a measure greater than 90° and less than 180°.

Octagon An eight-sided polygon.

Odd number A whole number that does not have 2 as a factor.

Opposites Two numbers whose sum is 0. $+5$ and -5 are opposites because $+5 + -5 = 0$.

Order property See Commutative property of addition and Commutative property of multiplication.

Ordered pair A number pair, such as (3, 5), in which 3 is the first number and 5 is the second number.

Ordinal number A number, such as *third*, used to tell order or position.

Output Any information that is produced by a computer.

Parallel lines Lines in the same plane that do not meet.

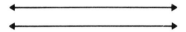

Parallelogram A quadrilateral with opposite sides parallel.

Pentagon A five-sided polygon.

Percent (%) A word indicating "hundredths" or "out of 100." 45 percent (45%) means 0.45 or $\frac{45}{100}$.

Perimeter The sum of the lengths of the sides of a polygon.

Perpendicular lines Two intersecting lines that form right angles.

Pi (π) The number obtained by dividing the circumference of any circle by its diameter. A common approximation for π is 3.14.

Place value In a number, the value given to the place in which a digit appears. In 683, 6 is in the hundreds place, 8 is in the tens place, and 3 is in the ones place.

Polygon A plane figure made up of segments called its *sides*, each side intersecting two other sides, one at each of its endpoints.

Polyhedron A space figure with all flat surfaces. The outline of each surface is a polygon.

Positive integer An integer greater than 0, such as +1, +2, +10, or +35.

Power 3^4 is read "3 to the fourth power." $3^4 = 3 \times 3 \times 3 \times 3 = 81$. The fourth power of 3 is 81. 4^2 is read "4 to the second power" or "4 squared." *See* Exponent.

Prime factor A factor that is a prime number. The prime factors of 10 are 2 and 5.

Prime number A whole number greater than 1, that has exactly two factors: itself and 1. 17 is a prime number.

PRINT An instruction to the computer to give certain output on the screen.

Prism A polyhedron with two parallel congruent faces, called *bases*. All other faces are parallelograms.

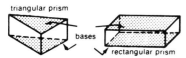

Probability A number that tells how likely it is that a certain event will happen.

Product The answer to a multiplication problem. In $3 \times 7 = 21$, the product is 21.

Pyramid The space figure formed by connecting points of a polygon to a point not in the plane of the polygon. The polygon and its interior is the *base*.

triangular pyramid   rectangular pyramid

Quadrilateral A four-sided polygon.

Quotient The answer to a division problem. In $48 \div 6 = 8$, the quotient is 8.

Radius (1) In a circle, a segment that connects the center of the circle with a point on the circle. (2) In a circle, the distance from the center to a point on the circle.

Ratio A pair of numbers that expresses a rate or a comparison.

Ray Part of a line that has one endpoint and goes on and on in one direction.

Reciprocals Two numbers whose product is 1. $\frac{3}{4}$ and $\frac{4}{3}$ are reciprocals because $\frac{3}{4} \times \frac{4}{3} = 1$.

Rectangle A parallelogram with four right angles.

Rectangular prism *See* Prism.

Rectangular pyramid *See* Pyramid.

Regular polygon A polygon with all sides congruent and all angles congruent.

regular hexagon   regular pentagon

REM A remark in a program that is intended to be read by someone who lists the program, but it does not affect the logic of the program.

Remainder When 20 is divided by 6, the remainder is 2.

REPEAT A LOGO command that causes a list of commands to be done many times.

Right angle An angle that has a measure of 90°.

RIGHT (RT) A LOGO command that directs the turtle to turn right to a specified number of turtle turns.

Right triangle A triangle with one right angle.

Rounded number A number expressed to the nearest 10, 100, 1,000, and so on. 352 rounded to the nearest 10 is 350.

Scale drawing A drawing that shows the shape of a figure but differs in size.

Scalene triangle A triangle with no two sides congruent.

Segment Part of a line, including the two endpoints.

Similar figures Figures with the same shape but not necessarily the same size.

Sphere A space figure with all of its points the same distance from a given point called the *center*.

Square A rectangle with all four sides congruent.

Standard form The standard form for 5 thousands 1 hundred 7 tens 6 ones is 5,176.

Subtrahend A number to be subtracted from another number. In $95 - 68 = 27$, the subtrahend is 68.

Sum The answer to an addition problem. In $8 + 4 = 12$, the sum is 12.

Surface area The sum of the areas of all the surfaces of a space figure.

Triangle A three-sided polygon.

Triangular prism *See* Prism.

Triangular pyramid *See* Pyramid.

Vertex (1) The common endpoint of two rays that form an angle. (2) The point of intersection of two sides of a polygon. (3) The point of intersection of the edges of a polyhedron.

(1)   (2)   (3)

Volume A number indicating the size of the inside of a space figure. The volume of this figure is 12 cubic units.

Whole number One of the numbers 0, 1, 2, 3, 4, and so on.

Working in Groups: Main Ideas

- There are 4 students in each group.
- Groups work as teams.
- Each member of the group must learn the material.
- Each member of the group may be assigned a letter. The group members are called T, E, A, and M.
- The teacher decides who is in each group and what their letters will be.
- Group members may be assigned special roles by the teacher.
- Skills for learning together are taught and practiced.

Working in groups gives you a chance to work and learn with other students.

Why work in groups? Which 3 reasons are most important to you?

1. Working in groups is a good change of pace.
2. I can get more help in a group.
3. I learn better when I explain to others.
4. I like being able to ask questions in a small group rather than in front of the whole class.
5. I get to know my classmates better.
6. I like to help others.
7. Working in groups makes math more fun.
8. Working in groups helps us learn to work as a team.

Which reason do you think was picked by the greatest number of students? Why?

Working in Groups: Description of a Group Activity

Here are the steps in a typical group activity.

Step 1: The students move into their groups. Remember, the teacher selects the students for each group. Stay with the same group until the teacher forms new groups.

Step 2: The class discusses one of the skills for learning together.

- Thinking Aloud
- Settling Disagreements Without Voting
- Locating and Analyzing Errors
- Asking Leading Questions
- Explaining with Pictures or Objects

Step 3: The teacher indicates what the groups will be working on.

Step 4: The teacher may assign a role to one or more students in the group. Here are some possible roles.

- **Reader** This student reads aloud while the others follow along silently.
- **Encourager** This student encourages other members to take part and to use the skills for learning together.
- **Summarizer** At different times, this student summarizes the group's thinking and may report to other groups.
- **Checker** This student may ask group members to explain their thinking or may ask others if they agree. The checker may go to an answer station or to another group to check the group's answer.
- **Materials Manager** This student gets any materials that are needed and returns them at the end of the period.

Step 5: The teacher gives any special instructions for how the group is to work. The group works on the task.

Step 6: The teacher checks how well the group worked together.

Step 7: The teacher checks how well the group understands the lesson.

Which role in Step 4 is your favorite? Why?

Pointers
1. Stay with the group. Don't move around.
2. Get involved.
3. Listen to others.
4. Remember to work as a team.

Working in Groups: Skills for Learning Together

Asking Leading Questions

When a group member doesn't understand, it may help to ask that person leading questions.

Example: A group member did not know how to solve this problem. "Mr. Sims bought three $17 shirts and four $9 ties. How much change did he get from $100?" The other students could ask leading questions such as:

"How much do the shirts cost?"

"How much do the ties cost?"

"What was the total cost?"

Leading questions help to point someone to the important parts of the problem. Asking questions keeps them trying. Telling the answer doesn't help. They still would not understand how to solve the problem.

Thinking Aloud

When you think aloud you tell how you would solve the problem. Thinking aloud helps you understand better. Your thinking aloud also helps those who are listening. If you run into trouble, they will know where your problem is. When help is needed or when the others disagree, they should only ask leading questions. They shouldn't tell you the answer.

Example: Michael thought aloud as he did an addition problem mentally.

Think aloud as you do this problem. Do you agree with Michael's thinking?

Working in Groups: More Skills for Learning Together

Locating and Analyzing Errors

It is easy to say that an answer is wrong.
It is harder to find the error and figure out how it was made.

Example: A group of students solved this problem.
In a race, Ann is 325 feet ahead of Jill, and Jill
is 287 feet ahead of Sue. Mary is 436 feet behind
Jill. How far apart are Ann and Sue?

Can you find the error? Explain how the error was made.

Settling Disagreements Without Voting

If group members disagree on an
answer, they should keep talking
until they all agree.

Explain why this is better than
voting on which answer is correct.

Explaining with Pictures or Objects

When someone has trouble solving a problem, it may help to
have that person or another group member explain the problem
or solution using pictures or objects.

How would you draw a picture for the problem at the top of this page?

Index

443